Fodor's

TWELFTH
New
EDITION

Vienna & the Danube Valley

// *"When it comes to information on regional history, what to see and do, and shopping, these guides are exhaustive."*

—*USAir Magazine*

"Valuable because of their comprehensiveness."
—*Minneapolis Star-Tribune*

"Fodor's always delivers high quality...thoughtfully presented...thorough."

—*Houston Post*

"An excellent choice for those who want everything under one cover."

—*Washington Post* //

Reprinted from *Fodor's Austria*

Fodor's Travel Publications, Inc.
New York • Toronto • London • Sydney • Auckland
http://www.fodors.com/

Fodor's Vienna & the Danube Valley

Editor: Robert I.C. Fisher

Area Editor: George W. Hamilton

Contributors: Alan Levy, Willibald Picard, Linda K. Schmidt, Mary Ellen Schultz, M.T. Schwartzman (Gold Guide editor), Dinah Spritzer, Earl Steinbicker, George Sullivan

Creative Director: Fabrizio La Rocca

Cartographer: David Lindroth; Eureka Cartography

Cover Photograph: Robert Lightfoot III/Nawrocki Stock Photo

Text Design: Between the Covers

Copyright

Twelfth Edition

ISBN 0–679–03592–3

Special Sales

CONTENTS

ON THE ROAD WITH FODOR'S

WE'RE ALWAYS THRILLED to get letters from readers, especially one like this:

It took us an hour to decide what book to buy and we now know we picked the best one. Your book was wonderful, easy to follow, very accurate, and good on pointing out eating places, informal as well as formal. When we saw other people using your book, we would look at each other and smile.

Our editors and writers are deeply committed to making every Fodor's guide "the best one"—not only accurate but always charming, brimming with sound recommendations and solid ideas, right on the mark in describing restaurants and hotels, and full of fascinating facts that make you view what you've traveled to see in a rich new light.

About Our Writers

Our success in achieving our goals—and in helping to make your trip the best of all possible vacations—is a credit to the hard work of our extraordinary writers and editors.

Even before **George W. Hamilton** first arrived in Vienna in 1960, his heart would beat in three-quarter time whenever he heard the intoxicating waltzes of Johann Strauss. Falling in love with the Austrian capital, George found a handy excuse to become a resident: he settled in as manager of the recording studio of the Vienna Symphony Orchestra. Along the way, our longtime area editor has helped found the orchestra's renowned Johann Strauss Ensemble and even discovered unrecorded waltzes. Among his favorite times in Austria are those brilliant spring days when the not-so-blue Danube manages to turn the proper Straussian shade. Music is not the only Austrian specialty George appreciates. His direct experience as hotelier and restaurateur served as the basis for the critical evaluations found in this guide's dining and lodging sections. "Whenever I pick up a cookbook on Austrian cuisine, I first check the recipe for goulash," he chuckles. "If it says any-

thing other than equal parts onion and meat, the book is bogus." Today, as a reporter for the *Economist* and the *Financial Times* research units specializing in travel and economics, he loves to dine out with guests at the Vier Jahreszeiten or—for a more *gemütlich* evening—at the atmospheric Ofenloch.

"To the age, its art; To art, its freedom" was the motto of the famous Vienna Secession group, and **George Sullivan** firmly believes in this maxim, as any reader of our Vienna tours can vouch. The history, art, and architecture of European cities have been his favorite subject since he spent a college summer in London many years ago. A native of Virginia, he gets to Europe as often as he can (he's also written about Florence for Fodor's) and is currently working on an architectural guide to Rome. Austria—the country that gave us "Silent Night, Holy Night"—is never too far from his thoughts: in addition to his writing assignments, he helps run his family's Christmas-tree farm.

Like a true Viennese, **Willibald Picard** believes that coffee drinking is a life's work. Updating our Vienna chapter, he rarely could resist stopping into his favorite coffeehouses, the Frauenhuber and the Haag, for a Mazagran—a glass of iced mocha topped with a maraschino cherry—and, of course, for the latest city news and gossip. A free-lance writer and art historian, Willibald also assisted our area editor in tackling the Danube Valley chapter. Considering the number of mountains he hiked up and down, he feels writing for Fodor's should be considered an Olympic track event.

New This Year

This year we've reformatted our guides to make them easier to use. Each chapter of *Vienna & the Danube Valley* begins with brand-new recommended itineraries to help you decide what to see in the time you have; a section called When to Tour points out the optimal time of day, day of the week, and season for your journey. You may also notice our fresh graphics, new in 1996. More readable and more helpful than ever? We think so—and we hope you do, too.

Like an intricate painting, Vienna takes careful study to fully appreciate its myriad wonders. To help you do that, we've dramatically expanded our Vienna chapter to uncover the city in a new way—from its broad, rough strokes down to the tiniest details that will capture the most demanding traveler's interest. We begin with an introduction that lets you in on the big picture, then introduce each neighborhood section and suggest—in A Good Walk—a wonderful way to discover it. Finally, we present all the neighborhood sights alphabetically. To allow you the delights of free-form touring, this helps you design your own personalized itinerary and also allows you to find your list of mustsees in a snap.

We've also subdivided the section on side trips from Vienna into a brand new chapter; with its seductive excursions to Baden, the Wine Country, Mayerling, and the Vienna Woods, it's a true day tripper's delight.

Check out Fodor's Web site (http://www.fodors.com/), where you'll find travel information on major destinations around the world and an ever-changing array of travel-savvy interactive features.

How to Use This Book

Organization

Up front is the **Gold Guide.** Its first section, **Important Contacts A to Z,** gives addresses and telephone numbers of organizations and companies that offer destination-related services and detailed information and publications. **Smart Travel Tips A to Z,** the Gold Guide's second section, gives specific information on how to accomplish what you need to in Austria as well as tips on savvy traveling. Both sections are in alphabetical order by topic.

The Vienna chapter is subdivided by neighborhood; each subsection recommends a walking tour and lists sights in alphabetical order. Each regional chapter is divided by geographical area; within each area, towns are covered in logical geographical order, and attractive stretches of road and minor points of interest between them are indicated by the designation *En Route.* Throughout, Off the Beaten Path

sights appear after the places from which they are most easily accessible. And within town sections, all restaurants and lodgings are grouped together. Each chapter covers exploring, then highlights regional topics such as shopping, outdoor activities and sports, dining and lodging, and nightlife and the arts.

To help you decide what to visit in the time you have, all chapters begin with recommended itineraries; you can mix and match those from several chapters to create a complete vacation. The **A to Z section** that ends all chapters covers getting there, getting around, and helpful contacts and resources.

Icons and Symbols

★ Our special recommendations
✗ Restaurant
🏠 Lodging establishment
✗🏠 Lodging establishment whose restaurant warrants a detour
♻ Good for kids (rubber duckie)
☞ Sends you to another section of the guide for more information
✉ Address
☎ Telephone number
☉ Opening and closing times
💰 Admission prices (those we give apply only to adults; substantially reduced fees are almost always available for children, students, and senior citizens)

Numbers in white and black circles—② and ❷, for example—that appear on the maps, in the margins, and within the tours correspond to one another.

The restaurants and lodgings we list are the cream of the crop in each price range: $$$$ Very Expensive; $$$ Expensive; $$ Moderate; $ Inexpensive. Price charts appear in the Pleasures and Pastimes section that follows each chapter introduction.

In all restaurant price charts, costs are per person for a three-course meal, with house wine, and usually including sales tax and service (but leaving an additional 5%–7% is customary). Meals in the top price categories usually include a dessert or cheese and coffee. In hotel price charts, rates are for standard double rooms, with city and state sales taxes, and service charges where applicable, during peak season (where applicable).

Hotel Facilities and Reservations

We always list the facilities that are available—but we don't specify whether they cost extra: When pricing accommodations, always ask what's included.

Today, many travelers make hotel reservations by telephone and follow-up fax. For those who decide to write, note that you will often come across hotels in this guide—generally based in smaller towns and villages—that use only postal codes (for example, A–3478) or have, in certain instances, *no* official street address at all. In such cases, simply post your letter with the hotel name, town, and Austrian province. **At all times, be sure to include the town's name when using addresses listed in the hotel reviews of this guide**—the postal code alone will not guarantee delivery. Assume that hotels operate on the **European Plan** (EP, with no meals) unless we note that they use a **full- or partial-board** plan (with some or all meals); other hotels operate on the **Continental Plan,** with a Continental breakfast daily. For complete information, inquire when booking.

A Note About Austrian Addresses

In many cases, they don't exist—to put it simply. Throughout this guide, you will find numerous churches, museums, castles, and other attractions with no discernable street address. As with hotels and restaurants, these sights often don't have definite addresses other than the postal code and town name. This is most often the case in smaller towns and villages, but this can also occur in cities. So when there is no street address listed, consult this book's map or just ask a passerby—the magic phrase is "*Entschuldigen Sie. Wo ist . . . ?* (Excuse me. Where is . . . ?).

Restaurant Reservations and Dress Codes

Reservations are always a good idea; we note only when they're essential or when they are not accepted. Book as far ahead as you can, and reconfirm when you get to town. Unless otherwise noted, the restaurants listed are open daily for lunch and dinner. We mention dress only when men are required to wear a jacket or a jacket and tie. Look for an overview of local habits under Dining in Smart Travel Tips A to Z and in the Pleasures and Pastimes section that follows each chapter introduction.

Credit Cards

The following abbreviations are used: **AE,** American Express; **DC,** Diners Club; **MC,** MasterCard; and **V,** Visa. Discover is not accepted outside the United States.

Don't Forget to Write

You can use this book in the confidence that all prices and opening times are based on information supplied to us at press time; Fodor's cannot accept responsibility for any errors. Time inevitably brings changes, so always confirm information when it matters—especially if you're making a detour to visit a specific place. In addition, when making reservations be sure to mention if you have a disability or are traveling with children, if you prefer a private bath or a certain type of bed, or if you have specific dietary needs or any other concerns.

Were the restaurants we recommended as described? Did our hotel picks exceed your expectations? Did you find a museum we recommended a waste of time? If you have complaints, we'll look into them and revise our entries when the facts warrant it. If you've discovered a special place that we haven't included, we'll pass the information along to our correspondents and have them check it out. So send your feedback, positive *and* negative, to the *Vienna & the Danube Valley* editor at 201 East 50th Street, New York, New York 10022—and have a wonderful trip!

Karen Cure
Editorial Director

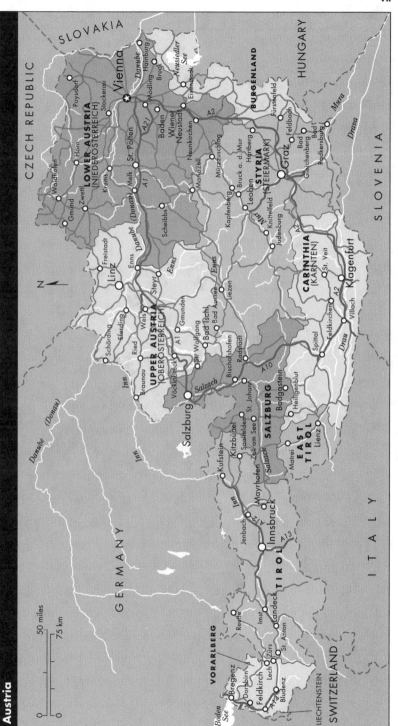

Austria

VIII

Vienna

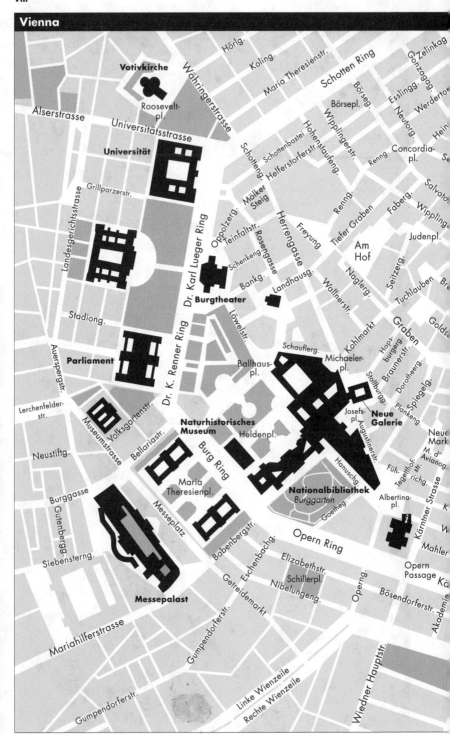

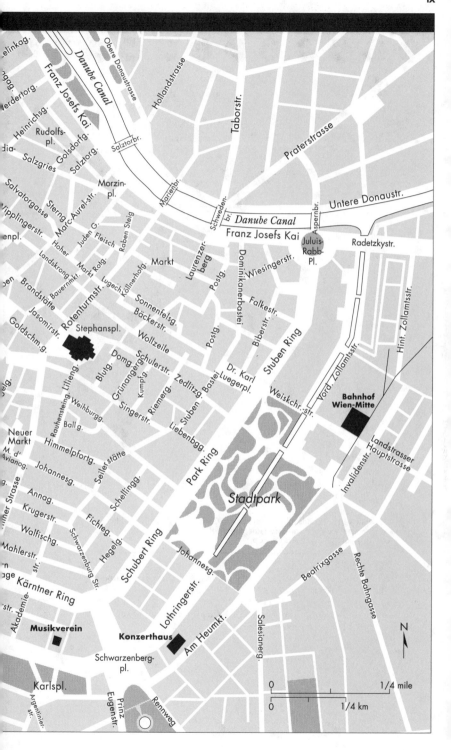

elinkag.

Franz Josefs Kai

Obere Donaustrasse

Danube Canal

Hollandstrasse

Taborstr.

Praterstrasse

nag.

Werdertorg.

Heinrichsg.

Rudolfs-
pl.

Golsdorfg.

Salztorg.

dia-

Salzgries

Salztorbr.

Morzin-
pl.

Marienbr.

Schweden-

br.

Danube Canal

Franz Josefs Kai

Untere Donaustr.

Salvatorgasse

Sterng.

Marc-Aurel-str.

Juden G. Fleisch

Raben Steig

Julius-
Rabb-
Pl.

Radetzkystr.

ipplingerstr.

enpl.

Hoher

Landskrong.

Markt Roig.

Bauernmkt.

Lugech.

Köllnerholg.

Markt

Laurenzer-
berg

Postg.

Wiesingerstr.

Dominikanerbastei

Aspernbr.

Hint. Zollamtsstr.

ben

Brandstätte

Rotenturmstr.

Sonnenfelsg.

Bäckerstr.

Falkestr.

Biberstr.

Jasomirstr.

Stephanspl.

Wollzeile

Postg.

Stuben Ring

Vord. Zollamtsstr.

Goldschm.g.

Domg.

Schulerstr.

Zedlitzg.

Bastei

Dr. Karl
Luegerpl.

**Bahnhof
Wien-Mitte**

belg.

Blutg.

Grünangerg.

Kumpfg.

Remerg.

Stuben

Weiskch.-str.

str.

Landstrasser
Hauptstrasse

Rauhensteing. Weihburgg.

Singerstr.

Liebenbgg.

Invalidenstr.

Neuer
Markt

Ball g.

Himmelpfortg.

Seilerstätte

Park Ring

Rechte Bahngasse

M. d'

Avianog.

Johannesg.

Schellingg.

Stadtpark

g.

Annag.

Krugerstr.

Fichteg.

Schubert Ring

Hegelg.

Johannesg.

Beatrixgasse

Walfischg.

Schwarzenburg Str.

Mahlerstr.

str.

rn

age

Kärntner Ring

Lothringerstr.

Salesianerg.

Akademie-

Musikverein

Konzerthaus

Am Heumkt.

N

str.

Schwarzenberg-
pl.

Karlspl.

Argentinier-

str.

Prinz
Eugenstr.

Rennweg

0   1/4 mile

0   1/4 km

x

World Time Zones

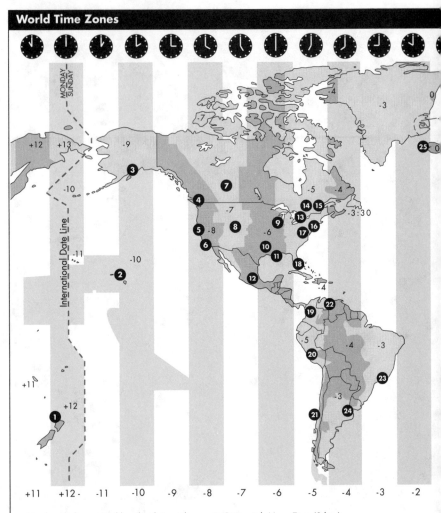

Numbers below vertical bands relate each zone to Greenwich Mean Time (0 hrs.).
Local times frequently differ from these general indications,
as indicated by light-face numbers on map.

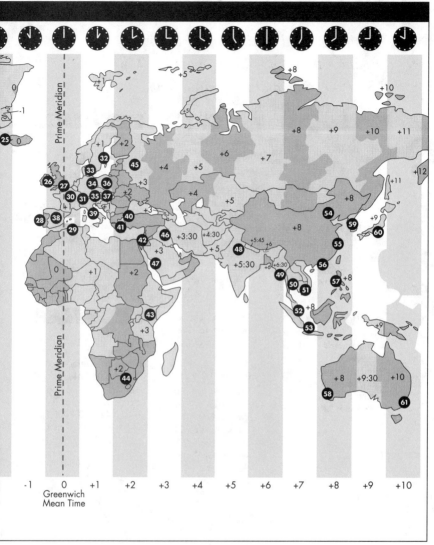

IMPORTANT CONTACTS A TO Z

An Alphabetical Listing of Publications, Organizations, and Companies that Will Help You Before, During, and After Your Trip

A

AIR TRAVEL

The major gateway to Vienna is Schwechat airport (☎ 011–43/1–71110), about 12 miles southeast of the city.

FLYING TIME

Flying time is 8 hours from New York, 11 hours from Chicago, and 13 hours from Los Angeles.

CARRIERS

Carriers serving Austria include **Austrian Airlines** (☎ 800/843–0002), **Delta** (☎ 800/221–1212), **Lauda Air** (☎ 800/325–2832), and **Air Canada** (☎ 416/925–2311 or 800/268–7240).

FROM THE U.K.

British Airways (☎ 0171/897–4000), **Austrian Airlines** (☎ 0171/439–0741), and **Lauda Air** (☎ 0171/494–0702) have nonstop service from London to Vienna.

COMPLAINTS

To register complaints about charter and scheduled airlines, contact the U.S. Department of Transportation's **Aviation Consumer Protection Division** (✉ C-75, Washington, DC 20590, ☎ 202/366–2220). Complaints about lost baggage or ticketing problems and safety concerns may

also be logged with the **Federal Aviation Administration (FAA) Consumer Hotline** (☎ 800/322–7873).

CONSOLIDATORS

For the names of reputable air-ticket consolidators, contact the **United States Air Consolidators Association** (925 L St., Suite 220, Sacramento, CA 95814, ☎ 916/441–4166, FAX 916/441–3520). For discount air-ticketing agencies, *see* Discounts & Deals, *below.*

PUBLICATIONS

For general information about charter carriers, ask for the Department of Transportation's free brochure **"Plane Talk: Public Charter Flights"** (✉ Aviation Consumer Protection Division, C-75, Washington, DC 20590, ☎ 202/366–2220). The Department of Transportation also publishes a 58-page booklet, **"Fly Rights,"** available from the Consumer Information Center (✉ Supt. of Documents, Dept. 136C, Pueblo, CO 81009; $1.75).

For other tips and hints, consult the Consumers Union's monthly **"Consumer Reports Travel Letter"** (✉ Box 53629, Boulder, CO 80322, ☎ 800/234–1970; $39 1st year).

B

BETTER BUSINESS BUREAU

For local contacts in the hometown of a tour operator you may be considering, consult the **Council of Better Business Bureaus** (✉ 4200 Wilson Blvd., Suite 800, Arlington, VA 22203, ☎ 703/276–0100, FAX 703/525–8277).

C

CAR RENTAL

The major car-rental companies represented in Vienna are **Alamo** (☎ 800/327–9633; in the U.K., 0800/272–2000), **Avis** (☎ 800/331–1084; in Canada, 800/879–2847), **Budget** (☎ 800/527–0700; in the U.K., 0800/181181), **Dollar** (☎ 800/800–4000; in the U.K., 0990/565656, where it is known as Eurodollar), **Hertz** (☎ 800/654–3001; in Canada, 800/263–0600; in the U.K., 0345/555888), and **National InterRent** (sometimes known as Europcar InterRent outside North America; ☎ 800/227–3876; in the U.K., 0345/222–525). Rates in Vienna begin at $48 a day and $347 a week for an economy car with unlimited mileage. This does not include tax on car rentals, which is 20% on car rentals plus a 1% contract tax. If you rent at the airport, you'll also pay a 9% surcharge. If you rent and pay before you arrive, you'll save a considerable amount of money (*see* Car Rental *in* Smart Travel Tips A to Z, *below*).

One of the cheapest local rental firms is **Autoverleih Buchbinder** (Schlachthausgasse 38, A–1030 Vienna, ☎ 0222/717–50–0, FAX 0222/717–5022).

RENTAL WHOLESALERS

Contact **Auto Europe** (☎ 207/828–2525 or 800/223–5555), **Europe by Car** (☎ 800/223–1516; in CA, 800/252–9401), or the **Kemwel Group** (☎ 914/835–5555 or 800/678–0678).

CHILDREN & TRAVEL

BABY-SITTING

In Vienna, you can call on the baby-sitters of the **Austrian Academic Guest Service** (Operngasse 24, A–1040, ☎ 0222/587–3525).

FLYING

Look into **"Flying with Baby"** (✉ Third Street Press, Box 261250, Littleton, CO 80163, ☎ 303/595–5959; $4.95 includes shipping), cowritten by a flight attendant. **"Kids and Teens in Flight,"** free from the U.S. Department of Transportation's Aviation Consumer Protection Division (✉ C-75, Washington, DC 20590, ☎ 202/366–2220), offers tips on children flying alone. Every two years the February issue of *Family Travel Times* (☞ Know-How, *below*) details children's ser-

vices on three dozen airlines. **"Flying Alone, Handy Advice for Kids Traveling Solo"** is available free from the American Automobile Association (AAA) (✉ send stamped, self-addressed, legal-size envelope: Flying Alone, Mail Stop 800, 1000 AAA Dr., Heathrow, FL 32746).

KNOW-HOW

Family Travel Times, published quarterly by Travel with Your Children (✉ TWYCH, 40 5th Ave., New York, NY 10011, ☎ 212/477–5524; $40 per year), covers destinations, types of vacations, and modes of travel.

CUSTOMS

IN THE U.S.

The **U.S. Customs Service** (✉ Box 7407, Washington, DC 20044, ☎ 202/927–6724) can answer questions on duty-free limits and publishes a helpful brochure, "Know Before You Go." For information on registering foreign-made articles, call 202/927–0540 or write U.S. Customs Service, Resource Management, 1301 Constitution Ave. NW, Washington DC, 20229.

COMPLAINTS➤ Note the inspector's badge number and write to the commissioner's office (✉ 1301 Constitution Ave. NW, Washington, DC 20229).

CANADIANS

Contact **Revenue Canada** (✉ 2265 St. Laurent Blvd. S, Ottawa, Ontario K1G 4K3, ☎ 613/993–0534)

for a copy of the free brochure **"I Declare/ Je Déclare"** and for details on duty-free limits. For recorded information (within Canada only), call 800/461–9999.

U.K. CITIZENS

HM Customs and Excise (✉ Dorset House, Stamford St., London SE1 9NG, ☎ 0171/202–4227) can answer questions about U.K. customs regulations and publishes a free pamphlet, **"A Guide for Travellers,"** detailing standard procedures and import rules.

D

DISABILITIES & ACCESSIBILITY

The **Austrian National Tourist Office** (*see* Visitor Information, *below*) can provide a guide to accessible Austrian hotels.

In Austria, check with the **Österreichischer Zivilinvalidenverband** (Brigittenauer Lände 42, A–1200 Vienna, ☎ 0222/330–6189) for more information. The **Sozialamt der Stadt Wien** (Gonzagagasse 23, A–1010, ☎ 0222/531–14–0) and the **Vienna Tourist Office** (Obere Augartenstr. 40, A–1025, ☎ 0222/211–14–0) also have a booklet on Vienna hotels and a city guide for travelers with disabilities.

COMPLAINTS

To register complaints under the provisions of the Americans with Disabilities Act, contact the U.S. Department of Justice's **Disability Rights Section** (✉ Box 66738,

Washington, DC 20035, ☎ 202/514–0301 or 800/514–0301, FAX 202/307–1198, TTY 202/514–0383 or 800/514–0383). For airline-related problems, contact the U.S. Department of Transportation's **Aviation Consumer Protection Division** (☞ Air Travel, *above*). For complaints about surface transportation, contact the Department of Transportation's **Civil Rights Office** (✉ 400 7th St., SW, Room 10215, Washington DC, 20590 ☎ 202/366–4648).

ORGANIZATIONS

TRAVELERS WITH HEAR-ING IMPAIRMENTS➤ The **American Academy of Otolaryngology** (✉ 1 Prince St., Alexandria, VA 22314, ☎ 703/836–4444, FAX 703/683–5100, TTY 703/519–1585) publishes a brochure, "Travel Tips for Hearing Impaired People."

TRAVELERS WITH MOBIL-ITY PROBLEMS➤ Contact **Mobility International USA** (✉ Box 10767, Eugene, OR 97440, ☎ and TTY 541/343–1284, FAX 541/343–6812), the U.S. branch of a Belgium-based organization (☞ *below*) with affiliates in 30 countries; **MossRehab Hospital Travel Information Service** (☎ 215/456–9600, TTY 215/456–9602), a telephone information resource for travelers with physical disabilities; the **Society for the Advancement of Travel for the Handicapped** (✉ 347 5th Ave., Suite 610, New York, NY 10016, ☎ 212/447–7284, FAX 212/725–8253; membership $45); and

Travelin' Talk (✉ Box 3534, Clarksville, TN 37043, ☎ 615/552–6670, FAX 615/552–1182) which provides local contacts world-wide for travelers with disabilities.

TRAVELERS WITH VISION IMPAIRMENTS➤ Contact the **American Council of the Blind** (✉ 1155 15th St. NW, Suite 720, Washington, DC 20005, ☎ 202/467–5081, FAX 202/467–5085) for a list of travelers' resources or the **American Foundation for the Blind** (✉ 11 Penn Plaza, Suite 300, New York, NY 10001, ☎ 212/502–7600 or 800/232–5463, TTY 212/502–7662), which provides general advice and publishes "Access to Art" ($19.95), a directory of museums that accommodate travelers with vision impairments.

IN THE U.K.

Contact the **Royal Association for Disability and Rehabilitation** (✉ RADAR, 12 City Forum, 250 City Rd., London EC1V 8AF, ☎ 0171/250–3222) or **Mobility International** (✉ rue de Manchester 25, B-1080 Brussels, Belgium, ☎ 00–322–410–6297, FAX 00–322–410–6874), an international travel-information clearing-house for people with disabilities.

PUBLICATIONS

Several publications for travelers with disabilities are available from the **Consumer Information Center** (✉ Box 100, Pueblo, CO 81009, ☎ 719/948–3334). Call or write for its free catalog of current titles. The Society for the Advancement of Travel for the

Handicapped (☞ Orga-nizations, *above*) pub-lishes the quarterly magazine **"Access to Travel"** ($13 for 1-year subscription).

The 500-page **Travelin' Talk Directory** (✉ Box 3534, Clarksville, TN 37043, ☎ 615/552–6670, FAX 615/552–1182; $35) lists people and organizations who help travelers with disabilities. For travel agents worldwide, consult the **Directory of Travel Agencies for the Disabled** (✉ Twin Peaks Press, Box 129, Van-couver, WA 98666, ☎ 360/694–2462 or 800/637–2256, FAX 360/696–3210; $19.95 plus $3 shipping).

TRAVEL AGENCIES & TOUR OPERATORS

The Americans with Disabilities Act requires that all travel firms serve the needs of all travelers. That said, you should note that some agencies and operators specialize in making travel ar-rangements for individu-als and groups with disabilities, among them **Access Adventures** (✉ 206 Chestnut Ridge Rd., Rochester, NY 14624, ☎ 716/889–9096), run by a former physical-rehab counselor.

TRAVELERS WITH MOBIL-ITY PROBLEMS➤ Contact **Flying Wheels Travel** (✉ 143 W. Bridge St., Box 382, Owatonna, MN 55060, ☎ 507/451–5005 or 800/535–6790), a travel agency specializing in Euro-pean cruises and tours; **Hinsdale Travel Service** (✉ 201 E. Ogden Ave., Suite 100, Hinsdale, IL 60521, ☎ 630/325–1335), a travel agency that benefits from the advice of wheelchair traveler Janice Perkins; and **Wheelchair Journeys** (⌧ 16979 Redmond Way, Redmond, WA 98052, ☎ 206/885–2210 or 800/313–4751), which can handle arrangements worldwide.

TRAVELERS WITH DEVELOPMENTAL DISABILITIES➤ Contact the nonprofit **New Directions** (⌧ 5276 Hollister Ave., Suite 207, Santa Barbara, CA 93111, ☎ 805/967–2841).

TRAVEL GEAR

The **Magellan's** catalog (☎ 800/962–4943, FAX 805/568–5406), includes a section devoted to products designed for travelers with disabilities.

DISCOUNTS & DEALS

AIRFARES

For the lowest airfares to Vienna, call 800/FLY–4–LESS.

CLUBS

Contact **Entertainment Travel Editions** (⌧ Box 1068, Trumbull, CT 06611, ☎ 800/445–4137; $28–$53, depending on destination), **Great American Traveler** (⌧ Box 27965, Salt Lake City, UT 84127, ☎ 800/548–2812; $49.95 per year), **Moment's Notice Discount Travel Club** (⌧ 7301 New Utrecht Ave., Brooklyn, NY 11204, ☎ 718/234–6295; $25 per year, single or family), **Privilege Card International** (⌧ 3391 Peachtree Rd. NE, Suite 110, Atlanta, GA 30326, ☎ 404/262–0222 or 800/236–9732; $74.95 per year), **Travel-**

ers **Advantage** (⌧ CUC Travel Service, 49 Music Sq. W, Nashville, TN 37203, ☎ 800/548–1116 or 800/648–4037; $49 per year, single or family), or **Worldwide Discount Travel Club** (⌧ 1674 Meridian Ave., Miami Beach, FL 33139, ☎ 305/534–2082; $50 per year for family, $40 single).

HOTEL ROOMS

For hotel room rates guaranteed in U.S. dollars, call **Steigenberger Reservation Service** (☎ 800/223–5652).

STUDENTS

Members of Hostelling International–American Youth Hostels (☞ Students, *below*) are eligible for discounts on car rentals, admissions to attractions, and other selected travel expenses.

PUBLICATIONS

Consult *The Frugal Globetrotter,* by Bruce Northam (⌧ Fulcrum Publishing, 350 Indiana St., Suite 350, Golden, CO 80401, ☎ 800/992–2908; $16.95 plus $4 shipping). For publications that tell how to find the lowest prices on plane tickets, *see* Air Travel, *above.*

Also see Fodor's *Affordable Europe* (available in bookstores, or ☎ 800/533–6478; $18.50 plus $4 shipping).

G

GAY & LESBIAN TRAVEL

In Austria, key information sources are **Homosexuelle Initiative** (Novaragasse 40, A–1020 Vienna, ☎ 0222/216–6604) and

Rosa Lila Villa (Linke Wienzeile 102, A–1060 Vienna, ☎ 0222/586–8150). The twice-monthly magazine *Xtra!* runs a calendar of daily events and addresses.

ORGANIZATIONS

The **International Gay Travel Association** (⌧ Box 4974, Key West, FL 33041, ☎ 800/448–8550, FAX 305/296–6633), a consortium of more than 1,000 travel companies, can supply names of gay-friendly travel agents, tour operators, and accommodations.

PUBLICATIONS

The 16-page monthly newsletter **"Out & About"** (⌧ 8 W. 19th St., Suite 401, New York, NY 10011, ☎ 212/645–6922 or 800/929–2268, FAX 800/929–2215; $49 for 10 issues and quarterly calendar) covers gay-friendly resorts, hotels, cruise lines, and airlines.

TOUR OPERATORS

Toto Tours (⌧ 1326 W. Albion Ave., Suite 3W, Chicago, IL 60626, ☎ 773/274–8686 or 800/565–1241, FAX 773/274–8695) offers group tours to worldwide destinations.

TRAVEL AGENCIES

The largest agencies serving gay travelers are **Advance Travel** (⌧ 10700 Northwest Fwy., Suite 160, Houston, TX 77092, ☎ 713/682–2002 or 800/292–0500), **Club Travel** (⌧ 8739 Santa Monica Blvd., W. Hollywood, CA 90069, ☎ 310/358–2200 or 800/429–8747), **Islanders/**

THE GOLD GUIDE / IMPORTANT CONTACTS

Kennedy Travel (✉ 183 W. 10th St., New York, NY 10014, ☎ 212/242–3222 or 800/988–1181), **Now Voyager** (✉ 4406 18th St., San Francisco, CA 94114, ☎ 415/626–1169 or 800/255–6951), and **Yellowbrick Road** (✉ 1500 W. Balmoral Ave., Chicago, IL 60640, ☎ 773/561–1800 or 800/642–2488). **Skylink Women's Travel** (✉ 2460 W. 3rd St., Suite 215, Santa Rosa, CA 95401, ☎ 707/570–0105 or 800/225–5759) serves lesbian travelers.

H

HEALTH

FINDING A DOCTOR

For its members, the **International Association for Medical Assistance to Travellers** (✉ IAMAT, membership free; 417 Center St., Lewiston, NY 14092, ☎ 716/754–4883; 40 Regal Rd., Guelph, Ontario N1K 1B5, ☎ 519/836–0102; 1287 St. Clair Ave. W., Toronto, Ontario M6E 1B8, ☎ 416/652–0137; 57 Voirets, 1212 Grand-Lancy, Geneva, Switzerland, no phone) publishes a worldwide directory of English-speaking physicians meeting IAMAT standards.

MEDICAL ASSISTANCE COMPANIES

The following companies are concerned primarily with emergency medical assistance, although they may provide some insurance as part of their coverage. For a list of full-service travel

insurance companies, *see* Insurance, *below*.

Contact **International SOS Assistance** (✉ Box 11568, Philadelphia, PA 19116, ☎ 215/244–1500 or 800/523–8930; Box 466, Pl. Bonaventure, Montréal, Québec H5A 1C1, ☎ 514/874–7674 or 800/363–0263; 7 Old Lodge Pl., St. Margarets, Twickenham TW1 1RQ, England, ☎ 0181/744–0033), **Medex Assistance Corporation** (✉ Box 5375, Timonium, MD 21094, ☎ 410/453–6300 or 800/537–2029), **Near Travel Services** (✉ Box 1339, Calumet City, IL 60409, ☎ 708/868–6700 or 800/654–6700), **Traveler's Emergency Network** (✉ 1133 15th St. NW, Suite 400, Washington DC, 20005, ☎ 202/828–5894 or 800/275–4836, FAX 202/828–5896), **TravMed** (✉ Box 5375, Timonium, MD 21094, ☎ 410/453–6380 or 800/732–5309), or **Worldwide Assistance Services** (✉ 1133 15th St. NW, Suite 400, Washington, DC 20005, ☎ 202/331–1609 or 800/821–2828, FAX 202/828–5896).

I

INSURANCE

IN CANADA

Contact **Mutual of Omaha** (✉ Travel Division, 500 University Ave., Toronto, Ontario M5G 1V8, ☎ 800/465–0267 (in Canada) or 416/598-4083).

IN THE U.S.

Travel insurance covering baggage, health, and trip cancellation or interruptions is available from **Access America**

(✉ 6600 W. Broad St., Richmond, VA 23230, ☎ 804/285–3300 or 800/334–7525), **Carefree Travel Insurance** (✉ Box 9366, 100 Garden City Plaza, Garden City, NY 11530, ☎ 516/294–0220 or 800/323–3149), **Tele-Trip** (✉ Mutual of Omaha Plaza, Box 31716, Omaha, NE 68131, ☎ 800/228–9792), **Travel Guard International** (✉ 1145 Clark St., Stevens Point, WI 54481, ☎ 715/345–0505 or 800/826–1300), **Travel Insured International** (✉ Box 280568, East Hartford, CT 06128, ☎ 203/528–7663 or 800/243–3174), and **Wallach & Company** (✉ 107 W. Federal St., Box 480, Middleburg, VA 22117, ☎ 540/687–3166 or 800/237–6615).

IN THE U.K.

The **Association of British Insurers** (✉ 51 Gresham St., London EC2V 7HQ, ☎ 0171/600–3333) gives advice by phone and publishes the free pamphlet **"Holiday Insurance and Motoring Abroad,"** which sets out typical policy provisions and costs.

L

LODGING

For information on hotel consolidators, *see* Discounts, *above*.

APARTMENT & VILLA RENTAL

Among the companies to contact are **Europa-Let/Tropical Inn-Let, Inc.** (✉ 92 N. Main St., Ashland, OR 97520, ☎ 541/482–5806 or 800/462–4486, FAX 541/482–0660), **Hometours International** (✉ Box

11503, Knoxville, TN 37939, ☎ 423/690–8484 or 800/367–4668), **Interhome** (✉ 124 Little Falls Rd., Fairfield, NJ 07004, ☎ 201/882–6864, FAX 201/808–1742), **Rent-a-Home International** (✉ 7200 34th Ave. NW, Seattle, WA 98117, ☎ 206/789–9377 or 800/488–7368, FAX 206/789–9379, rentahome-international@msn.com), or **Villas International** (✉ 605 Market St., Suite 510, San Francisco, CA 94105, ☎ 415/281–0910 or 800/221–2260, FAX 415/281–0919). Members of the travel club **Hideaways International** (✉ 767 Islington St., Portsmouth, NH 03801, ☎ 603/430–4433 or 800/843–4433, FAX 603/430–4444, info@hideaways.com; $99 per year) receive two annual guides plus quarterly newsletters and arrange rentals among themselves.

HOME EXCHANGE

Some of the principal clearinghouses are **HomeLink International/Vacation Exchange Club** (✉ Box 650, Key West, FL 33041, ☎ 305/294–1448 or 800/638–3841, FAX 305/294–1148; $78 per year), which sends members five annual directories, with a listing in one, plus updates; and **Loan-a-Home** (✉ 2 Park La., Apt. 6E, Mount Vernon, NY 10552, ☎ 914/664–7640; $40–$50 per year), which specializes in long-term exchanges.

ROMANTIK HOTELS

For the coziest, most personal accommodations in elegant surroundings, ask for the

Romantik Hotels & Restaurants. Among agents who can book are AAA travel agencies as well as **Euro-Connection** (Box 2397, 1819 207th Place SW, Lynwood, WA 98036, ☎ 206/670–1140 or 800/645–EURO), **DER Tours** (11933 Wilshire Blvd., Los Angeles, CA 90025, ☎ 310/479–4140 or 800/421–4343), **MLT Vacations** (5130 Highway 101, Minnetonka, MN 55345, ☎ 612/474–2540 or 800/362–3520, **Romantik Travel and Tours** (16932 Woodinville-Redmond Rd., Suite A107, Box 1278, Woodinville, WA 98072, ☎ 206/486–9394 or 800/826–0015).

M
MONEY

ATMS

For specific foreign **Cirrus** locations, call 800/424–7787; for foreign **Plus** locations, consult the Plus directory at your local bank.

CURRENCY EXCHANGE

If your bank doesn't exchange currency, contact **Thomas Cook Currency Services** (☎ 800/287–7362 for locations). **Ruesch International** (☎ 800/424–2923 for locations) can also provide you with foreign banknotes before you leave home and publishes a number of useful brochures, including a "Foreign Currency Guide" and "Foreign Exchange Tips."

WIRING FUNDS

Funds can be wired via **MoneyGram℠** (for locations and informa-

tion in the U.S. and Canada, ☎ 800/926–9400) or **Western Union** (for agent locations or to send money using MasterCard or Visa, ☎ 800/325–6000; in Canada, 800/321–2923; in the U.K., 0800/833833; or visit the Western Union office at the nearest major post office).

P
PACKING

For strategies on packing light, get a copy of *The Packing Book,* by Judith Gilford (✉ Ten Speed Press, Box 7123, Berkeley, CA 94707, ☎ 510/559–1600 or 800/841–2665, FAX 510/524–4588; $7.95 plus $3.50 shipping).

PASSPORTS & VISAS

IN THE U.S.

For fees, documentation requirements, and other information, call the State Department's **Office of Passport Services** information line (☎ 202/647–0518).

CANADIANS

For fees, documentation requirements, and other information, call the Ministry of Foreign Affairs and International Trade's **Passport Office** (☎ 819/994–3500 or 800/567–6868).

U.K. CITIZENS

For fees, documentation requirements, and to request an emergency passport, call the **London Passport Office** (☎ 0990/210410).

PHOTO HELP

The **Kodak Information Center** (☎ 800/242–

THE GOLD GUIDE / IMPORTANT CONTACTS

2424) answers consumer questions about film and photography. The *Kodak Guide to Shooting Great Travel Pictures* (available in bookstores; or contact Fodor's Travel Publications, ☎ 800/533–6478; $16.50 plus $4 shipping) explains how to take expert travel photographs.

S

SAFETY

"Trouble-Free Travel," from the AAA, is a booklet of tips for protecting yourself and your belongings when away from home. Send a stamped, self-addressed, legal-size envelope to Trouble-Free Travel (✉ Mail Stop 75, 1000 AAA Dr., Heathrow, FL 32746).

SENIOR CITIZENS

CLUBS

Sears's **Mature Outlook** (✉ Box 10448, Des Moines, IA 50306, ☎ 800/336–6330; annual membership $14.95) includes a lifestyle/travel magazine and membership in ITC-50 travel club, which offers discounts of up to 50% at participating hotels and restaurants. (☞ Discounts & Deals *in* Smart Travel Tips A to Z).

EDUCATIONAL TRAVEL

The nonprofit **Elderhostel** (✉ 75 Federal St., 3rd Floor, Boston, MA 02110, ☎ 617/426–7788), for people 55 and older, has offered inexpensive study programs since 1975. Courses cover everything from marine science to Greek mytho-

logy and cowboy poetry. Costs for two- to three-week international trips—including room, board, and transportation from the United States—range from $1,800 to $4,500.

Interhostel (✉ University of New Hampshire, 6 Garrison Ave., Durham, NH 03824, ☎ 603/862–1147 or 800/733–9753), for travelers 50 and older, has two- to three-week trips; most last two weeks and cost $2,000–$3,500, including airfare.

ORGANIZATIONS

Contact the **American Association of Retired Persons** (✉ AARP, 601 E St. NW, Washington, DC 20049, ☎ 202/434–2277; annual dues $8 per person or couple). Its Purchase Privilege Program secures discounts for members on lodging, car rentals, and sightseeing.

STUDENTS

GROUPS

The major tour operators specializing in student travel are **Contiki Holidays** (✉ 300 Plaza Alicante, Suite 900, Garden Grove, CA 92640, ☎ 714/740–0808 or 800/266–8454) and **AESU Travel** (✉ 2 Hamill Rd., Suite 248, Baltimore, MD 21210-1807, ☎ 410/323–4416 or 800/638–7640).

HOSTELING

In Austria, youth hostels are coordinated through the Österreichische **Jugendherbergverband** (Schottenring 28, A–1010 Vienna, ☎ 0222/533–5353, FAX 0222/535–0861), which can

help you plan a hostel holiday of hiking, cycling, or camping.

In the United States, contact **Hostelling International–American Youth Hostels** (✉ 733 15th St. NW, Suite 840, Washington, DC 20005, ☎ 202/783–6161, FAX 202/783–6171); in Canada, **Hostelling International–Canada** (✉ 205 Catherine St., Suite 400, Ottawa, Ontario K2P 1C3, ☎ 613/237–7884); and in the United Kingdom, the **Youth Hostel Association of England and Wales** (✉ Trevelyan House, 8 St. Stephen's Hill, St. Albans, Hertfordshire AL1 2DY, ☎ 01727/855215 or 01727/845047). Membership (in the U.S., $25; in Canada, C$26.75; in the U.K., £9.30) gives you access to 5,000 hostels in 77 countries that charge $5–$40 per person per night.

ORGANIZATIONS

A major contact is the **Council on International Educational Exchange** (✉ mail orders only: CIEE, 205 E. 42nd St., 16th Floor, New York, NY 10017, ☎ 212/822–2600, FAX 212/822–2699, info@ciee.org). The **Educational Travel Centre** (✉ 438 N. Frances St., Madison, WI 53703, ☎ 608/256–5551 or 800/747–5551, FAX 608/256–2042) offers rail passes and low-cost airline tickets, mostly for flights that depart from Chicago.

In Canada, also contact **Travel Cuts** (✉ 187 College St., Toronto, Ontario M5T 1P7, ☎

416/979–2406 or 800/
667–2887).

PUBLICATIONS

Check out the *Berkeley Guide to Europe* (available in bookstores; or contact Fodor's Travel Publications, ☎ 800/533–6478; $18.95 plus $4 shipping).

T

TELEPHONES

The country code for Austria is 43. For local access numbers abroad, contact **AT&T** USADirect (☎ 800/874–4000), **MCI** Call USA (☎ 800/444–4444), or **Sprint** Express (☎ 800/793–1153).

TOUR OPERATORS

Among the companies that sell tours and packages to Vienna, the following are nationally known, have a proven reputation, and offer plenty of options.

GROUP TOURS

SUPER-DELUXE➤ **Abercrombie & Kent** (✉ 1520 Kensington Rd., Oak Brook, IL 60521-2141, ☎ 708/954–2944 or 800/323–7308, FAX 708/954–3324), and **Travcoa** (✉ Box 2630, 2350 S.E. Bristol St., Newport Beach, CA 92660, ☎ 714/476–2800 or 800/992–2003, FAX 714/476–2538).

DELUXE➤ **Globus** (✉ 5301 S. Federal Circle, Littleton, CO 80123, ☎ 303/797–2800 or 800/221–0090, FAX 303/795–0962), **Maupintour** (✉ Box 807, 1515 St. Andrews Dr., Lawrence, KS 66047, ☎ 913/843–1211 or 800/255–4266, FAX 913/843–8351), and **Tauck Tours** (✉ Box

5027, 276 Post Rd. W, Westport, CT 06881, ☎ 203/226–6911 or 800/468–2825, FAX 203/221–6828).

FIRST-CLASS➤ **Brendan Tours** (✉ 15137 Califa St., Van Nuys, CA 91411, ☎ 818/785–9696 or 800/421–8446, FAX 818/902–9876), **Caravan Tours** (✉ 401 N. Michigan Ave., Chicago, IL 60611, ☎ 312/321–9800 or 800/227–2826), **Central Holidays** (✉ 206 Central Ave., Jersey City, NJ 07307, ☎ 201/798–5777 or 800/935–5000), **Collette Tours** (✉ 162 Middle St., Pawtucket, RI 02860, ☎ 401/728–3805 or 800/832–4656, FAX 401/728–1380), **Delta Dream Vacations** (☎ 800/872–7786), **DER Tours** (✉ 11933 Wilshire Blvd., Los Angeles, CA 90025, ☎ 310/479–4411 or 800/937–1235), **General Tours** (✉ 53 Summer St., Keene, NH 03431, ☎ 603/357–5033 or 800/221–2216, FAX 603/357–4548), **Insight International Tours** (✉ 745 Atlantic Ave., Boston MA 02111, ☎ 617/482-2000 or 800/582–8380), and **Trafalgar Tours** (✉ 11 E. 26th St., New York, NY 10010, ☎ 212/689–8977 or 800/854–0103, FAX 800/457–6644).

BUDGET➤ **Cosmos** (☞ Globus, *above*) and **Trafalgar Tours** (☞ *above*).

PACKAGES

Independent vacation packages are available from major airlines and tour operators. Contact **Austrian Airlines** (☞

Central Holidays *above*) and **Delta Dream Vacations** (☎ 800/872–7786). Also try the companies listed under Group Tours, above.

THEME TRIPS

Travel Contacts (✉ Box 173, Camberley, GU15 1YE, England, ☎ 011/44/1/27667–7217, FAX 011/44/1/2766–3477), which represents 150 tour operators, can satisfy just about any special interest in Austria.

BARGE/RIVER CRUISES➤ For cruises on the Danube that spend a day in Vienna, contact **KD River Cruises of Europe** (✉ 2500 Westchester Ave., Purchase, NY 10577, ☎ 914/696–3600 or 800/346–6525, FAX 914/696–0833).

CHRISTMAS/NEW YEAR'S➤ Contact **Smolka Tours** (✉ 82 Riveredge Rd., Tinton Falls, NJ 07724, ☎ 908/576–8813 or 800/722–0057) for festive holiday-season tours that include concerts and gala balls.

FOOD AND WINE➤ **Herzerl Tours** (✉ 355 Lexington Ave., New York, NY 10017, ☎ 212/867–4830 or 800/684–8488, FAX 212/986–0717) specializes in Austria and offers trips to Vienna.

GARDEN TOURS➤ *See* **Herzel Tours,** *above.*

HISTORY AND ART➤ For tours that highlight Vienna's artistic treasures, contact **Five Star Touring** (✉ 60 E. 42nd St., #612, New York, NY 10165, ☎ 212/

818–9140 or 800/792–7827, FAX 212/818–9142), **I.S.T. Cultural Tours** (✉ 225 W. 34th St., #913, New York, NY 10122-0994, ☎ 212/563–1202 or 800/833–2111, FAX 212/594–6953), or **Smolka Tours** (☞ Christmas/New Year's, *above*). **Herzerl Tours** (☞ Food and Wine, *above*) offers tours that examine the art of Vienna in depth, and **Smithsonian Study Tours and Seminars** (✉ 1100 Jefferson Dr. SW, Room 3045, MRC 702, Washington, DC 20560, ☎ 202/357–4700, FAX 202/633–9250) often has itineraries focused on Vienna.

MUSIC➤ **Dailey-Thorp Travel** (✉ 330 W. 58th St., #610, New York, NY 10019-1817, ☎ 212/307–1555 or 800/998–4677, FAX 212/974–1420) specializes in classical music and opera programs. **I.S.T. Cultural Tours** (☞ Food and Wine, *above*) visits the cities and homes of the great classical composers and also features performances and seminars. Performing arts tickets and packages in Vienna are also available from **Smolka Tours** (☞ Christmas/New Year's, *above*).

ORGANIZATIONS

The **National Tour Association** (✉ NTA, 546 E. Main St., Lexington, KY 40508, ☎ 606/226–4444 or 800/755–8687) and the **United States Tour Operators Association** (✉ USTOA, 211 E. 51st St., Suite 12B, New York, NY 10022, ☎ 212/750–7371) can

provide lists of members and information on booking tours.

PUBLICATIONS

Contact the USTOA (☞ Organizations, *above*) for its **"Smart Traveler's Planning Kit."** Pamphlets in the kit include the "Worldwide Tour and Vacation Package Finder," "How to Select a Tour or Vacation Package," and information on the organization's consumer protection plan. Also get copy of the Better Business Bureau's **"Tips on Travel Packages"** (✉ Publication 24-195, 4200 Wilson Blvd., Arlington, VA 22203; $2).

DISCOUNT PASSES

Austrian passes are available through travel agents and **Rail Europe** (226-230 Westchester Ave., White Plains, NY 10604, ☎ 914/682–5172 or 800/438–7245; 2087 Dundas E., Suite 105, Mississauga, Ontario L4X 1M2, ☎ 416/602–4195, **DER Tours** (Box 1606, Des Plaines, IL 60017, ☎ 800/782–2424, FAX 800/282–7474), or **CIT Tours Corp.** (342 Madison Ave., Suite 207, New York, NY 10173, for rail passes 212/697-1482 or ☎ 800/223–7987; for packages ☎ 212/697–2100 or 800/248–8687 or 800/248–7245 in western U.S.).

For travel apparel, appliances, personal-care items, and other travel necessities, get a free catalog from **Magellan's** (☎ 800/962–4943, FAX 805/568–5406), **Orvis**

Travel (☎ 800/541–3541, FAX 540/343–7053), or **TravelSmith** (☎ 800/950–1600, FAX 415/455–0554).

ELECTRICAL CONVERTERS

Send a self-addressed, stamped envelope to the **Franzus Company** (✉ Customer Service, Dept. B50, Murtha Industrial Park, Box 142, Beacon Falls, CT 06403, ☎ 203/723–6664) for a copy of the free brochure "Foreign Electricity Is No Deep, Dark Secret."

For names of reputable agencies in your area, contact the **American Society of Travel Agents** (✉ ASTA, 1101 King St., Suite 200, Alexandria, VA 22314, ☎ 703/739–2782), the **Association of Canadian Travel Agents** (✉ Suite 201, 1729 Bank St., Ottawa, Ontario K1V 7Z5, ☎ 613/521–0474, FAX 613/521–0805) or the **Association of British Travel Agents** (✉ 55-57 Newman St., London W1P 4AH, ☎ 0171/637–2444, FAX 0171/637–0713).

U

The U.S. Department of State's American Citizens Services office (✉ Room 4811, Washington, DC 20520; enclose SASE) issues **Consular Information Sheets** on all foreign countries. These cover issues such as crime, security, political climate, and health risks as well as listing embassy locations, entry requirements, currency regulations, and providing other useful information. For the latest information, stop in at any U.S. passport office, consulate, or embassy; call the interactive hot line (☎ 202/647–5225, FAX 202/647–3000); or, with your PC's modem, tap into the department's computer bulletin board (☎ 202/647–9225).

V
VISITOR
INFORMATION

Contact the **Austrian National Tourist Office.**

In Canada: ✉ 2 Bloor St. E, Suite 3330, Toronto, Ontario M4W 1A8, ☎ 416/967–3381, FAX 416/967–4101; ✉ 1010 Sherbrooke St. W, Suite 1410, Montréal, Québec H3A 2R7, ☎ 514/849–3709, FAX 514/849–9577; ✉ 200 Granville St., Suite 1380, Granville Sq., Vancouver, BC V6C 1S4, ☎ 604/683–5808 or 604/683–8695, FAX 604/662–8528.

In the U.K.: ✉ 30 St. George St., London W1R 0AL, ☎ 0171/629–0461, FAX 0171/499–6038. From a Touch-Tone phone you can get snow conditions and other taped information.

In the U.S.: ✉ 500 5th Ave., 20th floor, New York, NY 10110, ☎ 212/944–6880, FAX 212/730–4568, or write to Box 1142, New York, NY 10108; ✉ 11601 Wilshire Blvd., Suite 2480, Los Angeles, CA 90025, ☎ 310/477–3332, FAX 310/477–5141, or write to Box 491938, Los Angeles, CA 90049; ✉ 500 N. Michigan Ave., Suite 1950, Chicago, IL 60611, ☎ 312/644–8029, FAX 312/644–6526; ✉ 1300 Post Oak Blvd., Suite 1700, Houston, TX 77056, ☎ 713/850–8888, FAX 713/850–7857; ✉ 1350 Connecticut Ave. NW, Suite 501, Washington DC 20036, ☎ 202/835–8962, FAX 202/835–8960.

IN THE U.K.

Austrian National Tourist Office (✉ 30 St. George St., London W1R 0AL, ☎ 0171/629–0461).

W
WEATHER

For current conditions and forecasts, plus the local time and helpful travel tips, call the **Weather Channel Connection** (☎ 900/932–8437; 95¢ per minute) from a Touch-Tone phone.

The *International Traveler's Weather Guide* (✉ Weather Press, Box 660606, Sacramento, CA 95866, ☎ 916/974–0201 or 800/972–0201; $10.95 includes shipping), written by two meteorologists, provides month-by-month information on temperature, humidity, and precipitation in more than 175 cities worldwide.

SMART TRAVEL TIPS A TO Z

Basic Information on Traveling in Vienna and Savvy Tips to Make Your Trip a Breeze

A

AIR TRAVEL

If time is an issue, **always look for nonstop flights,** which require no change of plane. If possible, **avoid connecting flights,** which stop at least once and can involve a change of plane, even though the flight number remains the same; if the first leg is late, the second waits.

For better service, **fly smaller or regional carriers,** which often have higher passenger satisfaction ratings. Sometimes they have such in-flight amenities as leather seats or greater legroom and they often have better food.

CUTTING COSTS

The Sunday travel section of most newspapers is a good place to look for deals.

MAJOR AIRLINES➤ The least-expensive airfares from the major airlines are priced for round-trip travel and are subject to restrictions. Usually, you must **book in advance and buy the ticket within 24 hours** to get cheaper fares, and you may have to **stay over a Saturday night.** The lowest fare is subject to availability, and only a small percentage of the plane's total seats is sold at that price. It's smart to **call a number of airlines, and when you are quoted a good price, book it on the spot**—the same fare may not be available on the same flight the next day. Airlines generally allow you to change your return date for a $25 to $50 fee. If you don't use your ticket, you can apply the cost toward the purchase of a new ticket, again for a small charge. However, most low-fare tickets are nonrefundable. To get the lowest airfare, **check different routings.** If your destination has more than one gateway, **compare prices to different airports.**

FROM THE U.K.➤ To save money on flights, **look into an APEX or Super-PEX ticket.** APEX tickets must be booked in advance and have certain restrictions. Super-PEX tickets can be purchased right at the airport.

CONSOLIDATORS➤ Consolidators buy tickets for scheduled flights at reduced rates from the airlines, then sell them at prices below the lowest available from the airlines directly—usually without advance restrictions. Sometimes you can even get your money back if you need to return the ticket. Carefully read the fine print detailing penalties for changes and cancellations. If you doubt the reliability of a consolidator, **confirm your reservation with the airline.**

ALOFT

AIRLINE FOOD➤ If you hate airline food, **ask for special meals when booking.** These can be vegetarian, low-cholesterol, or kosher, for example; commonly prepared to order in smaller quantities than standard fare, they can be tastier.

JET LAG➤ To avoid this syndrome, which occurs when travel disrupts your body's natural cycles, try to maintain a normal routine. At night, **get some sleep.** By day, move about the cabin to **stretch your legs, eat light meals, and drink water—not alcohol.**

SMOKING➤ Smoking is not allowed on flights of six hours or less within the continental United States. Smoking is also prohibited on flights within Canada. For U.S. flights longer than six hours or international flights, **contact your carrier regarding their smoking policy.** Some carriers have prohibited smoking throughout their system; others allow smoking only on certain routes or even certain departures of that route.

B

BUSINESS HOURS

Banks are open weekdays 8–3, Thursday until 5:30 PM. Smaller bank offices close from 12:30 to 1:30. All are closed on Saturday, but you can change money at various locations (such as American

Express offices on Saturday morning and major railroad stations around the clock).

Museum hours vary from museum to museum; if there's a closing day, it is usually Monday. Few museums are open at night.

In general, you'll find **shops** open weekdays from 8:30 or 9 AM until 6 PM. Many food stores, bakeries, and small grocery shops are from 7 or 7:30 AM until 6 or 6:30 PM. On Saturday, shops stay open until noon or 1 PM, except on the first Saturday of the month, when (except for food stores) they stay open until 5, a few until 6 PM. Barbers and hairdressers traditionally take Monday off, but there are exceptions.

NATIONAL HOLIDAYS

All banks and shops are closed on national holidays: Jan. 1, New Year's Day; Jan. 6, Epiphany; Mar. 30–31, Easter Sunday and Monday; May 1, May Day; May 8, Ascension Day; May 18–19, Pentecost Sunday and Monday; May 29, Corpus Christi; Aug. 15, Assumption; Oct. 26, National Holiday; Nov. 1, All Saints' Day; Dec. 8, Immaculate Conception; Dec. 25–26, Christmas. Museums are open on most holidays and closed on Good Friday and Dec. 24. Banks and offices are closed on Dec. 8, but most shops are open.

C

CAMERAS, CAMCORDERS, & COMPUTERS

IN TRANSIT

Always **keep your film, tape, or disks out of the sun;** never put these on the dashboard of a car. Carry an extra supply of batteries, and **be prepared to turn on your camera, camcorder, or laptop computer for security personnel** to prove that it's real.

X-RAYS

Always **ask for hand inspection at security.** Such requests are virtually always honored at U.S. airports, and are usually accommodated abroad. Photographic film becomes clouded after successive exposure to airport x-ray machines. Videotape and computer disks are not harmed by X-rays, but **keep your tapes and disks away from metal detectors.**

CUSTOMS

Before departing, **register your foreign-made camera or laptop with U.S. Customs.** If your equipment is U.S.-made, call the consulate of the country you'll be visiting to find out whether it should be registered with local customs upon arrival.

CAR RENTAL

CUTTING COSTS

To get the best deal, **book through a travel agent who is willing to shop around.** Ask your agent to **look for fly-drive packages,** which also save you money, and **ask if local taxes**

are included in the rental or fly-drive price. These can be as high as 20% in some destinations. Don't forget to find out about required deposits, cancellation penalties, drop-off charges, and the cost of any required insurance coverage.

Also **ask your travel agent about a company's customer-service record.** How has it responded to late plane arrivals and vehicle mishaps? Are there often lines at the rental counter, and—if you're traveling during a holiday period—does a confirmed reservation guarantee you a car?

Always **find out what equipment is standard** at your destination before specifying what you want; automatic transmission and air-conditioning are usually optional—and very expensive.

Be sure to **look into wholesalers**—companies that do not own their own fleets but rent in bulk from those that do and often offer better rates than traditional car-rental operations. Prices are best during off-peak periods; rentals booked through wholesalers must be paid for before you leave the United States.

INSURANCE

When driving a rented car, you are generally responsible for any damage to or loss of the rental vehicle. Before you rent, **see what coverage you already have** under the terms of your personal auto insurance policy and credit cards.

If you do not have auto insurance or an umbrella insurance policy that covers damage to third parties, purchasing CDW or LDW is highly recommended.

Collision policies that car-rental companies sell for European rentals typically do not cover stolen vehicles. Before you buy additional coverage for theft, find out if your credit card or personal auto insurance will cover the loss.

LICENSE REQUIREMENTS

In Austria your own driver's license is acceptable. An International Driver's Permit is a good idea; it's available from the American or Canadian automobile associations, or, in the United Kingdom, from the AA or RAC.

SURCHARGES

Before you pick up a car in one city and leave it in another, **ask about drop-off charges or one-way service fees,** which can be substantial. Note, too, that some rental agencies charge extra if you return the car before the time specified on your contract. To avoid a hefty refueling fee, **fill the tank just before you turn in the car**—but be aware that gas stations near the rental outlet may overcharge.

CHILDREN & TRAVEL

When traveling with children, **plan ahead** and **involve your youngsters** as you outline your trip. When packing, **include a supply of things to keep them**

busy en route (☞ Children & Travel *in* Important Contacts A to Z). On sightseeing days, try to **schedule activities of special interest to your children,** like a trip to a zoo or a playground. If you **plan your itinerary around seasonal festivals,** you'll never lack for things to do. In addition, **check local newspapers for special events** mounted by public libraries, museums, and parks.

BABY-SITTING

For recommended local sitters, **check with your hotel desk.**

DRIVING

If you are renting a car, don't forget to **arrange for a car seat when you reserve.** Sometimes they're free. Seats are required for small children.

FLYING

As a general rule, infants under two not occupying a seat fly at greatly reduced fares and occasionally for free. If your children are two or older **ask about special children's fares.** Age limits for these fares vary among carriers. Rules also vary regarding unaccompanied minors, so again, check with your airline.

BAGGAGE➤ In general, the adult baggage allowance applies to children paying half or more of the adult fare. If you are traveling with an infant, **ask about carry-on allowances** before departure. In general, for infants charged 10% of the adult fare you are allowed one carry-on bag and a collapsible

stroller, which may have to be checked; you may be limited to less if the flight is full.

SAFETY SEATS➤ According to the FAA, it's a good idea to **use safety seats aloft** for children weighing less than 40 pounds. Airline policies vary. U.S. carriers allow FAA-approved models but usually require that you buy a ticket, even if your child would otherwise ride free, since the seats must be strapped into regular seats. However, some U.S. and foreign-flag airlines may require you to hold your baby during takeoff and landing—defeating the seat's purpose. Other foreign carriers may not allow infant seats at all, or may charge a child rather than an infant fare for their use.

FACILITIES➤ When making your reservation, **request for children's meals or freestanding bassinets** if you need them; the latter are available only to those seated at the bulkhead, where there's enough legroom. If you don't need a bassinet, **think twice before requesting bulkhead seats**—the only storage space for in-flight necessities is in inconveniently distant overhead bins.

GAMES

Milton Bradley and Parker Brothers have travel versions of some of their most popular games, including Yahtzee, Trouble, Sorry, and Monopoly. Prices run $5 to $8. Look for them in the travel section of your local toy store.

LODGING

Most hotels allow children under a certain age to stay in their parents' room at no extra charge; others charge them as extra adults. Be sure to **ask about the cutoff age.**

CUSTOMS & DUTIES

To speed your clearance through customs, **keep receipts for all your purchases abroad** and **be ready to show the inspector what you've bought.** If you feel that you've been incorrectly or unfairly charged a duty, you can **appeal assessments in dispute.** First ask to see a supervisor. If you are still unsatisfied, **write to the port director** at your point of entry, sending your customs receipt and any other appropriate documentation. The address will be listed on your receipt. If you still don't get satisfaction, you can take your case to customs headquarters in Washington.

IN VIENNA

Travelers over 17 coming from European countries—regardless of citizenship—may bring in duty-free 200 cigarettes or 50 cigars or 250 grams of tobacco, 2 liters of wine and 1 liter of spirits, one bottle of toilet water (approx. 300 ml), and 50 milliliters of perfume. These limits may be liberalized or eliminated under terms of the European Union agreement. Travelers from all other countries (such as those coming directly from the United States or Canada) may bring in twice these amounts. All visitors may bring gifts or other purchases valued at up to AS2,500 (about $235), although in practice you'll seldom be asked.

IN THE U.S.

You may bring home $400 worth of foreign goods duty-free if you've been out of the country for at least 48 hours and haven't already used the $400 allowance, or any part of it, in the past 30 days.

Travelers 21 or older may bring back 1 liter of alcohol duty-free, provided the beverage laws of the state through which they reenter the United States allow it. In addition, regardless of their age, they are allowed 100 non-Cuban cigars and 200 cigarettes. Antiques, which the U.S. Customs Service defines as objects more than 100 years old, are duty-free. Original works of art done entirely by hand are also duty-free. These include, but are not limited to, paintings, drawings, and sculptures.

Duty-free, travelers may mail packages valued at up to $200 to themselves and up to $100 to others, with a limit of one parcel per addressee per day (and no alcohol or tobacco products or perfume valued at more than $5); on the outside, the package must be labeled as being either for personal use or an unsolicited gift, and a list of its contents and their retail value must be attached. Mailed items do not affect your duty-free allowance on your return.

IN CANADA

If you've been out of Canada for at least seven days, you may bring in C$500 worth of goods duty-free. If you've been away for fewer than seven days but for more than 48 hours, the duty-free allowance drops to C$200; if your trip lasts between 24 and 48 hours, the allowance is C$50. You cannot pool allowances with family members. Goods claimed under the C$500 exemption may follow you by mail; those claimed under the lesser exemptions must accompany you.

Alcohol and tobacco products may be included in the seven-day and 48-hour exemptions but not in the 24-hour exemption. If you meet the age requirements of the province or territory through which you reenter Canada, you may bring in, duty-free, 1.14 liters (40 imperial ounces) of wine or liquor *or* 24 12-ounce cans or bottles of beer or ale. If you are 16 or older, you may bring in, duty-free, 200 cigarettes, 50 cigars or cigarillos, and 400 tobacco sticks or 400 grams of manufactured tobacco. Alcohol and tobacco must accompany you on your return.

An unlimited number of gifts with a value of up to C$60 each may be mailed to Canada duty-free. These do not affect your duty-free allowance on your return. Label the package "Unsolicited Gift—Value Under $60." Alcohol and tobacco are excluded.

IN THE U.K.

If your journey was wholly within European Union (EU) countries, you no longer need to pass through customs when you return to the United Kingdom. If you plan to bring back large quantities of alcohol or tobacco, check in advance on EU limits.

D
DINING

Austrians often eat up to five meals a day: a very early Continental breakfast of rolls and coffee; *Gabelfrühstück,* a slightly more substantial breakfast with eggs or cold meat—possibly even a small goulash—at mid-morning (understood to be 9, sharp); a main meal, usually served between noon and 2; afternoon *Jause* (coffee with cake) at teatime; and, unless dining out, a light supper to end the day, between 6 and 9, tending toward the later hour. Many restaurant kitchens close in the afternoon, but some post a notice saying *Durchgehend warme Küche,* meaning that hot food is available even between regular mealtimes.

When dining out, you'll get best value at the simpler restaurants. Most post menus with prices outside. If you begin with the *Würstelstand* (sausage vendor) on the street, the next category would be the *Imbiss-Stube,* for simple, quick snacks. Many

meat stores serve soups and a daily special at noon; a blackboard menu will be posted outside. A number of cafés also offer lunch, but watch the prices; some can turn out to be more expensive than restaurants. *Gasthäuser* are simple restaurants or country inns. Viennese hotels have some of the best restaurants in the country, often with outstanding chefs.

Wine cellars and wine gardens, or *Heurige* (for new wine), are a special category among Austrian eateries. They serve everything from a limited selection of cold cuts and cheeses to full meals. Some wine cellars are known as much for their food as for their wines.

WHAT TO WEAR

If you plan to spend much time in cities or the better resorts and go to top-notch places, you will find Austrians more formal, on the whole, than Americans and Britons. While a jacket and tie are generally advised for restaurants only in the top price categories, many dining establishments smile on gentlemen in jackets and invariably sit them at better tables. For lower priced restaurants, casual-smart resort wear is fine, although in Vienna jacket and tie are preferred in some moderate (**$$**) restaurants at dinner. When in doubt, it's best to dress up. Remember that if you are going to investigate any high altitudes (and it's pretty hard not to in Austria), you will find evenings chilly even in

midsummer, so carry a warm sweater.

DISABILITIES & ACCESSIBILITY

The Austria National Tourist Office in New York has a guide to Vienna for people with disabilities and a special map of the city's accessible sights. The Hilton, InterContinental, and Marriott chain hotels plus a number of smaller ones are accessible. The railroads are both understanding and helpful. If prior arrangements have been made, taxis and private vehicles are allowed to drive right to the train platform; railway personnel will help with boarding and leaving trains; and with three days' notice, a special wheelchair can be provided for getting around train corridors. If you're traveling by air, ask in advance for assistance or a wheelchair at your destination. A number of stations in the Vienna subway system have only stairs or escalators, but elevators are being added at major stations.

When discussing accessibility with an operator or reservationist, **ask hard questions.** Are there any stairs, inside *or* out? Are there grab bars next to the toilet *and* in the shower/tub? How wide is the doorway to the room? To the bathroom? For the most extensive facilities, meeting the latest legal specifications, **opt for newer accommodations,** which more often have been designed with access in mind. Older properties or ships must usually be retrofitted and may offer more limited facilities as a result. Be sure to **discuss your needs before booking.**

You shouldn't have to pay for a discount. In fact, you may already be eligible for all kinds of savings. Here are some time-honored strategies for getting the best deal.

LOOK IN YOUR WALLET

When you **use your credit card to make travel purchases,** you may get free travel-accident insurance, collision damage insurance, medical or legal assistance, depending on the card and bank that issued it. American Express, Visa, and MasterCard provide one or more of these services, so **get a copy of your card's travel benefits.** If you are a member of the AAA or an oil-company-sponsored road-assistance plan, always **ask hotel or car-rental reservationists for auto-club discounts.** Some clubs offer additional discounts on tours, cruises, or admission to attractions. And don't forget that auto-club membership entitles you to free maps and trip-planning services.

SENIORS CITIZENS & STUDENTS

As a senior-citizen traveler, you may be eligible for special rates, but you should mention your senior-citizen status up front. If you're a student or under 26 you can also get discounts, especially if you have an official ID card (☞ Senior-Citizen Discounts *and* Students on the Road, *below*).

DIAL FOR DOLLARS

To save money, **look into "1-800" discount reservations services,** which often have lower rates. These services use their buying power to get a better price on hotels, airline tickets, and sometimes even car rentals. When booking a room, always **call the hotel's local toll-free number** (if one is available) rather than the central reservations number—you'll often get a better price. Ask the reservationist about special packages or corporate rates, which are usually available even if you're not traveling on business.

JOIN A CLUB?

Discount clubs can be a legitimate source of savings, but you must use the participating hotels and visit the participating attractions in order to realize any benefits. Remember, too, that you have to pay a fee to join, so **determine if you'll save enough to warrant your membership fee.** Before booking with a club, **make sure the hotel or other supplier isn't offering a better deal.**

GET A GUARANTEE

When shopping for the best deal on hotels and car rentals, **look for guaranteed exchange rates,** which protect you against a falling dollar. With your rate locked in, you won't pay more even if the price goes up in the local currency.

Travel insurance can protect your monetary investment, replace your luggage and its contents, or provide for medical coverage should you fall ill during your trip. Most tour operators, travel agents, and insurance agents sell specialized health-and-accident, flight, trip-cancellation, and luggage insurance as well as comprehensive policies with some or all of these coverages. Comprehensive policies may also reimburse you for delays due to weather—an important consideration if you're traveling during the winter months. Some health-insurance policies do not cover preexisting conditions, but waivers may be available in specific cases. Coverage is sold by the companies listed in Important Contacts A to Z; these companies act as the policy's administrators. The actual insurance is usually underwritten by a well-known name, such as The Travelers or Continental Insurance.

Before you make any purchase, **review your existing health and homeowner's policies** to find out whether they cover expenses incurred while traveling.

BAGGAGE

Airline liability for baggage is limited to $1,250 per person on domestic flights. On international flights, it amounts to $9.07 per pound or $20 per kilogram for checked baggage (roughly $640 per 70-pound bag) and $400 per passenger for unchecked baggage. Insurance for losses exceeding the terms of your airline ticket can be bought directly from the airline at check-in for about $10 per $1,000 of coverage; note that it excludes a rather extensive list of items, shown on your airline ticket.

COMPREHENSIVE

Comprehensive insurance policies include all the coverages described above plus some that may not be available in more specific policies. If you have purchased an expensive vacation, especially one that involves travel abroad, comprehensive insurance is a must; **look for policies that include trip delay insurance,** which will protect you in the event that weather problems cause you to miss your flight, tour, or cruise. A few insurers will also sell you a waiver for preexisting medical conditions. Some of the companies that offer both these features are Access America, Carefree Travel Insurance, Travel Insured International, and Travel Guard International (☞ Insurance *in* Important Contacts A to Z).

FLIGHT

You should **think twice before buying flight insurance.** Often purchased as a last-minute impulse at the airport, it pays a lump sum when a plane crashes, either to a beneficiary if the insured dies or sometimes to a surviving passenger who loses his

or her eyesight or a limb. Supplementing the airlines' coverage described in the limits-of-liability paragraphs on your ticket, it's expensive and basically unnecessary. Charging an airline ticket to a major credit card often automatically provides you with coverage that may also extend to travel by bus, train, and ship.

HEALTH

Medicare generally does not cover health care costs outside the United States; nor do many privately issued policies. If your own health insurance policy does not cover you outside the United States, **consider buying supplemental medical coverage.** It can reimburse you for $1,000– $150,000 worth of medical and/or dental expenses incurred as a result of an accident or illness during a trip. These policies also may include a personal-accident, or death-and-dismemberment, provision, which pays a lump sum ranging from $15,000 to $500,000 to your beneficiaries if you die or to you if you lose one or more limbs or your eyesight, and a medical-assistance provision, which may either reimburse you for the cost of referrals, evacuation, or repatriation and other services, or automatically enroll you as a member of a particular medical-assistance company. (☞ Health Issues *in* Important Contacts A to Z.)

U.K. TRAVELERS

You can buy an annual travel insurance policy valid for most vacations

during the year in which it's purchased. If you are pregnant or have a preexisting medical condition make sure you're covered before buying such a policy.

TRIP

Without insurance, you will lose all or most of your money if you cancel your trip regardless of the reason. Especially if your airline ticket, cruise, or package tour is nonrefundable and cannot be changed, it's essential that you **buy trip-cancellation-and-interruption insurance.** When considering how much coverage you need, look for a policy that will cover the cost of your trip plus the nondiscounted price of a one-way airline ticket should you need to return home early. Read the fine print carefully, especially sections that define "family member" and "preexisting medical conditions." Also **consider default or bankruptcy insurance,** which protects you against a supplier's failure to deliver. Be aware, however, that if you buy such a policy from a travel agency, tour operator, airline, or cruise line, it may not cover default by the firm in question.

L
LANGUAGE

German is the official national language in Austria. In larger cities and in most resort areas, you will have no problem finding people who speak English; hotel and restaurant staffs in particular speak it reasonably well, and most young Austrians speak it at least passably.

LODGING

You can live like a king in a real castle in Austria or get by on a modest budget. Starting at the lower end, you can find a room in a private house or dormitory space in a youth hostel. Next up the line come the simpler pensions, many of them identified as *Frühstückspension,* meaning bed-and-breakfast. The fancier pensions in the cities can often cost as much as hotels; the difference lies in the services they offer. Most pensions, for example, do not staff the front desk around the clock. Among the hotels, you can find accommodations ranging from the most modest, with a shower and toilet down the hall, to the most elegant, with every possible amenity.

Overcapacity has dimmed the outlook for construction of new four-and five-star hotels. With many expensive chain hotels discounting heavily, it pays to **ask about price when you make reservations as deals are often available.** More capacity is gradually being added in the three-star category, adequate lodgings for all but those who want (and are willing to pay for) the luxuries of the top categories.

Assume that hotels operate on the European Plan (EP, with no meals) unless we note differently. Most hotels—except the most

expensive options—include a free breakfast. In rural and resort areas, however, some hotels opt for half-board basis (breakfast and one meal a day must be taken), particularly in the Western Alps region—we note if this is the case in our reviews. Top resort hotels throughout the country can insist on half or even full board in peak season; at other times, you can set your own terms.

All hotel prices include service charges (usually 10% but occasionally higher) and federal and local taxes—and in a few places, a small local tourism tax is added later. Some country hotels may add a heating supplement in winter.

APARTMENT & VILLA RENTAL

If you want a home base that's roomy enough for a family and comes with cooking facilities, **consider taking a furnished rental.** This can also save you money, but not always—some rentals are luxury properties (economical only when your party is large). Home-exchange directories list rentals—often second homes owned by prospective house swappers—and some services search for a house or apartment for you (even a castle if that's your fancy) and handle the paperwork. Some send an illustrated catalog; others send photographs only of specific properties, sometimes at a charge; up-front registration fees may apply.

HOME EXCHANGE

If you would like to find a house, an apartment, or some other type of vacation property to exchange for your own while on holiday, **become a member of a home-exchange organization,** which will send you its updated listings of available exchanges for a year, and will include your own listing in at least one of them. Arrangements for the actual exchange are made by the two parties involved, not by the organization.

M
MAIL

Within Europe, all mail goes by air, so there's no supplement on letters or postcards. A letter of up to 20 grams (about ¾ ounce) takes AS7, a postcard AS6. To the United States or Canada, a letter of up to 20 grams takes AS10 minimum, plus AS1.50 per 5 grams for airmail. If in doubt, mail your letters from a post office and have the weight checked. The Austrian post office also adheres strictly to a size standard; if your letter or card is outside the norm, you'll have to pay a surcharge. Postcards via airmail to the United States or Canada need AS8.50. Post offices have air-letter (aerogram) forms for AS12 to any overseas destination.

RECEIVING MAIL

When you don't know where you'll be staying, American Express mail service is a great convenience, with no charge to anyone either holding an American Express credit card or carrying American Express traveler's checks. Offices are at Kärntner Str. 21–23, A–1015 Vienna, ☎ 0222/515–40–0. You can also have mail held at any Austrian post office; letters should be marked *Poste Restante* or *Postlagernd.* You will be asked for identification when you collect mail. In Vienna, if not addressed to a specific district post office, this service is handled through the main post office (Fleischmarkt 19, A–1010 Vienna, ☎ 0222/515–09–0).

MEDICAL ASSISTANCE

No one plans to get sick while traveling, but it happens, so **consider signing up with a medical assistance company.** These outfits provide referrals, emergency evacuation or repatriation, 24-hour telephone hot lines for medical consultation, cash for emergencies, and other personal and legal assistance. They also dispatch medical personnel and arrange for the relay of medical records. Coverage varies by plan, so **read the fine print carefully.**

MONEY

The Austrian unit of currency is the schilling (AS), subdivided into 100 groschen. At press time (spring 1996), the exchange rate was about AS10.4 to the dollar, AS15.9 to the pound sterling. These rates can and will vary. The schilling is pegged

to the German mark at a constant 7-to-1 ratio.

There are Austrian coins for 5, 10, and 50 groschen and for 1, 5, 10, and 20 schillings. The paper notes have AS20, AS50, AS100, AS500, AS1,000, and AS5,000 face value. There is little visible difference between the 100- and 500-schilling notes; **be careful, since confusion could be expensive!** Legally, foreign exchange is limited to licensed offices (banks and exchange offices); in practice, the rule is universally ignored.

ATMS

CASH ADVANCES➤ Before leaving home, **make sure that your credit cards have been programmed for ATM use in Vienna.** Note that Discover is accepted mostly in the United States. Local bank cards often do not work overseas either; **ask your bank about a MasterCard/Cirrus or Visa debit card,** which works like a bank card but can be used at any ATM displaying a MasterCard/Cirrus or Visa logo.

TRANSACTION FEES➤ Although fees charged for ATM transactions may be higher abroad than at home, Cirrus and Plus exchange rates are excellent, because they are based on wholesale rates offered only by major banks.

COSTS

A cup of coffee in a café will cost about AS25; a half-liter of draft beer, AS27–40; a glass of wine, AS35; a Coca-Cola, AS25; an open-

face sandwich, AS25; a mid-range theater ticket AS200; a concert ticket AS250–500; an opera ticket AS600 upwards; a 1-mile taxi ride, AS35. Outside the hotels, laundering a shirt costs about AS30; dry cleaning a suit costs around AS130–140; a dress, AS100–120. A shampoo and set for a woman will cost around AS350–450, a manicure about AS150–180; a man's haircut (without shampoo) will cost about AS200–250.

EXCHANGING CURRENCY

For the most favorable rates, **change money at post offices or banks.** You won't do as well at exchange booths in airports or rail and bus stations, in hotels, in restaurants, or in stores, although you may find their hours more convenient. To avoid lines at airport exchange booths, **get a small amount of the local currency before you leave home.**

TAXES

VAT➤ Austrian prices include 20% value-added tax (VAT) on most items, 10% on some goods and services. If you buy goods totaling AS1,000 or more in one shop, **ask for the appropriate papers when you make the purchase,** and you can get a refund of the VAT either at the airport when you leave or by mail. Note that the VAT refund does *not* apply to those living in other EU countries. You can have the refund credited to your credit card account and not have to worry about the exchange rates.

TRAVELER'S CHECKS

Whether or not to buy traveler's checks depends on where you are headed; **take cash to rural areas and small towns, traveler's checks to cities.** The most widely recognized checks are issued by American Express, Citicorp, Thomas Cook, and Visa. These are sold by major commercial banks for 1%–3% of the checks' face value—it pays to **shop around.** Both American Express and Thomas Cook issue checks that can be countersigned and used by either you or your traveling companion. So you won't be left with excess foreign currency, **buy a few checks in small denominations** to cash toward the end of your trip. Before leaving home, **contact your issuer for information on where to cash your checks** without a incurring a transaction fee. Record the numbers of all your checks, and keep this listing in a separate place, crossing off the numbers of checks you have cashed.

WIRING MONEY

For a fee of 3%–10%, depending on the amount of the transaction, you can have money sent to you from home through Money-Gram^{SM} or Western Union (☞ Money Matters *in* Important Contacts A to Z). The transferred funds and the service fee can be charged to a Master-Card or Visa account.

P
PACKING FOR
VIENNA

Austrians dress conservatively; slacks on women are as rare as loud sport shirts are on men. That noted, jeans are ubiquitous in Austria as everywhere, but are considered inappropriate at concerts (other than pop) or formal restaurants. For concerts and opera, women may want a skirt or dress, and men a jacket; even in summer, gala performances at small festivals tend to be dressy. And since an evening outside at a *Heuriger* (wine garden) may be on your agenda, be sure to take a sweater or light wrap. Unless you're staying in an expensive hotel or will be in one place for more than a day or two, **take hand-washables;** laundry service gets complicated. Austria is a walking country, in cities and mountains alike. So **pack sturdy, comfortable shoes.** You'll need flat heels to cope with the cobblestones.

Bring an extra pair of eyeglasses or contact lenses in your carry-on luggage, and if you have a health problem, **pack enough medication** to last the trip or have your doctor write you a prescription using the drug's generic name, because brand names vary from country to country (you'll then need a duplicate prescription from a local doctor). It's important that you **don't put prescription drugs or valuables in luggage to be checked,** for it could go astray. To avoid

problems with customs officials, carry medications in the original packaging. Also, don't forget the addresses of offices that handle refunds of lost traveler's checks.

ELECTRICITY

To use your U.S.-purchased electric-powered equipment, **bring a converter and an adapter.** The electrical current in Austria is 240 volts, 50 cycles alternating current (AC); wall outlets take continental-type plugs, with two round prongs.

If your appliances are dual-voltage, you'll need only an adapter. Hotels sometimes have 110-volt outlets for low-wattage appliances near the sink, marked FOR SHAVERS ONLY; don't use them for high-wattage appliances like blow-dryers. If your laptop computer is older, carry a converter; new laptops operate equally well on 110 and 220 volts, so you need only an adapter.

LUGGAGE

Airline baggage allowances depend on the airline, the route, and the class of your ticket; ask in advance. In general, on domestic flights and on international flights between the United States and foreign destinations, you are entitled to check two bags. A third piece may be brought on board, but it must fit easily under the seat in front of you or in the overhead compartment. In the United States, the FAA gives airlines broad latitude regarding carry-on allowances, and they tend to tailor them to different aircraft and operational conditions. Charges for excess, oversize, or overweight pieces vary.

If you are flying between two foreign destinations, note that baggage allowances may be determined not by piece but by weight— generally 88 pounds (40 kilograms) in first class, 66 pounds (30 kilograms) in business class, and 44 pounds (20 kilograms) in economy. If your flight between two cities abroad *connects* with your transatlantic or transpacific flight, the piece method still applies.

SAFEGUARDING YOUR LUGGAGE➤ Before leaving home, **itemize your bags' contents** and their worth, and label them with your name, address, and phone number. (If you use your home address, cover it so that potential thieves can't see it readily.) Inside each bag, **pack a copy of your itinerary.** At check-in, **make sure that each bag is correctly tagged** with the destination airport's three-letter code. If your bags arrive damaged—or fail to arrive at all—file a written report with the airline before leaving the airport.

PASSPORTS & VISAS

If you don't already have one, **get a passport.** It is advisable that you **leave one photocopy of your passport's data page** with someone at home and keep another with you, separated from your passport, while travel-ing. If you lose your passport, promptly call the nearest embassy or consulate and the local police; having the data page information can speed replacement.

IN THE U.S.

All U.S. citizens, even infants, need only a valid passport to enter Austria for stays of up to 90 days. Application forms for both first-time and renewal passports are available at any of the 13 U.S. Passport Agency offices and at some post offices and courthouses. Passports are usually mailed within four weeks; allow five weeks or more in spring and summer.

CANADIANS

You need only a valid passport to enter Austria for stays of up to 90 days. Passport application forms are available at 28 regional passport offices, as well as post offices and travel agencies. Whether for a first or a renewal passport, you must apply in person. Children under 16 may be included on a parent's passport but must have their own to travel alone. Passports are valid for five years and are usually mailed within two to three weeks of application.

U.K. CITIZENS

Citizens of the United Kingdom need only a valid passport to enter Austria for stays of up to 90 days. Applications for new and renewal passports are available from main post offices and at the passport offices in Belfast, Glasgow, Liverpool, London, Newport, and Peterborough. You may apply in person at all passport offices, or by mail to all except the London office. Children under 16 may travel on an accompanying parent's passport. All passports are valid for 10 years. Allow a month for processing.

S

SENIOR-CITIZEN DISCOUNTS

Austria has so many senior citizens that facilities almost everywhere cater to the needs of older travelers, with discounts for rail travel and museum entry. **Check with the Austrian National Tourist Office** to find what form of identification is required, but generally if you're 65 or over (women 62), once you're in Austria the railroads will issue you a *Seniorenpass* (you'll need a passport photo and passport or other proof of age) entitling you to the senior citizen discounts regardless of nationality.

To qualify for age-related discounts, **mention your senior-citizen status up front** when booking hotel reservations, not when checking out, and before you're seated in restaurants, not when paying the bill. Note that discounts may be limited to certain menus, days, or hours. When renting a car, **ask about promotional car-rental discounts**—they can net even lower costs than your senior-citizen discount.

SHOPPING

In general, such locally produced goods as

textiles, crystal, porcelain figurines, leather goods, wood carvings, and other handicrafts are good value. Prices are similar throughout the country, but higher, of course, in the major tourist centers. Shops will ship your purchases, but if you can, take them with you. If you do ship goods, be sure you know the terms in advance, how the items will be sent, and when you can expect to receive them, and get all these details in writing.

STUDENTS ON THE ROAD

To save money, **look into deals available through student-oriented travel agencies.** To qualify, you'll need to have a bona fide student ID card. Members of international student groups are also eligible (☞ Students *in* Important Contacts A to Z).

T

TELEPHONES

Austria's telephone service is in a state of change as the country converts to a digital system. We make every effort to keep numbers up to date, but do recheck the number if you have problems getting the connection you want (a sharp tone indicates no connection or that the number has been changed). All numbers given in this guide include the city or town area code; if you are calling within that city or town, dial the local number only. Note that if you're calling Vienna from within Austria the city area code is 0222; if you call

from outside Austria, it's 01.

Basic telephone numbers in Austria are three to seven digits; longer numbers are the basic number plus a direct-dial extension of two to five digits.

LONG-DISTANCE

You can dial direct to almost any point on the globe from Austria. However, it costs more to telephone *from* Austria than it does to telephone *to* Austria. Calls from post offices are always the least expensive and you can get helpful assistance in placing a long-distance call; in large cities, these centers at main post offices are open around the clock.

The long-distance services of AT&T, MCI, and Sprint make calling home relatively convenient, but in many hotels you may find it impossible to dial the access number. The hotel operator may also refuse to make the connection. Instead, the hotel will charge you a premium rate—as much as 400% more than a calling card—for calls placed from your hotel room. To avoid such price gouging, travel with more than one company's long-distance calling card—a hotel may block Sprint but not MCI. If the hotel operator claims that you cannot use any phone card, ask to be connected to an international operator, who will help you to access your phone card. You can also dial the international operator yourself. If none of this works, try calling your phone

company collect in the United States. If collect calls are also blocked, call from a pay phone in the hotel lobby. Before you go, **find out the local access codes** for your destinations.

To make a collect call—you can't do this from pay phones—dial the operator and ask for an R-Gespräch (pronounced air-ga-*shprayk*). Most operators speak English; if yours doesn't, you'll be passed to one who does.

The international access code for the United States and Canada is 001, followed by the area code and number. For Great Britain, first dial 0044, then the city code *without the usual "0"* (171 or 181 for London), and the number. Other country and many city codes are given in the front of telephone books (in Vienna, in the *A-H* book).

When placing a long-distance call to a destination within Austria, you'll need to **know the local area codes,** which can often be found by consulting the telephone numbers that are listed in this guide's regional chapters. The following are area codes for Austria's major cities: Vienna, 0222; Graz, 0316; Salzburg, 0662; Innsbruck, 0512; Linz, 0732. When dialing from outside Austria, the 0 should be left out. Note that calls within Austria are one-third cheaper between 6 PM and 8 AM on weekdays and from 1 PM on Saturday to 8 AM on Monday.

OPERATORS AND INFORMATION

For information on local calls, dial 1611 or 08; for assistance with long-distance service, dial 1616 or 09; and for information on direct dialing out of Austria, call 08 or 1613.

PAY PHONES

Coin-operated pay telephones are numerous and take AS1, 5, 10, and 20 coins. A three-minute local call costs AS1. Drop in the one-schilling piece, pick up the receiver and dial; when the party answers, push the indicated button and the connection will be made. If there is no response, your coin will be returned into the bin to the lower left. Most pay phones have instructions in English on them. Add AS1 when time is up to continue the connection.

If you plan to make many calls from pay phones, a *Wertkarte* is a convenience. You can buy this electronic credit card at any post office for AS190, AS95, or AS48, which allows AS200, AS100, or AS50 worth of calls from any *Wertkartentelephon*. You simply insert the card and dial; the cost of the call is automatically deducted from the card. A few public phones in the cities also take American Express, Diners, MasterCard, and Visa credit cards.

TIPPING

Although virtually all hotels and restaurants include service charges in their rates, tipping is still customary, but at a level lower than in the United States. Tip the hotel doorman AS10 per bag, and the porter who brings your bags to the room another AS10 per bag. In family-run establishments, tips are generally not given to immediate family members, only to employees. Tip the hotel concierge only for special services or in response to special requests. Room service gets AS10–AS20 for snacks or ice, AS20 for full meals. Maids normally get no tip unless your stay is a week or more or service has been special.

In restaurants, round up the bill by AS5 to AS50 or 5%–7%, depending on the size of the check and the class of the restaurant. Big tips are not usual in Austrian restaurants, since 10% has already been included in the prices. Hat-check attendants get AS7–AS15, depending on the locale. Washroom attendants get about AS2–AS5. Wandering musicians and the piano player get AS20, AS50 if they've filled a number of requests.

Round up taxi fares to the next AS5 or AS10; a minimum AS5 tip is customary. If the driver offers (or you ask for) special assistance, such as carrying your bags beyond the curb, an added tip of AS5–AS10 is in order.

TOUR OPERATORS

A package or tour to Vienna can make your vacation less expensive and more hassle-free. Firms that sell tours and packages reserve airline seats, hotel rooms, and rental cars in bulk and pass some of the savings on to you. In addition, the best operators have local representatives available to help you at your destination.

A GOOD DEAL?

The more your package or tour includes, the better you can predict the ultimate cost of your vacation. Make sure you know exactly what is covered, and **beware of hidden costs.** Are taxes, tips, and service charges included? Transfers and baggage handling? Entertainment and excursions? These can add up.

Most packages and tours are rated deluxe, first-class superior, first class, tourist, or budget. The key difference is usually accommodations. If the package or tour you are considering is priced lower than in your wildest dreams, **be skeptical.** Also, **make sure your travel agent knows the accommodations** and other services. Ask about the hotel's location, room size, beds, and whether it has a pool, room service, or programs for children, if you care about these. Has your agent been there in person or sent others you can contact?

BUYER BEWARE

Each year a number of consumers are stranded or lose their money when operators—even very large ones with excellent reputations—go out of business. To avoid becoming one of them, take the time to **check out the operator—**

find out how long the company has been in business and ask several agents about its reputation. Next, **don't book unless the firm has a consumer-protection program.** Members of the USTOA and the NTA are required to set aside funds for the sole purpose of covering your payments and travel arrangements in case of default. Non-member operators may instead carry insurance; look for the details in the operator's brochure—and for the name of an underwriter with a solid reputation. Note: When it comes to tour operators, **don't trust escrow accounts.** Although there are laws governing those of charter-flight operators, no governmental body prevents tour operators from raiding the till.

Next, **contact your local Better Business Bureau and the attorney general's offices** in both your own state and the operator's; have any complaints been filed? Finally, **pay with a major credit card.** Then you can cancel payment, provided that you can document your complaint. Always **consider trip-cancellation insurance** (☞ Insurance, *above*).

BIG VS. SMALL➤ Operators that handle several hundred thousand travelers per year can use their purchasing power to give you a good price. Their high volume may also indicate financial stability. But some small companies provide more personalized service; because they tend to

specialize, they may also be more knowledgeable about a given area.

USING AN AGENT

Travel agents are excellent resources. In fact, large operators accept bookings made only through travel agents. But it's good to **collect brochures from several agencies** because some agents' suggestions may be skewed by promotional relationships with tour and package firms that reward them for volume sales. If you have a special interest, **find an agent with expertise in that area;** ASTA can provide leads in the United States. (Don't rely solely on your agent, though; agents may be unaware of small-niche operators, and some special-interest travel companies only sell direct.)

SINGLE TRAVELERS

Prices are usually quoted per person, based on two sharing a room. If traveling solo, you may be required to pay the full double-occupancy rate. Some operators eliminate this surcharge if you agree to be matched up with a roommate of the same sex, even if one is not found by departure time.

TRAIN TRAVEL

DISCOUNT PASSES

If you plan to travel outside of Vienna by train, **consider purchasing an Austrian Rail Pass,** which allows four days of unlimited train travel in a 10-day. Prices begin at $111 in second-class or $165 for first-class. Pass-

holders **get a discount on river boats traveling between Passau, Linz, and Vienna.** You get a similar discount on bicycle rentals in more than 160 rail stations throughout the country.

TRAVEL GEAR

Travel catalogs specialize in useful items that can **save space when packing** and make life on the road more convenient. Compact alarm clocks, travel irons, travel wallets, and personal-care kits are among the most common items you'll find. They also carry dual-voltage appliances, currency converters and foreign-language phrase books. Some catalogs even carry miniature coffeemakers and water purifiers.

U

U.S.

GOVERNMENT

The U.S. government can be an excellent source of travel information. Some of this is free and some is available for a nominal charge. When planning your trip, **find out what government materials are available.** For just a couple of dollars, you can get a variety of publications from the Consumer Information Center in Pueblo, Colorado. Free consumer information also is available from individual government agencies, such as the Department of Transportation or the U.S. Customs Service. For specific titles, see the appropriate publications entry in Important Contacts A to Z, *above*.

THE GOLD GUIDE / SMART TRAVEL TIPS

W
WHEN TO GO

Austria has two main tourist seasons. The weather usually turns glorious around Easter to mark the start of the summer season and holds until about mid-October, often later. May and early June, September, and October are the pleasantest months for travel; there is less demand for restaurant tables, and hotel prices tend to be lower.

An Italian invasion takes place between Christmas and New Year's Day and over the long Easter weekend, and hotel rooms in Vienna are at a premium; otherwise July and August and the main festivals (*see* Festivals and Seasonal Events *in* Chapter 1) are the most crowded times.

The winter-sports season starts in December, snow conditions permitting, and runs through April. You can ski as late as mid-June on the high glaciers, at altitudes of 2,500 meters (8,200 feet) or more. Although reservations are essential in the major ski resorts in season, travelers can frequently find rooms in private houses or small pensions if they're prepared to take a slight detour from the beaten path.

CLIMATE

Austria has four distinct seasons, all fairly mild. But because of altitudes and the Alpine divide, temperatures and dampness vary considerably from one part of the country to another; for example, northern Austria's winter is often overcast and dreary, while the southern half of the country basks in sunshine. In winter it's wise to check with the automobile clubs for weather conditions, since mountain roads are often blocked, and ice and fog are hazards.

Climate in Vienna

Jan.	34F	1C	May	66F	19C	Sept.	68F	20C
	25	− 4		50	10		52	11
Feb.	37F	3C	June	73F	23C	Oct.	57F	14C
	27	− 3		57	14		45	7
Mar.	46F	8C	July	77F	25C	Nov.	45F	7C
	34	1		59	15		37	3
Apr.	59F	15C	Aug.	75F	24C	Dec.	37F	3C
	43	6		59	15		30	− 1

1 Destination: Vienna and the Danube Valley

BEYOND THE SCHLAG

TODAY'S AUSTRIA—and in particular its capital, Vienna—reminds me of a formerly fat man who is now at least as gaunt as the rest of us, but still allows himself a lot of room and expects doors to open wide when he goes through them. After losing two world wars and surviving amputation, annexation, and occupation, a nation that once ruled Europe now endures as a tourist mecca and a neutralized, somewhat balkanized republic.

It takes any foreign resident in Austria, even a German or Swiss, the whole first year to find out what questions one should be asking. It takes the second year to start getting answers; beginning with the third year, one can sift the merits of the answers. This is why I tell our friends from embassies, agencies, banks, and businesses—people doing two- or three-year stints in Austria— that they need a minimum of five years here to liquidate the investment of effort and utilize the contacts they've made. To tourists, I have just three words of advice: "Don't even try." Were you to succeed in thinking like the Viennese, for example, you would be a prime candidate for Doctor Freud's couch at Berggasse 19; but he and it aren't there anymore—the house is now the Sigmund Freud Museum, and the couch is in London.

Sitting in a loge in the Vienna State Opera in the 1970s, my wife and I gasped with dismay when a young ballerina slipped and fell, but while we applauded the girl's quick recovery, the ancient dowager next to me merely murmured: "In the days of the monarchy, she'd have been taken outside and shot."

I hope it was hyperbole, but she had a point. In a world of tattered glitter and tacky taste, jet-lagged superstars and under-rehearsed choruses, opera and operetta aren't what they used to be (though Viennese ballet has climbed steadily uphill in the decades since that girl's fall).

Still, there are oases of perfection, such as those Sunday mornings from September

to June when—if you've reserved months in advance—you can hear (but not see) those "voices from heaven," the Vienna Choir Boys, sing mass in the marble-and-velvet royal chapel of the Hofburg. Lads of 8 to 13 in sailor suits, they peal out angelic notes from the topmost gallery, and you might catch a glimpse of them after mass as you cut across the Renaissance courtyard for the 10:45 performance of the Lippizaner stallions in the Spanish Riding School around the corner. Beneath crystal chandeliers in a lofty white hall, expert riders in brown uniforms with gold buttons and black hats with gold braid put these aristocrats of the equine world through their classic paces.

Just past noon, when the Spanish Riding School lets out, cross the Michaelerplatz and stroll up the Kohlmarkt to No. 14: Demel's, the renowned and lavish pastry shop founded shortly after 1848 by the court confectioner. It was an instant success with those privileged to dine with the emperor, for not only was Franz Josef a notoriously stodgy and paltry eater, but, when he stopped eating, protocol dictated that all others stop, too. Dessert at Demel's became a must for hungry higher-ups. Today's Demel's features a flawless midday buffet offering venison en croûte, chicken in pastry shells, beef Wellington, meat tarts, and frequent warnings to "leave room for the desserts."

Closer to the less costly level of everyday existence, my family and I laid on a welcoming meal for visitors just off plane or train: a freshly baked slab of *Krusti Brot* to be spread with *Liptauer*, a piquant paprika cream cheese, and *Kräuter Gervais*, Austria's answer to cream cheese and chives, all washed down by a youngish white wine. Such simple pleasures as a jug of wine, a loaf of bread, and a spicy cheese or two are what we treasure as Austrian excellence in democratic days. Though our visitors managed to live well back home without Grüner Veltliner and Rheinriesling to drink or Liptauer and Kräuter Gervais to eat, they did find it hard to rejoin the outside world of white bread that wiggles. And if they really carried on about our wine, we could take them on the weekend to the farm it was from, for going to the source is one of the virtues of living in this small, unhomogenized land of 7.5 million people that is modern Austria.

"Is it safe to drink the water?" is still the question I'm asked most by visitors to Vienna. "It's not only safe," I reply, "it's recommended." Sometimes they call back to thank me for the tip. Piped cold and clean via Roman aqueducts from a couple of Alpine springs, the city's water has been rated the best in the world by such connoisseurs and authorities as the Austrian Academy of Sciences and an international association of solid-waste-management engineers. Often on a summer evening, when our guests looked as though a cognac after dinner might be too heavy, I brought out a pitcher of iced tap water, and even our Viennese visitors smacked their lips upon tasting this refreshing novelty. But don't bother to try for it in a tavern; except for a few radical thinkers and the converts I've made, virtually all Viennese drink bottled mineral water, and few waiters will condescend to serve you any other kind.

People say that after two decades in Vienna one must feel very Viennese, and maybe they're right, because here I am chatting about food and drink, which is the principal topic of Viennese conversation. So, before leaving the capital for the provinces, let me call your attention to three major culinary inventions that were all introduced to Western civilization in Vienna in the watershed year of 1683: coffee, the croissant, and the bagel.

That was the year the second Turkish siege of Vienna was at last repelled, when King Jan Sobieski of Poland and Duke Charles of Lorraine rode to the rescue, thereby saving the West for Christianity. The Sultan's armies left behind their silken tents and banners, some 25,000 dead, and hundreds of huge sacks filled with a mysterious brownish bean. The victorious Viennese didn't know what to make of it—whether to bake, boil, or fry it. But one of their spies, Franz George Kolschitzky, a wheeler-dealer merchant who had traveled in Turkey and spoke the language, had sampled in Constantinople the thick black brew of roasted coffee beans that the Turks called *"Kahve."* Though he could have had almost as many sacks of gold, he settled for beans— and opened history's first Viennese coffeehouse. Business was bad, however, until Kolschitzky tinkered with the recipe and experimented with milk, thus inventing the *Mélange:* taste sensation of the 1680s and still the most popular local coffee drink of the 1990s.

While Kolschitzky was roasting his reward, Viennese bakers were celebrating with two new creations that enabled their customers truly to taste victory over the Muslims: a bun curved like a crescent, the emblem of Islam (what Charles of Lorraine might have called *croissant,* Austrians call *Kipferl*), and a roll shaped like Sobieski's stirrup, for which the German word was *Bügel.* The invention of the bagel, however, proved less significant, for it disappeared swiftly and totally, only to resurface in America centuries later, along with Sunday brunch.

T HOUGH VIENNA'S is more a wine culture than a beer culture, in its hundreds of *Heurigen* (young-wine taverns identified by a bush over their door) the Viennese male indulges in a beer-garden ritual that I call "airing the paunch." With one or two buttons open, he exposes his belly to sun or moon or just passing admiration. One would be hard put to tell our sometimes smug and self-satisfied Viennese gentleman that Wien (the German name for the capital) is not the navel of the universe, let alone of Austria, but the person who could tell it to him best would be a Vorarlberger. The 305,600 citizens of Austria's westernmost province live as close to Paris as they do to Vienna, which tries to govern them; their capital, Bregenz, is barely an hour's drive from Zürich, but eight or more from Vienna, and the natives sometimes seem more Swiss than Austrian.

The Kleinwalsertal, a remote valley of Vorarlberg that juts into Bavaria, cannot be reached directly from Austria by car, bus, or train. A few summers ago, I joined some intrepid Austrians on a strenuous and sometimes treacherous two-day up- and downhill climb from Lech am Arlberg to the Kleinwalsertal. Along the way, we saw an eagle, vultures, and marmots—and I wouldn't have traded the trip for a sack of coffee beans; nor would I ever undertake such a venture again. When we tried to buy some coffee, the locals were reluctant to accept our schillings because the Deutschmark is their official currency. While the rest of Austria aspires to enter the European Union, the Kleinwalsertal, through monetary union, has been quietly living in it from its outset.

The northern reaches of Tirol and the western parts of Upper Austria also border on Germany and have a heartier, beerier character than the eastern and southern provinces. (There are nine provinces in all; Vienna, the capital, counts as a state, too, and its mayor is also a governor.) Although the glittering city of Salzburg, capital of rugged Salzburg province, perches right on the German border 16 miles from Berchtesgaden, Austrian traditions, folk customs and costumes, and the music of native son Mozart flourish there as nowhere else in the country—revered and cherished, revived and embroidered. And defended! Once, sitting at sundown in the Café Winkler high up on the Mönchsberg, watching the lights of the city come on below, I heard a man from Munich exclaim in admiration of the same view: "Ah, Salzburg! Still the most beautiful of Bavarian cities." From three sides of the restaurant, three glasses smashed in Austrian hands. The man from Munich hastily paid up and left.

AUSTRIA BORDERS not just on Germany and Switzerland, but also on Liechtenstein, Italy, Slovenia, the Czech Republic, Slovakia, and Hungary. In Austria's greenest province, Styria, one side of the road is sometimes in Slovenia, and you're never far from Hungary or Italy. Styria is so prickly about its independence, even from Austria, that it maintains its own embassies in Vienna and Washington. It is the source of Schilcher, Austria's best rosé wine, which you almost never see in Viennese restaurants. A few years ago, at a

farmhouse near Graz, the Styrian capital, I was sipping some Schilcher that went with some wonderful lamb. "Where is this lamb from?" I asked my host.

"Right here," he replied. "Styrian lamb wins all kinds of prizes."

"Then why can't we find it in Vienna?" I wondered. "When we do get lamb, it comes all the way from New Zealand and costs a fortune."

"That's because we don't grow lambs or Schilcher for export," he replied, dead serious.

The influx and tastes of Balkan and Turkish workers have made lamb cheaper and plentiful all over Austria, and now, since the crumbling of the Iron Curtain, Austria is reluctantly becoming even more of a melting pot than it was in the days of the Habsburg empire. The most assimilable province will surely be Burgenland, which used to be part of Hungary. It retains much of its Magyar character in villages where you open a door and find, instead of a courtyard, a whole street full of steep-roofed houses, people, and life. With the dissolution of the Austro-Hungarian empire after World War I, Burgenland was ceded to Austria, pending a plebiscite in 1921. The population voted overwhelmingly to stay Austrian—except for the people of Ödenburg, which was then its capital and is now Sopron in Hungary. Later, but too late, it was discovered that Ödenburg's pro-Hungarians had registered the inhabitants of several cemeteries to achieve a majority. By enlisting their ancestors, they doomed their descendants to two generations behind the Iron Curtain and a difficult job of catching up. Their move also meant, until lately, that to go from one point in Burgenland to another 20 kilometers (12½ miles) away, Westerners sometimes had to detour up to 100 kilometers (62 miles).

Burgenland also boasts a culturally active Croatian minority, while Carinthia, Austria's southernmost province, has a proud Slovenian minority that is still fighting for the legal right not to Germanize the names of its villages.

The ultimate identity problem, however, belonged until recently to the province of Lower Austria, which is neither low nor south but takes its name from the part of the Danube it dominates on the map. Before 1986, Lower Austria had no capital city; its state offices were scattered around Vienna, the metropolis it envelops with forest. Upon its selection as the provincial seat, the small city of St. Pölten, with a core of lovely churches and cloisters that swirl around you like a Barococo ballet, danced onto the map of tourist destinations. Already coming to life as a sightseeing attraction, St. Pölten is starting to thrive as a center of government, though Lower Austria's bureaucrats in Vienna are relocating slowly and grudgingly, if at all; many are contemplating early retirement.

Any day of the year, you can take an express train at Wien's Westbahnhof for an eight-hour, 770-kilometer (480-mile) east–west crossing of most of the country, stopping at five of Austria's nine provincial capitals: St. Pölten; Linz, the Upper Austrian seat; Salzburg; Innsbruck in Tirol; and Bregenz in Vorarlberg. But you would be well rewarded, as the pages that follow will demonstrate, by disembarking at each one and giving it a day or two or more of your life.

—Alan Levy

Now editor-in-chief of the *Prague Post*, Alan Levy lived in Vienna for 20 years.

WHAT'S WHERE

Poised in the very heart of the continent, Austria is as topographically diverse as it is historically wealthy. What it may lack in size, it makes up for in diversity, for it has some of just about everything: a 1,000-year recorded history; an Alpine region that—as the setting for *The Sound of Music*—remains one of the most beloved regions in all Europe; and, arguably one of the great cities of the world, Vienna. If you take a Grand Tour of the country, you'll learn there are as many Austrias as there are crystals on a chandelier in a Viennese ballroom. Its Alps rival those of neighboring Switzerland; its vineyards along the Danube match those of the Rhine and Mosel River valleys; its museums and Baroque churches are without peer for old-world splendor.

In addition, nowhere else are there such pastry shops!

For most people, Austria is Vienna or Innsbruck or Salzburg or the Tirol region. These places have grandeur, plus all that is superlative in style and scenery. But some half dozen other vacation areas exist, and there is a good case for spending some time in these areas. You will even find that many of the smaller country towns reproduce in miniature the glories of the great centers. Although it is one of Europe's smallest countries, Austria manages to pack within its border as many mountains, lakes, and picturesque cities as countries five times its size. Here is a quick overview to help you travel civilized roads, both back in time and forward.

Vienna

Think of Vienna and you think of operettas and psychoanalysis, *Apfelstrudel* and marble staircases, Strauss waltzes and Schubert melodies. Baroque and imperial, it goes without saying that the city (Wien, in German) has an old-world charm—a fact that the natives are both ready to acknowledge and yet hate being reminded of. Today, Vienna is a white-gloved yet modern metropolis, a place where Andrew Lloyd Webber's *Phantom of the Opera* plays in the same theater that premiered Mozart's *Magic Flute*. A walk through the city's neighborhoods—many dotted with masterpieces of Gothic, Baroque, and Secession architecture—offers a fascinating journey thick with history and peopled by the spirits of Empress Maria Theresa, Haydn, Beethoven, Metternich, Mozart, and Klimt.

Most visitors start along the Ring, the grand boulevard that surrounds the inner city; here, you'll find art treasures in the Fine Arts Museum, magnificent spectacles at the Vienna State Opera (one reason why Vienna remains for many the musical capital of the world), and the Hofburg, Vienna's gigantic Imperial Palace, whose chapel showcases the Vienna Boys Choir and whose stables shelter the Lipizzaner stallions (when they aren't prancing at the Spanish Riding School). The city comes alive during the "Merry Season"—the first two months of the year—when raised trumpets and opera capes adorn its great

Fasching balls; then more than ever, Vienna moves in three-quarter time. Near the city are the legendary Vienna Woods, with the famous spa of **Baden,** the **Weinviertel** (Wine District), and poetic **Mayerling,** where Crown Prince Rudolf and his lover met a tragic end.

The Danube Valley

The scenes along a trip down the Austrian Danube unfold like a picture-book of history. In a parade of sights, Roman ruins, Baroque monsteries with "candle-snuffer" cupolas, and innumerable medieval castles-in-air dot the length of the river, stoking the imagination with their legends and myths. Here is where Richard the Lion Hearted spent years locked in a dungeon and where the Nibelungs—immortalized by Wagner—caroused at the top of their lungs in battlemented forts. Clearly, the Danube is liquid history, and you can enjoy drifting eight hours downriver in a steamer or—even better—18 hours upriver against the current.

Along the way you discover **the Wachau** Valley—"crown jewel of the Austrian landscape"—the Baroque abbey of **Melk,** and the robber castles of Studen and Werfenstein. A convenient base point is **Linz,** Austria's third-largest city (and its most underrated): its Old Town is filled with architectural treasures, glockenspiel chimes, and pastry shops that offer the best linzertortes around. The town is right on the Danube, which, if you catch it on a bright summer day, takes on the proper shade of Johann Strauss "blau."

PLEASURES AND PASTIMES

Mozart Mania

Somewhere, at almost any hour, an orchestra will be playing his music; somewhere, shoulders will be swaying, fingers tapping. It may be at a gala evening concert, an outdoor festival, or an Easter Mass. But chances are the music of Johannes Chrysostomus Theophilus Wolfgang Amadeus Mozart will be traveling through the air when you visit Austria. The most purely inspired of any composer crammed a prodigious amount of composing into his short 35-year life. Today—thanks to Tom Hulce's characterization in the film *Amadeus*—this youthful genius and native son of Salzburg wears the crown of the rock star of the 18th century.

Schnitzels, Strudels, and Sachertortes

Travelers in Austria can be faced with a moveable feast of enticing choices. There are the four-star dining establishments that are proud to feature the latest in *Neue Küche,* or Viennese nouvelle cuisine. Some visitors head first for those Hungarian-themed eateries that specialize in Genghis Khan's Flaming Sword, plum brandy, Turkish coffee, and a Primaś, a gypsy orchestra in which the leading violinist plays your favorite song. Others skip right to dessert and check out a *Konditorei*—such as Demel's, where you can feast on pastries that are among the gastronomic wonders of Europe. There are *gemütlich* wine taverns, *Heurigen,* where you can always get a bite to eat and listen to *Schrammel* music. Then there are those who swear the best meal in Austria is a simple *Frankfurter und Pfefferminz* at the street corner *Wurstelstand* (sausage vendor).

Whatever your pick, restaurant food in Austria ranges from fine (and expensive) offerings at elegant restaurants to simple, inexpensive, and wholesome meals in small country inns. Wherever you go, you will find traditional restaurants, with all the atmosphere typical of such places—good value included. If you crave a Big Mac you can find it, and you can even get a bad meal in Austria, but it will be the exception; the simplest *Gasthaus* takes pride in its cooking, no matter how standard it may be. Some Austrians even believe you have a better chance getting a wonderful meal at a simple neighborhood *Beisel* than at a *nobel* four-star establishment.

Austrian cuisine is heavily influenced by that of its neighbors. This accounts for the cross-fertilization of tastes and flavors, with Hungarian, Czech, Slovak, Polish, Yugoslav, and Italian cooking all in the mix. The delicious, thick Serbian bean soup came from an area of the former Yugoslavia; the bread dumpling (*Knödel*) that accompanies many standard dishes has its parentage in the former Czechoslovakia; the exquisitely rich (more butter than sugar) *Dobostorte* comes straight from Hungary.

All too often justice is not done to the relatively few Austrian national dishes. You're likely to get a soggy *Wiener schnitzel* as often as a supreme example, lightly pan-fried in a dry, crisp breading. Austrian cooking on the whole is more solid than delicate. Try *Tafelspitz* (boiled beef); when properly done it is outstanding in flavor and texture. Reflecting the Italian influence, Austrian cooking also leans heavily on pastas and rice. *Schinkenfleckerl* is a good example: a casserole of confettilike flecks of ham baked with pasta. A standard roast of pork (*Schweinsbraten*) served hot or cold can be exquisite. As for other dishes, here's a list of traditional Austrian favorites: *Leberknödelsuppe,* a meat broth with liver dumplings; *Fischbeuschlsuppe,* a thick, piquant, Viennese soup made from freshwater fish; *Fogosch,* pike, and *Krebs,* succulent little crawfish, all from the lakes and rivers of Austria; the various Schnitzels—*Holsteiner, Pariser, Natur;* pork specialities such as *Schweinscarrée,* a very special cut; *Rehrücken,* or venison; especially pheasant and wild-boar (incidentally, today's nouvelle chefs are serving up sublime prosciuttos of the latter); *Gulyas* (goulash), seasoned with superlative Hungarian paprika; *Backhuhn* or *Backhendl,* young chicken breaded and fried to a golden brown; and *Steirisches Brathuhn,* chicken roasted on a spit. And don't forget those wonderful Austrian sausages.

Austrian vintage wines range from good to outstanding. Don't hesitate to ask waiters for advice, even in the simpler restaurants. The best whites come from the Wachau and Kamptal, Weinviertel (Lower Austria), Styria, and the area around Vienna. Grüner Veltliner, a light dry-to-medium-dry wine that goes well with many foods, is the most popular. The Welschriesling is a slightly heavier, fruitier wine. The favored Austrian reds are those of Burgenland. Blauer Portugieser and Zweigelt tend to be lighter. For a slightly heavier red, select a Blaufränkisch, Blauer Burgunder, or St. Laurent. These are all good value, and there is little difference among the years.

Most of these wines can be bought by the glass. Look for labels from vintners Beck in Gols, Bründlmayer in Langenlois, Hirtzberger in Spitz/Donau, Jamek in Joching, Nikolaihof in Mautern, Sonnhof in Langenlois, Dolle in Strass, Wieninger in Vienna, and Freie Weingärtner Wachau in Dürnstein.

Souvenirs, Austrian-Style

Not so long ago, almost any store on Vienna's Kärntnerstrasse could boast that it once created its exquisite jewelry, fine leather goods, or petit-point handbags (as Viennese as St. Stephen's Cathedral) for the imperial Habsburgs. This may no longer be the case, but rest assured, Miss Average Tourist will receive service fully as gracious as that once accorded to Their Imperial Majesties the Emperor and Empress. For the most lasting souvenir, however, visitors might consider a foray into the realm of Austrian arts and crafts. Of great age and agelessness, these objects are often made outside Vienna. For instance, the world-famous firm of Riedel, based in the charming town of Kufstein—between Salzburg and Innsbruck—produces glassware with the thinnest of stems and designs that can be strikingly contemporary (even though the company was founded in 1756). Perhaps you'll agree that wine tastes better in a Riedel glass.

Northeast of Salzburg on the shores of Lake Traum is Count Hohenberg's Gmundner Keramic, celebrated for its 16th-century green-and-white *Grüngeflammt* pattern ceramics. Choose a sturdy beer stein, or for a splurge, buy a reproduction *Knöde-Schüssel*—a gigantic platter on which a 16th-century family would divvy up the communal Sunday meal. For the best in linen nightwear, dirndls, and lodels, head for Lanz of Austria, the No. 1 choice of chic Salzburgers. Lanz changes its motifs—deer, farmhouse, or flower—from year to year on its skirts and aprons. Part *Trachten* (folk dress), part *Haute Confection* (what Austrians call high-quality fashion), these very designs have been known to inspire Yves Saint Laurent. For furnishings, check out rural antique dealers for a rustic "Empire Peasant" painted wooded chest. Or try to buy the most unique Austrian souvenir of all—one of those colored and mirrored glass orbs, garden ornaments typical of the Biedermeier era, and the Austrians' right-on version of a scarecrow.

The Great Outdoors

Austria is one of the most participant-sport-minded countries in the world. Babies barely out of diapers practically learn to walk on skis. At a snowflake's notice, half the population takes to the slopes; in summer, water sports are just as popular. New attractions are appearing; golf and snowboarding are sweeping the country. One "sport"—an activity we are all experts at—is an Austrian passion: walking. Austria is a walker's El Dorado, and its sights—once you're off the Autobahn—are amazing: valleys that inspired Anton Bruckner's symphonies; alleés of linden trees immortalized in Klimt's paintings; gorgeous medieval villages such as Steyr; and Sound-of-Music meadows that make you want to spread your arms and whirl around. Because Austrians so love *das Wandern* (as they refer to walking and hiking), you can be sure there will be complete information about the country's many trails—including the famous "Romantic Road" running from Salzburg through the Salzkammergut to the Danube Region—from National Tourist Offices.

NEW AND NOTEWORTHY

The music never stops in Vienna. The 1997 year opens with a burst, with the annual New Year's Day concert by the Vienna Philharmonic, conducted by Riccardo Muti, and a performance of Beethoven's Ninth Symphony by the Vienna Symphony under Roger Norrington, which promises to be an outstanding if possibly controversial experience. Both concerts are scheduled for New Year's Eve and repeated on the morning of New Year's Day. The Vienna State Opera, the Volksoper, and opera houses in other cities mount Strauss' comic opera, *Die Fledermaus,* on New Year's Eve. Other cities have followed Vienna's lead and also offer New Year's concerts.

The **Vienna Festival this year moves into the historic Konzerthaus.** This year marks

the 200th anniversary of the birth of Franz Schubert, meaning that the festival will be overflowing with his works. At the Vienna opera, new productions include two rarities, Richard Strauss's *Die Schweigsame Frau* and Boito's *Mephistophles,* with Samuel Ramey in the title role. Ballet under director Renato Zanella will present a "Viennese Evening," complete with Balanchine's *La Valse.*

Highlights of the ball season in Vienna will include the Philharmonic Ball on January 16 in the Musikverein and the Opera Ball on February 6, which takes place in the elegantly decorated Opera House. The main ball season runs through *Fasching,* the carnival period, which ends on Ash Wednesday. As always, the Imperial Ball in the Hofburg wraps up the year in style on December 31.

The main musical event of 1997 is the **200th anniversary of the birth of Franz Schubert.** The Biedermeier-era composer was born in 1797 and died tragically (from typhoid) at the age of 31 in 1828. Schubert's music reflects the soul of Vienna as Mozart's does that of Salzburg, so the capital, fittingly, will lead the festivities with its annual **Schubertiade,** along with a major Schubert show in the Historical Museum of the City of Vienna, an international choral competition in November, and special concerts at both the Festwochen (mid-May–late-June) and the Klangbogen/Musikalischer Sommer (July–September)—the city's two major summer music festivals. Other focal points for special commemorative concerts (small, given the spaces involved) will be his birthplace in Nudorfer Strasse and his brother's house, where he died, in Kettenbruckengasse.

The **Vienna Card** is proving to be a popular success. It includes unlimited travel on public transportation for 72 hours, reduced museum entrance fees, shopping discounts, and a number of other attractions, all for AS180.

Driving still remains one of the best ways to see the countryside, but **highways are showing signs of heavy congestion** of late, particularly on weekends and holidays and on the major north–south routes that carry transit traffic between Germany and Italy. **More towns and cities are adding pedestrian zones,** so check on access and parking possibilities with your hotel before you arrive. Cars have been almost totally banned from such resorts as Zürs and Lech; parking in the center of Vienna is restricted, with whole squares cleared of cars. Where you're forced to walk—in the inner city of Vienna, for example—remember that this is really the best way to capture the feeling and flavor of those places anyway.

Also, **cycling is increasingly the way to go.** Bikers are supported by maps, repair shops, friendly overnight lodging possibilities, and transport of heavier, bulkier bags between destinations. Routes will take you along the Danube—in most places, you've a choice of north or south bank—or to other more challenging parts of Austria.

Austria's membership in the European Union is taking longer to be digested than most officials in Vienna had hoped. The public had been promised instantly lower prices which have not materialized—a fact travelers will notice at every turn. A recent austerity budget extends into 1997 and has served to hold the government together and, at least, kept the lid on inflation. Austria remains one of Europe's most expensive countries. However, the good news is that the exchange rate is looking slightly more favorable for the dollar (at press time). Already, CNN Travel News has reported Austria could be one of Europe's three hottest destinations for the coming year.

FODOR'S CHOICE

No two people agree on what makes a perfect vacation, but it's fun and helpful to known what others think. Here's a compendium from the must-see lists of hundreds of Austrian travelers. For detailed information about these memories-in-the-making, refer to the appropriate chapters in this book.

Quintessential Austria

★**New Year's Day concert in Vienna's Musikverein.** You've seen it on television, but now you're *here* in the Golden Hall—its gilt bare-breasted ladies supporting the balconies, the walls festooned with floral displays—sharing in the excitement of a Vienna Philharmonic concert seen and heard by millions around the world.

★**Waltzing around the clock at a Fasching ball.** Whether you go to the Opera Ball or the Zuckerbäckerball (sponsored by pastry cooks), remember that gala etiquette states a gentleman can kiss only a lady's hand.

★**High Mass on Sunday in the Augustinerkirche in Vienna.** Particularly if it's a mass by Mozart or Haydn, the soaring music and the church architecture elevate the event to a soulful experience as you focus on the great altar and the pomp of the ceremony.

★**The most festive Christmas delights.** In Vienna, head for Demel's pastry shrine to try the *Mohr im Hemd*—a heavenly hot chocolate and whipped cream pudding called "Moor in a Shirt," and in most every town, check out the outdoor *Christkindlmarkt,* or gift market.

★**The Lippizaner stallions at the Spanish Riding School.** Where else can you see horses dance a minuet to Mozart? For sheer elegance, the combination of the chestnut-colored riding habits of the trainers and the pure white of the horses' coats can't be beat.

Top Art

★**Brueghel's *Hunters in the Snow.*** The confrontation alone is dramatic: You've seen this painting, and most of the other Brueghels that are hung in Vienna's Kunsthistorisches Museum, reproduced a thousand times over. It's incredible detail could keep you fascinated for hours, even if you're not an art aficionado.

★**Klimt's *The Kiss.*** Arguably Austria's greatest painter, Gustav Klimt fuses high romanticism with eye-knocking pattern to create one of his—and the 20th century's—most memorable images, on view in the Österreichische Galerie of Vienna's Belvedere Palace.

Unforgettable Drive

★**The Wachau when its apricot trees are in blossom.** In spring, the narrow Danube Valley becomes a riot of fruit trees in delicate pastel blossom sweeping up hillsides from the very river banks.

Great Hotel

★**Bristol, Vienna.** The Bristol is a classic that has moved with the times; service is impeccable and at no time will a guest feel anything but the luxury of old-world traditions tempered by contemporary comforts. *$$$$*

Memorable Restaurants

★**Hedrich, Vienna.** When owner-chef Richard Hedrich cooks, for his own as well as his guests' pleasure, the results are outstanding in a city of fine dining establishments. The plainness of the single, smallish room allows better concentration on the creations emanating from the kitchen. *$$$$*

★**Landhaus Bacher, Mautern.** Understatement is the rule here, where frills and decoration never get in the way of the superb food quality. Whether inside or outside in the shaded garden, the atmosphere is relaxed and service exemplary, making the excursion into the countryside all the more worthwhile. While other top chefs have skyrocketed only to burn out quickly, Lisl Bacher-Wagner maintains her talent for innovation with a steady keel. *$$$$*

Historic Towns and Picturesque Squares

★**Hauptplatz, Linz.** The spacious main square of the Upper Austrian capital has been handsomely restored; church spires rather than skyscrapers shape the skyline. The square is the site for local markets just as it was centuries ago, with many of the same buildings gracing the scene.

★**Steyr, Upper Austria.** Wonderfully colorful decorative facades address the main square, brooded over by the castle above. Tiny, half-concealed stairways lead upward to the castle area, other stone steps take you down the opposite side to the riverbank. The setting is an ensemble worthy of Hollywood; in this case, it's all charmingly real.

Classic Cafés

★**Hawelka, Vienna.** No visit to Vienna is complete without a stop at this famous landmark, virtually unchanged since Herr Hawelka got it running again in 1945. This remains the artists' stylishly shabby, smoky hangout in name if not always in fact.

★**Schwarzenberg, Vienna.** This winner among the city's hundreds of cafés, with its brass-topped tables, is a favorite meeting place or the spot for an after-work wine at the tables outside facing the Ring. Piano music at cocktail hour lends a classic Viennese touch.

Churches and Abbeys

★**Melk, Lower Austria.** Probably the most impressive of Europe's abbeys, Melk perches like a magnificent yellow-frosted wedding cake overlooking the Danube, its ornate library holding rows of priceless treasures. If you can visit only one abbey in all of Europe, Melk should be among the top contenders.

★**St. Florian, Upper Austria.** This abbey, where composer Anton Bruckner was organist, is impressive for its sheer size alone. Add to the symmetrical structure the glorious church and the representational rooms, and you have one of Austria's religious highlights.

★**St. Stephen's Cathedral, Vienna.** The country's spiritual life centers on St. Stephen's, rebuilt after disastrous ruin in the last days of World War II. Today known as the "skyscraper," the church has witnessed many notable events, including the marriage of Mozart. Inside, the penumbral light means that the nave's sweeping heights are felt but seldom seen.

Garden

★**Schönbrunn, Vienna.** Was the palace an excuse for the gardens, or vice versa? The manicured trees, the symmetrical walkways, the discoveries at various intersections, all add to the pleasure of exploration here. Climb to the Gloriette for a sweeping perspective of the gardens and the city beyond.

GREAT ITINERARIES

The Wine Country

Austria's vineyards, spread out over the northern and eastern countryside, offer a splendid excuse to see areas that are well off the usual tourist routes. Here you can sample local wines, many of which are very good indeed but, because the output is low, don't travel far beyond private wine cellars. The countryside is relaxed and rolling in the north, a bit more dramatic as you head south. Although public transport penetrates these areas, you will do much better by car.

Length of Trip: 4 to 6 days

Getting Around

BY CAR➤ The trip by car will run about 800 kilometers (500 miles), and the total driving time will be 13–16 hours.

BY PUBLIC TRANSPORTATION➤ Klosterneuburg and Krems can be reached from Vienna by train. A local train goes up the Kamp Valley to Horn, where a post-office bus goes on to Retz and back to Vienna. Laa an der Thaya is served by bus from Vienna; so is Poysdorf. A train runs from Bruck an der Leitha via Neusiedl to Eisenstadt. While the southernmost section of this itinerary can be covered by post-office bus, the service is infrequent. A train from Graz goes to Bad Gleichenberg. The vineyards south of Vienna in Mödling, Baden, Gumpoldskirchen, and Bad Vöslau are easily reached by rail or bus.

The Main Route

ONE NIGHT➤ **Krems.** A wine-tasting in Kloster Und will give some idea of the wines of the area. The Göttweig abbey, across the river, also produces wines and sells them by the bottle in the abbey shop.

ONE NIGHT➤ **Laa an der Thaya.** For variety, you might visit the beer museum associated with the Hubertus brewery, in business since 1454. The "Weinschlössl" offers tastings of area wine specialties.

ONE NIGHT➤ **Eisenstadt.** The road down from Jois is part of the "Red Wine Highway" through Burgenland's best vineyards. At Donnerkirchen, the Vinarium (Leisserhof) has tastings of local wines. A side trip to the "Weinakademie" in Rust offers the opportunity to sample the wines of the Rust and Lake Neusiedl region. Nearby Siegendorf produces outstanding wines.

ONE NIGHT➤ **Bad Gleichenberg.** There's no wine involved, but don't overlook nearby Riegersburg Castle. The north–south

valleys lying to the west are covered with vineyards. Parallel to Route 66 to the east, from Höflach south to Halbenrain, lies the Klöcher wine highway. West of Strass on Route 69, Gamlitz is the northern end of the South Styrian Wine Road. Off Route 74 west of Leibnitz, Kitzeck in Sausal, at the lower end of the Sausal Wine Road, boasts a wine museum.

ONE NIGHT➤ **Baden.** The region around Bad Vöslau is home to one of Austria's most widely known white wines, Gumpoldskirchner, named for a nearby town. Traiskirchen hosts a wine festival in the city park near the beginning of July, and from spring to late fall hundreds of vintners offer their wares at tiny Heurigen cellars throughout the area.

Information: See Chapters 3 and 4.

Castles Against the Invaders

During the Middle Ages, hordes of invaders periodically swept down from the north into what is now Lower Austria. Lacking natural defenses such as mountains or a river, local rulers set up a chain of castles to protect their lands and to display their wealth and position. To visit these fortifications is to appreciate what life was like for the ruling elite more than 300 years ago. The chain includes the castles at Ottenstein, Weitra, Gmünd, Heidenreichstein, Raabs an der Thaya, Riegersburg, and Hardegg.

Length of Trip: 2 to 3 days

Getting Around

BY CAR➤ The distance by car is about 340 kilometers (215 miles), and the total driving time will be more than 6 hours.

BY PUBLIC TRANSPORTATION➤ Trains run from Vienna to Gmünd, and bus service is available from Gmünd to Weitra and Heidenreichstein. Raabs can be reached by bus from Horn. Post-office buses connect Riegersburg and Hardegg with Retz, which has a bus link to Vienna.

The Main Route

ONE NIGHT➤ **Heidenreichstein.** Neunagelberg, on the Czech border southwest of Heidenreichstein, is a center of handmade ornamental glass in the old tradition, and several glassworks are open to the public. In Heidenreichstein you can easily spend the better part of a morning or an afternoon in the moated castle and its grounds.

ONE NIGHT➤ **Raabs an der Thaya.** The idyllic setting alongside the Thaya River, with the castle perched on a promontory above, is a splendid place for relaxation. Nearby is the mysterious ruin of Kollmitz Castle. At Hardegg, the castle tour (allow two hours) includes kitchens and other utility areas as well as the more elegant reception rooms.

Information: *See* Chapter 3.

In Pursuit of the Great Abbeys

Austria's abbeys were centers of learning and education, repositories of books and documents, scientific papers, music manuscripts, and art. The church's special position allowed the abbeys the freedom to engage in commercial activities in order to support less worldly pursuits. The archbishopric in Salzburg ruled over a vast area, drawing on income from the salt mines to pay for elaborate libraries and galleries. A visit to these abbeys, still very much in operation, can give you a feeling for the sequestered life of 100–200 years ago and the magnificence these treasuries hold. Our tour highlights Klosterneuburg, Göttweig, and Melk in Lower Austria; St. Florian and Kremsmünster in Upper Austria; Admont and Seckau in Styria; and St. Paul in Lavantal in Carinthia. The St. Paul abbey was rescued from ruin in the 1930s when the abbots sold a Gutenberg Bible to the U.S. Library of Congress for $250,000; the abbey library still holds priceless treasures.

Length of Trip: 3 to 4 days

Getting Around

BY CAR➤ A car is the only practical way to tackle this tour. The itinerary covers 825 kilometers (515 miles) and will take about 13–15 hours to drive.

BY PUBLIC TRANSPORTATION➤ Klosterneuburg is easily reached by fast suburban train from Vienna. Göttweig lies some distance from public transport. Melk is reached by train from Vienna. Buses run to St. Florian and Kremsmünster from Linz. Post-office buses go to Admont and St. Paul. Seckau is off the usual path.

The Main Route

ONE NIGHT➤ **Krems.** Klosterneuburg and Melk can be seen in a day, Göttweig as well if you hurry. Yet Krems is a pleasant base for a more leisurely visit to Göttweig, and you'll want time to stroll Krems's old streets and squares.

ONE NIGHT➤ **Bad Hall.** This spa near Kremsmünster offers a refreshing stop after a busy day of sightseeing.

Information: *See* Chapter 5.

The Danube from Passau to Vienna

The Danube's tranquility contrasts markedly with the busy character of the Rhine and Main rivers in Germany, but the relative quiet of today will soon disappear as freight traffic increases from the Netherlands and Germany via the Rhine-Main-Danube canal. Now may be a good time to enjoy the river before commercial shipping gets the upper hand. On the Austrian stretch down to Vienna the river is in places docile and a bit insignificant; in other places it is the kind of mighty stream you'd associate with one of the great rivers of the world. The course through the Wachau is as impressive as any part of the Rhine, and the Danube also boasts its Lorelei.

Length of Trip: 2 to 3 days

Getting Around

BY CAR➤ This tour is a little more than 300 kilometers (190 miles) long and will take 13–15 hours to drive.

BY PUBLIC TRANSPORTATION➤ From early May to late October you can travel the stream itself on the comfortable river ships run by the tongue-twisting DDSG (*Donaudampfschiffahrtsgesellschaft*). You have the choice of deck or cabin passage, with a change in ship and line in Linz on the Passau run. From Melk to Krems, local services crisscross the river from town to town. The main rail line from Passau via Linz to Vienna parallels the river closely as far as Melk, but you miss the intimacy when you see the Danube fleetingly through a train window. The Tulln–Vienna rail line also hugs the riverbank, sharing it with the highway.

The Main Route

ONE NIGHT➤ **Eferding or Linz.** The choice depends on whether you prefer a smaller city or the attractions of a major center.

ONE NIGHT➤ **Krems.** Outings to Dürnstein, Weissenkirchen, Spitz, and Melk—by car, boat, or public transportation—are easy from this convenient base. If you're driving, don't overlook the Göttweig abbey across the river or the wine cellars around nearby Langenlois.

Information: *See* Chapter 4.

FESTIVALS AND SEASONAL EVENTS

WINTER

JAN. 1➤ The **New Year** opens in Vienna with the world-famous concert by the Vienna Philharmonic Orchestra, this year under the direction of Riccardo Muti (✉ Vienna Philharmonic, Musikverein, Bösendorferstr. 12, A–1010 Vienna, ☎ 0222/505–6525; write a year—or more—in advance). Those who can't get into the Philharmonic concert can try for one of the performances of the Johann Strauss operetta *Die Fledermaus* in the State Opera and Volksoper (✉ Bundestheaterverband, Goethegasse 1, A–1010 Vienna, ☎ 0222/513–1513) or for Beethoven's Ninth (Choral) Symphony by the Vienna Symphony Orchestra with the controversial conductor Roger Norrington (✉ Konzerthaus, Lothringerstr. 20, A–1030 Vienna, ☎ 0222/712–1211). Those who want to dance their way into the new year can do so at the Kaiserball in the elegant rooms of the Hofburg (✉ WKV, Hofburg, Heldenplatz, A–1014 Vienna, ☎ 0222/587–3666–14).

FEB. 13➤ The Opera House in Vienna is transformed into the world's most elegant ballroom for the annual **Opera Ball.**

SPRING

MID-MAY–MID-JUNE➤ The **Wiener Festwochen** takes place in Vienna—a festival of theater, music, films, and exhibitions (✉ Lehargasse 11, A–1060 Vienna, ☎ 0222/582–2222).

SUMMER

JUNE 2➤ The religious holiday **Corpus Christi** is celebrated throughout Austria with colorful processions and parades.

JUNE 21➤ **Midsummer Night** is ablaze with bonfires throughout the country, with some of the liveliest celebrations taking place in the Wachau region along the Danube in Lower Austria.

JULY–AUG.➤ **Musical Summer/Klangbogen** in Vienna has nightly recitals in one of the city's many palaces or orchestral concerts in the courtyard of the city hall (✉ Klangbogen Wien, Laudongasse 29, A–1080 Vienna, ☎ 0222/4000–8410).

AUTUMN

SEPT. 1➤ This date marks the start of the **theater and music season** in Vienna (✉ Wiener Fremdenverkehrsverband, Obere Augartenstr. 40, A–1020 Vienna, ☎ 0222/211–140–14–0).

EARLY SEPT.➤ A series of **trade fairs** packs Vienna during the first weeks of the month; the most interesting is the Hit consumer electronics show, where new products are showcased.

The **International Bruckner Festival** makes Linz come alive: Theater, concerts, fireworks, and art exhibits extend to the St. Florian monastery, where the composer Anton Bruckner worked and is buried (✉ Untere Donaulände 7, A–4010 Linz, ☎ 0732/775230).

MID-OCT.➤ **Viennale** in Vienna shows films ranging from the avant-garde to retrospectives (✉ Wiener Filmfestwochen Viennale, Stiftsgasse 6, A–1070 Vienna, ☎ 0222/526–5947).

NOV. 11➤ **St. Martin's Day** is as good as a holiday; restaurants throughout the country serve traditional roast goose and red cabbage in honor of the patron saint of publicans and innkeepers. Called *Martinigansl* or *Ganslessen* ("Martin's goose" or "goose eating"), it's much more than a feast of goose; people celebrate with parties and processions, church services, and village parades.

DEC. 6➤ On **St. Nicholas's Day** the patron saint of children is honored at *Christkindl* (Christchild) festivals, open-air markets throughout the country selling toys, favors, decorations, and food.

DEC. 24➤ **Christmas Eve midnight mass** at St. Stephen's cathedral in Vienna is an impressive, if crowded, event; get an entrance pass at the cathedral in advance.

2 Vienna

Magnificent, magnetic, and magical, Vienna beguiles one and all with old-world charm and courtly grace. It is a place where head waiters still bow as if saluting a Habsburg prince, where Lipizzaner stallions dance minuets to Mozart—a city that waltzes and works in three-quarter time. Like a well-bred grande dame, Vienna doesn't hurry and neither should you. Saunter through its stately streets—peopled by the spirits of Beethoven and Strauss, Metternich, and Freud—marvel at its Baroque palaces, and dream an afternoon away at a cozy Kaffeehaus.

By George H.
Sullivan

Revised and
updated by
Willibald
Picard

THE CITIZENS OF VIENNA, it has been said, properly waltz only from the waist down, whirling around the crowded dance floor while holding their upper bodies motionless and ramrod straight. The sight can be breathtaking in its sweep and splendor, and its elegant coupling of freewheeling exuberance and rigid formality—of license and constraint—is quintessentially Viennese.

Architecture is frozen music, said the German poet Goethe, and the closest that European architecture ever came to embodying the Viennese waltz, appropriately enough, is the Viennese town palace. Built mostly during the 18th century, these Baroque mansions can be found all over the inner city, and they present in stone and stucco the same artful synthesis of license and constraint as the dance that was so often performed inside them. They make Vienna a Baroque city that is, at its best, an architectural waltz.

Today, visitors who tour Vienna can easily feel they're doing so in three-quarter time. As they explore its churches filled with statues of golden saints and pink-cheeked cherubs, wander through its treasure-packed museums, or while away the afternoon in those multitudinous meccas of mocha (those inevitable cafés) they can begin to feel lapped in lashings of rich, delicious, whipped cream—the beloved *Schlagobers* that garnishes most Viennese pastries. The ambience of the city is predominantly ornate and fluffy: white horses dancing to elegant music; snow frosting the opulent draperies of Empress Maria Theresa's monument, set in the formal patterns of "her" lovely square; a gilded Johann Strauss, playing gracefully among a grove of green trees; rich decorations, secretly filling the interior courtyards of town houses that present a severe face to the outside world; the transformation of grim Greek legends by the voluptuous music of Richard Strauss; the tangible, geometric impasto of Klimt's paintings; the stately pavane of a mechanical clock. All these will create in the visitor the sensation of a metropolis that likes to be visited and admired—and which indeed is well worth admiring and visiting.

For many centuries, this has been the case. One of the great capitals of Europe, Vienna was for centuries home to the Habsburg rulers of the Austro-Hungarian Empire. Today the empire is long gone, but many reminders of the city's imperial heyday remain, carefully preserved by the tradition-loving Viennese. When it comes to the arts, the glories of the past are particularly evergreen, thanks to the cultural legacy created by the many artistic geniuses nourished here.

From the late 18th century on, Vienna's culture—particularly its musical forte—was famous throughout Europe. Haydn, Mozart, Beethoven, Schubert, Brahms, Strauss, Mahler, and Bruckner all lived in the city, producing music that is still played in concert halls all over the world. And at the tail end of the 19th century the city's artists and architects—Gustav Klimt, Egon Schiele, Oskar Kokoschka, Josef Hoffmann, Otto Wagner, and Adolf Loos among them—brought about an unprecedented artistic revolution, a revolution that swept away the past and set the stage for the radically experimental art of the 20th century.

At the close of World War I the Austro-Hungarian Empire was dismembered, and Vienna lost its cherished status as the seat of imperial power. Its influence was much reduced, and (unlike most of Europe's other great cities) its population began to decline, from around 2 million to the current 1.7 million. Today, however, the city's future looks brighter, for with the collapse of the Iron Curtain, Vienna may at long last regain its traditional status as the hub of central Europe.

For many first-time visitors, the city's one major disappointment concerns the Danube River. The inner city, it turns out, lies not on the river's main stream but on one of its narrow offshoots, known as the Danube Canal. As a result, the sweeping river views expected by most newcomers fail to materialize.

The Romans are to blame, for when Vienna was founded as a Roman military encampment around AD 100, the walled garrison was built not on the Danube's main stream but rather on the largest of the river's eastern branches, where it could be bordered by water on three sides. The wide, present-day Danube did not take shape until the late 19th century, when its various branches were rerouted and merged to prevent flooding.

The Romans maintained their camp for some 300 years (the emperor Marcus Aurelius is thought to have died in Vindobona, as it was called, in AD 180) and finally abandoned the site around AD 400. The settlement survived the Roman withdrawal, however, and by the 13th century growth was sufficient to require new city walls to the south. According to legend, the walls were financed by the English: In 1192 the local duke kidnapped King Richard I the Lionhearted, en route from the Third Crusade, and held him prisoner in Dürnstein, upriver, for two years until he was expensively ransomed.

Vienna's third set of walls dates from 1544, when the existing walls were improved and extended. The new fortifications were built by the Habsburg dynasty, which ruled the Austro-Hungarian Empire for an astonishing 640 years, beginning with Rudolf I in 1273 and ending with Karl I in 1918. The walls stood until 1857, when Emperor Francis Joseph finally decreed that they be demolished and replaced by the famous tree-lined Ringstrasse (Ring Street).

During medieval times the city's growth was relatively slow, and its heyday as a European capital did not begin until 1683, after a huge force of invading Turks laid siege to the city for two months, to be finally routed by an army of Habsburg allies. Among the supplies that the fleeing Turks left behind were sacks filled with coffee beans. It was these beans, so the story goes, that gave a local entrepreneur the idea of opening the first public coffeehouse; they remain a Viennese institution to this day.

The passing of the Turkish threat produced a Viennese building boom, and the Baroque style was the architectural order of the day. Flamboyant, triumphant, joyous, and extravagantly ostentatious, the new art form—imported from Italy—transformed the city into a vast theater in the 17th and 18th centuries. Life became a dream—the gorgeous dream of the Baroque, with its gilded madonnas and cherubs, its soaring, twisted columns, its painted heavens on the ceilings, its sumptuous domes. In the 19th century, a reaction set in—the Biedermeier epoch, when middle-class industriousness and sober family values set a new style. Then came the Strauss era—that lighthearted period that conjures up imperial balls, "Wine, Women, and Song," heel-clicking, and hand-kissing. Today, visitors will find that all these eras have left their mark on Vienna, making it a city possessed of a special grace. It is this grace that gives Vienna the distinctive architectural character that sets the city so memorably apart from its great rivals—London, Paris, and Rome.

Pleasures and Pastimes

Café Society

They used to say that there were more cafés and coffeehouses in Vienna than there were banks in Switzerland. Whether or not this can still be claimed, you can't savor the true flavor of Vienna without visiting some of its Meccas of Mocha. Every afternoon at 4, the coffee-and-pastry ritual of *Kaffeejause* takes place from one end of the city to the other. Regulars take their *Stammtisch* (usual table) and sit until they go home for dinner. They come to gossip, read the papers, negotiate business, play cards, meet a spouse (or someone else's), or—who knows?—just have a cup of coffee. Whatever the reason, Viennese use cafés and coffeehouses as club, pub, bistro, and even a home-away-from-home. (Oldtimers recall the old joke: "Pardon me, would you mind watching my seat for awhile so I can go out for a cup of coffee?")

In fact, to savor the atmosphere of the coffeehouse, you must allow time. There is no need to worry about outstaying one's welcome, even over a single small cup of Mokka—so set aside a morning or afternoon, and take along this book. For historical overtones, head for the Café Central—where Stalin and Trotsky hatched the Russian Revolution; for Old-World charm, check out the opulent Café Landtmann (even it's plush velvet interior is chocolate-colored) or the elegant Café Sacher (famous for its cake); for an art scene, go to the Café Hawelka. Wherever you go, never ask for just a cup of coffee; request, at the very least, a Mocha *mit Obers*—with whipped cream—from the "Herr Ober" or any of the other delightful variations discussed within the Cafés section in the Dining listings below.

The Heurigen

It is a memorable experience to sit at the edge of a vineyard on the Kahlenberg with a tankard of young white wine, and listen to the *Schrammel* quartet playing sentimental Viennese songs. How far-sighted of the Emperor Joseph to decree in 1784 that winegrowers could sell their wines together with cold food to customers whenever they liked. At the same time, the Viennese discovered that it was cheaper to go out to the wine than to bring it inside the city walls where taxes were levied. Mutual interest has thus made an institution of these Heurigen polka-dotting the hills surrounding Vienna.

Today, in such villages as Sievering, Nussdorf, and Grinzing, there seem to be more heurigen than homes. The heuriger owner is supposed to be licensed to served only the produce of his own vineyard, a rule long more honored in the breach than in the observance (it would take a sensitive palate indeed to differentiate among the various vineyards). Head for the taverns that mark their doorways with a green branch, spend a wonderfully relaxing afternoon or evening over a mug or two of wine and you'll truly learning the full Austrian meaning of the German term gemütlichkeit. There are so many of these taverns that it would be frivolous to single any out: everyone in Vienna has his favorite which is also, of course, the best. Beethoven, however, knew a good thing when he lived at his house on the Pfarrplatz in Heiligenstadt for some time. Now belonging to the Mayer family, this noted address houses a Heuriger, the Mayer, which really serves its own wines and has long been a favorite of many famous Viennese. If you go to this region in the fall, try a glass of *Sturm,* a cloudy drink halfway between grape juice and wine, with a delicious yeasty fizz. A word of warning: Heuriger wine tastes like water at first. Newcomers blithely say, "I can drink a barrel of this." Then, after the first liter has gone down, it feels as if a little man comes up from behind and slugs you on the skull.

Jugendstil Jewels

From 1897 to 1907, the Vienna Secession movement gave rise to one of the most spectacular manifestations of the pan-European style known as Art Nouveau. Viennese took to calling the look "Jugenstil," or the "young style." In such dazzling edifices as Otto Wagner's Wienzeile majolica-adorned mansion or Adolf Loos's Looshaus, Jugendstil architects rebelled against the prevailing 19th-century historicism that had created so many imitation Renaissance town houses and faux Grecian temples. Josef Maria Olbrich, Josef Hoffman, and Otto Schönthal took William Morris's Arts and Crafts movement, added dashes of Charles Rennie Mackintosh and flat-surface Germanic geometry, and came up with a luxurious style that shocked turn-of-the-century Viennese (and infuriated Emperor Francis Joseph). Many artists united to form the Vienna Secession—whose most famous member was painter Gustav Klimt—and the Wiener Werkstätte, which transformed the objects of daily life with a sleek modern look. Today, Jugendstil buildings are among the most fascinating structures in Vienna. The shrine of the movement is the world-famous Secession Pavilion—the work of Josef Maria Olbrich—the cynosure of all eyes on the Friedrichstrasse.

Museums and Marvels

You could spend months just perusing Vienna's 90 museums. Subjects range alphabetically from Art to Wine, and in between are found such oddities as bricks and burials, such marvels as carriages and clocks, and such memorials as Mozart and martyrs. If your time is short, the one museum not to be overlooked is the *Kunsthistorisches,* Vienna's famous art museum. Here you'll discover the originals of paintings you've otherwise seen only on calendars or in books. The most famous room of all is, of course, the one given over to masterpieces by Pieter Brueghel the Elder, the famed 16th-century Netherlandish painter, including his *Peasant Wedding, Peasant Dance,* and the unforgettable *Hunters in the Snow.*

Given a little more time, the *Schatzkammer,* or Imperial Treasury, is well worth a visit, for its opulent bounty of crown jewels, regal attire, and other trappings of court. The sparkling new museum of court silver and tableware is fascinating for its "behind the scenes" views of state banquets and other elegant representational affairs. The best-known museums tend to crowd up in late morning and mid-afternoon hours; you can beat the mobs by going earlier or around the noon hour, at least to the larger museums that are open without a noontime break.

The Sound—and Sights—of Music

What closer association to Vienna is there but music? Boasting one of the world's greatest concert halls (Musikverein), two of the world's greatest symphony orchestras (Vienna Philharmonic and Vienna Symphony), and one of the top opera houses (Staatsoper), it's no wonder that music and the related politics are subjects of daily conversation. During July and August—just in time for tourists—the city hosts the Vienna Summer of Music, with numerous special events and concerts.

For the musical tourist who is excited at the prospect of treading in the footprints of the mighty, seeing where masterpieces were committed to paper, or standing where a long-loved work was either praised or damned at its first appearance, Vienna is tops: The city is saturated with musical history. There is the apartment where Mozart wrote his last three symphonies, the house where Schubert was born, and, just a tram ride away, the path that inspired Beethoven's Pastoral Symphony. Just below, you'll find a handy list of these musical landmarks.

Of course, there is also music to delight as well as inspire. The statue of Johann Strauss II in the Stadtpark tells all. To see him, violin tucked under his chin, is to imagine those infectious waltzes, "Wine, Women, and Song," "Voices of Spring," and best of all, the "Emperor." But quite possibly you will not need to imagine them. Chances are, somewhere in the distance, an orchestra will be playing them. Head for the Theatre an der Wien to hear great operetta (*Die Fledermaus* and *The Merry Widow* both premiered here) or to the Volksoper. While the traditional classics are the main fare for the conservative, traditional Viennese, acceptance of modern music is growing, as are the audiences for pop and jazz.

Musicians' residences abound and many are open as museums. The most famous are Mozart's Figarohaus and Beethoven's Pasqualatihaus, which are discussed in the city sections below. Vienna has many other music landmarks scattered over the city—here's a Whitman's Sampler. Schubert—a native of the city, unlike most of Vienna's other famous composers—was born at Nussdorferstrasse 54 (☎ 01/317–3601, U-Bahn (subway) U2/Schottenring then Streetcar 37 or 38 to Canisiusgasse), in the Ninth District, and died in the Fourth District at Kettenbrückengasse 6 (☎ 01/581–6730, U-Bahn U4/Kettenbrückengasse). Joseph Haydn's house, which includes a Brahms memorial room, is at Haydngasse 19 (☎ 01/596–1307, U-Bahn U4/Pilgramgasse or U3/Zieglergasse) in the Sixth District; Beethoven's Heiligenstadt residence, where at age 32 he wrote the "Heiligenstadt Testament," an anguished cry of pain and protest against his ever-increasing deafness, is at Probusgasse 6 in the 19th District (☎ 01/375408, U-Bahn U4/Heiligenstadt then Bus 38A to Wählamt). The home of the most popular composer of all, waltz king Johann Strauss the Younger, can be visited at Praterstrasse 54 (☎ 01/214–0121, U-Bahn U4/Nestroypl.), in the Second District; he lived here when he composed "The Blue Danube Waltz" in 1867. All the above houses contain commemorative museums. ⌧ AS25, *block of 10 AS25 tickets for city museums AS160.* ☉ *Tues.–Sun. 9–12:15 and 1–4:30.*

One of the most delightful musicians' residences is the Lehár Villa (✉ Hackhofergasse 18, ☎ 01/371–8213), generally open by appointment only. For a wistful experience, phone ahead and arrange to visit the exquisite house where the composer Franz Lehár lived and worked. Parts of the miniature *Schloss* date to the 1600s; from 1802–1812 it belonged to Emanuel Schikaneder, who wrote the libretto for Mozart's *The Magic Flute.* The main sitting room is given over to Lehár memorabilia, including his dreadfully out-of-tune piano. Ask to see the charming front garden and the tiny chapel (in which the singer Richard Tauber was married). To get to the villa, take U2/Schottenring, then Streetcar D to Nussdorferplatz.

Stepping Out in Three-Quarter Time

Ever since the 19th-century Congress of Vienna—when pundits laughed *"Elle danse, mais elle ne marche pas"* (the city "dances, but it never gets anything done")—Viennese extravagance and gaiety have been world famous. Fasching, the season of Prince Carnival, was given over to court balls, opera balls, masked balls, Chambermaids' and Bakers' balls, and a hundred other gatherings, many held within the glittering interiors of Baroque theaters and palaces. Presiding over the dazzling evening gowns and gilt-splashed uniforms, towering headresses, flirtatious fans, *chambres séparées,* "Wine, Women, and Song," *Die Fledermaus,* "Blue Danube," hand-kissing and gay abandon, was the baton of the waltz emperor, Johann Strauss. White-gloved women and men in white tie would glide over marble floors to his heavenly melodies. They still do. Now, as in the days of Francis Joseph, Vienna's old three-quarter-time rhythm strikes up anew each year during Carnival time, from New Year's Eve until Mardi Gras.

During January and February, as many as 40 balls may be held in a single evening, the most exclusive being Prince Willi Thurn und Taxis's Ball der Silbernen Rose and the most famous—some say too famous—being the Opernball. On February 6, this event transforms the Vienna Opera House into the world's most beautiful ballroom (and transfixes all of Austria when shown live on national television). For a price, anyone can attend, but corporate interests often buy up most of the tickets. The invitation to the Opernball reads, "Frack mit Dekorationen," which means that it's time to dust off your Legion of Honor medal and women mustn't wear white (reserved for debutantes). Remember that you must dance the *Linkswalzer*—the counter-clockwise, left-turning waltz that is the only way to dance in Vienna. After your gala evening, finish off the morning with a Kater Frühstuck—a hangover breakfast—of goulash soup. For a run-down on the major balls that the public can attend during the winter season, *see* Nightlife *in* Nightlife and the Arts, *below.*

EXPLORING VIENNA

To the Viennese, the most prestigious address of Vienna's 23 *Bezirke,* or districts, is the First District (the inner city, bounded by the Ringstrasse and the Danube Canal). The Second through Ninth districts surround the inner city (starting with the Second District across the Danube Canal and running clockwise); the 10th through 23rd districts form a second concentric ring of suburbs. The vast majority of sightseeing attractions is to be found in the First District. For hard-core sightseers who wish to supplement the key attractions that follow, the tourist office (☞ Contacts and Resources *in* Vienna A to Z, *below*) has a booklet by the same name, "Vienna from A–Z" (AS60), that gives short descriptions of some 250 sights around the city, all numbered and keyed to a fold-out map at the back, as well as to numbered wall plaques on the buildings themselves. Note that the nearest U-Bahn (subway) stop to most city attractions described below is included at the end of the service information (for a handy map of the Vienna subway system, *see* the map *in* Getting Around *in* Vienna A to Z, *below*). The more important churches have coin-operated (AS10) tape machines that give an excellent commentary in English on the history and architecture of the church.

Vienna is a city to explore and discover on foot. The description of the city on the following pages is divided into seven areas: six that explore the architectural riches of central Vienna, and a seventh that describes Schönbrunn Palace and its gardens. Above all, *look up* as you tour Vienna: Some of the most fascinating architectural and ornamental bits are on upper stories or atop the city's buildings.

Great Itineraries

IF YOU HAVE 1 DAY

Touring Vienna in a single day is a proposition as strenuous as it is unlikely, but those with more ambition than time should first get a quick view of the lay of the city by taking a streetcar ride around the Ringstrasse, the wide boulevard that encloses the heart of the city. Then spend the time until early afternoon exploring the city center, starting at Vienna's cathedral, the **Stephansdom**, and including the neighboring streets. About 2 PM, head for **Schönbrunn Palace** to spend the afternoon touring the magnificent royal residence, then return to the city center to take

a quick look at the most famous art treasures in town, the legendary
Pieter Brueghel paintings at the **Kunsthistoriches Museum** (who could
possibly visit Vienna and not see Brueghel's *Hunters in the Snow*?). After
the museum closes at 6 PM, relax over coffee at a café, then spend a musical evening at a concert, opera, or operetta, or a convivial evening at
a Heuriger, one of the wine restaurants for which Vienna is also famous.

IF YOU HAVE 3 DAYS
Given more time, day one can be a little less hectic, and in any case,
you'll want more time for the city center. Rather than the do-it-your-
self streetcar ride around the Ringstrasse, take an organized sightseeing tour, which will describe the highlights. Plan to spend a full
afternoon at the **Schönbrunn Palace.** Reserve the second day for art,
and tackle the rest of the exciting **Kunsthistoriches Museum** (having taken
in the Brueghels on your first day) before lunch and the magnificent

collection of Old Master drawings of the **Albertina,** the impressive
Belvedere Palace for a contrasting step into modern art in the afternoon—don't miss Klimt's legendary *The Kiss.* Do as the Viennese do,
and fill in any gaps with stops at cafés, reserving evenings for relaxing over music or wine. On the third day, head for the world famous
Spanish Riding School and watch the Lipizzaners prance through morning training. While you're in the neighborhood, view the sparkling court
jewels in the **Schatzkammer**—the imperial treasury—and the glitzy **Silberkammer,** the museum of court silverware and table settings, and
take in one of Vienna's most spectacular Baroque settings, the glorious Grand Hall of the **Hofbibliothek Prunksaal** (National Library). For
a total contrast, head out to the **Prater** amusement park in late afternoon for a ride on the giant Ferris wheel and end the day in a wine
restaurant on the outskirts, such as Sievering or Nussdorf.

IF YOU HAVE 7 DAYS
Spend your first three days as outlined in the itinerary above. Then begin
your fourth day getting better acquainted with the Fourth District—
the heart of the city. Treasures here range from Roman ruins to the
residences of Mozart and Beethoven, and, slightly afield, **Sigmund Freud's
apartment** (in the Ninth District) or the oddball **Hunderwasserhaus**

(in the Third). Put it all in contemporary perspective with a backstage
tour of the magnificent **Staastoper,** the opera house. For a country break
on the fifth day, take a tour of the **Vienna Woods** or the Danube Valley, particularly the glorious **Wachau district** where vineyards sweep
down to the river's edge. On the sixth day, fill in some of the blanks
with a stroll around the **Naschmarkt** food market district, taking in
the nearby **Secession Building** with Gustav Klimt's famous Beethoven
Frieze. Don't overlook the superb **Jugendstil** buildings on the north side
of the market. If you're still game for museums, head for any one of
the less usual offerings, such as the Jewish Museum, the Musical Instruments or Ephesos museums in **the Hofburg,** or the city's **Historical
Museum**; by now, you'll have acquired a good concept of the city and
its background, so the exhibits will make more sense. Cap the day by
visiting the **Kaisergruft** in the Kapuzinerkirche to view the serried
ranks of Habsburgs responsible for so much of Vienna.

The Inner City: Historic Heart of Vienna

A good way to break the ice on your introduction to Vienna is to get
a general picture of its layout as presented to the cruising bird or air-
plane pilot. There are several beautiful vantage points from which you
can look down and over the city—including the terrace of the Upper
Belvedere Palace—but the city's preeminent lookout point, offering fine
views in all directions, is gained from **Stephansdom** (St. Stephen's

Cathedral) by toiling up the 345 steps of "Alt Steffl" (Old Stephan, its south tower) to the observation platform. The young and agile will make it up in 8 to 10 minutes; the slower-paced will make it in closer to 20. An elevator, and no exertion, will present you with much the same view from the terrace. From atop, you can see that St. Stephen's is the veritable hub of the city's wheel.

Most of Vienna lies roughly within an arc of a circle, with the straight line of the Danube as its chord. Its heart, the *Innere Stadt* (Inner City) or First District—in medieval times, the entire city of Vienna—is bounded by the Ringstrasse (Ring), which forms almost a circle, with a narrow arc cut off by the Danube Canal, diverted from the main river just above Vienna and flowing through the city to rejoin the parent stream just below it. The city spreads out from the Stephansdom, accented by the series of magnificent buildings erected—beginning in the 1870s, when Vienna reached the zenith of its imperial prosperity—around the Ringstrasse: the Opera House, the National Art Gallery and the National Museum of Natural History, the "New Wing" of the Hofburg, the House of Parliament, the Rathaus, the University, and the Votivkirche. For more than eight centuries, the enormous bulk of the cathedral has remained the nucleus around which the city has grown. The bird's-eye view can be left until the last day of your visit when the city's landmarks will be more familiar. First day or last, the vistas are memorable, especially if you catch them as the cathedral's famous "Pummerin" (Boomer) bell is tolling.

Numbers in the text correspond to numbers in the margin and on the Vienna map.

A Good Walk

Stephansplatz, in the heart of the city, is the logical starting point from which to track down Vienna's past and present, as well as any acquaintance (natives believe that if you wait long enough at this intersection of eight streets you'll run into anyone you're searching for). Although it's now in what is mainly a pedestrian zone, **Stephansdom** ①, the mighty cathedral, marks the point from which distances to and from Vienna are measured. Visit the cathedral (it's quite impossible to view all its treasures, so just soak up its reflective Gothic spirit) and consider climbing its 345-step Alt Steffl tower or descending into its Habsburg crypt. Then wander up the Wollzeile, cutting through the narrow Essiggasse and right into the Backerstrasse, to the **Universitätskirche** ② or Jesuitenkirche, a lovely Jesuit church—the pink and green interior is topped by a trompe l'oeil ceiling painted by Andrea Pozzo in 1705— where masses are sung in Latin on many Sunday mornings. Note the contrasting **Academy of Science** diagonally opposite (Beethoven premiered his Battle Symphony in its Ceremonial Hall). Follow the Sonnenfelsgasse, ducking through one of the tiny alleys on the right to reach the Backerstrasse; turn right at Gutenbergplatz into the Köllnerhofgasse, right again into tiny Grashofgasse and through the gate into the surprising **Heiligenkreuzerhof square** ③, a peaceful oasis (unless a a handicrafts market is taking place). Through the square, enter the Schönlaterngasse (Beautiful Lantern Street) to admire the house fronts—film companies at times block this street to make shots in the picturesque atmosphere— on your way to the **Dominikanerkirche** ④, the Dominican church with its marvelous Baroque interior. Following Predigergasse and Falkestrasse, in back of the church is the architectural contrast of the **Post Office Savings Bank** ⑤ and former **War Ministry,** facing each other. Retrace your steps, following Postgasse into **Fleischmarkt** ⑥. Nearby Hoher Markt, reached by taking Rotenturmstrasse west to Lichtensteg or Bauernmarkt, was part of the early Roman encampment, witness the Roman Ruins under **Hoher Markt** ⑦. The extension of Fleischmarkt ends in a set of stairs leading up past the eccentric Kornhäusal Tower. Up the stairs to the right on Ruprechtsplatz is **Ruprechtskirche** ⑧, St. Rupert's Church, allegedly the city's oldest. Take Sterngasse down the steps, turn left into Marc Aurel-Strasse and right into Salvatorgasse to discover the lacework **Maria am Gestade** ⑨, Maria on the Banks, which once sat above a small river, now underground.

TIMING

If you're pressed for time and happy with facades rather than what's behind them, this route could take half a day, but if you love to look inside, stop to ponder and explore the myriad narrow alleys, figure at least a day for this walk. During services, wandering around the churches will be limited, but otherwise, you can tackle this walk about any time at your convenience.

Sights to See

Basilikenhaus (House of the Basilik). One of the most intriguing houses in Vienna is the House of the Basilik, located at Schönlaterngasse (Beautiful Lantern Street)—once part of Vienna's medieval *Quartier Latin* and rapidly becoming so again. Along the street's Baroque houses (note the colorfully painted facades) and chic shops you'll find the house known as the Basiliskenhaus, at No. 7. According to legend, it was first built for a baker; on June 26, 1212, a foul-smelling basilisk (half-rooster, half-toad, with a glance that could kill) took up residence in the courtyard well, poisoning the water. An enterprising apprentice dealt with the problem by climbing down the well armed with a mirror; when the basilisk saw its own reflection it turned to stone. The petrified creature can still be seen in a niche on the building's facade. Today, modern science accounts for the contamination with a more prosaic explanation: natural-gas seepage. Be sure to take a look in the house's miniature courtyard for a trip back to medieval Vienna (the house itself is private). The picturesque street is named for the ornate wrought-iron wall lantern at No. 6. Just a few steps from the Basilikenhaus, take a look into the Baroque courtyard at No. 8—one of the city's prettiest—and at No. 9, you'll find the **Alte Schmiede**, the Old Smithy, a blacksmith workshop that is now a museum.

❹ **Dominikanerkirche** (Dominican Church). The Postgasse, to the east of Schönlaterngasse, introduces an unexpected visitor from Rome: the Dominikanerkirche. Built in the 1630s, some 50 years before the Viennese Baroque building boom, its facade is modeled after any number of Roman churches of the 16th century. The interior illustrates why the Baroque style came to be considered the height of bad taste during the 19th century and still has many detractors today. "Sculpt till you drop" seems to have been the motto here, and the viewer's eye is given no respite. This sort of Roman architectural orgy never really gained a foothold in Vienna, and when the great Viennese architects did pull out all the decorative stops—Hildebrandt's interior at the Belvedere Palace, for instance, they did it in a very different style and with far greater success. ⊠ *Postgasse 4,* ☎ *01/512–7460. U-Bahn: U3 Stubentor/Dr. Karl-Lueger-Pl.*

❻ **Fleischmarkt No. 11.** Fleischmarkt and the picturesque tiny Griechengasse just beyond the glittering 19th-century Greek Orthodox church are part of the city's oldest core. This corner of the inner city has a medieval feel that is quite genuine; there has been a tavern at No. 11 for some 500 years. The wooden carving on the facade of the current Griechenbeisl restaurant commemorates Max Augustin—best known today from the song "Ach du lieber Augustin"—an itinerant musician who sang here during the plague of 1679.

26

Academy of Fine
Arts, **43**
Albertina Museum, **41**
Belvedere Palace, **47**
Blutgasse quarter, **37**
Bohemian Court
Chancery, **10**
Burgtheater, **32**
Café Central, **17**
Demel's, **24**
Dominikanerkirche, **4**
Figarohaus, **38**
Fleischmarkt No. 11, **6**
Freud's Apartment, **35**
Heiligenkreuzerhof, **3**
Historisches Museum
der Stadt Wien, **46**
Hofburg, **25**
Hoher Markt, **7**
Jewish Museum, **20**
Justizpalast, **29**
Kaisergruft, **40**
Karlskirche, **45**
Kinsky Palace, **13**
Kirche Am Hof, **11**
Kohlmarkt, **23**
Kunsthistorisches
Museum, **26**
Looshaus, **19**
Maria am Gestade, **9**
Michaelerplatz, **18**
Ministry of
Finance, **39**
Minoritenkirche, **16**
Museum Moderner
Kunst, **36**
Palais Ferstel, **12**
Parliament, **30**
Pasqualatihaus, **15**
Peterskirche, **22**
Postsparkasse, **5**
Rathaus, **31**
Ruprechtskirche, **8**
Schottenkirche, **14**
Secession Pavilion, **44**
Spittelberg quarter, **27**
Stock-im-Eisen, **21**
St. Stephen's
Cathedral, **1**
State Opera House, **42**
Universität, **33**
Universitätskirche, **2**
Volksgarten, **28**
Votivkirche, **34**

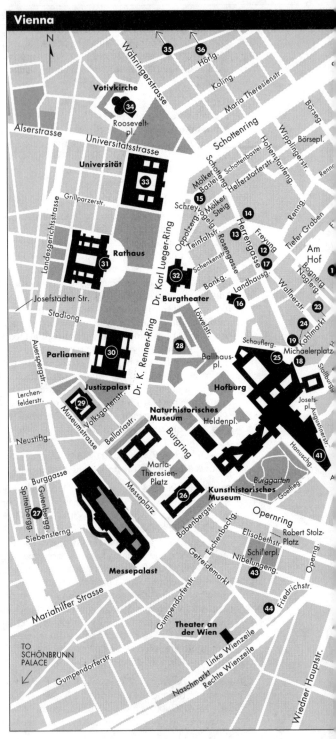

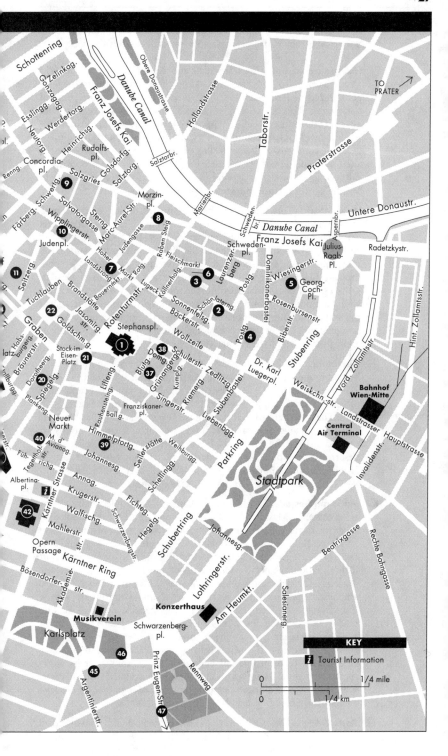

Schottenring

Gonzagag.

Zelinkag.

Esslingg.

Neutorg.

Werdertorg.

Heinrichsg.

Renng.

Concordia-
pl.

Färberg.

Schwertg.

Rudolfs-
pl.

Salzgries

Goldorfg.

Salztorg.

Salvatorgasse

Sterng.

Judenpl.

Wipplingerstr.

Seitzerg.

Tuchlauben

Brandstätte

Landskrong.

Hoher
Markt

Bauernmkt.

Marc-Aurel-Str.

Judengasse

Morzin-
pl.

Raben Steig

Fleischmarkt

Lugeck

Kollnerhofg.

Sonnenfelsg.

Köllnerhofg.

Schön laterng.

Franz Josefs Kai

Danube Canal

Obere Donaustrasse

Danube Canal

Franz Josefs Kai

Hollandstrasse

Taborstr.

Praterstrasse

TO
PRATER

Untere Donaustr.

Radetzkystr.

Julius-
Raab-
Pl.

Wiesingerstr.

Georg-
Coch-
Pl.

Rosenbursenstr

Dominikanerbastei

Biberstr.

Stubenring

Dr. Karl
Luegerpl.

Weiskchn-str.

Vord Zollamtsstr.

Landstrasser

Hauptstrasse

Invalidenstr.

Hint. Zollamtsstr.

Bahnhof
Wien-Mitte

Central
Air Terminal

Graben

Goldschm.g.

Jasomirg.

str.

Rotenturmstr.

Stephanspl.

Wollzeile

Bäckerstr.

Schulerstr.

Domg.

Zedlizg.g.

Singerstr.

Riemerg.

Stubenbastei

Liebenbgg.

Lauenzer-
berg

Postg.

Postg.

Schwedenpl.

Habs-
burgerg.

Bräunerstr.

Dorotheerg.

Spiegelg.

Plankeng.

Stock-im-
Eisen-
Platz

Lilieng.

Rauhensteing.

Ball g.

Franziskaner-
pl.

Grünang.

B.luig.

Domg.g.

Neuer
Markt

M d
Aviang.

Tegetthof-

richg.

Annag.

Krugerstr.

Himmelpfortg.

Johannesg.

Seilerstätte

Weihburgg.

Weihburgg.

Scheflingg.

Fichteg.

Hegelg.

Parkring

Stadtpark

Johannesg.

Beatrixgasse

Rechte Bahngasse

Albertina-
pl.

Führich-

Kärntner Strasse

Walfischg.

Mahlerstr.

Opern
Passage

str.

Bösendorfer-
str.

Akademie-
str.

Kärntner Ring

Schwarzenbergstr.

Schubertring

Lothringerstr.

Am Heumkt.

Schlesianerg.

Musikverein

Karlsplatz

Konzerthaus

Schwarzenberg-
pl.

Prinz Eugen-Str.

Rennweg

Argentinierstr.

NEED A
BREAK?   Take a pause for coffee at the corner of Fleischmarkt and Wolfengasse,
at the **Café Vienne** (✉ Fleischmarkt 20, ☎ 01/512–4457) famous for
baking what may be the biggest and most enticing cakes in the city.

❸ **Heiligenkreuzerhof.** Tiny side streets and alleys run off of Sonnenfelsgasse, parallel to Bäckerstrasse. Amid the narrow streets is Heiligenkreuzerhof (Holy Cross Court), one of the city's most peaceful
backwaters. This complex of buildings dates from the 17th century but
got an 18th-century face-lift. Appropriately, the restraint of the architecture—with only here and there a small outburst of Baroque spirit—
gives the courtyard a distinct feeling of retreat. The square is a favorite
site for seasonal markets at Easter and Christmas, and for occasional
outdoor art shows. Just around the bend is **Schönlaterngasse**, one of
Vienna's most picturesque streets (☞ Basilikhaus, *above*).

❼ **Hoher Markt.** This square was badly damaged during World War II,
but the famous Anker Clock at the east end survived the artillery fire.
The huge mechanical timepiece took six years (1911–17) to build and
still attracts crowds at noon when the full panoply of mechanical figures representing Austrian historical personages parades by. The figures are identified on a plaque to the bottom left of the clock. The
graceless buildings erected around the square since 1945 are not aging
well and do little to show off the square's lovely Baroque centerpiece,
the St. Joseph Fountain (portraying the marriage of Joseph and Mary),
designed in 1729 by Joseph Emanuel Fischer von Erlach, son of the
great Johann Bernhard Fischer von Erlach.

The Hoher Markt does harbor one wholly unexpected attraction,
however: **underground Roman ruins.** This was once the main east–west
axis of the Roman encampment of Vindobona, and the foundations
of several officers' houses built in the 2nd century have been uncov-
ered. The officers lived well: their houses even had central heating, and
you can see the pipes that carried the hot water. The excavations are
entered through the sushi snack bar in the passageway at No. 3; a short
descriptive pamphlet in English is available at the ticket table. ✉
Hoher Markt/Fischhof 3, ☎ *01/535–5606.* 🖭 *AS25.* ☉ *Tues.–Sun.
9–12:15 and 1–4:30. U-Bahn: U1, U3 Stephansplatz.*

❾ **Maria am Gestade** (St. Mary on the Banks). The middle-Gothic, seven-
sided tower of Maria am Gestade, crowned by a delicate cupola, is a
sheer joy to the eye, and dispels the idea that Gothic must necessarily
be autere. Built around 1400 (but much restored in the 17th and 19th
centuries), the church incorporated part of the Roman city walls into
its foundation; the north wall, as a result, takes a slight but noticeable
dogleg to the right halfway down the nave. Like St. Stephen's, Maria
am Gestade is rough-hewn Gothic, with a simple but forceful facade.
The church is especially beloved, however, because of its unusual details—the pinnacled and saint-bedecked gable that tops the front facade, the stone canopy that hovers protectively over the front door, and
(most appealing of all) the intricate openwork lantern atop the south-
side bell tower. Appropriately enough in a city famous for its pastry,
the lantern lends its tower an engaging suggestion of a sugar caster,
while some see an allusion to hands intertwined in prayer. ✉ *Passauer
Pl./Salvatorgasse. U-Bahn: U1, U3 Stephansplatz.*

❺ **Postsparkasse** (Post Office Savings Bank). The Post Office Savings Bank
is one of modern architecture's greatest curiosities. It was designed in
1904 by Otto Wagner, whom many consider the father of 20th-century
architecture. In his famous manifesto, *Modern Architecture,* Wagner con-
demned 19th-century revivalist architecture and pleaded for a modern
style that honestly expressed modern building methods. Accordingly, the

exterior walls of the Post Office Savings Bank are mostly flat and undecorated; visual interest is supplied merely by varying the pattern of the bolts that were used to hold the marble slabs in place on the wall surface during construction. Later architects were to embrace Wagner's beliefs wholeheartedly, although they used different, truly modern building materials: glass and concrete rather than marble. The Post Office Savings Bank was indeed a bold leap into the future, but unfortunately the future took a different path and today the whole appears a bit dated. Go inside for a look at the restored and functioning *Kassa-Saal,* or central cashier's hall, to see how Wagner carried his concepts over to interior design. ⊠ *Georg-Coch-Pl. 2,* ☎ *01/51400.* ☉ *Lobby weekdays 8–3.*

OFF THE
BEATEN PATH

HUNDERTWASSERHAUS – To see one of Vienna's most amazing buildings, travel eastward from Schwendenplatz or Julius-Raab Platz along Radetzkystrasse to the junction of Kegelgasse and Löwengasse. Here, you'll find the Hundertwasserhaus, a 50-apartment public-housing complex designed by Friedensreich Hundertwasser, Austria's best-known living painter. The structure looks as though it had been decorated by a crew of mischievous circus clowns wielding giant crayons. The building caused a sensation when it was erected in 1985 and still draws crowds of sightseers. ⊠ *Löwengasse/Kegelgasse. U-Bahn: U1 or U4/Schwedenpl., then Streetcar N to Hetzgasse.*

Nearby, you'll find another Hundertwasser project, the **KunstHaus Wien** art museum, which mounts outstanding international exhibits in addition to showings of the colorful Hundertwasser works. Like the apartment complex nearby, the building itself is pure Hundertwasser, with irregular floors, windows with trees growing out of them, and sudden architectural surprises, a wholly appropriate setting for modern art. ⊠ *Untere Weissgerberstr. 13,* ☎ *01/712–0491–0.* ☉ *Daily 10–7. U-Bahn: U1 or U4/Schwedenpl., then Streetcar N to Radetzkypl..*

❽ **Ruprechtskirche** (St. Ruprecht's Church). Ruprechtsplatz, another of Vienna's time-warp backwaters, lies to the north of the Kornhäusel Tower. The church in the middle, Ruprechtskirche, is the city's oldest. According to legend it was founded in 740; the oldest part of the present structure (the lower half of the tower) dates from the 11th century. Set on the ancient ramparts overlooking the Danube Canal, it is serene and unpretentious. Try the one door, though it's usually locked. You can look in through the grill, but the lack of windows generally obscures what can be seen of the arcaded, unadorned interior. ⊠ *Ruprechtspl. U-Bahn: U1, U4 Schwedenpl.*

❶ **Stephansdom** (St. Stephen's Cathedral). This soaring structure enshrines the heart of Vienna, although it is curious to note that in its earliest days, as the parish church which was built in the years 1144–1147, it stood outside the walls of the city. Vienna can thank a period of hard times for the Mother Church for the distinctive silhouette of the cathedral. Originally the structure was to have had matching 445-foot-high spires, a standard design of the era, but funds ran out, and the north tower to this day remains a happy reminder of what gloriously is not. The lack of symmetry creates an imbalance that makes the cathedral instantly identifiable from its profile alone. The cathedral, as well as the Staastoper and some other major buildings, were very heavily damaged in World War II. Since then, it has risen from the fires of destruction like a phoenix, and as with the phoenix, it is a symbol of regeneration.

It is difficult now, sitting quietly in the shadowed peace, to tell what was original and what parts of the walls and vaults were reconstructed.

No matter: its history-rich atmosphere is dear to all Viennese. That noted, St. Stephen's possesses a fierce presence that is blatantly un-Viennese. It is a stylistic jumble ranging from 13th-century Romanesque to 15th-century Gothic. Like the exterior, St. Stephen's interior lacks the soaring unity of Europe's greatest Gothic cathedrals, with much of its decoration dating from the later Baroque era.

The wealth of decorative sculpture in St. Stephen's can be demoralizing to the nonspecialist, so if you wish to explore the cathedral in detail, you may want to buy the admirably complete English-language description sold in the small room marked *Schriften und Opferkerzen* (Pamphlets and Votive Candles). One particularly masterly work, however, should be seen by everyone: the stone pulpit attached to the second freestanding pier on the left of the central nave, carved by Anton Pilgram around 1510. The delicacy of its decoration would in itself set the pulpit apart, but even more intriguing are its five sculpted figures. Carved around the outside of the pulpit proper are the four Latin Fathers of the Church (from left to right: Saint Augustine, Saint Gregory, Saint Jerome, and Saint Ambrose), and each is given an individual personality so sharply carved as to suggest satire, perhaps of living models. There is no satire suggested by the fifth figure, however; below the pulpit's stairs Pilgram sculpted a fine self-portrait, showing himself peering out a half-open window. Note the toads, lizards, and other creatures climbing the spiral rail alongside the steps up to the pulpit. As you walk among the statues and aisles, remember that many notable events occurred here, including the marriage of Mozart in 1782 and his funeral in December 1791.

St. Stephen's was devastated by fire in the last days of World War II, and the extent of the damage may be seen by leaving the cathedral through the south portal, where a set of prereconstruction photographs commemorates the disaster. Restoration was protracted and difficult, but today the cathedral once again dominates the center of the city. The bird's-eye views from the cathedral's beloved **Alte Steffl** (Old Steven) tower will be a highlight for some. The tower is 450 feet high and was built between 1359 and 1433. The climb or elevator ride up is rewarded with vistas that extend to the rising slopes of the Wienerwald. ⊠ *Stephanspl.,* ☎ *01/515–52–526.* 🎫 *Each tour AS40, elevator AS40.* ☉ *Daily 6 AM–10 PM; tour Mon.–Sat. at 10:30 and 3, and Sun. and holidays at 3; evening tour July and Aug., daily at 7; catacombs tour Mon.–Sat. at 10, 11, 11:30, 2, 2:30, 3:30, 4, and 4:30, and Sun. and holidays at 2, 2:30, 3:30, 4, and 4:30; North Tower elevator to "Pummerin" bell Apr.–Sept., daily 9–6, and Oct.–Mar., daily 8–5. U-Bahn: U1, U3 Stephanspl.*

Vienna of the Middle Ages is encapsulated in the streets in back of St. Stephen's cathedral. You could easily spend half a day or more just prowling the narrow streets and passageways—Wollzeile, Bäckerstrasse, Blutgasse—typical remnants of an early era. Café Alt Wien at Bäckerstrasse 9 is a true original and a hangout for artists and students young and old. Other cafés, bars, and small restaurants along the street are equally worth a visit. Don't overlook the amusing, 18th-century cow playing checkers painted on the facade of the house at No. 12.

❷ Universitätskirche (Jesuit Church). The east end of Bäckerstrasse is punctuated by Dr.-Ignaz-Seipel-Platz, named for the theology professor who was chancellor of Austria during the 1920s. On the north side is the Universitätskirche, or Jesuitenkirche, built around 1630. Its flamboyant Baroque interior contains a fine trompe l'oeil ceiling fresco by that master of visual trickery, Andrea Pozzo, who was imported from Rome in 1702 for the job. You may hear a Mozart or Haydn mass sung here in Latin on many Sundays. ⊠ *Dr. Ignaz-Seipl-Pl.,* ☎ *01/512–5232. U-Bahn: U3 Stubentor/Dr. Karl-Lueger-Pl.*

OFF THE
BEATEN PATH

PRATER – Vienna's most famous park and most beloved attraction for children can be found by heading out northeast from the historic city center, across the Danube Canal along Praterstrasse: the famous Prater, or more correctly, Volksprater (or as the Viennese call it, *Wurstelprater*), the city's foremost amusement park. In 1766, to the dismay of the aristocracy, Emperor Joseph II decreed that the vast expanse of imperial parklands known as the Prater would henceforth be open to the public. East of the inner city between the Danube Canal and the Danube proper, the Prater is a public park to this day, notable for its long promenade (the Hauptallee, more than 4½ kilometers, or 3 miles, in length, its sports facilities (a golf course, a stadium, a race track, and a swimming pool, for starters), and the *Wurstelprater* with its giant Ferris wheel (Riesenrad), the traditional, modern amusement-park rides, plus a number of less innocent indoor, sex-oriented attractions, a planetarium, and a small but interesting museum devoted to the Wurstelprater's long history. If you look carefully, you can discover a handful of children's rides dating to the 1920s and 30s which survived the fire that consumed most of the Volksprater in 1945. The best-known attraction is the 200-foot Ferris wheel that figured so prominently in the 1949 film *The Third Man.* One of three built in Europe at the end of the last century (the others were in England and France, but have long since been dismantled), the wheel was badly damaged during World War II and restored shortly thereafter. Its progress is slow and stately (a revolution takes 10 minutes), and the views from its cars magnificent, particularly toward dusk. ☎ *01/729–5430.* 🎫 *AS45.* ⊗ *Apr., daily 10 AM–11 PM; May–Sept., daily 9 AM–midnight; Oct., daily 10–10; Nov., daily 10–8; Dec., weekends 10–6. U-Bahn: U1/Praterstern.*

Bittersweet Vienna: Baroque Gems and Cozy Cafés

As the city developed and expanded, the core quickly outgrew its early confines. New urban centers sprang up, to be ornamented by government buildings and elegant town residences. Since Vienna was the beating heart of a vast empire, nothing was spared to make the edifices as exuberant as possible, with utility often a secondary consideration. The best architects of the day were commissioned to create impressions as well as buildings, and they did their job well. That so much has survived is a testimony to the solidity both of the designs and of the structures on which the ornamentation has been overlaid.

Those not fortunate enough to afford town palaces were relegated to housing that was often confining and far less than elegant. Rather than suffer the discomfitures of a disruptive household environment, the city's literati and its philosophers and artists took refuge in cafés, which in effect became their combined salons and offices. To this day, cafés remain an important element of Viennese life. Many residents still have their *Stammtisch*, or regular table, at which they appear daily. Talk still prevails—but increasingly so do handy radio telephones and even laptops.

A Good Walk

Start in the Wipplingerstrasse at the upper (west) end of Hohe Markt to find touches of both the imperial and the municipal Vienna. On the east side is the **Altes Rathaus,** which served as the city hall until 1885; on the west, the **Bohemian Court Chancery** ⑩, once diplomatic headquarters for Bohemia's representation to the Habsburg court. Turn south into the short Fütterergasse to reach **Judenplatz,** in the Middle Ages, center of Judaism in Vienna. A clockwatcher's delight is down at the end of Kurrentgasse in the form of the **Uhrenmuseum** (Clock Museum); around the corner through the Parisgasse to Schulhof, a children's delight is the **Puppen- und Spielzeug-Museum** (Doll and Toy Museum). Follow Schulhof into the huge **Am Hof** square, boasting the **Kirche am Hof** ⑪ and what must be the world's most elegant fire station. The square hosts an antiques and collectibles market most of the year on Thursdays and Friday, plus other ad hoc events. Take the miniscule Irisgasse from Am Hof into the Naglergasse, noting the mosaic Jugendstil facade on the pharmacy in the Bognergasse, to your left. Around a bend in the narrow Naglergasse is **Freyung,** an irregular square bounded on the south side by two wonderfully stylish palaces including **Palais Ferstel** ⑫, now a shopping arcade, and the elegantly restored **Palais Harrach** next door, now an outpost of the Kunsthistoriches Museum. Opposite, the privately-run **Kunstforum** art museum mounts varied and outstanding exhibitions. The famous **Kinsky Palace** ⑬ at the beginning of Herrengasse is still partly a private residence. The north side of Freyung is watched over by the **Schottenkirche** ⑭, the Scottish church in fact established by Irish monks. The complex also houses a small but worthwhile museum of the order's treasures. Follow Teinfaltstrasse from opposite the Schottenkirche, turning right into Schreyvogelgasse. Climb the ramp on your right past the so-called Dreimäderlhaus at Schreyvogelgasse 10—note the ornate facade of this pre-Biedermeier patrician house—to reach Molker Bastei, where Beethoven lived in the **Pasqualatihaus** ⑮, now housing a museum memorializing the composer. Follow the ring south to Löwelstrasse, turning left into Bankgasse, then turn right into Abraham-a-Santa Clara-Gasse (our map doesn't show this street by name—for obvious reasons of space!—but it's the tiny street that runs off the Bankgasse) to Minoritenplatz and the **Minoritenkirche** ⑯, the Minorite church with its odd, hat-less tower. Inside is a kitschy mosaic Last Supper. Landhausgasse will bring you to Herrengasse, and diagonally across the street, in the back corner of the Palais Ferstel, is the **Café Central** ⑰, one of Vienna's hangouts for the famous. Going south up the Herrengasse on the left is the odd Hochhaus, a twentieth-century building once noted as Vienna's skyscraper. Opposite are elegant Baroque former town palaces, now used as museum and administration buildings by the province of Lower Austria.

TIMING

The actual distances in this walk are relatively short, and you could cover the route in 1½ hours or so. But if you take time to linger in the museums and sample a Kaffee mit schlag in the Café Central, you'll develop a much better understanding of the contrasts between old and newer in the city. You could easily spend a day following this walk, if you were to take in all of the museums; note that these, like many Viennese museums, are closed on Mondays.

Sights to See

⑩ **Bohemian Court Chancery.** One of the architectural jewels of the Inner City can be found at No. 7 Wipplingerstrasse, the former Bohemian Court Chancery, built between 1708 and 1714 by Johann Bernhard Fischer von Erlach. Fischer von Erlach and his contemporary, Johann Lukas von Hildebrandt, were the reigning architectural geniuses of Baroque Vienna; they designed their churches and palaces during the building boom that followed the defeat of the Turks in 1683. Both had studied architecture in Rome, and both were deeply impressed by the work of the great Italian architect Francesco Borromini, who had brought to his designs a wealth and freedom of invention that was looked upon with horror by most contemporary Romans. But for Fischer von Erlach and Hildebrandt, Borromini's ideas were a source of triumphant

architectural inspiration, and when they returned to Vienna they produced between them many of the city's most beautiful buildings. Alas,
narrow Wipplingerstrasse allows little more than a oblique view of this
florid facade. The back side of the building, on Judenplatz, is less
elaborate but gives a better idea of the design concept. The building
first served as diplomatic and representational offices of Bohemia (now
a part of the Czech republic) to the Vienna-based monarchy, and,
today, still houses government offices.

Altes Rathaus (Old City Hall). Opposite the Bohemian Chancery (☞
above) stands the Altes Rathaus, dating from the 14th century but sport-
ing 18th-century Baroque motifs on its facade. The interior passageways and courtyards, which are open during the day, house a Gothic
chapel (open at odd hours), a much-loved, Baroque wall-fountain
(Georg Raphael Donner's **Andromeda Fountain** of 1741), and display
cases exhibiting maps and photos illustrating the city's history.

Am Hof. Am Hof is one of the city's oldest squares. In the Middle Ages
the ruling Babenberg family built their castle on the site of No. 2; hence
the name of the square, which means simply "at court" (the grand residence hosted such luminaries as Barbarossa and Walter vonder Vogel-
weide, the famous Minnesinger who features in Wagner's *Tannhauser*).
The Baroque **Column of Our Lady** in the center dates from 1667, marking the Catholic victory over the Swedish Protestants in the Thirty Years'
War (1618–48). The onetime **Civic Armory** at the northwest corner has
been used as a fire station since 1685 (the high-spirited facade, with its
Habsburg eagle, was "Baroqued" in 1731) and today houses the headquarters of Vienna's fire department. The complex includes a firefighting museum (open only on Sunday and holiday mornings). Presiding over
the east side of the square is the noted Kirche Am Hof church (☞
below). In Bognergasse to the right of the Kirche Am Hof, around the
corner from the imposing Bank Austria headquarters building, at No.
9 is the **Engel Pharmacy,** with a Jugendstil mosaic depicting winged
women collecting the elixir of life in outstretched chalices. At the turn
of the century the inner city was dotted with storefronts decorated in a
similar manner; today this is the sole survivor. Around the bend from
the Naglergasse is the picturesque Freyung square (☞ Palais Kinsky, *below*).

⓱ **Café Central.** Part of the Ferstel Palace complex, at the corner of Herrengasse and Strauchgasse, the Café Central is one of Vienna's more
famous cafés, its full authenticity blemished only by complete restoration in recent years. In its prime (before World War I), the café was
home—in the literal as well as the figurative sense—to some of the
most famous literary figures of the day. In that era, housing was one
of the city's most intractable problems. As a result, many of Vienna's
artists and writers spent as little time as possible in their "homes" and
instead ensconced themselves at a favorite café, where they ate, so-
cialized, worked, and even received mail. The denizens of the Central
favored political argument; indeed, their heated discussions became
so well known that in October 1917, when Austria's foreign secre-
tary was informed of the outbreak of the Russian Revolution, he dismissed the report with a facetious reference to a well-known local
Marxist, the chess-loving (and presumably harmless) "Herr Bronstein from the Café Central." The remark was to become famous all
over Austria, for Herr Bronstein had disappeared and was about to
resurface in Russia bearing a new name: Leon Trotsky. No matter how
crowded the café may become, you can linger as long as you like over
a single cup of coffee and a newspaper from the huge international
selection provided. Across Herrengasse at No. 17 is the Café Central
Konditorei, an excellent pastry and confectionery shop associated

with the café. ⊠ *Herrengasse 14,* ☏ *01/5333–3726–26. AE, DC, MC, V. Closed Sun. U-Bahn: U3 Herrengasse.*

The Freyung. Naglergasse, at its curved end, flows into Heidenschuss, which in turn leads down a slight incline from Am Hof to one of Vienna's most prominent squares, the Freyung, meaning "freeing." The square was so named because for many centuries the monks at the adjacent Scottish Church (☞ *below*) possessed the privilege of offering sanctuary for three days. In the center of the square stands the allegorical **Austria Fountain** (1845), notable because its Bavarian designer, one Ludwig Schwanthaler, had the statues cast in Munich and then supposedly filled them with cigars to be smuggled into Vienna for black-market sale. Around the sides of the square are some of Vienna's greatest patrician residences, including the Ferstel, Harrach, and Kinsky Palaces (☞ *below*).

Judenplatz. From the 13th to the 15th century, Judenplatz—off Wipplingerstrasse—was the center of Vienna's Jewish ghetto. Today the square's centerpiece is a rectangular block intended as a Holocaust memorial; the architect's concept was a stylized stack of books to recall Jewish strivings toward learning. Nearby is a statue of the 18th-century Jewish playwright Gotthold Ephraim Lessing, erected after World War II; disconcertingly, the statue suggests the underground comics of the American artist R. Crumb.

⓭ Kinsky Palace. Just one of the architectural treasures that comprises the urban set piece of the Freyung, the Palais Kinsky is the square's best-known palace, one of the most sophisticated pieces of Baroque architecture in the city. Located at Freyung 4, it was built between 1713 and 1716 by Hildebrandt. Its only real competition comes a few yards farther on: the Greek temple facade of the Schottenhof (☞ *below*), which is at right angles to the Schottenkirche church, up the street from the Kinsky Palace.

⓫ Kirche am Hof (Church of the Nine Choirs of Angels). The Kirche Am Hof, on the east side of the Am Hof square, is identified by its sprawling Baroque facade, designed by Carlo Carlone in 1662. The somber interior lacks appeal but the checkerboard marble floor may remind you of Dutch churches. ⊠ *Am Hof 1. U-Bahn: U3 Herrengasse.*

⓰ Minoritenkirche (Church of the Minorite Order). The Minoritenplatz is named after its centerpiece, the Minoritenkirche, a Gothic affair with a strange stump of a tower, built mostly in the 14th century. The front is brutally ugly, but the back is a wonderful (if predominantly 19th-century) surprise. The interior contains the city's most imposing piece of kitsch: a large mosaic reproduction of Leonardo da Vinci's *Last Supper,* commissioned by Napoléon in 1806 and later purchased by Emperor Francis I. ⊠ *Minoritenpl. 2a,* ☏ *01/533–4162. U-Bahn: U3 Herrengasse.*

⓬ Palais Ferstel. At Freyung 2 stands the recently restored Palais Ferstel, which is not a palace at all but a commercial shop-and-office complex designed in 1856 and named for its architect, Heinrich Ferstel. The facade is Italianate in style, harking back, in its 19th-century way, to the Florentine palazzi of the early Renaissance. The interior is unashamedly eclectic: vaguely Romanesque in feel and Gothic in decoration, with here and there a bit of Renaissance or Baroque sculpted detail thrown in for good measure. Such eclecticism is sometimes dismissed as mindlessly derivative, but here the architectural details are so respectfully and inventively combined that the interior becomes a pleasure to explore. The 19th century stock exchange rooms upstairs are now gloriously restored and used for conferences and concerts.

Next door to the Palais Fersel is the newly renovated **Palais Harrach,** part of which now houses a small but worthwhile gallery of paintings and art objects from the main Kunsthistorisches Museum (which has far more treasures than space in which to display them) as well as special exhibits. ⊠ *Freyung 3,* ☎ *01/523–7593.* ▭ *Combined ticket with Kunsthistorisches Museum AS45.* ⊙ *Wed.–Mon. 10–5.*

The huge gold ball atop the doorway across the Freyung at the corner of Renngasse marks the entrance to the **Kunstforum,** an extensive art gallery run by Bank Austria featuring outstanding temporary exhibitions. ⊠ *Freyung 8,* ☎ *01/711–91–5742.* ▭ *AS90.* ⊙ *Thurs.–Tues. 10–6, Wed. 10–9. U-Bahn: U3 Herrengasse.*

⓯ Pasqualatihaus. Beethoven lived in the Pasqualatihaus while he was composing his only opera, *Fidelio,* as well as his Seventh Symphony and Fourth Piano Concerto. Today his apartment houses a small commemorative museum (in distressingly modern taste). After navigating the narrow and twisting stairway, you might well ask how he maintained the jubilant spirit of the works he wrote there. This house is around the corner from the Third Man Portal (☞ *below*). ⊠ *8 Mölker Bastei,* ☎ *01/535–8905.* ▭ *AS25.* ⊙ *Tues.–Sun. 9–12:15 and 1–4:30. U-Bahn: U2 Schottentor.*

☺ Puppen und Spielzeugmuseum (Doll and Toy Museum). As appealing as the clockworks of the Uhrenmuseum located just next door is this doll and toy museum, with its collections of dolls, dollhouses, teddies, and trains. ⊠ *Schulhof 4,* ☎ *01/535–6860.* ▭ *AS60.* ⊙ *Tues.–Sun. 10–6. U-Bahn: U1, U3 Stephansplatz.*

Schottenhof. Found on the Freyung square and designed by Joseph Kornhäusel in a very different style from his Fleischmarkt tower, the Schottenhof facade typifies the change that came over Viennese architecture during the Biedermeier era (1815–48). The Viennese, according to the traditional view, were at the time so relieved to be rid of the upheavals of the Napoléonic Wars that they accepted without protest the iron-handed repression of Prince Metternich, chancellor of Austria, and retreated into a cozy and complacent domesticity. Restraint also ruled in architecture, with Baroque license rejected in favor of a new and historically "correct" style that was far more controlled and reserved. Kornhäusel led the way in Vienna; his Schottenhof facade is all sober organization and frank repetition. But in its marriage of strong and delicate forces it still pulls off the great Viennese-waltz trick of successfully merging seemingly antithetical characteristics. *U-Bahn: U2 Schottentor.*

NEED A BREAK? In summer, **Café Haag** and **Wienerwald** restaurant share the tree-shaded courtyard of the Schottenhof (☞ *above*), ideal for a relaxing coffee or a glass of wine.

⓮ Schottenkirche. In 1758–61 the famous Italian painter Canaletto painted the Freyung square looking north toward the Schottenkirche; the pictures hang in the Kunsthistorisches Museum and the similarity to the view you see about 240 years later is arresting. In fact, a church has stood on the site of the Schottenkirche since 1177; the present edifice dates to the mid-1600s when it replaced its predecessor, which had collapsed after the architects of the time had built on weakened foundations. The interior, with its ornate ceiling and a decided surplus of cherubs and angels' faces, is in stark contrast to the plain exterior. The adjacent small **Museum im Schottenstift** includes the best of the monastery's art works, including the celebrated late-Gothic high altar dating to about 1470. The winged altar is fascinating for its portrayal of the Holy Family in flight into Egypt—with Vienna clearly identifiable in the background. ⊠ *Freyung 6,* ☎ *01/534–9820; museum, 01/534–9860–0.* 🖅 *AS40.* ☉ *Thurs.–Sat. 10–5, Sun. noon–5. U-Bahn: U2 Schottentor.*

"Third Man" Portal. The doorway at No. 8 Schreyvogelgasse (up the incline) was made famous in 1949 by the classic film *The Third Man;* it was here that Orson Welles, as the malevolently knowing Harry Lime, stood hiding in the dark, only to have his smiling face illuminated by a sudden light from the upper-story windows of the house across the alley. The film enjoys a renaissance each summer in the Burg Kino and is fascinating for its portrayal of a postwar Vienna still in ruins. To get here from the nearby and noted Schottenkirche (☞ *above*), follow Teinfaltstrasse one block west to Schreyvogelgasse on the right.

Uhrenmuseum (Clock Museum). Kurrentgasse leads south from the east end of Judenplatz; the beautifully restored 18th-century houses on its east side make this one of the most unpretentiously appealing streets in the city. And at the far end of the street is one of Vienna's most appealing museums: the Uhrenmuseum, or Clock Museum (enter to the right on the Schulhof side of the building). The museum's three floors display a splendid array of clocks and watches—more than 3,000 timepieces—dating from the 15th century to the present. The ruckus of bells and chimes on any hour is impressive, but try to be here at noon for the full cacophony. Right next door is the Puppen und Spielzeugmuseum (☞ *above*). ⊠ *Schulhof 2,* ☎ *01/533–2265.* 🖅 *AS50.* ☉ *Tues.–Sun. 9–4:30. U-Bahn: U1, U3 Stephansplatz.*

Vienna's Shop Window: From Michaelerplatz to the Graben

The compact area bounded roughly by the back side of the Hofburg palace complex, the Kohlmarkt, the Graben, and Kärntner Strasse belongs to the oldest core of the city. Remains of the Roman city are just below the present-day surface. This was and still is the commercial heart of the city, with shops and markets for various commodities; today, the Kohlmarkt and Graben in particular offer the choicest luxury shops, overflowing into the Graben end of Kärnter Strasse. The area is marvelous for its visual treats, ranging from the squares and varied architecture to window shopping. The evening view down Kohlmarkt from the Graben is an inspiring classic, with the night-lit gilded dome of Michael's Gate to the palace complex as the glittering backdrop.

A Good Walk

Start your walk through this fascinating quarter at **Michaelerplatz** ⑱, one of Vienna's most evocative squares, where the feel of the imperial city remains very strong; the buildings around the perimeter present a synopsis of the city's entire architectural history: medieval church spire, Renaissance church facade, Baroque palace facade, 19th-century apartment house, and 20th-century bank. Look in on **Michaelerkirche** (St. Michael's Church). Opposite the church is the once-controversial **Looshaus** ⑲, considered a breakthrough in modern architecture (visitors are welcome to view the restored lobby). From Michaelerplatz, take the small passageway to the right of the church; in it on your right is a relief dating to 1480 of Christ on the Mount of Olives. Follow the Stallburggasse through to Dorotheergasse, and turn right to discover the **Dorotheum,** the government-run auction house and the Vienna equivalent of Christie's or Sotheby's. On your right in the Dorotheergasse toward the Graben is the enlarged **Jewish Museum** ⑳, which includes a bookstore and café. On the left is the famous **Café Hawelka,** home to the contemporary art and literature crowd. Turn right in the Graben to come to **Stock-im-Eisen Platz** ㉑; the famous nail-studded tree trunk is encased in the corner of the building with the Bank Austria offices. Opposite and impossible to overlook is the agressive **Neues Haas Haus,** an upmarket restaurant and shopping complex. Wander back through the Graben for the full effect of this harmonious square and, above all, look up to see the ornamentation on the buildings. Pass the **Pestsäule** (Plague Column), which shoots up from the middle of the Graben like a geyser of whipped cream. Just off to the north side is **Peterskirche** ㉒, St. Peter's Church, a Baroque gem almost hidden by its surroundings. At the end of the Graben, turn left into the **Kohlmarkt** ㉓ for the classic view of the domed arch leading to the Hofburg, the imperial palace complex. Even if your feet aren't calling a sit-down strike, finish up at **Demel's** ㉔, at Kohlmarkt 14, with some of the best *patisserie* in the world.

TIMING

Inveterate shoppers, window or otherwise, will want to take time to pause before or in many of the elegant shops during this walk, which then could easily take most of a day or even longer. If you're content with facades and general impressions, the exercise could be done in a bit over an hour, but it would be a shame to bypass the narrow side streets. In any case, look into St. Michael's and consider the fascinating Dorotheum, itself easily worth an hour or more.

Sights to See

Café Hawelka. At No. 6 Dorotheergasse, hidden behind an unprepossessing doorway, the Café Hawelka is one of the few famous inner-city cafés that has survived without major restoration. The Hawelka's air of romantic shabbiness—originally the product of Viennese *Fortwursteln,* or "muddling through," now sacrosanct literally as a national monument—is especially evocative. The smoky room has been home to most of Austria's leading artists and writers since 1945, and the Hawelka family has amassed an enviable art collection by taking paintings in lieu of cash from destitute artists who later became famous. ✉ *Dorotheergasse 6,* ☎ *01/512–8230.* ☼ *Wed.–Sat., Mon. 8 AM–2 AM. No credit cards. U-Bahn: U1, U3 Stephanspl.*

Dorotheum. The narrow passageway just to the right of St. Michael's, with its large 15th-century relief depicting Christ on the Mount of Olives, leads into the Stallburggasse. The area is dotted with antiques stores, attracted by the presence of the Dorotheum, the famous Viennese auction house that began as a state-controlled pawnshop in 1707 (affectionately known as "Aunt Dorothy" to its patrons). Merchandise coming up for auction is on display at Dorotheergasse 17. The showrooms—packed with everything from carpets and pianos to cameras and jewelry and postage stamps—are well worth a visit. Some wares are not for auction but for immediate sale. ✉ *Dorotheergasse 17,* ☎ *01/515–60–0.* ☼ *Weekdays 8–6, Sat. 8–noon. U-Bahn: U1, U3 Stephanspl.*

The Graben. One of Vienna's major crossroads, the Graben, leading west from Stock-im-Eisen-Platz, is a street whose unusual width gives it the presence and weight of a city square. Its shape is due to the Romans, who dug the city's southwestern moat here, adjacent to the original city walls. The Graben's centerpiece is the effulgently Baroque **Pestsäule,** or Plague Column, erected by Emperor Leopold I between 1687 and 1693 in thanks to God for delivering the city from a particularly virulent plague. Today the representation looks more like a host of cherubs doing their best to cope with the icing of a wedding cake wilting in the hot sunshine. Staunch Protestants may be shocked to learn that the foul figure of the Pest stands also for the heretic plunging away from the "True Faith" into the depth of hell. But they will have to get used to the fact that the Catholic Church has triumphed over Protestantism in Austria and frequently recalls the fact on stone and on canvas.

㉒ Jewish Museum. The former Eskeles Palace, once an elegant private residence, is now home to the city's Jüdisches Museum der Stadt Wien. New permanent exhibitions tell of the momentous role that Viennese-born Jews played in realms from music to medicine, art to philosophy, both in Vienna—until abruptly halted in 1938—and in the world at large. Changing exhibits add contemporary touches. The museum complex includes a café and bookstore. ⊠ *Dorotheergasse 11,* ☎ *01/ 535–0431.* ⊠ *AS70.* ☽ *Sun.–Fri. 10–6, Thurs. 10–9. U-Bahn: U1, U3 Stephansplatz.*

㉓ Kohlmarkt. The Kohlmarkt, aside from its classic view of the domed entryway to the imperial palace complex of the Hofburg, is best known as Vienna's most elegant shopping street. The shops, not the buildings, are remarkable, although there is an entertainingly ironic odd-couple pairing: No. 11 (early 18th century) and No. 9 (early 20th century). The mixture of architectural styles is similar to that of the Graben, but the general atmosphere is low-key, as if the street were consciously deferring to the showstopper dome at the west end. The composers Haydn and Chopin lived in houses on the street, and indeed, the Kohlmarkt lingers in the memory when flashier streets have faded.

NEED A
BREAK?

㉔ Demel (⊠ Kohlmarkt 14, ☎ 01/535–1717-0), Vienna's best-known (and priciest) pastry shop, offers a dizzying selection, and if you possess a sweet tooth, a visit will be worth every penny of the extra cost. Chocolate lovers will want to participate in the famous Viennese Sacher-torte debate by sampling Demel's version and then comparing it with its rival at the Sacher Café, which is in Hotel Sacher. For considerably less elegance with a touch of the Formica-cool '50s, but excellent coffee and pastries as well as value, go instead to the **Arabia** café (⊠ Kohlmarkt 5, ☎ 01/503–0929).

⑲ Looshaus. In 1911, Adolf Loos, one of the founding fathers of 20th-century modern architecture, built the Looshaus on august Michaelerplatz, facing the Imperial Palace entrance. It was considered nothing less than an architectural declaration of war. After two hundred years of Baroque and neo-Baroque exuberance, the first generation of 20th-century architects had had enough. Loos led the revolt against architectural tradition; *Ornament and Crime* was the title of his famous manifesto, in which he inveighed against the conventional architectural wisdom of the 19th century. Instead, he advocated buildings that were plain, honest, and functional. When he built the Looshaus for Goldman and Salatsch (men's clothiers) in 1911, the city was scandalized. Archduke Franz Ferdinand, heir to the throne, was so offended that he vowed never again to use the Michaelerplatz entrance to the Imperial Palace. Today the Looshaus has lost its power to shock, and the facade seems quite innocuous; argument now focuses on the post-modern Neues Haas-Haus (☞ *below*) opposite St. Stephen's cathedral. The recently restored interior of the Looshaus remains a breathtaking surprise; the building now houses a bank and you can go inside to see the stylish chambers and staircase. ⊠ *Michaelpl. 3. U-Bahn: U3 Herrengasse.*

⑱ Michaelerplatz. In Michaelerplatz, one of Vienna's most historic squares, the buildings seem to crowd in toward the center of the small plaza as if acceding to the center of the small plaza. Rightly so, for this is now the site of an excavation revealing Roman plus 18th and 19th century layers of the past. The excavations are a latter-day distraction from the

Michaelerplatz's most noted claim to fame—the eloquent entryway to the palace complex of the Hofburg. *U-Bahn: U3 Herrengasse.*

Neues Haas-Haus. Stock-im-Eisen-Platz is home to central Vienna's (for the moment, at least) most controversial piece of architecture: the Neues Haas-Haus designed by Hans Hollein, one of Austria's best-known living architects. Detractors consider its aggressively contemporary style out of place opposite St. Stephen's, seeing the cathedral's style parodied by being stood on its head; advocates consider the contrast enlivening. Whatever the ultimate verdict, the new building has not been the expected commercial success; its restaurants may be thriving, but its boutiques are not. ⊠ *Stephanspl. 12.* ☉ *Shops weekdays 9–6, Sat. 9–noon.*

㉒ **Peterskirche** (St. Peter's Church). Considered the best example of church Baroque in Vienna—certainly the most theatrical—the Peterskirche was constructed between 1702 and 1708 by Lucas von Hildebrandt. According to legend, the original church on this site was founded in 792 by Charlemagne, a tale immortalized by the relief plaque on the right side of the church. The facade possesses angled towers, graceful towertops (said to have been inspired by the tents of the Turks during the siege of 1683), and an unusually fine entrance portal. Inside the church, the Baroque decoration is elaborate, with some fine touches (particularly the glass-crowned galleries high on the walls to either side of the altar and the amazing tableau of the martyrdom of St. John Nepomuk), but the lack of light and years of accumulated dirt create a prevailing gloom, and the much-praised ceiling frescoes by J. M. Rottmayr are impossible to make out. Just before Christmastime each year, the basement crypt is filled with a display of nativity scenes. The church is shoehorned into tiny Petersplatz, just off the Graben. ⊠ *Peterspl. U-Bahn: U1, U3 Stephanspl.*

㉑ **Stock-im-Eisen.** In the southwest corner of Stock-im-Eisen-Platz, set into the building on the west side of Kärntnerstrasse, is one of the city's odder relics: the Stock-im-Eisen, or the "nail-studded stump." Chronicles first mention the Stock-im-Eisen in 1533, but it is probably far older, and for hundreds of years any apprentice metalsmith who came to Vienna to learn his trade hammered a nail into the tree trunk for good luck. During World War II, when there was talk of moving the relic to a museum in Munich, it mysteriously disappeared; it reappeared, perfectly preserved, after the threat of removal had passed.

An Imperial City: The Hofburg and the Ringstrasse

The Hofburg

A walk through the Imperial Palace, known as the **Hofburg** ㉕, brings you back to the days when Vienna was the capital of a mighty empire in which the sun never set. You can still find in Vienna shops vintage postcards and prints that show the revered and be-whiskered Emperor Francis Joseph starting out on a morning drive from his Hofburg palace in his carriage; Today, at the palace—which faces Kohlmarkt on the opposite side of Michaelerplatz—you can walk in his very footsteps, as well as gaze at the old tin bath the emperor kept under his simple iron bedstead and marvel at his bejeweled christening robe. Let alone, of course, feast your eyes on great works of art, impressive armor, and some of the finest Baroque interiors in Europe along the way.

Until 1918 the Hofburg was the home of the Habsburgs, rulers of the Austro-Hungarian Empire. As a current tourist mecca, it has become a vast smorgasbord of sightseeing attractions: the Imperial Apartments, two Imperial treasuries, *six* museums, the National Library, and the famous Winter Riding School all vie for attention. The entire complex takes a minimum of a full day to explore in detail; if your time is limited (or if you want to save most of the interior sightseeing for a rainy day), you should omit the Imperial Apartments and all the museums mentioned below except the Kunsthistorisches (the Museum of Art History), the new Museum of Court Silver and Tableware, and probably the Schatzkammer (Crown Jewels and Court Treasury). An excellent multilingual, full-color booklet describing the palace in detail is for sale at most ticket counters within the complex; it gives a complete list of attractions and maps out the palace's complicated ground plan and building history wing by wing.

Vienna took its imperial role seriously, as evidenced by the sprawling Hofburg complex, today, as then, the seat of government. But this is generally understated power; while the buildings cover considerable area, the treasures lie inside, not to be flamboyantly flaunted. Certainly under Francis Joseph II, the reign was beneficient—witness the broad Ringstrasse he ordained and the array of museums and public buildings it hosts. With few exceptions (Vienna City Hall and the Votive Church), rooflines are kept to an even level, creating an ensemble effect that helps integrate the palace complex and its parks into the urban landscape without making a domineering statement. Diplomats still bustle in and out of high-level international meetings in the elegant halls. Horse-drawn carriages still traverse the Ring and the roadway that cuts thorugh the complex. Ignore the cars and tour buses and you can easily imagine yourself in a Vienna of a hundred or more years ago.

Architecturally, the Hofburg—like St. Stephen's—is far from refined. It grew up over a period of 700 years (its earliest mention in court documents is 1279, at the very beginning of Habsburg rule), and its spasmodic, haphazard growth kept it from attaining any sort of unified identity. But many of the bits and pieces are fine, and one interior (the National Library) is a tour de force.

After a tour of the Hofburg complex this chapter concludes with an exploration of Vienna's famed Ringstrasse and the major attractions of its environs, including the Kunsthistoriches Museum and Freud's Apartment. The walks found below split up the marvels and museums of this area into two digestible bites.

Numbers in the text correspond to numbers in the margin and on the Hofburg map.

A GOOD WALK

When you begin to explore the Hofburg you realize that the palace complex is like a nest of boxes, courtyards opening off courtyards and wings (*trakts*) spreading far and wide. First tackle **Josefsplatz** ①, the remarkable square that interrupts Augustinerstrasse, ornamented by the equestrian **statue of Josef II** ②—many consider this Vienna's loveliest square. Indeed, the beautifully restored imperial decor adorning the roof of the buildings forming Josefsplatz are one of the few visual demonstrations of Austria's one-time widespread power and influence. On your right to the north is the **Spanische Reitschule** ③, the Spanish Riding School—one part of Vienna known throughout the world—where the famous white horses reign. Across Reitschulgasse under the arches are the **Imperial Stables** ④. To the south stands the **Augustinerkirche** ⑤, St. Augustine's Church, where the Habsburg rulers' hearts are preserved in urns. The grand main hall of the **Hofbibliothek Prunksaal** ⑥, the National Library, is one of the great Baroque treasures of Europe, a sight not to be missed (enter from the southwest corner of Josefsplatz).

Under the Michaelerplatz dome is the entrance to the **Imperial Apartments** ⑦, hardly the elegance you would normally associate with roy-

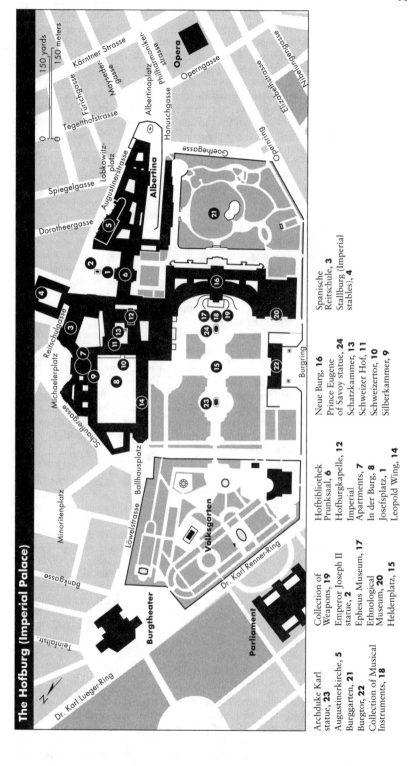

The Hofburg (Imperial Palace)

150 yards
150 meters

Kärntner Strasse

Opera

Opergasse

Albertinaplatz

philharmoniker-strasse

Nibelungengasse

Fürichgasse

Tegetthofstrasse

Mayseder-gasse

Hanuschgasse

Operngasse

Opernring

Elizabethstrasse

Lobkowitz-platz

Augustinerstrasse

Albertina

Goethegasse

Spiegelgasse

Dorotheergasse

Reitschulgasse

Michaelerplatz

Schauflergasse

Ballhausplatz

Löwelstrasse

Minoritenplatz

Bankgasse

Volksgarten

Dr. Karl Renner-Ring

Burgring

Dr. Karl Lueger-Ring

Teinfaltst.

Burgtheater

Parliament

Archduke Karl statue, **23**
Augustinerkirche, **5**
Burggarten, **21**
Burgtor, **22**
Collection of Musical Instruments, **18**

Collection of Weapons, **19**
Emperor Joseph II statue, **2**
Ephesus Museum, **17**
Ethnological Museum, **20**
Heldenplatz, **15**

Hofbibliothek Prunksaal, **6**
Hofburgkapelle, **12**
Imperial Apartments, **7**
In der Burg, **8**
Josefsplatz, **1**
Leopold Wing, **14**

Neue Burg, **16**
Prince Eugene of Savoy statue, **24**
Schatzkammer, **13**
Schweizer Hof, **11**
Schweizertor, **10**
Silberkammer, **9**

Spanische Reitschule, **3**
Stallburg (Imperial stables), **4**

alty, but Francis Joseph II, the residing emperor from 1848 to 1916, was anything but ostentatious in his personal life. For the representational side, however, go through into the **In der Burg courtyard** ⑧ and look in at the elegant **Silberkammer** ⑨ museum of court silver and crystal. Go through the **Schweizertor** ⑩, the Swiss gate, to the south off of In der Burg, to reach the small **Schweizer Hof** ⑪ courtyard with stairs leading to the **Hofburgkapelle** ⑫, the Imperial Chapel where the Vienna Boys Choir makes its regular Sunday appearances. In a back corner of the courtyard is the entrance to the **Schatzkammer** museum ⑬, the Imperial Treasury, overflowing with jewels, robes, and royal trappings. From In der Burg, the roadway leads under the **Leopold Wing** ⑭ of the complex into the vast park known as **Heldenplatz** ⑮, or Hero's Square. The immediately obvious heroes are the equestrian **statues of Archduke Karl** ㉓, toward to the city hall, and closer, the **statue of Prince Eugene of Savoy** ㉔. The Hofburg wing to the south with its concave facade is the **Neue Burg** ⑯, the "new" section of the complex, now housing four specialized museums. Depending on your interests, consider the **Ephesus Museum** ⑰, with Roman antiquities, the **Collection of Musical Instruments** ⑱, where you also hear what you see, the impressive **Weapons Collection** ⑲, with tons of steel armor, or the **Ethnological Museum** ⑳, including Montezuma's headdress. Ahead, the **Burgtor** ㉒ gate separates the Hofburg complex from the Ringstrasse. The quiet oasis in back of the Neue Burg is the **Burggarten** ㉑. Catch your breath and marvel that you've only seen a small part of the Hofburg—a large part of it still houses the offices of the Austrian Government and cannot be visited by the public.

Timing: If you were simply to combine the two walks in this section as one, you'd need over half a day—that's without taking in any of the museums. How much time you will need with museum stops is an individual affair. You could spend a day in the Hofburg complex alone, another half to full day in the Kunsthistoriches Museum (found in the Ringstrasse walk, below). For most of the smaller museums, figure on anything from an hour upward.

SIGHTS TO SEE

❺ **Augustinerkirche** (Church of the Augustinian Order). Across Josefsplatz from the Riding School is the entrance to the Augustinerkirche, built during the 14th century and possessing the most unified Gothic interior in the city. But the church is something of a fraud; the interior, it turns out, dates from the late 18th century, not the early 14th. A historical fraud the church may be, but a spiritual fraud it is not. The view from the entrance doorway is stunning: a soaring harmony of vertical piers, ribbed vaults, and hanging chandeliers that makes Vienna's other Gothic interiors look earthbound by comparison. The imposing Baroque organ sounds as fine as it looks, and the Sunday morning high mass—frequently by Mozart or Haydn—sung here can be the highlight of a trip. To the right of the main altar in the small Loreto Chapel stand silver urns in serried ranks; they contain the hearts of Habsburg rulers. This rather morbid sight is viewable after early mass on Sunday, Monday, or by appointment. ⊠ *Josefspl.,* ☎ *01/533–7099–0. U-Bahn: U3 Herrengasse.*

㉑ **Burggarten.** The intimate Burggarten in back of the Neue Burg is a quiet oasis which includes a statue of a contemplative Kaiser Francis Joseph and an elegant statue of Mozart, moved here from the Albertinaplatz after the war, when the city's charred ruins were rebuilt. The former greenhouses under the wall to the Augustine church are being restored into a café complex replete with palms and winter garden setting. ⊠

Access from Opernring and Hanuschgasse/Goethegasse. U-Bahn: U2 Babenbergerstr.

❻ **Hofbibliothek Prunksaal** (National Library). This is one of the grandest Baroque libraries in the world, in every sense a cathedral of books. Its centerpiece is the spectacular Prunksaal—the Grand Hall of the National Library—which probably contains more book treasures than any comparable collection outside the Vatican. The main entrance to the ornate reading room is in the left corner of Josefsplatz. Designed by Fischer von Erlach the Elder just before his death in 1723 and completed by his son, the Grand Hall is full-blown High Baroque, with trompe l'oeil ceiling frescoes by Daniel Gran. The library may not be to everyone's taste, but in the end it is the books themselves that come to the rescue. They are as lovingly displayed as the gilding and the frescoes, and they give the hall a warmth that the rest of the palace decidedly lacks. On the third floor is an intriguing museum of globes that should not be overlooked. ⊠ *Josefspl. 1, at top of stairs inside; library,* ☎ *01/534–10–397; museum,* ☎ *01/534–10–297.* 🎟 *Library AS20, museum AS10.* ☉ *Library Nov.–May, Mon.–Sat. 10–noon; June–Oct., Mon.–Sat. 10–4 (hrs vary depending on exhibitions); museum Mon.–Wed. and Fri. 11–noon, Thurs. 2–3. U-Bahn: U3 Herrengasse.*

⓬ ⓾ **Hofburgkapelle** (Chapel of the Imperial Palace). The ancient **Schweizertor,** or Swiss Gate (dating from 1552 and decorated with some of the earliest classical motifs in the city), leads from In der Burg through to the oldest section of the palace, a small courtyard known as the **⓫** **Schweizer Hof**—named after the Swiss Guards who were once stationed here. In the southeast corner (at the top of the steps) is the entrance to **⓬** the **Hofburgkapelle,** or Imperial Chapel, where the **Vienna Boys Choir** (Wiener Sängerknaben) sings Mass at 9:15 on Sunday, Monday, and holidays from September to June. Alas, the arrangement is such that you *hear* the choirboys but don't see them; their soprano and alto voices peal forth from a gallery behind the seating area. ⊠ *Hofburg, Schweizer Hof,* ☎ *01/533–9927.*

❽ **In der Burg Courtyard.** A prominent courtyard of the Hofburg complex, it features a statue of Francis II and the noted **Schweizertor** gateway—built in 1552 and painted maroon, black, and gold, it gives a fine Renaissance flourish to its building facade. Also note the **clock** on the far upper wall at the north end of the courtyard: it tells time by the sun dial, also gives the time mechanically, and even, above the clock face, indicates the phase of the moon.

❶ **Josefsplatz.** Josefsplatz is the most imposing of the Hofburg courtyards, with an **equestrian monument to namesake Emperor Joseph II** (1807) in the center.

❼ **Kaiserappartements** (Imperial Apartments). The domed rotunda on Michaelerplatz signals the entrances to two of the Hofburg museums. To the left under the dome is the access to the Kaiserappartements. The long, repetitive suite of conventionally luxurious rooms has a sad and poignant feel. The decoration (19th-century imitation of 18th-century Rococo) tries to look regal, but much like the empire itself in its latter days, it is only going through the motions and ends up looking merely official. Among the few signs of genuine life are Emperor Francis Joseph's spartan, iron field bed, on which he slept every night, and the Empress Elisabeth's wooden gymnastics equipment, on which she exercised every morning. Amid all the tired splendor they look decidedly forlorn. ⊠ *Hofburg, Schweizer Hof,* ☎ *01/587–5554–515.* 🎟 *AS70, combination ticket with Museum of Court Silver AS90, tour AS20 per museum.* ☉ *Daily 9–5. U-Bahn: U2 Herrengasse.*

⓰ Neue Burg. The Neue Burg stands today as a symbol of architectural overconfidence. Designed for Emperor Francis Joseph in 1869, this "new chateau" was part of a much larger scheme that was meant to make the Hofburg rival the Louvre, if not Versailles. The German architect Gottfried Semper planned a twin of the present Neue Burg on the opposite side of the Heldenplatz, with arches connecting the Neue Burg and its twin with the other pair of twins on the Ringstrasse, the Kunsthistorisches Museum (Museum of Art History) and the Naturhistorisches Museum (Museum of Natural History). But World War I intervened, and with the Empire's collapse the Neue Burg became merely the last in a long series of failed attempts to bring architectural order to the Hofburg. The failure to complete the Hofburg building program left the Heldenplatz without a discernible shape, and today it is amorphous, with the **Burgtor** (the old main palace gate) stranded in the middle. The space nevertheless is punctuated by two superb equestrian statues of **Archduke Karl** and **Prince Eugene of Savoy.**

⓮ Neue Burg Museums. A long tract of offices known as the **Leopold Wing** ⓯ separates the In der Burg courtyard from the vast **Heldenplatz.** The older section on the north includes the offices of the federal president. The long wing with the concave bay on the south is the youngest section of the palace, called the Neue Burg. (From its main balcony, in April, 1938, Adolf Hitler, telling a huge cheering crowd below of his plan for the new German empire, declared that Vienna "is a pearl! I am going to put it into a setting of which it is worthy!") Today, visitors flock to the Neue Burg because it houses no fewer than four specialty museums: the **Ephesus Museum,** containing exceptional Roman antiquities unearthed by Austrian archaeologists in Turkey at the turn of the century; the listenable **Collection of Musical Instruments,** including pianos that belonged to Brahms, Schumann, and Mahler (an acoustic guided tour allows you to actually hear the various instruments on headphones as you move from room to room); the **Ethnological Museum** (Museum für Völkerkunde), devoted to anthropology (Montezuma's feathered headdress is a highlight of its collection); and the **Collection of Weapons,** rivaling the armory in Graz as one of the most extensive arms-and-armor collections in the world. The first three museums are entered at the triumphal arch set into the middle of the curved portion of the facade; the Ethnological Museum is entered farther along, at the west end pavilion. ✉ *Heldenpl.,* ☎ *01/521–77–0.* 🎫 *Combination ticket for Ephesus, Musical Instrument, and Weapons museums AS30; Ethnological Museum AS30.* ⏱ *Ephesus, Musical Instrument, and Weapons museums Tues.–Sun. 10–6; Ethnological Museum Wed.–Mon. 10–4. U-Bahn: U2 Babenbergerstrasse.*

⓭ Schatzkammer (Imperial Treasury). The entrance to the Schatzkammer, or Imperial Treasury, with its 1,000 years of treasures is tucked away at ground level behind the staircase to the Hofburgkapelle. The elegant display is a welcome antidote to the monotony of the Imperial Apartments, for the entire Treasury was completely renovated in 1983–87, and the crowns and relics and vestments fairly glow in their new surroundings. Here you'll find such marvels as the Holy Lance—reputedly the lance that pierced Jesus's side—the Imperial Crown (a sacred symbol of sovereignty once stolen on Hitler's orders), and the Saber of Charlemagne. Don't miss the Burgundian Treasure, connected with that most romantic of medieval orders of chivalry, the Order of the Golden Fleece. ✉ *Schweizer Hof,* ☎ *01/533–7931.* 🎫 *AS60.* ⏱ *Wed. and Fri.–Mon. 10–6, Thurs. 10–9. U-Bahn: U2 Herrengasse.*

➒ Silberkammer (Museum of Court Silver and Tableware). The large courtyard on the far side of the Michaelertor rotunda is known as In der

Burg; here on the west side is the entrance to the sparkling new Silberkammer. There's far more than forks and fingerbowls here; stunning decorative pieces vie with glittering silver and gold for attention. Highlights include Francis Joseph's vermeil banqueting service, the Jardinière given to the Empress Elisabeth by Queen Victoria, and gifts from Marie-Antonette to her brother, Josef II. The presentation of full table settings gives an idea of court life both as a daily routine and on festive occasions. ⊠ *Hofburg, Michalertrakt,* ☎ *01/533–1044.* ▣ *AS70, combination ticket with Imperial Apartments AS90.* ☉ *Daily 9–5.*

★ ❸ **Spanische Reitschule** (Spanish Riding School). Located between Augustinerstrasse and the Josefsplatz is the world famous Spanish Riding School, a favorite for centuries, and no wonder: who can resist the sight of the stark white Lipizzaners going through their masterful paces? For the last 300 years they have been perfecting their *haute école* riding demonstrations to the sound of Baroque music in an ballroom that seems to be a crystal-chandeliered stable. The breed was started in 1580 and proved themselves in battle as well as in the complicated "dances" for which they are famous. The interior of the riding school, the 1735 work of Fischer von Erlach the Younger, is itself an attraction—surely Europe's most elegant sports arena—and if the prancing horses begin to pall, move up to the top balcony and examine the ceiling. The School's popularity is hardly surprising, and tickets to some performances must be ordered in writing many weeks in advance. Information offices have a brochure with the detailed schedule (performances are usually from March through December, with the school on vacation in July and August). Generally the full, 80-minute shows take place Sunday at 10:45 AM plus selected Wednesdays at 7 PM. Check for hour-long morning performances on Saturday at 10; tickets for Saturday shows are only available from ticket and travel agencies (a list of these agencies is included in a free leaflet about the Spanish Riding School available from the Austrian National Tourist Office; the leaflet also includes the full year schedule of performances). Morning training sessions (without music) held Tuesday through Saturday, with a few in February and August on Mondays as well, are usually open to the public. Tickets can *only* be bought at the door for these morning training sessions—in other words, no reservations (the relocated entrance is currently next to the Schweizertor, in the In der Burg courtyard, but might be moved back to Josefsplatz, so check), and the line starts forming between 9 and 9:30 for the opening at 10; most sightseers are unaware that visitors may come and go as they please between 10 and noon. Note, however, there are special training sessions on Saturday mornings that are accompanied by music—these tickets are available only by reservation through ticket agencies. Note that ticket agencies (legally) add a commission of 22%–25% to the face price of the ticket. For Sunday and Wednesday performance ticket orders, write to Spanische Reitschule (⊠ Hofburg, A-1010 Vienna). Pick up reserved tickets at the office under the Michaelerplatz rotunda dome. ⊠ *Michaelerpl. 1, Hofburg,* ☎ *01/533–9031–0,* 🖷 *01/535–0186.* ▣ *Seats AS240–AS800, standing room AS190, Saturday morning training session with music AS240, other morning training session AS100.* ☉ *Mar.–June and Sept.–mid-Dec.; closed tour wks.*

The Ringstrasse and Its Environs

Along with the Hofburg, the Ringstrasse is Vienna's major urban set piece. This grand series of thoroughfares bounds the heart of Vienna, the Innere Stadt (Inner City) or First District. It follows the lines of what, until an imperial decree ordered their leveling in 1857, were the defenses of the city. By the 1870's, Vienna had reached the zenith of her imperial prosperity, and this found ultimate expression in the series of magnificent buildings erected around the Ringstrasse—the Opera House, the Kunsthistoriches Museum, the Natural History Museum, and the Rathaus, University, and Votivkirche. Here follows the major sights and attractions on and around the Ringstrasse.

Numbers in the text correspond to numbers in the margin and on the Vienna map.

A GOOD WALK

Is there a best way to explore the Ring? You can walk it from one end to the other—from where it begins at the Danube Canal to where it returns to the Canal after its curving flight. Or you can explore it whenever you happen to cross it on other missions (while it is a pleasant sequence of boulevards, seeing its succession of rather pompous buildings all in one walk can be a bit overpowering). Or you can obtain the best of both options by following this suggested itinerary, which leavens the bombast of the Ring with some of Vienna's most fascinating sights. Immediately across the Ringstrasse from the Hofburg are two twin buildings, both museums. To the west is the **Natural History Museum,** to the east, the **Kunsthistorisches Museum** ㉖, the art museum packed with world-famous treasures. Allow ample time for exploration here. Further to the west of the museum square is the compact **Spittelberg Quarter** ㉗ of tiny streets between Burggasse and Sibensterngasse, often site of handicraft and seasonal fairs. The **Volksgarten** ㉘ on the inside of the Ringstrasse to the north of the museum square numbers a café and rose garden among its attractions; look also for the small memorial to Francis Joseph's wife Empress Elisabeth in the back corner. Tackle the Ringstrasse buildings by starting with the **Justizpalast** ㉙, the ministry of justice, moving along to **Parliament** ㉚, the **Rathaus** ㉛, the Vienna city hall, the **Burgtheater** ㉜ opposite on the inside of the Ring, then the **Universität** ㉝, the main building of Vienna's university, beyond, again on the outside of the Ring. Next to the university stands the neo-Gothic **Votivkirche** ㉞. If you've still time and energy, walk farther along the Ring to discover the Börse at the corner of the Ring and Wipplingerstrasse. The outside end of Hohenstaufengasse leads into Liechtensteinstrasse, which will bring you to Berggasse. Turn right to reach No. 19, the **Sigmund Freud Apartment** ㉟, now a museum and research facility. By continuing along Liechtensteinstrasse four blocks or taking the "D" streetcar two stops from the Böre, you will arrive at Fürstengasse, where the **Museum of Modern Art** ㊱ is incongruously housed in the legendary Palais Liechtenstein.

Timing: If you can, plan for Vienna's Louvre—the Kunsthistorisches Museum—early in the day before the crowds arrive, although the size of crowds depends greatly on whatever special shows the museum may be exhibiting. As for the main sights off the Ringstrasse, you could easily lump visits to the Sigmund Freud Apartment and the Museum of Modern Art together, figuring on about a half day for the two combined.

SIGHTS TO SEE

㉟ **Freud's Apartment.** Not far from the historic Hofburg district, beyond the Votive Church at the Schotterning along the Ringstrasse, you can skip over several centuries and visit that outstanding symbol of 20th-century Vienna: Sigmund Freud's Apartment at Berggasse 19 (Apartment 6, one flight up; ring the bell and push the door simultaneously); this was his residence from 1891 to 1938. The five-room collection of memorabilia is mostly a photographic record of Freud's life, with some documents, publications, and a portion of his collection of antiquities also on display. The waiting room furniture is authentic, but the consulting room and study furniture (including the famous couch) can be seen only in photographs. ⊠ *Berggasse 19,* ☎ *01/319–1596.* 💶 *AS60.* ☉ *July–Sept., daily 9–6; Oct.–June, daily 9–4. U-Bahn: U2 Schottentor.*

㉖ **Kunsthistorisches Museum** (Museum of Fine Art) One of the finest art collections in the world, the Kunsthistorisches Museum is the jewel of Vienna's museums, and lies across the street from the Hofburg's Neue Burg museum complex. The collection was assembled by the ruling Habsburgs over several hundred years, and even a cursory description would run on for pages. Invidious as it might be to try to select from this incredible wealth of pictures, a brief selection might help you to steer around the maze of galleries (the rooms are numbered in two sequences and around two courtyards). One trick to keep in mind: the large rooms have all the big-scale paintings—some of them striking, some merely pompous; the smaller rooms contain most of the jewel-like pictures, also many of the best portraits. So if you suffer from museumitis or are short on time, do the small rooms first! Head of the list, of course, is Room X, where you enter the world of Pieter Brueghel the Elder, one of the greatest painters of all time. Here, in one salon, you'll see more than half of Brueghel's surviving output. Here are the landscapes vividly changing with the seasons (pride of place goes to the winter view, *Hunters in the Snow*) and his panels swarming with throngs of animated 16th-century peasants. In other rooms, most of the great European old masters are represented (although some of the masterpieces are disgracefully dirty). Even the shortest list of highlights must include Rogier van der Weyden's *Crucifixion Triptych,* Raphael's *Madonna in the Meadow,* Holbein's *Portrait of Jane Seymour, Queen of England,* Correggio's *Jupiter Embracing Io,* Parmegianino's *Cupid Cutting a Bow,* Caravaggio's *Madonna of the Rosary,* a fine selection of Rembrandt portraits, Rubens's *Nude of Helene Fourment,* and Vermeer's peerless *Allegory of the Art of Painting.* Benvenuto Cellini's famous gold saltcellar—certainly one of the most sumptuous pieces of tableware ever created—is on display amid the treasures of the applied-arts wing. ⊠ *Maria-Theresien-Pl.,* ☎ *01/521–77–0.* 💶 *AS45 (higher for special exhibits).* ☉ *Tues.–Sun. 10–6, picture gallery Thurs. 6–9* PM.

Museum für angewandte Kunst, or MAK (Museum of Applied Arts). This museum contains a large collection of Austrian furniture and art objects; the Jugendstil display devoted to Josef Hoffman and his followers at the Wiener Werkstätte is particularly fine. The museum also features a number of changing exhibitions of contemporary arts and crafts, ranging from Chris Burden to Nam June Paik. ⊠ *Stubenring 5,* ☎ *01/711–36–0.* 💶 *Standing exhibits AS30, special exhibits AS90.* ☉ *Tues., Wed., and Fri.–Sun. 10–6, Thurs. 10–9. U-Bahn: U3 Stubentor.*

㊱ **Museum Moderner Kunst** (Museum of Modern Art). Housed in the celebrated **Palais Liechtenstein,** the Museum Moderner Kunst's official address may be at Fürstengasse 1, but Liechtensteinstrasse is the address by which most Viennese know it. The large 18th-century mansion was originally the Liechtenstein Summer Palace; today it houses the national collection of 20th-century art and the outstanding private Ludwig collection, mainly of Austrian artists. Artists from Gustav Klimt to Robert Rauschenberg and Nam June Paik are represented, and a more inappropriate environment for modern art would be hard to imagine. Twentieth-century art and 18th-century architecture here declare war on each other and fight to an uneasy draw. Still, if you can shut out the architecture (or the art, depending on your taste), the museum is well worth a visit. ⊠ *Fürstengasse 1,* ☎ *01/317–6900.* 💶 *AS45.* ☉ *Tues.–Sun. 10–6. U-Bahn: U2 Schottentor, then Streetcar D to Fürstengasse.*

Naturhistorisches Museum (Natural History Museum). The formal museum complex just outside the Ring has two elements—to the east is the celebrated Kunsthistorisches Museum, to the west is the Naturhistorisches Museum, or Natural History Museum. This is home of, among other artifacts, the famous Venus of Willendorf, a tiny statuette thought to be some 20,000 years old and symbol of the Iron Age Hallstatt civilization. The reconstructed dinosaur skeletons understandably draw the greatest attraction. ⊠ *Maria-Theresien-Pl.*, ☏ *01/521–77–0.* 🎫 *AS30.* ☉ *Wed.–Mon. 9–6; winter, ground floor only, Wed.–Mon. 9–3. U-Bahn: U2, U3 Volkstheater.*

㉘–㉞   Ringstrasse. The **Volksgarten,** just opposite the Hofburg, is a green oasis with a beautifully planted rose garden, a 19th-century Greek temple, and a rather wistful white marble monument to the Empress Elisabeth—Francis Joseph's Bavarian wife who died of dagger wounds inflicted by a martyr in Geneva in 1898. If not overrun with latter-day hippies, these can offer appropriate spots to sit for a few minutes and consider Vienna's most ambitious piece of 19th-century city planning: the famous Ringstrasse. Late in 1857, Emperor Francis Joseph issued a decree announcing the most ambitious piece of urban redevelopment Vienna had ever seen. The inner city's centuries-old walls were to be torn down, and the *glacis*—the wide expanse of open field that acted as a protective buffer between inner city and outer suburbs—was to be filled in. In their place was to rise a wide, tree-lined boulevard, upon which would stand an imposing collection of new buildings that would reflect Vienna's special status as the political, economic, and cultural heart of the Austro-Hungarian Empire. During the 50 years of building that followed, many factors combined to produce the Ringstrasse as it now stands, but the most important was the gradual rise of liberalism after the failed Revolution of 1848. By the latter half of the Ringstrasse era, support for constitutional government, democracy, and equality—all the concepts that liberalism traditionally equates with progress—was steadily increasing. As the Ringstrasse went up, it became the definitive symbol of this liberal progress; as Carl E. Schorske put it in his *Fin-de-Siècle Vienna,* it celebrated "the triumph of constitutional *Recht* (right) over Imperial *Macht* (might), of secular culture over religious faith. Not palaces, garrisons, and churches, but centers of constitutional government and higher culture dominated the Ring."

But what should these centers of culture look like? The answer was the result of a new passion among the intelligentsia: architectural historicism. Greek temples, it was argued, reminded the viewer of the cradle of democracy; what could be more appropriate than a Parliament building designed in Greek Revival style? Gothic architecture, on the other hand, suggested the church and the rise of the great medieval city-states; the new Votive Church and the new City Hall would therefore be Gothic Revival. And the Renaissance Era, which produced the unprecedented flowering of enlightenment and creativity that put an end to the Middle Ages, was most admired of all; the style of the new centers of high culture—the museums, the theaters, and the university—would be Renaissance Revival. In building after building, architectural style was dictated by historical association, and gradually the Ringstrasse of today took shape.

The highest concentration of public building occurred in the area around the Volksgarten, where are clustered (moving from south to north, from Burgring to Schottenring) the ☞ **Museum of Art History,** the ☞ **Museum of Natural History,** the **Justizpalast** (Palace of Justice), the **Parliament** (Parliament), the **Rathaus** (City Hall), the **Burgtheater** (National Theater), the **Universität** (University of Vienna), the **Votivkirche,** and slightly farther along, the **Börse** (Stock Exchange) on Schottenring. As an ensemble, the collection is astonishing in its architectural presumption: it is nothing less than an attempt to assimilate and summarize the entire architectural history of Europe. As critics were quick to notice, however, the complex suffers from a serious organizational flaw: Most of the buildings lack effective context. Rather than being the focal points of an organized overall plan, they are plunked haphazardly down on an avenue that is itself too wide to possess a unified, visually comprehensible character.

To some, the monumentality of it all is overbearing; others however find the architectural panorama exhilarating, and growth of the trees over 100 years has served to put the buildings into different perspective. There is no question but that the tree-lined boulevard with its broad sidewalks gives the city a unique ribbon of green and certainly the distinction that the emperor sought. *U-Bahn for Volksgarten: U2 Lerchenfelder Strasse.*

㉗ **Spittelberg Quarter.** The Spittelberg quarter, one block northwest of Maria-Theresien-Platz off of the Burggasse, offers a fair visual idea of Vienna outside of the city walls a century ago. Most buildings have been replaced, but the engaging 18th-century survivors at Burggasse Nos. 11 and 13 are adorned with religious and secular decorative sculpture, the latter with a niche statue of St. Joseph, the former with cherubic work-and-play bas-reliefs. For several blocks around—walk down Gutenberggasse and back up Spittelberggasse—the 18th-century houses have been beautifully restored. The sequence from No. 5 to No. 19 Spittelberggasse is an especially fine array of Viennese plain and fancy. Around holiday times, particularly Easter and Christmas, the Spittelberg quarter, known for arts and handicrafts, hosts seasonal markets offering unusual and interesting items.

Monarchs and Mozart: From St. Stephen's to the Opera House

The cramped, ancient quarter behind St. Stephen's Cathedral offers a fascinating contrast to the luxurious expanses of the Ringstrasse and more recent parts of Vienna. This was—and still is—concentrated residential territory in the heart of the city. Mozart lived here; later, Prince Eugene and others built elegant town palaces as the smaller buildings were replaced. Here you get a feeling of old and newer Vienna in contrast over the centuries. Streets, now mostly reserved for pedestrians, are narrow and tiny alleysways abound. Facades open into courtyards that once housed the carriages and horses. The west side of the Kärnter Strasse which since time immemorial has formed a north–south axis through the heart of the city, brings you face-to-face with the former monarchs, their remains and their monuments. Musically, you might encounter Mozart again, at the magnificent State Opera House, which shares with St. Stephen's the honor of being one of the city's most familiar and beloved landmarks.

A Good Walk

To pass through these streets is to take a short journey through history and art. In the process—as you visit haunts of Mozart, kings, and emperors—you can be easily impressed with a sense of exactly how Vienna's glittering Habsburg centuries unfolded. Start from St. Stephen's Cathedral by walking down Singerstrasse to Blutgasse and turn left into the **Blutgasse district** ㊲—a neighborhood redolent of the 19th century. At the north end in Domgasse is the so-called **Figarohaus** ㊳, now a memorial museum, the house in which Wolfgang Amadeus Mozart lived when he wrote the opera *The Marriage of Figaro*. Follow Domgasse east to Grünangergasse, which will bring you to Franziskanerplatz and the Gothic-Renaissance Franziskanerkirche (St. Francis Church). Follow the ancient Ballgasse to Rauhensteingasse, turning left onto **Himmelpfortgasse**—"The Gates of Heaven Street." Prince Eugene of Savoy had his town palace here at No. 8, now the **Ministry of Finance** ㊴, living here when he wasn't enjoying his other residence, the Belvedere Palace. Continue down Himmelpfortgasse to Seilerstätte, and turn right into **Annagasse** and its beautiful houses, which brings you back to the main shopping street **Kärnter Strasse,** where you can find everything from Austrian jade to the latest Jill Sander turnouts. Turn left, walking north two blocks and take the short Donnergasse to reach **Neuer Markt** square and the Providence Fountain. At the southwest corner of the square is the **Kaisergruft** ㊵ in the **Kapuzinerkirche,** the burial vault for rows of once-ruling Habsburgs. Tegetthofstrasse south will bring you to Albertinaplatz, the square noted for the obvious war memorial but more for the **Albertina** ㊶, one of the world's great collections of Old Master drawings and prints. The southeast side of the square is bounded by the famous **Staatsoper** ㊷, the State Opera House; check for tour possibilities or, better, book tickets for a great *Der Rosenkavalier.*

TIMING

A simple walk of this route could take you a full half day, assuming you stop occasionally to survey the scene and take it all in. The restyled Figarohaus is worth a visit, but note the odd closing hours and schedule accordingly. The Kaisergruft in the Kapuziner church is impressive for its shadows of past glories, but there are crowds, and you may have to wait to get in; the best times are early morning or around lunchtime. Tours of the State Opera House take place in the afternoons; check the schedule posted outside one of the doors on the arcaded Kärtner Strasse side. Figure about an hour each for the various visits and tours.

Sights to See

41 **Albertina Museum.** On the west side of Albertinaplatz stands the Albertina Museum, an unpretentious affair housing one of the world's finest collections of drawings, engravings, and prints by leading Old Masters. The Albertina is currently undergoing extensive renovations, but some of its most famous works (for example, Albrecht Dürer's *Praying Hands*) are too popular to be hidden away in security archives and are on view. The monthly city information brochure lists Albertina events and times. ✉ *Augustinerstr. 1,* ☎ *01/534–83–0.* ⏲ *Call for hrs during renovation. U-Bahn: U1, U3 Stephansplatz.*

NEED A BREAK?

Take a coffee break at one of the nearby cafés. The **Café Sacher** (✉ Hotel Sacher, ☎ 01/512–1487. ⏲ Daily 6:30 AM–10:30 PM) on Philharmonikerstrasse—the street directly behind the Opera House leading east from the south end of Albertinaplatz—is the most formal of them all (no shorts allowed inside during the summer); its famous Sachertorte can also be purchased at a small Kärntner Strasse shop on the hotel's east side. The **Café Tirolerhof** (✉ Tegetthoffstr. 8, ☎ 01/512-7833. ⏲ Mon.–Sat. 7 AM–9 PM, Sun. 9:30 AM–8 PM), on the north side of Albertinaplatz, is a less upscale (but more typically Viennese) alternative, with good desserts as well.

37 **Blutgasse District.** The small block bounded by Singerstrasse, Grünangergasse, and Blutgasse is known as the Blutgasse District. Nobody knows for certain how the gruesome name—Blut is German for blood—originated, although one legend has it that Knights Templar were slaughtered here when their order was abolished in 1312, although in later years the narrow street was known in those unpaved days as Mud Lane. Today the block is a splendid example of city renovation and restoration, with cafés, small shops and galleries tucked into the corners. You can look inside the courtyards to see the open galleries that connect var-

ious apartments on the upper floors, the finest example being at Blutgasse No. 3. At the corner of Singerstrasse sits the 18th-century **Neupauer-Breuner Palace,** with its monumental entranceway and inventively delicate windows. Opposite at No. 17 is the **Rottal Palace,** attributed to Hildebrandt, with its wealth of classical wall motifs. For a contrast, turn up the narrow Blutgasse, with its simple 18th-century facades.

38 **Figarohaus.** One of Mozart's 11 rented Viennese residences, the Figarohaus has its entrance at No. 5 Domgasse, the tiny alley behind St. Stephen's (although the facade on Schulerstrasse is far more imposing). It was in this house that Mozart wrote *The Marriage of Figaro* and the six quartets dedicated to Joseph Haydn (who once called on Mozart here, saying to Leopold, Mozart's father, ". . . your son is the greatest composer that I know in person or by name."). The apartment he occupied now contains a small commemorative museum—"created," alas, by an architect more interested in graphic blandishment than a sense of history; you'll have to use your imagination to picture how Mozart lived and worked here. ✉ *Domgasse 5,* ☎ *01/513–6294.* 🎟 *AS25.* ⊙ *Tues.–Sun. 10–12:15 and 1–4:30. U-Bahn: U1, U3 Stephansplatz.*

39 **Finanzministerium** (Ministry of Finance). The architectural jewel of Himmelpfortgasse, this imposing abode—designed by Fischer von Erlach in 1697 and later expanded by Hildebrandt—was originally the town palace of Prince Eugene of Savoy. As you study the Finanzministerium, you'll realize its Baroque details are among the most inventively conceived and beautifully executed in the city; all the decorative motifs are so softly carved that they appear to have been freshly squeezed from a pastry tube. The Viennese are lovers of the Baroque in both their architecture and their pastry, and here the two passions seem visibly merged. Such Baroque elegance may seem inappropriate for a finance ministry, but the contrast between place and purpose could hardly be more Viennese. ✉ *8 Himmelpfortgasse 8.*

Himmelpfortgasse. The maze of tiny streets including Ballgasse, Rauhensteingasse, and Himmelpfortgasse (literally, "The Gates of Heaven Street") masterfully conjures up the Vienna of the 19th century. The most impressive house on the street is the Ministry of Finance (☞ *above*). The back side of the Steffl department store on Rauhensteingasse now marks the site of the house in which Mozart died in 1791. There's a commemorative plaque that once identified the streetside site together with a small memorial corner to Mozart on the 5th floor of the store.

40 **Kaisergruft** (Imperial Burial Vault). In the basement of the **Kapuzinerkirche,** or Capucin church (on the southwest corner of the Neuer Markt), is one of the more intriguing sights in Vienna: the Kaisergruft, or Imperial Burial Vault. The crypts contain the partial remains of some 140 Habsburgs (the hearts are in the Augustinerkirche and the entrails in St. Stephen's) plus one non-Habsburg governess ("She was always with us in life," said Maria Theresa, "why not in death?"). Perhaps this is the wrong way to approach the Habsburgs in Vienna, starting with their tombs, but it does give you a chance to get their names in sequence as they lie in their serried ranks, their coffers ranging from the simplest though positive explosions of funerary conceit with decorations of skulls and other morbid symbols to the lovely and distinguished tomb of Maria Theresa and her husband. Designed while the couple still lived, their monument shows the empress in bed with her husband—awaking to the Last Judgment as if it were just another weekday morning, while the remains of her son (the ascetic Josef II) lie in a simple casket at the foot of the bed as if he were the family dog. ✉ *Neuer Markt/Tegetthoffstr. 2,* ☎ *01/512–6853–0.* 🎟 *AS40.* ⊙ *Daily 9:30–4. U-Bahn: U1, U3 Stephansplatz.*

Kärntner Strasse. The Kärntner Strasse remains Vienna's leading central shopping street. These days Kärntner Strasse is much maligned. Too commercial, too crowded, too many tasteless signs, too much gaudy neon—the complaints go on and on. Nevertheless, when the daytime tourist crowds dissolve, the Viennese arrive regularly for their evening promenade, and it is easy to see why. Vulgar the street may be, but it is also alive and vital, possessing an energy that the more tasteful Graben and the impeccable Kohlmarkt lack. For the sightseer beginning to suffer from an excess of art history, classic buildings, and museums, a Kärntner Strasse window-shopping pause will be welcome.

Neuer Markt. The centerpiece in the Neuer Markt square, Georg Raphael Donner's **Providence Fountain,** has not had a happy life. Put up in 1739, it was at the time the very latest word in civic improvement, with elegantly mannered nude statuary meant to personify the Danube and four of its tributaries. The Empress Maria Theresa, however, was offended; she disapproved of nudity in art. The figures were removed and put away and later nearly melted down for munitions. They were finally restored in 1801, but were once again taken away (to be replaced by the present copies) in 1873. The original figures can be studied in quiet at the Lower Belvedere Palace.

㊷ **Staatsoper** (State Opera House). The famous Vienna Staatsoper on the Ring vies with the cathedral for the honor of marking the emotional heart of the city—it is a focus for Viennese life and one of the chief symbols of resurgence after the cataclysm of World War II. Its directorship is virtually the top job in Austria, almost as important as that of president, and one that comes in for even more public attention. Everyone thinks they could do it just as well and, since the huge salary comes out of the taxes, they feel they have every right to criticize, often and loudly. The first of the Ringstrasse projects to be completed (in 1869), the opera house suffered disastrous bomb damage in the last days of World War II (only the outer walls, the front facade, and the main staircase area behind it survived). The auditorium is plain when compared to the red and gold eruptions of London's Covent Garden or some of the Italian opera houses, but it has an elegant individuality that shows to best advantage when the stage and auditorium are turned into a ballroom for the great Opera Ball.

The construction of the Opera House is the stuff of legend. When the foundation was laid, the plans for the Opernring were not yet complete, and in the end the avenue turned out to be several feet higher than originally planned. As a result, the Opera House lacked the commanding prospect that its architects, Eduard van der Nüll and August Sicard von Sicardsburg, had intended, and even Emperor Francis Joseph pronounced the building a bit low to the ground. For the sensitive van der Nüll (and here the story becomes a bit suspect), failing his beloved emperor was the last straw. In disgrace and despair, he committed suicide. Sicardsburg died of grief shortly thereafter. And the emperor, horrified at the deaths his innocuous remark had caused, limited all his future artistic pronouncements to a single immutable formula: *Es war sehr schön, es hat mich sehr gefreut* ("It was very nice, it pleased me very much").

Rebuilt after the war, it is unable to belie its 1950s look, for the cost of fully restoring the 19th-century interior decor was prohibitive. The original basic design was followed in the 1945–55 reconstruction, meaning that sight lines from some of the front boxes are poor at best. These disappointments hardly detract from the fact that this is one of the world's half dozen greatest opera houses, and experiencing a performance here can be the highlight of a trip to Vienna. Tours of the Opera House are given regularly, but starting times vary according to opera rehearsals; the current schedule is posted at the east side entrance under the arcade on the Kärntner Strasse marked GUIDED TOURS, where the tours begin. Alongside under the arcade is an information office that also sells tickets to the main opera and the Volksoper. ⊠ *Opernring 2,* ☎ *01/514–44–0 or 01/51444–2656.* ☞ *Tour AS50.* ☉ *Weekdays 10–1 hr before performance begins, Sat. 9–2. U-Bahn: U1, U2, U4 Karlsplatz.*

Pomp and Circumstance: South of the Ring to the Belvedere

City planning in the late 1800s and early 1900s clearly was essential to manage the growth of the burgeoning imperial capital. The elegant Ringstrasse alone was not a sufficient showcase, and anyway, it focused on public rather than private buildings. The city fathers as well as private individuals commissioned the architect Otto Wagner to plan and undertake a series of projects. The area around Karlsplatz and the fascinating open food market remains a classic example of unity of design. Not all of Wagner's concept for Karlsplatz was realized, but enough remains to be convincing and to convey the impression of what might have been. The unity concept predates Wagner's time in the former garden setting of Belvedere Palace, one of Europe's greatest architectural triumphs.

A Good Walk

The often overlooked **Academy of Fine Arts** ㊸ is an appropriate starting point for this walk, as it puts into perspective the artistic arguments being raised around the turn of the century. While the Academy represented the conservative viewpoint, a group of modernist revolutionaries broke away and founded the Secessionist movement, with its culimination in the gold-crowned **Secession Building** ㊹. Their achievement, now housing changing exhibits and Gustav Klimt's provocative *Beethoven Frieze*, stands appropriately close by the Academy; from the Academy, take Makartgasse south one block. The famous **Naschmarkt** open food market starts diagonally south from the Secession; follow the rows of stalls southwest. Pay attention to the northwest side of the Linke Wienzeile as you go; at the intersection with Millöckergasse stands the Theater an der Wien, an opera house–theater in which Mozart and Beethoven personally premiered some of their finest works. The Otto Wagner gems on the street are the apartment blocks at No. 38 and 40— the famous "Majolica House"—Jugendstil in fullest bloom. Wagner also designed the stations on what is now the U4 line; a good example is at Kettenbrückengasse; opposite is the market office, another Jugendstil prize. Head back north through the Naschmarkt; at the top end, cross Wiedner Hauptstrasse to your right into the park complex that forms Karlsplatz, creating a setting for the classic **Karlskirche** ㊺, St. Charles's Church. Around the park, note the **Technical University** on the south side, the Otto Wagner subway station buildings on the north. Across Lothringer Strasse on the north side are the **Künstlerhaus** art exhibit hall and the **Musikverein,** the superb concert hall from which the New Year's Day concerts are broadcast worldwide. The out-of-place and rather undistinguished modern building to the left of Karlskirche houses the worthwhile **Historisches Museum der Stadt Wien** ㊻, the Museum of the City of Vienna. Cut through Symphonikerstrasse (a passageway through the modern complex) and take Brucknerstrasse to **Schwarzenbergplatz.** The Jugendstil edifice on your left is the **French Embassy**; ahead is the **Russian War Memorial.** On a rise behind the memorial sits **Schwarzenberg Palais,** a jewel of a one-time summer palace and now a luxury hotel. Follow Prinz Eugen-Strasse up to the entrance of the **Belvedere Palace** ㊼ complex on your left. Admire the baroque ornamentation: cake decoration everywhere but without being overdone, held together by the symmetry of the building itself. Here, you'll find the noted entry hall—a Baroque fantasia where huge supporting columns rising out of the stone floors are transformed into muscular giants. Besides the palace itself are other structures and, off to the east side, a remarkable botanical garden. After viewing the palace and the grounds, you can exit the complex from the lower building, Untere Belvedere, into Rennweg, which will steer you back to Schwarzenbergplatz.

TIMING

The first part of this walk, taking in the Academy of Fine Arts and the Secession, plus the Naschmarkt and Karlsplatz, can be accomplished in an easy half day. The Museum of the City of Vienna is good for a couple of hours, more if you understand some German. Give the Belvedere Palace and grounds as much time as you can. Organized tours breeze in and out—without as much as a glance at the outstanding modern art museum—in a half hour or so, not even scratching the surface of this fascinating complex. If you can, budget up to a half day here, but plan to arrive fairly early in the morning or afternoon before the busloads descend. Bus tourists aren't taken to the Lower Belvedere, so you'll have that and the formal gardens to yourself.

Sights to See

㊸ **Academy of Fine Arts.** An outsized statue of the German author Schiller announces the Academy of Fine Arts on Schillerplatz. (Turn around and note his more famous contemporary Goethe, pompously seated in an overstuffed chair, facing him from across the Ring.) The Academy was founded in 1692 but the present Renaissance Revival building dates to the late 19th century. The idea was conservatism and traditional values, even in the face of a growing Arts and Crafts movement that scorned formal rules. It was here in the 1920s that an aspiring Adolf Hitler was refused acceptance on grounds of insufficient talent. The academy includes a museum focusing on Old Masters. The collection is mainly of interest to specialists, but Hieronymus Bosch's famous *Last Judgment* tryptich hangs here, an imaginative if gruesome speculation of the hereafter. ⊠ *Schillerpl. 3,* ☎ *01/588–16–225.* ☒ *AS30.* ⊙ *Tues., Thurs., and Fri. 10–2; Wed. 10–1 and 3–6; weekends and holidays 9–1. U-Bahn: U1, U2, U4 Karlsplatz.*

★ ㊼ **Belvedere Palace.** Baroque architect Lucas von Hildebrandt's most important Viennese work is wedged between Rennweg (entry at No. 6A) and Prinz Eugen-Strasse (entry at No. 27): the Belvedere Palace. In fact the Belvedere is two palaces with extensive gardens between. Built outside the city fortifications between 1714 and 1722, the complex originally served as the summer palace of Prince Eugene of Savoy; much later it became the home of Archduke Franz Ferdinand, whose assassination in 1914 precipitated World War I. Though the lower palace is impressive in its own right, it is the much larger upper palace, used for state receptions, banquets, and balls, that is Hildebrandt's acknowledged masterpiece. The usual tourist entrance for the Upper Belvedere is the gate on Prinz-Eugen-Strasse, for the Lower Belvedere, the Rennweg gate—but for the most impressive view of the upper palace, approach it from the south garden closest to the South Rail Station. The upper palace displays a remarkable wealth of architectural invention in its facade, avoiding the main design problem common to all palaces because of their excessive size: monotony on the one hand and pomposity on the other. Hildebrandt's decoration here approaches the Rococo, that final style of the Baroque era when traditional classical motifs all but disappeared in a whirlwind of seductive asymmetric fancy. The main interiors of the palace go even farther: Columns are transformed into muscle-bound giants, pilasters grow torsos, capitals sprout great piles of symbolic Imperial paraphernalia, and the ceilings are set aswirl with ornately molded stucco. The result is the finest Rococo interior in the city.

Today both the upper and lower palaces of the Belvedere are noted museums devoted to Austrian painting. The **Österreichisches Barockmuseum** (Austrian Museum of Baroque Art) in the lower palace at Rennweg 6a displays Austrian art of the 18th century (including the original figures from Georg Raphael Donner's *Providence Fountain* in the Neuer Markt)—and what better building to house it! Next to the Baroque Museum (outside the west end) is the converted Orangerie, devoted to works of the medieval period. The main attraction is the upper palace's **Österreichische Galerie** (Austrian Gallery), the legendary collection of 19th- and 20th-century Austrian paintings, centering on the work of Vienna's three preeminent early 20th-century artists: Gustav Klimt, Egon Schiele, and Oskar Kokoschka. Klimt was the oldest, and by the time he helped found the Secession movement, he had forged a highly idiosyncratic painting style that combined realistic and decorative elements in a way that was completely revolutionary. *The Kiss*—his greatest painting and one of the icons of modern art—is here on display. Schiele and Kokoschka went even farther, rejecting the decorative appeal of Klimt's glittering abstract designs and producing works that completely ignored conventional ideas of beauty. Today they are considered the fathers of modern art in Vienna. Modern music, too, has roots in the Belvedere complex: the composer Anton Bruckner lived and died here in 1896 in a small garden house now marked by a commemorative plaque. ⊠ *Upper Belvedere, Prinz-Eugen-Str. 27, Lower Belvedere, Rennweg 6A,* ☎ *01/798–0700.* ⊠ *All Belvedere museums AS60.* ⊘ *Tues.–Sun. 10–5. U-Bahn: U1, U2, U4 Karlsplatz; then for upper Belvedere, Streetcar D to Belvederegasse.*

㊻ Historisches Museum der Stadt Wien (Museum of Viennese History). Housed in an incongrously modern building at the east end of the regal Karlsplatz, this museum possesses a dazzling array of Viennese historical artifacts and treasures: models, maps, documents, photographs, antiquities, stained glass, paintings, sculpture, crafts, and reconstructed rooms. Paintings include Klimts and Schieles, and there's a life-size portrait of the composer Alban Berg painted by his contemporary Arnold Schönberg. Alas, display information and designations in the museum are only in German, and there's no guidebook in English. ⊠ *Karlspl.,* ☎ *01/505–8747–0.* ⊠ *AS50.* ⊘ *Tues.–Sun. 9–4:30. U-Bahn: U1, U2, U4 Karlsplatz.*

★ **㊺ Karlskirche.** Dominating the Karlsplatz is one of Vienna's greatest buildings, the Karlskirche, dedicated to St. Charles Borromeo. At first glance, the church seems like a fantastic vision—one blink and you half expect the building to vanish. For before you is a giant Baroque church framed by enormous free-standing columns, mates to the famous Trajan's Column of Rome's ancient Forum. These columns may be out of keeping with the building as a whole, but were conceived with at least two functions in mind; one was to portray scenes from the life of the patron saint, carved in imitation of Trajan's triumphs, and thus help to emphasize the Imperial nature of the building; and the other was to symbolize the Pillars of Hercules, suggesting the right of the Habsburgs to their Spanish dominions which the Emperor had been forced to renounce. Whatever the reason, the end result is an architectural tour de force.

The Karlskirche was built in the early 18th century on what was then the bank of the river Wien and is now the southeast corner of the park complex. The church had its beginnings in a disaster. In 1713 Vienna was hit by a brutal plague outbreak, and Emperor Charles VI made a vow: If the plague abated, he would build a church dedicated to his namesake Saint Charles Borromeo, the 16th-century Italian bishop who was famous for his ministrations to Milanese plague victims. In 1715 construction began, using an ambitious design by Johann Bernhard Fischer von Erlach that combined architectural elements from ancient Greece (the columned entrance porch), ancient Rome (the Trajaneseque columns), contemporary Rome (the Baroque dome), and contemporary Vienna (the Baroque towers at either end). When it was finished, the church received a decidedly mixed press. History, incidentally, delivered a negative verdict: In its day the Karlskirche spawned no imitations, and it went on to become one of European architecture's most famous curiosities. Notwithstanding, seen lit at night, the building is magical in its setting.

The main interior of the church utilizes only the area under the dome, and is surprisingly conventional given the unorthodox facade. The space and architectural detailing are typical High Baroque; the fine vault frescoes, by J. M. Rottmayr (1725–30), depict Saint Charles Borromeo imploring the Holy Trinity to end the plague. ✉ *Karlspl.,* ☎ *01/504–61–87.* ☉ *Weekdays 7:30–7, Sat. 8–7, Sun. 9–7. U-Bahn: U1, U2, U4 Karlspl.*

Karlsplatz. Like the space now occupied by the Naschmarkt, Karlsplatz was formed when the River Wien was covered over at the turn of the century. At the time Wagner expressed his frustration with the result—too large a space for a formal square and too small a space for an informal park—and the awkwardness persists to this day. The buildings surrounding the Karlsplatz, on the other hand, are quite sure of themselves: the area is dominated by the classic **Karlskirche** (☞ *above*), the less dramatic for the unfortunate reflecting pool with its Henry Moore sculpture, wholly out of place, in front. On the south side of the Resselpark, that part of Karlsplatz named for the inventor of the ship's screw propeller, stands the **Technical University** (1816–18). In a house that occupied the space closest to the church, Italian composer Antonio Vivaldi died in 1741; a plaque marks the spot. On the north side across the heavily-traveled roadway are the **Künstlerhaus** (the exhibition hall in which the Secessionists refused to exhibit, built in 1881 and still in use) and the **Musikverein** (☞ Music *in* the Arts, *below*). The latter building, finished in 1869, is now home to the Vienna Philharmonic. The downstairs lobby and the two halls upstairs have been gloriously restored and glow with fresh gilding. The main hall has what may be the world's finest acoustics; this is the site of the annual, globally televised New Year's Day concert.

Some of Otto Wagner's finest Secessionist work can be seen two blocks east on the northern edge of Karlsplatz. In 1893 Wagner was appointed architectural supervisor of the new Vienna City Railway, and the matched **pair of small pavilions** he designed for the Karlsplatz station in 1898 are among the city's most ingratiating buildings. Their structural framework is frankly exposed (in keeping with Wagner's belief in architectural honesty), but they are also lovingly decorated (in keeping with the Viennese fondness for architectural finery). The result is Jugendstil at its very best, melding plain and fancy with grace and insouciance. The pavilion to the southwest is utilized as a small, specialized museum. In the course of redesigning Karlsplatz, it was Wagner, incidentally, who proposed moving the fruit and vegetable market to what is now the Naschmarkt (☞ *below*).

Naschmarkt. The area between Linke and Rechte Wienzeile has for 80 years been home to the Naschmarkt, Vienna's main outdoor produce market, certainly one of Europe's—if not the world's—great open-air markets, where packed rows of polished and stacked fruits and vegetables compete for visual appeal with braces of fresh pheasant in season; the nostrils meanwhile are accosted by spice fragrances redolent of Asia or the Middle East. *U-Bahn: U1, U2, U4 Karlsplatz.*

NEED A
BREAK?

Who can resist exploring the Naschmarkt without picking up a snack as you go along. The stands marked *Imbiss* (Snack) will sell you a *Hühner-schnitzel-Semmel* (chicken schnitzel inside a Viennese roll); **Heindl & Co. Palatschinkenkuch'l** (pancake kitchen) sells a wide variety of meat and dessert crepes; and the **Naschmarkt Bäckerei** has pastry. You can find a "Stehkaffee" (literally, standup coffee)—limited seats but high tables on which to lean—at the **Anker** pastry and bakery shops.

Otto Wagner Houses. The Ringstrasse-style apartment houses that line the Wienzeile are an attractive if generally somewhat standard lot, but two stand out: **Linke Wienzeile Nos. 38 and 40**—the latter better known as the "Majolica House"—designed (1898–99) by the grand old man of Viennese fin-de-siècle architecture, Otto Wagner, during his Secessionist phase. A good example of what Wagner was rebelling against can be seen next door, at **Linke Wienzeile No. 42,** where decorative enthusiasm has blossomed into Baroque Revival hysteria. Wagner had come to believe that this sort of display was nothing but empty pretense and sham; modern apartment houses, he wrote in his pioneering text *Modern Architecture,* are entirely different from 18th-century town palaces, and architects should not pretend otherwise. Accordingly, he banished classical decoration and introduced a new architectural simplicity, with flat exterior walls and plain, regular window treatments meant to reflect the orderly layout of the apartments behind them. There the simplicity ended. For exterior decoration, he turned to his younger Secessionist cohorts Joseph Olbrich and Koloman Moser, who designed the ornate Jugendstil patterns of red majolica-tile roses (No. 40) and gold stucco medallions (No. 38) that gloriously brighten the facades of the adjacent houses—so much so that their Baroque-period neighbor is ignored. The houses are private.

OFF THE
BEATEN PATH

AM STEINHOF CHURCH – Otto Wagner's most exalted piece of Jugendstil architecture is not in the inner city but in the suburbs to the west: the Am Steinhof Church, designed in 1904 during his Secessionist phase (head out to the church by taking the U4 subway line, which is adjacent to the Wagner houses discussed above). On the grounds of the Vienna City Psychiatric Hospital, Wagner's design unites mundane functional details (rounded edges on the pews to prevent injury to the patients and a slightly sloped tile floor to facilitate cleaning) with a soaring, airy dome and glittering Jugendstil decoration (stained glass by Koloman Moser). The church is open once a week for guided tours (in German). ⊠ *Baumgartner Höhe 1,* ☎ *01/910-60-2391.* 🎟 *Free.* ⊙ *Sat. 3–4. U-Bahn: U4/Unter-St.-Veit, then Bus 47A to Psychiatrisches Krankenhaus; or U2/Volkstheater, then Bus 48A.*

Schwarzenbergplatz. A remarkable urban ensemble, the Schwarzenbergplatz comprises some notable sights. The center of the lower square off the Ring is marked by an oversized equestrian Prince Schwarzenberg—he was a 19th century field marshal for the imperial forces. Admire the overall effect of the square and see if you can guess which building is the newest; it's the one on the northeast corner (No. 3) at Lothringer Strasse, an exacting reproduction of a building destroyed by war damage in 1945, and dating only to the 1980s. The military monument occupying the south end of the square behind the fountain is the **Russian War Memorial,** set up at the end of World War II by the Soviets; the Viennese, remembering the Soviet occupation, call its unknown soldier "the unknown plunderer." South of the memorial is the stately **Schwarzenberg Palace,** designed as a summer residence by Johann Lukas von Hildebrandt in 1697, completed by Fischer von Erlach father and son, and now (in part) a luxury hotel (☞ Dining and Lodging, *below*). The delightful formal gardens wedged between Prinz Eugen–Strasse and the Belvedere gardens can be enjoyed from the hotel restaurant's veranda.

OFF THE
BEATEN PATH
CENTRAL CEMETERY – Taking a streetcar out of Schwarzenbergplatz, music lovers will want to make a pilgrimage to the **Zentralfriedhof** (Central Cemetery, ✉ 11th District on Simmeringer Hauptstr.), which contains the graves of most of Vienna's great composers: Ludwig van Beethoven, Franz Schubert, Johannes Brahms, the Johann Strausses (father and son), and Arnold Schönberg, among others. The monument to Wolfgang Amadeus Mozart is a memorial only; the approximate location of his unmarked grave can be seen at the now deconsecrated St. Marx-Friedhof at Leberstrasse 6–8. *Streetcar 71 to St. Marxer Friedhof, or on to Zentralfriedhof Haupttor/2.*

★ ㊹ **Secession Pavilion.** If the Academy of Fine Arts represents the conservative attitude toward the arts in the late 1800s, then its antithesis can be found immediately behind it to the southeast: the Secession Pavilion. Restored in the mid-1980s after years of neglect, the Secession building is one of Vienna's preeminent symbols of artistic rebellion. Rather than looking to the architecture of the past like the revivalist Ringstrasse, it looked to a new anti-historicist future. It was, in its day, a riveting trumpet-blast of a building, and is today considered by many to be Europe's first example of full-blown 20th-century architecture.

The Sezession—to use the German spelling—began in 1897 when 20 dissatisfied Viennese artists, headed by Gustav Klimt, "seceded" from the Künstlerhausgenossenschaft, the conservative artists' society associated with the Academy of Fine Arts. The movement promoted the radically new kind of art known as Jugendstil, which found its inspiration in both the organic, fluid designs of Art Nouveau and the related but more geometric designs of the English Arts and Crafts Movement. (The Secessionists founded an Arts-and-Crafts workshop of their own, the famous Wiener Werkstätte, in an effort to embrace the applied arts.) The Secession building was the movement's exhibition hall, designed by the architect Joseph Olbrich and completed in 1898. The lower story, crowned by the entrance motto *Der Zeit Ihre Kunst, Der Kunst Ihre Freiheit* (To Every Age Its Art, To Art Its Freedom), is classic Jugendstil: The restrained but assured decoration (by Koloman Moser) beautifully complements the facade's pristine flat expanses of cream-color wall. Above the entrance motto sits the building's most famous feature, the gilded openwork dome that the Viennese were quick to christen "the golden cabbage" (Olbrich wanted it to be seen as a dome of laurel, a subtle classical reference meant to celebrate the triumph of art). The plain white interior—"shining and chaste," in Olbrich's words—was also revolutionary; its most unusual feature was movable walls, allowing the galleries to be reshaped and redesigned for every show. One early show, in 1902, was an exhibition devoted to art celebrating the genius of Beethoven; Gustav Klimt's *Beethoven Frieze,* painted for the occasion, has now been restored and is permanently installed in the building's basement. ⊠ *Friedrichstr. 12,* ☎ *01/587–5307–0.* ⌦ *AS60.* ☉ *Tues.–Fri. 10–6, weekends and holidays 10–4. U-Bahn: U1, U2, U4 Karlsplatz.*

Splendors of the Habsburgs: A Visit to Schönbrunn Palace

The glories of Imperial Austria are nowhere brought together more convincingly than in the Schönbrunn Palace (Schloss Schönbrunn) complex. Brilliant "Maria Theresia Yellow"—she, in fact, caused Schöbrunn to be built—is everywhere in evidence. Imperial elegance flows unbroken throughout the grounds and the setting, and the impression even today is interrupted only by ceaseless hiccups of tourists. This, after all, one of Austria's primary tourist sites, although sadly, few stay long enough to discover the real Schönbrunn (including the little maiden with the water jar, after whom the complex is named). While the assorted outbuildings might seem eclectic, they served as centers of entertainment when the court moved to Schönbrunn in the summer, accounting for the zoo, the priceless theater, the fake Roman ruins, the greenhouses, and the walkways. In Schönbrunn, you step back three hundred years into the heart of a powerful and growing empire and follow it through to defeat and demise in 1917.

Numbers in the text correspond to numbers in the margin and on the Schönbrunn Palace and Park map.

A Good Walk

The usual start for exploring the Schönbrunn complex is the main palace. There's nothing wrong with that approach, but as a variation, consider first climbing to the **Gloriette** on the hill overlooking the site, for a bird's-eye view to put the rest in perspective (take the stairs to the Gloriette roof for the ultimate experience). While at the Gloriette, take a few steps west to discover the **Tiroler House** ⑳ and follow the zigzag path downhill to the palace; note the picturebook views of the main building through the woods. Try to take the full tour of the **palace** ㊺ rather than the shorter, truncated version. Check whether the ground floor back rooms (*Berglzimmer*) are open to viewing. After the palace guided tour, take your own walk around the grounds. The "Schöner Brunner," the namesake fountain, is hidden in the woods to the southeast; continue along to discover the convincing (but fake) Roman Ruins. At the other side of the complex to the west are the excellent **Tiergarten** ㊾ (zoo), the **Palmenhaus** ㊽ (tropical greenhouse), and the attached **Schmetterlinghaus** (butterfly house). Closer to the main entrance, both the **Wagenburg** ㊻ (carriage museum) and **Schlosstheater** (palace theater) are frequently overlooked treasures. Before heading back to the city center, visit the **Hofpavillion** ㊼, the private subway station built for Emperor Francis Joseph, located to the west across Schönbrunner Schlossstrasse.

TIMING

If you're really pressed for time, the shorter guided tour will give you a fleeting impression of the palace itself, but try to budget at least half a day to take the full tour and include the extra roooms and grounds as well. The 20-minute hike up to the Gloriette is a bit strenuous but worthwhile, and there's now a café as reward at the top. The zoo is worth as much as much time as you can spend, and figure on at least a half hour to an hour each for the other museums. Tour buses begin to unload for the main building about mid-morning; start early or utilize the noon lull to avoid the worst crowds. The other museums and buildings in the complex are far less crowded.

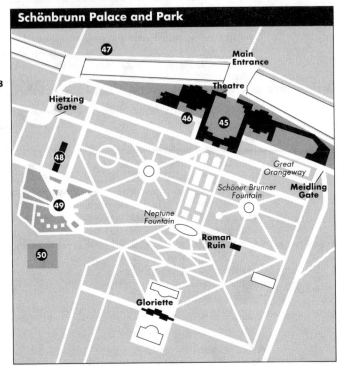

Schönbrunn Palace and Park

Sights to See

Hofpavillon. The most unusual interior of the palace complex, the restored Imperial subway station known as the Hofpavillon is just outside the palace grounds (at the northwest corner, a few yards east of the Hietzing subway station). Designed by Otto Wagner in conjunction with Joseph Olbrich and Leopold Bauer, the Hofpavillon was built in 1899 for the exclusive use of the Emperor Francis Joseph and his entourage. Exclusive it was: The emperor used the station only once. The exterior, with its proud architectural crown, is Wagner at his best, and the lustrous interior is one of the finest examples of Jugendstil decoration in the city. ⊠ *Schönbrunner Schloss-Str., next to Hietzing subway station*, ☎ *01/877–1571.* 🎫 *AS25.* 🕓 *Tues.–Sun. 9–12:15 and 1–4:30. U-Bahn: U4 Hietzing.*

★ ㊺ **Schönbrunn Palace.** Designed by Johann Bernhard Fischer von Erlach in 1696, Schönbrunn Palace, the huge Habsburg summer residence lies well within the city limits, just a few subway stops west of Karlsplatz on line U4. The vast and elegantly planted gardens are open daily from dawn till dusk, and multilingual guided tours of the palace interior are offered daily. A visit inside the palace is not included in most general city sightseeing tours, which offer either a mercilessly tempting drive past or else an impossibly short half hour or so to explore. The four-hour commercial sightseeing bus tours of Schönbrunn offered by tour operators cost several times what you'd pay if you tackled the easy excursion yourself; their advantage is that they get you there and back with less effort. Go on your own if you want time to wander the magnificent grounds.

The most impressive approach to the palace and its gardens is through the front gate, located on Schönbrunner Schloss-Strasse halfway between the Schönbrunn and Hietzing subway stations. The vast main courtyard is ruled by a formal design of impeccable order and rigorous symmetry: Wing nods at wing, facade mirrors facade, and every part stylistically complements every other. The courtyard, however, turns out to be a mere appetizer; the feast lies beyond. The breathtaking view that unfolds on the other side of the palace is one of the finest set pieces in all Europe and one of the supreme achievements of Baroque planning. Formal *allées* (garden promenades) shoot off diagonally, the one on the right toward the zoo, the one on the left toward a rock-mounted obelisk and a fine false Roman ruin. But these, and the woods beyond, are merely a frame for the astonishing composition in the center: the sculpted fountain, the carefully planted screen of trees behind, the sudden almost vertical rise of the grass-covered hill beyond. At the crest of the hill, topping it all off, sits a Baroque masterstroke: Johann Ferdinand von Hohenberg's incomparable **Gloriette,** now restored to its original splendor. Perfectly scaled for its setting, the Gloriette—a palatial pavilion that once offered royal guests a place to rest and relax on their tours of the palace grounds and that now houses an equally welcome café—holds the whole vast garden composition together, and at the same time crowns the ensemble with a brilliant architectural tiara.

Within the palace, the magisterial state salons are quite up to the splendor of the gardens, but note the contrast between these chambers and the far more modest rooms in which the rulers—particularly Francis Joseph—lived and spent most of their time. Of the 1,400 rooms, 40 are open to the public on the regular tour, and two are of special note: the Hall of Mirrors, where the six-year-old Mozart performed for the Empress Maria Theresa in 1762, and the Grand Gallery, where the Congress of Vienna (1815) danced at night after carving up Napoléon's collapsed empire during the day. Ask about viewing the ground-floor living quarters (*Berglzimmer*), where the walls are fascinatingly painted with palm trees, exotic animals, and tropical views. As you go through the palace, take an occasional glance out the windows; you'll be rewarded by a better impression of the beautiful patterns of the formal gardens, punctuated by hedgerows and fountains. These window vistas were enjoyed by rulers from Maria Theresa and Napoléon to Francis Joseph. ✉ *Schönbrunner Schloss-Str.,* ☎ *01/811–13–239.* 🎫 *Grand tour of palace interior (40 rooms) AS140, self-guided grand tour (40 rooms) AS110, self-guided imperial tour (20 rooms) AS80.* ⊙ *Apr.–Oct., daily 8:30–5; Nov.–Mar., daily 8:30–4:30. U-Bahn: U4 Schönbrunn.*

Schönbrunn Palace Park. The palace grounds boast a bevy of splendid divertissements, including a grand zoo (☞ Tiergarten, *below*) and carriage museum (☞ Wagenburg, *below*). Climb to the Gloriette for a panoramic view out over the city as well as the palace complex. If you're exploring on your own, seek out the intriguing Roman ruin, now used as a backdrop for outdoor summer opera. The marble *"schöner Brunnen"* (beautiful fountain) with the young girl pouring water from an urn is nearby. The fountain gave the name to the palace complex. **50** The charming **Tiroler House** to the west of the Gloriette was a favorite retreat of Empress Elisabeth; it now includes a small restaurant (open according to season and weather). 🎫 *Gloriette roof AS20.* ⊙ *May–Oct., daily 9–5. U-Bahn: U4 Schönbrunn.*

48 On the grounds to the west of Schönbrunn Palace is the **Palmenhaus,** a huge greenhouse filled with exotic trees and plants. ✉ *Nearest entrance Hietzing,* ☎ *01/877–5087–406.* 🎫 *AS40, combination ticket with Schmetterlinghaus AS65.* ⊙ *May–Sept., daily 9:30–6 (last admission 5:30); Oct.–Apr., daily 9:30–5 (last admission 4:30).*

Close by the Palmenhaus is another Schönbrunn Palace favorite, the **Schmetterlinghaus,** given over to hordes of live butterflies, orchids, and other floral displays. ⊠ *Nearest entrance Hietzing,* ☎ *01/877–5087–421.* ⌑ *AS40, combination ticket with Palmenhaus AS65.* ☉ *May–Sept., daily 10–5 (last admission 4:30); Oct.–Apr., daily 10–3:30 (last admission 3).*

🐾 **49** Claimed to be the world's oldest, the **Tiergarten** (Zoo) has retained its original Baroque decor and, today, has acquired world class recognition under director Helmut Pechlaner. New settings have been created for both animals and public; in one case, the public looks out into a new natural display area from one of the Baroque former animal houses. The zoo is constantly adding new attractions and undergoing renovations, so there's plenty to see. ☎ *01/877–1236–0.* ⌑ *AS90.* ☉ *Nov.–Jan., daily 9–4:30; Oct. and Feb., daily 9–5; Mar., daily 9–5:30; Apr., daily 9–6; May–Sept., daily 9–6:30. U-Bahn: U4.*

🐾 **46** Most of the carriages in the **Wagenburg** (Carriage Museum) are still road-worthy and, indeed, Schönbrunn dusted off the gilt-and-black royal funeral carriage that you see here for the burial ceremony of Empress Zita in 1989. ⊠ *Wagenburg,* ☎ *01/877–3244.* ⌑ *AS30.* ☉ *Nov.–Mar., Tues.–Sun. 10–4; Apr.–Oct., daily 9–6. U-Bahn: U4 Schönbrunn.*

DINING

Whether the locale be one of the city's finest or a modest neighborhood *Beisl,* the Viennese take their dining seriously and can tell you to a crumb what they've had to eat for at least the last fortnight. This development is remarkable since, not so long ago, Vienna was a culinary backwater. In recent years, however, Vienna has produced a new generation of chefs willing to slaughter sacred cows and create a New Vienna Cuisine. The movement is well past the "less is more" stage that nouvelle cuisine traditionally demands (and to which most Viennese vociferously objected), relying now on lighter versions of the old standbys and clever combinations of such traditional ingredients as liver pâtés and sour cream.

In a first-class restaurant you will pay as much as in most other major Western European capitals. But you can still find good food at refreshingly low prices in the simpler restaurants, particularly at neighborhood *Gasthäuser* in the suburbs. If you eat your main meal at noon (as the Viennese do), you can take advantage of the luncheon specials.

Vienna's restaurant fare ranges from Arabic to Yugoslav, with strong doses of Chinese, Italian, and Japanese, but assuming you've come for what makes Vienna unique, our listings focus not on the exotic but on places where you'll meet the Viennese and experience Vienna.

Many restaurants are closed one or two days a week (often weekends), and most serve meals only 11:30–2:30 and 6–10. An increasing number now serve after-theater dinners, but reserve in advance. The pocket-sized paperback book *Wien wie es isst* (in German; from almost any bookstore) gives up-to-date information on the restaurant, café, and bar scene. For an overview on the pleasures of Austrian cuisine, *see* "Schnitzels, Strudels, and Sachertortes" *in* Pleasures and Pastimes *in* Chapter 1.

CATEGORY	COST*
$$$$	over AS500
$$$	AS300–AS500
$$	AS150–AS300
$	under AS150

*per person, including a small glass of open house wine or beer, service (usually 10%), sales tax (10%), and additional small tip (5%–7%)

Restaurants

$$$$ ✕ **Korso.** For many, this is Vienna's top restaurant, in the Bristol Hotel;
★ you're surrounded by subdued dark-paneled and gold elegance; tables
are set with fine linen, glassware, and silver. The food matches the setting; chef Reinhard Gerer is one of Austria's great creative cooks; unfortunately the kitchen is occasionally left to the second brigade, hardly
a disaster, but not up to the master's achievements. Try such specialties
as roast duck with savoy cabbage or *Rehnüsschen,* tiny venison fillets.
Ask sommelier Christian Zach to recommend an appropriate wine; the
choice is international, although the Austrian list is outstanding. ⊠
Mahlerstr. 2, ☏ *01/515–16–546,* 𝔽𝔸𝕏 *01/515–16–550. Reservations essential. Jacket and tie. AE, DC, MC, V. Closed Aug. No lunch Sat.*

$$$$ ✕ **Palais Schwarzenberg.** This restaurant, in a former private palace,
has one of the most impressive settings in Vienna, but be sure to book
a table on the glassed-in terrace; you'll be surrounded inside by green-
ery, with a view out over the formal gardens. The food is a notch or two
below Korso's (☞ *above*), but still extremely good, and new top chef
Christian Petz gives promise of even better. The service may lag if the
restaurant is full, so be prepared to relax and enjoy the setting. You can't
go wrong with the fillet of beef in red wine sauce, medallions of lamb,
or the delicate pike. ⊠ *Schwarzenbergpl. 9,* ☏ *01/798–4515–600,* 𝔽𝔸𝕏
01/798–4714. Reservations essential. Jacket and tie. AE, DC, MC, V.

$$$$ ✕ **Steirer Eck.** Critics are in agreement that this is Austria's top restau-
★ rant. You dine handsomely in classical elegance, among businesspeople at noon, amid politicians and personalities at night. Tables are set
with flower arrangements and elegant crystal, with a flair that matches
the food. Chef Helmut Österreicher is a genius at combining ideas and
tastes; lobster with artichoke is a successful example, venison with leek
and mushrooms another, but creations are constantly changing. The
fixed-price menu at noon is an outstanding value. The house wine list
is overwhelming; you can ask sommelier Adolf Schmid for advice with
the assurance that it will be good. ⊠ *Rasumofskygasse 2,* ☏ *01/713–
3168,* 𝔽𝔸𝕏 *01/713–5168–2. Reservations essential. Jacket and tie. AE,
DC, MC, V. Closed weekends.*

$$$$ ✕ **Vier Jahreszeiten.** The Inter-Continental's restaurant is an excellent
★ if conservative choice for both the ample noontime buffet and evening
dining. The atmosphere is elegant without being overdone. Service, too,
is attentive but discreet, the wine list impressive but not overwhelming. The delicate roast lamb is consistently delicious; so is the fillet of
beef with raw mushrooms. For dessert, ask for a *Mohr im Hemd,* literally, a moor in a shirt, a chocolate sponge-cake confection with
chocolate sauce and whipped cream. ⊠ *Johannesgasse 28,* ☏ *01/711–
22–143,* 𝔽𝔸𝕏 *01/713–4489. Reservations essential. Jacket and tie. AE,
DC, MC, V. Closed weekends, 2 wks in Jan., and 3 wks in July.*

$$$$ ✕ **Zu den Drei Husaren.** The Three Hussars is again solidly in the ranks
of Vienna's gourmet temples; despite redecoration producing a brighter
ambience, the house remains embalmed in its draped green-yellow velvet and gold. If you don't mind the heavy hand (which occasionally
carries over to the food and service), you'll probably enjoy this touch
of "old" Vienna, evening piano music included. Evenings are enjoyed
by celebrities, lunchtime is for business, and both are for tourists. The
noontime limited menu offers sufficient choice and is good value. Be
warned of the enticing but unpriced evening hors d'oeuvre trolley; a
single dip here can double your bill. The Husaren does best with the
classic standards: *Leberknödelsuppe* (liver-dumpling soup), Wiener
schnitzel, roast beef, and the like. Finish with *Husarenpfannkuchen,*
the house crepes. ⊠ *Weihburggasse 4,* ☏ *01/512–1092,* 𝔽𝔸𝕏 *01/512–*

64

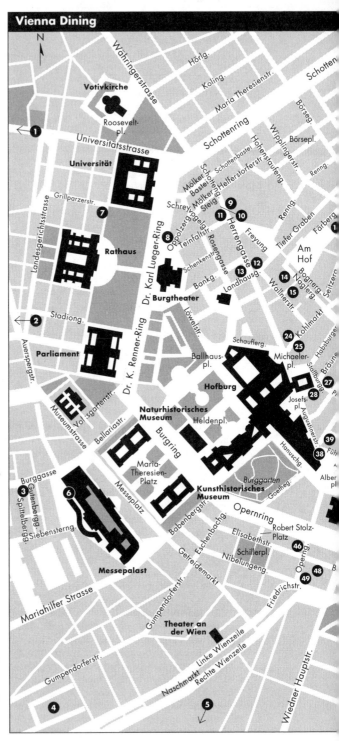

Vienna Dining

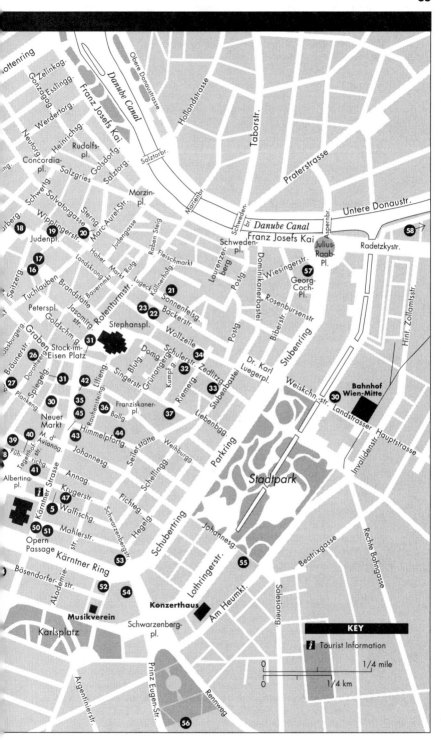

Danube Canal

Obere Donaustrasse

Franz Josefs Kai

Hollandstrasse

Taborstr.

Praterstrasse

Untere Donaustr.

ottenring
G. Zelinkag.
Gonzaga.
Esslingg.
Werdertorg.
Neutorg.
Heinrichsg.
Rudolfs-pl.
Concordia-pl.
Salzgries
Goldorfg.
Salztorg.
Schweng.
Salvatorgasse
Sterng.
Marc-Aurel-Str.
Morzin-pl.
Salztorbr.

Marienbr.

Schwedenbr.

Schweden-pl.

Franz Josefs Kai

Danube Canal

Aspernbr.
Julius-Raab-Pl.
Radetzkystr.

58

18
Wipplingerstr.
20
Judengasse
Raben Steig
17
16
Seitzerg.
Tuchlauben
Brandstätte
Hoher Markt
Landskrong.
Bauernmkt.
Rotg.
Judenpl.
Fleischmarkt
Laurenzer-berg
Postg.
Schwarzen-
Wiesingerstr.
57
Georg-Coch-Pl.
Rosenbursenstr.
Dominikanerbastei
Biberstr.

Peterspl.
Jasomirg.str.
Goldschm.g.
Graben
Augsburgerg.
Bräunerstr.
26
Dorotheerg.
27
Spiegelg.
Plankeng.
30
31
Stock-im-Eisen Platz
31
42
Lilieng.
Singerstr.
Grünangerg.
Kumpfg.
Rauhenstein
Domg.
Schulerstr.
Blutg.
34
Zedlitzg.
32
Riemerg.
33
Stubenbastei
Weiskirchnerstr.
Stubenring
Dr. Karl Luegerpl.

Rotenturmstr.
Lugeck
Köllnerhof.g.
21
Sonnenfelsg.
23 **22**
Bäckerstr.
Wollzeile
Stephanspl.
Postg.

35
45
Neuer Markt
Franziskaner-pl.
Ballg.
36
37
Liebenbgg.
Parkring
Stadtpark

39
40
M. d' Avianog.
43
Himmelpfortg.
44
Seilerstätte
Weihburgg.
8
Tegetthof.
.richg.
41
Johannesg.
Annag.
Krugerstr.
Schelling.
Ficheg.
Hegelg.

30
Bahnhof Wien-Mitte
Landstrasser Hauptstrasse
Invalidenstr.

Hint. Zollamtsstr.

Albertina-pl.
i
47
Kärntner Strasse
5
Walfischg.
50 **51**
Mahlerstr.
str.
Opern Passage
Kärntner Ring
Bösendorfer-str.
Akademie.str.
53
52
54
Musikverein
Karlsplatz
Schwarzenberg-pl.
Prinz Eugen-Str.
Argentinierstr.

Konzerthaus
Am Heumkt.
Johannesg.
55
Lothringerstr.
Schubertring
Schwarzenbergstr.

Salesianerg.
Beatrixgasse
Rechte Bahngasse

Rennweg
56

KEY

i Tourist Information

0   1/4 mile
0   1/4 km

1092–18. Reservations essential. Jacket and tie. AE, DC, MC, V. Closed mid-July–mid-Aug.

$$$ ✕ **Hedrich.** This tiny, unassuming restaurant offers astonishingly fine
★ food. Richard Hedrich, the owner and chef, decided to go into busi-
ness for himself and cook to his and his guests' pleasure; his wife looks
after the tables and the guests, including giving wine recommendations.
The menu changes regularly, so ask for recommendations; recent of-
ferings have included a fragrant whipped basil soup and medallions
of pork in a cheese dough crust. ⊠ *Stubenring 2,* ☎ *01/512–9588.
Reservations essential. No credit cards. Closed Fri., weekends, and Aug.*

$$$ ✕ **Imperial Café.** In the Imperial Hotel, the café is much more than
★ just a (very good) meeting spot for coffee or *Torte*; both lunch and after-
concert supper are popular and reasonably priced. The rooms are understated by local standards; crystal and velvet are evident but not
overdone. The city's politicians, attorneys, and business types gather
here for solid Viennese fare, selecting either from the choice daily specialties, which generally include a superb cream soup, or relying on such
standards as *Leberknödelsuppe* and *Tafelspitz,* Viennese boiled beef.
In summer, the terrace outside is enticing but noisy. ⊠ *Kärntner Ring
16,* ☎ *01/501–10–359,* ℻ *01/501–10–410. AE, DC, MC, V.*

$$$ ✕ **Plachutta.** In two settings that pleasantly mix traditional and mod-
ern, attention focuses on the excellent Tafelspitz, various cuts of beef
cooked and served in their own delicious soup, for which you order
the "supplement," perhaps thin pancake strips (*Frittaten*) or liver
dumpling (*Leberknödel*). Steaks or grilled fish are alternatives. To fin-
ish, select a rhubarb strudel or fresh fruit. The traditional accompa-
niment to Tafelspitz is beer, but the house open wines are excellent.
The otherwise top service may lag a bit as the evening comes to a close.
⊠ *Wollzeile 38,* ☎ *01/512–1577,* ℻ *01/512–1577–20;* ⊠ *Heiligen-
städter Str. 179,* ☎ *01/374125,* ℻ *01/374125–20. Reservations es-
sential. MC, V. Closed last wk of July–mid-Aug.*

$$$ ✕ **Schnattl.** If you're not outdoors in the idyllic courtyard, the setting
could be described as cool postmodern: the main room has now ac-
quired a warmer patina but is relatively unadorned, letting you con-
centrate instead on the attractively set tables and excellent cuisine
(which offers occasional surprises such as medallions of mountain
ram). Traditional dishes like roast pork are transformed with such
touches as a light mustard sauce, lamb with a trace of rosemary, with
offerings dependent on season and availability of fresh ingredients. ⊠
Lange Gasse 40, ☎ *01/405–3400. AE, DC. Closed Sun., 2 wks around
Easter, and late Aug.–mid-Sept. No lunch Sat.*

$$$ ✕ **Sirk.** This comfortable restaurant in traditional style is ideal for a light
lunch or an evening snack. The glassed-in sidewalk terrace is perfect for
afternoon coffee and dessert, but for more privacy, take a table upstairs;
those overlooking the Opera House are best, but at noon you'll have to
fight Vienna's business establishment for one of them. The daily menu
is excellent value, or you might choose the rare roast beef with black-
mushroom sauce. The post-opera menu is consistently good. ⊠ *Kärnt-
ner Str. 53,* ☎ *01/515–16–552,* ℻ *01/515–16–550. AE, DC, MC, V.*

$$$ ✕ **Zum Kuckuck.** This intimate, wood-paneled restaurant, in a build-
ing many hundreds of years old, draws its clientele from the ministries
in the neighborhood at noon. The kitchen does such variations on regional themes as fillet of veal in mushroom sauce and fillet of venison
in puff pastry. Try the warm fig cake with rum sauce for dessert. ⊠
Himmelpfortgasse 15, ☎ *01/512–8470,* ℻ *01/523–3818. AE, DC,
MC, V. Closed weekends.*

$$ ✕ **Bastei Beisl.** You'll find good basic Viennese cuisine in this unpretentious,
friendly, pine-paneled restaurant. Try the *Zwiebelrostbraten,* a rump steak
smothered in fried onions. The tables outside in summer add to the plea-

sure at noon or in the evening. ⊠ *Stubenbastei 10,* ☎ *01/512–4319. AE, DC, MC. Closed Sat. July and Aug., Sun., and holidays.*

$$ ✕ **Bei Max.** The decor is somewhat bland, but the tasty Carinthian specialties—the cheese-and-meat-filled ravioli known as *Käsnudeln* and *Fleischnudeln* in particular—pack this friendly restaurant, a favorite with officials from neighboring government offices and with students alike. You'll also find such classic standards as Tafelspitz, as well as outstanding desserts. The *Kletzennudeln,* a form of bread pudding with dried fruit and cinnamon, is a house feature. Both bottled and open wines are good and generally reasonable, and the beer is excellent. ⊠ *Landhausgasse 2/Herrengasse,* ☎ *01/533–7359. No credit cards. Closed weekends, last wk of July, and 1st 3 wks of Aug.*

$$ ✕ **Figlmüller.** If you'll accept the style of the house (you sit at a series
★ of benches elbow-to-elbow with the other guests), this is *the* spot for Wiener schnitzel—one that overhangs the plate. (Waiters understand the doggie-bag principle.) Other choices are somewhat limited, and you'll have to take wine or mineral water with your meal because no beer or coffee is served. No desserts are offered; you probably couldn't manage one anyway. But Figlmüller is an experience you'll want to repeat. ⊠ *Wollzeile 5,* ☎ *01/512–6177. No credit cards.*

$$ ✕ **Glacis-Beisl.** This restaurant, tucked beneath a section of the old city
★ wall, is no longer the secret it once was, but the charm of the indoor rooms is still appealing, and its garden under grape arbors is unique. Alas, a proposed rebuilding of the Messepalast (dubbed the Museumquartier, a venue used for art exhibits and theater events) into a cultural complex threatens the existence of this fascinating corner of Vienna. The menu is long; ask the waiter for help. You'll find most of the Viennese standards, but the place seems right for grilled chicken (*Brathendl*) and a mug of wine. ⊠ *Messepalast (follow signs to rear right corner), Messepl. 1,* ☎ *01/526–6795. Reservations essential. No credit cards. Closed Sun., Jan.–mid-Feb., and holidays.*

$$ ✕ **Gösser Bierklinik.** The rooms go on and on in this upstairs (more formal) and downstairs (preferred) complex that dates back four centuries. The fare is as solid as the house; the Wiener schnitzel here is first class. The salad bar is new. And there's a menu in English. The beer, of course, is Austrian, from the Gösser brewery in Styria. ⊠ *Steindlgasse 4,* ☎ *01/535–6897. AE, DC, MC, V. Closed Sun. and holidays.*

$$ ✕ **Gösser Brau.** This vast *Keller* (cellar) with a faux copper brewing vat is a noontime hangout of businesspeople who appreciate the good food and generally prompt service. Go for the game when it's available. *Rehrücken* (rack of venison) is a specialty. The appropriate accompaniment is Gösser beer, of course. ⊠ *Elisabethstr. 3,* ☎ *01/587–4750. AE, DC, MC, V.*

$$ ✕ **Königsbacher bei der Oper.** The small, paneled and arched rooms
★ or the tables outside seem just right for Viennese standards such as schnitzel and roast pork. The daily special—this might be ravioli or meat loaf—is an excellent value. Service is friendly, beer is German, and the open wines are good. ⊠ *Walfischgasse 5,* ☎ *01/513–1210. No credit cards. Closed Sun. No dinner Sat.*

$$ ✕ **Myer's Kaiserwalzer-Bräu.** Traces of the elegant "old Vienna" atmosphere remain in this former town house with its wood paneled rooms inside and large dining garden out front. The menu is as eclectic as the decor but both are genuine. You'll find standards such as Tafelspitz alongside relative exotica like *Vitello tonnato,* roast veal with a delicate tuna fish and capers sauce. The shorter menu changes weekly according to season. The excellent beer comes from Salzburg, the wines mainly from Austria. ⊠ *Esterházygasse 9,* ☎ *01/587–0494,* FAX *01/587–0494. AE, DC, MC, V. No lunch.*

$$ ✕ **Ofenloch.** Unique for its turn-of-the-century ambience, this restau-
★ rant features waitresses in costume and a menu in miniature newspaper
form. The fare is based on original recipes and the offerings change pe-
riodically according to what's in season. Garlic fans will find the
Vanillerostbraten, a rump steak prepared not with vanilla but with
garlic, delicious. The misleading name came about because in early days,
no one would admit to ordering anything with garlic. Desserts—try the
Palatschinken, cream-filled crepes ladled with chocolate sauce—are
consistently good and utterly seductive. ✉ *Kurrentgasse 8,* ☎ *01/533–
8844. Reservations essential. AE, DC, MC, V.*

$$ ✕ **Stadtbeisl.** The smallish dark-paneled rooms are packed at noon,
as is the summer garden amid the ivy outside. Better say "no" to the
waiter's (expensive) offer of a *Schnaps* (liquor) to start. Take the game
in season; otherwise try one of the good Viennese standards. ✉ *Naglergasse 21,* ☎ *01/533–3507. V.*

$$ ✕ **Zu den Drei Hacken.** This is one of the last of the old *Gasthäuser*
in the center of town; Schubert, among other luminaries of the past,
is alleged to have dined here. You will find excellent Viennese fare, from
schnitzel to Tafelspitz. The outdoor garden is attractive but jammed.
✉ *Singerstr. 28,* ☎ *01/512–5895. AE, DC, MC, V. Closed Sun.*

$$ ✕ **Zu ebener Erde und im ersten Stock.** This gem of a historic house
★ has an upstairs/downstairs combination: In the tiny room upstairs, done
in Biedermeier old Vienna decor, the cuisine reflects the setting, with
Viennese favorites and others such as medallions of lamb or rump steak
with bread crust. The selection concentrates on a narrower range of
excellently-prepared dishes. There's simpler (and cheaper) fare on the
ground floor. ✉ *Burggasse 13,* ☎ *01/523–6254. Reservations essential. AE, V. Closed Sat. afternoon, Sun., Mon., and 1st 3 wks of Aug.*

$ ✕ **Brezlg'wölb.** Casual food—soups in mini-tureen portions and salad
plates—and a cozy, friendly atmosphere draw the crowds here. If you
sit in the quiet courtyard between Am Hof and Judenplatz, you look
up at classical facades; inside, small, brick-vaulted rooms offer a comfortable interlude to diners. Downstairs, many come just to enjoy the
excellent wine, beer, and coffee in the candle-lit cellar rooms. ✉ *Led-
ererhof 9,* ☎ *01/533–8811. No credit cards.*

$ ✕ **Gigerl.** This charming and original wine restaurant offers a hot and
★ cold buffet, specializing in vegetable and pasta dishes; try the maca-
roni salad or the *Schinkenfleckerl,* a baked noodle and ham dish. They
go remarkably well with the light wines that the costumed waitresses
keep pouring into your glass. In winter the rooms can get smoky and
stuffy; in summer, the outside tables are delightful. ✉ *Rauhensteingasse
3/Blumenstockgasse 2,* ☎ *01/513–4431. AE, DC, MC, V.*

$ ✕ **Göttweiger Stiftskeller.** In this traditional, basic restaurant, look for
grilled and fried chicken, schnitzel variants, tasty liver dishes such as
Leberknödelsuppe plus occasional surprises like oxtail soup. The food
helps compensate for the rather unexciting rooms. The wines, on the
other hand, are outstanding. ✉ *Spiegelgasse 9,* ☎ *01/512–7817. No
credit cards. Closed weekends.*

$ ✕ **Gulaschmuseum.** The original idea behind this modern restaurant
is literally dozens of tasty variants on the theme of goulash. They're
just right for a between-meal snack, although most of the goulashes
served are filling enough for a complete meal. There are alternatives
as well. ✉ *Schulerstr. 20,* ☎ *01/512–1017. No credit cards.*

$ ✕ **Lustig Essen.** The name means "amusing dining." The concept in
these modern rooms involves smaller portions (although generous
enough for most) at remarkably reasonable prices, so that you can sample more of the outstanding dishes on the menu. Try the cream of garlic soup, the lamb ragout, or grilled shrimp. ✉ *Salvatorgasse 6,* ☎ *01/
533–3037. No credit cards.*

$ ✕ **Naschmarkt.** In this attractive cafeteria the food is good, of excellent value, and of far more variety than at the next-door McDonald's. Look for the daily specials on the blackboard. You'll also find good soups (gazpacho on hot summer days), sandwiches, a salad bar, and a no-smoking area. ✉ *Schwarzenbergpl. 16,* ☎ *01/505–3115;* ✉ *Schottengasse 1,* ☎ *01/533–5186. No credit cards. No dinner Sun. at Schottengasse.*

$ ✕ **Pantherbräu.** This neighborhood *Gasthaus* is packed at noon with government officials, businessmen, and students who come for the comfortable if relatively unadorned environment, good beer, and honest food with no pretensions. This is a fine place for standards such as roast pork with mushroom sauce or, in season, venison. The standard menu card is available in English, but ask about the daily specials. In summer, the tables outside on the square are in great demand. ✉ *Judenpl. 10,* ☎ *01/533–4428. No credit cards. Closed weekends.*

$ ✕ **Reinthaler.** The atmosphere is thick enough to cut in this convenient neighborhood establishment, full of regulars. The fare is genuine Viennese: schnitzel, chicken, roast pork with *Knödel* (bread dumpling), and such. The ivy-fenced tables outside in summer are particularly popular. ✉ *Glückgasse 5,* ☎ *01/512–3366. No credit cards. Closed weekends. No dinner Fri.*

$ ✕ **Rosenberger Marktrestaurant.** Downstairs under a huge (artificial) tree you'll find a cluster of cafeteria islands offering soups, excellent grilled specialties, vegetables, pastas, salads, desserts, and fresh juices and other beverages, all prepared to order and attractively (if somewhat confusingly) presented. You can leave your valuables in one of the free lockers while you make and enjoy your selection. Look for seasonal specialties such as asparagus and fresh chilled melon. Take your choice to any of the side rooms, some decorated with musical instruments, some with antique kitchenware and dishes. ✉ *Maysedergasse 2/Fürichgasse 3,* ☎ *01/512–3458. No credit cards.*

$ ✕ **Schnitzelhaus.** This local self-service chain specializes in pork schnitzel (pork cutlet breaded, deep fried), but you could have a turkey schnitzel, schnitzel cordon bleu or a schnitzelburger as an alternative. And there are smaller portions for children. The decor is relatively unadorned, but the schnitzels are certainly not bad (choose fries over the traditional but sometimes soggy potato salad accompaniment), and prices rock-bottom. Beer and wine in mini-bottles are available in addition to soft drinks. All items are available for take-out. ✉ *Krugerstr. 6,* ☎ *01/513–2560;* ✉ *Kettenbrückengasse 19,* ☎ *01/586–1774;* ✉ *Billrothstr. 18;* ✉ *Favoritenstr. 145;* ✉ *Brigittapl. 22. No credit cards.*

$ ✕ **Trzesniewski.** "Unpronounceably good" is the (correct) motto of this tiny sandwich shop, a Viennese tradition for decades. If a quick snack will suffice, three or four of the open sandwiches and a *Pfiff* (⅛ liter, or ¹⁄₁₀ quart) of beer, or a vodka, may be just the needed pickup. Share one of the few tables, or stand up at one of the counters. You'll be surprised at the elegance of many of the customers. ✉ *Dorotheergasse 1,* ☎ *01/512–3291. No credit cards. Closed Sun. No dinner Sat.*

Wine Taverns

In-town wine restaurants cannot properly be called *Heurigen,* since they are not run by the vintner, so the term is "wine restaurant," or "cellar" (*Keller*). Many of them extend a number of levels underground, particularly in the older part of the city. Mainly open in the evening, they are intended primarily for drinking, though you can always get something to eat from a buffet, and increasingly, full dinners are available. As at their country cousins, wine is served by the mug. Some of the better wine restaurants follow; no credit cards are accepted except where noted.

$$ ✕ **Augustinerkeller.** This ground-floor-and-upstairs Keller is open at
★ noontime as well. The grilled chicken is excellent, as is the filling *Stelze* (roast knuckle of pork). The open wines are first-class. ✉ *Augustinerstr. 1/Albertinerpl.,* ☎ *01/533–1026. MC, V.*

$$ ✕ **Esterházykeller.** This maze of rooms offers some of the best Keller
★ wines in town plus a typical Vienna menu noontime and evenings plus hot and cold buffet, but the atmosphere may be too smoky for some. ✉ *Haarhof 1,* ☎ *01/533–3482. Stüberl closed Sat., Keller closed weekends. No lunch Sun. at Stüberl.*

$$ ✕ **Melker Stiftskeller.** Down and down you go, into one of the friendli-
★ est Kellers in town, where Stelze is a popular feature, along with outstanding wines by the glass or rather, mug. ✉ *Schottengasse 3,* ☎ *01/533–5530. MC. Closed Sun. No lunch.*

$ ✕ **Zwölf Apostel-Keller.** You pass a huge wood statue of St. Peter on the way downstairs to the two underground floors in this deep-down cellar in the oldest part of Vienna. The young crowd comes for the good wines and the atmosphere, and there's buffet food as well. ✉ *Sonnenfelsgasse 3,* ☎ *01/512–6777. No lunch.*

Heurigen

Few cities the size of Vienna boast wine produced within city limits, even fewer offer wines ranging from good to outstanding. But in various suburban villages—once well outside the center but now now parts of the urban complex—the fringes of the city have spawned characteristic wine taverns and restaurants, sometimes located in the vineyards themselves. Called *Heurigen* (the single appelation is a *Heuriger*) for the new wine that they serve, they are very much a part of and typical of the city (although not unique to Vienna). Heurigen sprang up in 1784 when Joseph II decreed that owners of vineyards could open their own private wine taverns.

These taverns in the wine-growing districts on the outskirts of the city vary from the simple front room of a vintner's house to ornate establishments. (The name means "new wine," and that's what is chiefly served.) The true Heuriger is open for only a few weeks a year to allow the vintner to sell a certain quantity of his production tax-free for consumption on his own premises. The commercial establishments keep to a somewhat more regular season, but still sell only wine from their own vines.

The choice is usually between a "new" and an "old" white wine and a red, but you can also ask for a milder or sharper wine according to your taste. Most Heurigen are happy to let you sample the wines before ordering. You can also order a *Gespritzter,* half wine and half soda water. The waitress will bring you the wine, usually in a ¼-liter mug or liter carafe, but you get your own food from the buffet. The wine tastes as mild as lemonade, but it packs a punch. If it isn't of good quality, you will know by a raging headache the next day.

Summer and fall are the seasons for visiting the Heurigen, though often the more elegant and expensive establishments, called *Noble-Heurige,* stay open year-round. No credit cards are accepted except where noted.

Heurige are concentrated in several outskirts of Vienna: Stammersdorf, Grinzing, Sievering, Nussdorf, Neustift, and a corner of Ottakring. Perchtoldsdorf, just outside Vienna, is also well known for its wine taverns.

Our favorite district is Stammersdorf, across the Danube. Try **Robert Helm** for good wines, a small but complete buffet including desserts from the house kitchen, and a wonderfully inviting tree-shaded garden. ⊠ *Stammersdorfer Str. 121,* ☎ *01/292–1244. Closed Sun., Mon., and other periods during yr.*

Wine and food are both outstanding at **Wieninger,** with its spacious garden and series of typical vintner's rooms. Wieningers's bottled wines are ranked among the country's best. ⊠ *Stammersdorfer Str. 78,* ☎ *01/292–4106. Closed Mon. and mid-Dec.–Jan. 2.*

The Grinzing district today suffers from mass tourism, with very few exceptions; one is **Zum Martin Sepp,** where the wine, food, service, and ambience are all good. ⊠ *Cobenzlgasse 32,* ☎ *01/324–4875. DC, V.*

East of the Grinzing village center, **Zimmermann** has excellent wines and buffet foods, an enchanting tree-shaded garden, and an endless collection of small paneled rooms and vaulted cellars. ⊠ *Armbrustergasse 5/Grinzinger Str.,* ☎ *01/318-8975. AE, DC, MC, V. Closed Sun. No lunch.*

In Sievering, vintner **Haslinger** offers both good wines and a small but tasty buffet. The atmosphere is plain but honest both indoors and in the small, typical vine-covered garden outside in summer. ⊠ *Agnesgasse 3,* ☎ *01/440–1347. Closed Mon.*

In Neustift, **Wolff** has an enticing garden and outstanding food, as well as good wine. The small rooms inside are intimate and attractive. ⊠ *Rathstr. 46,* ☎ *01/440–2335.*

In Nussdorf seek out **Schübel-Auer** for its series of atmospheric rooms and good wines. ⊠ *Kahlenberger Str. 22,* ☎ *01/372222. Closed Sun., Jan., and July.*

Heiligenstadt is home to **Mayer am Pfarrplatz**—the legendary heuriger in Beethoven's former abode—where the atmosphere in the collection of rooms is genuine, the á la carte offerings and buffet more than abundant, and the house wines excellent. You'll even find some Viennese among the tourists. ⊠ *Heiligenstädter Pfarrpl. 2,* ☎ *01/371287. AE, DC, MC, V. No lunch weekdays or Sat.*

Cafés

One of the quintessential Viennese institutions, the coffeehouse, or café, is club, pub, and bistro all rolled into one. For decades, a substantial part of Austrian social life has revolved around them (though now less than in the past) as Austrians by and large are rather reluctant to invite strangers to their homes and prefer to meet them in the friendly, but noncommittal, atmosphere of the café.

To savor the atmosphere of the coffeehouses you must take your time; set aside an afternoon, a morning, or at least a couple of hours, and settle down in one of your choice. Read or catch up on your letter writing: There is no need to worry about outstaying one's welcome, even over a single small cup of coffee, better identified as a *kleiner Schwarzer* (black) or *kleiner Brauner* (with milk). (Of course, in some of the more opulent coffeehouses, this cup of coffee can cost as much as a meal.)

Coffee is not just coffee in Austria. It comes in many forms and under many names. Morning coffee is generally *Melange* (half coffee, half milk), or with little milk, a *Brauner.* The usual after-dinner drink is *Mokka,* very black, and most Austrians like it heavily sweetened. Restaurants that serve Balkan food offer *Türkischer,* or Turkish coffee, a strong, thick brew. Most delightful are the coffee-and-whipped-cream concoctions, universally cherished as *Kaffee mit Schlag,* a taste that is easily acquired and a menace to all but the very thin. The coffee may be either hot or cold. A customer who wants more whipped cream than coffee asks for a *Doppelschlag*. Hot black coffee in a glass with one knob of whipped cream is an *Einspänner* (one-horse coach). Then you can go to town on a *Mazagran,* black coffee with ice and a tot of rum, or *Eiskaffee,* cold coffee with ice cream, whipped cream, and biscuits. Or you can simply order a *Portion Kaffee* and have an honest pot of coffee and jug of hot milk.

The typical Viennese café, with polished brass or marble-topped tables, bentwood chairs, supplies of newspapers, and tables outside in good weather, is a fixed institution of which there are literally hundreds. All cafés serve pastries and light snacks in addition to beverages. Many offer a menu or fixed lunch at noon, but be aware that some can get rather expensive. No credit cards are accepted except where noted.

Of course, when tourists think of Viennese cafés, Demel's and Café Sacher leap to mind, but they are hardly typical—for information on them, see the Kohlmarkt and the Albertina sections in the Exploring Vienna section, *above.* When you want a quick (but excellent) coffee and dessert, look for an **Aida** café; they are scattered throughout the city. Here's a sampling of the best of the traditional cafés. **Alte Backstübe** (⊠ Lange Gasse 34, ☎ 01/406−1101), in a gorgeous Baroque house—with a café in front and restaurant in back—was once a bakery and is now a museum as well. **Bräunerhof** (⊠ Stallburggasse 2, ☎ 01/512−3893) has music on some afternoons. **Café Central** (⊠ Herrengasse 14, ☎ 01/535−4176−0) is where Stalin and Trotsky played chess. **Frauenhuber** (⊠ Himmelpfortgasse 6, ☎ 01/512−4323) has its original turn-of-the-century interior and a good choice of desserts. **Haag** (⊠ Schottengasse 2, ☎ 01/533−1810), with crystal chandeliers and a shaded courtyard garden in summer, serves snacks and desserts. **Landtmann** (⊠ Dr. Karl Lueger-Ring 4, ☎ 01/532−0621) is where government officials gather. **Museum** (⊠ Friedrichstr. 6, ☎ 01/586−5202), original interior by the architect Adolf Loos, draws a mixed crowd and has lots of newspapers. **Schwarzenberg** (⊠ Kärntner Ring 17, ☎ 01/512−7393), with piano music in late afternoons, is highly popular, particularly its sidewalk tables in summer. **Tirolerhof** (⊠ Tegetthoffstr. 8/Albertinapl., ☎ 01/512−7833), with ample papers and its excellent desserts, is popular with students.

Café Hawelka (⊠ Dorotheergasse 12, ☎ 01/512−8230) deserves special mention; whole books have been written at and about this gathering place. Its international clientele ranges from artists to politicians; Hawelka is jammed any time of day, so you share a table (and the smoky atmosphere). In a city noted for fine coffee, Hawelka's is superb, even more so when accompanied by a freshly baked *Buchterln* (sweet roll, evenings only).

Pastry Shops

Viennese pastries are said to be the best in the world. In all shops you can buy them to enjoy on the premises, usually with coffee, as well as to take out. **Kurkonditorei Oberlaa** (⊠ Neuer Markt 16, ☎ 01/513−2936; ⊠ Landstrasser Hauptstr. 1, ☎ 01/714−6502) has irresistible confections, cakes, and bonbons, as well as light lunches and salad plates, served outdoors in summer. Traditionalists and tourists with fat pocketbooks still go to **Demel** (⊠ Kohlmarkt 14, ☎ 01/533−5516−0), where the value is arguable but turn-of-the-century atmosphere prevails among velvet and polished brass in the older front rooms, stark modern in the new inner court, open in summer, covered in winter. The newer **Demel Vis-à-vis** opposite its mother shop (⊠ Kohlmarkt 11, ☎ 01/533−6020) has an elegant buffet and stand-up tables, plus a mail-order service for Demel specialties. **Gerstner** (⊠ Kärntner Str. 15, ☎ 01/

512–4963–0), while hardly inexpensive, is also recommended. **Heiner** (✉ Kärntner Str. 21-23, ☎ 01/512–6863–0; ✉ Wollzeile 9, ☎ 01/512–4838–0) is dazzling for its crystal chandeliers as well as for its pastries. **Sluka** (✉ Rathauspl. 8, ☎ 01/406–8896–0) has special dietetic desserts, snacks, and an appetizer buffet and serves outdoors in summer.

LODGING

In Vienna's best hotels the staff seems to anticipate your wishes almost before you express them. Such service of course has its price, and if you wish, you can stay in Vienna in profound luxury. For those with more modest requirements, ample rooms are available in less expensive but entirely adequate hotels. Pensions, mainly bed-and-breakfast establishments often managed by the owner, generally represent good value. A number of student dormitories are run as hotels in summer, offering about the most reasonable quarters of all. And several apartment-hotels accommodate those who want to stay longer.

When you have only a short time to spend in Vienna, you will probably want to stay in the inner city (the First District, or 1010 postal code) or fairly close to it, within walking distance of the most important sights, restaurants, and shops. Although most of the hotels there are in the upper categories, excellent and reasonable accommodations can be found in the Eighth District, which borders the First and puts you close to the major museums. You'll also find a group of moderate ($$) and inexpensive ($) hotels in the Mariahilfer Strasse–Westbahnhof area, within easy reach of the city center by subway.

For the high season, Easter through September, and around the Christmas–New Year holidays, make reservations a month or more in advance. Vienna is continually the site of some international convention or other, and the city fills up quickly.

Our hotel categories correspond more or less to the official Austrian rating system, with five stars the equivalent of our very expensive ($$$$) category. All rooms have bath or shower unless otherwise stated; color television is usual in the top two categories; breakfast is included with all *except* the highest category. Air-conditioning is rare except in the larger, newer chain hotels. These seem constantly to be hosting convention or seminar groups, making service somewhat less personal, but there are exceptions, as noted.

CATEGORY	COST*
$$$$	over AS2,700
$$$	AS1,200–AS2,700
$$	AS950–AS1,200
$	under AS950

All prices are for two persons in a standard double room, including local taxes (usually 10%), service (15%), and breakfast (except in many $$$$ hotels).

$$$$ 🏨 **Ambassador.** This superbly located dowager (from 1866) wears well. An air of decadent elegance radiates from the red velvet and crystal chandeliers in the high-ceilinged guest rooms. The trade-off is room air conditioners and rather stuffy period furniture. But what was once good enough for Mark Twain—yes, he stayed here, but long before the 1990–91 renovations—is still very good, and you will know instantly that you are in Vienna. Unless you want the excitement of a direct view into the lively pedestrian Kärntner Strasse, ask for one of the quieter rooms on the Neuer Markt side. ✉ *Neuer Markt 5/Kärnt-*

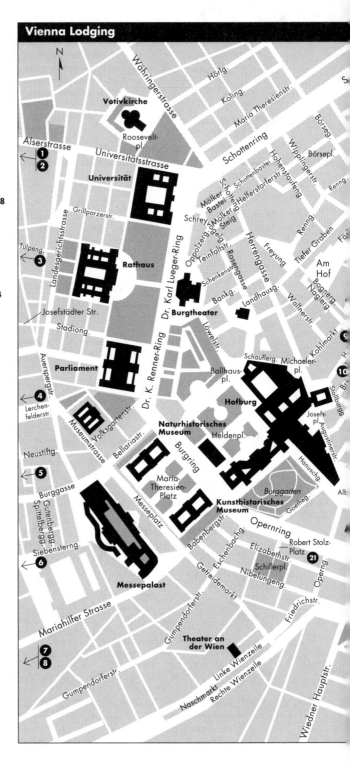

Vienna Lodging

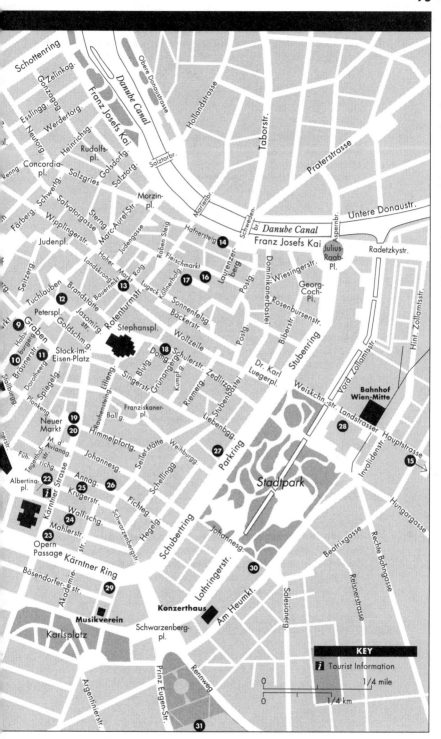

ner Str. 22, A–1010, ☎ 01/514–66–0, ℻ 01/513–2999. 107 rooms. Restaurant, bar. AE, DC, MC, V.

$$$$ ⊞ Bristol. This hotel has one of the finest locations in Europe, on the
★ Ring next to the Opera House. The accent here is on tradition, from the brocaded walls to the Biedermeier period furnishings in the public rooms and many of the bedrooms. The house dates from 1896; renovations have left no trace of the fact that the Bristol was the U.S. military headquarters during the 1945–55 occupation. Like an old shoe, the hotel is seductively comfortable from the moment you arrive. The rooms on the Mahlerstrasse (back) side of the house are quieter, but the view isn't as gratifying as from rooms on the Kärntner Strasse or the Ring. ⊠ *Kärntner Ring 1, A–1010, ☎ 01/515–16–0, ℻ 01/515–16–550. 146 rooms. 2 restaurants, bar, sauna, exercise room. AE, DC, MC, V.*

$$$$ ⊞ Hilton. The public areas have been restyled for a more contemporary look, and the air-conditioned bedrooms are a cut above the usual Hilton standard in size and individuality of decor. The suites are particularly spacious; who could resist breakfast on a suite balcony with a 180-degree view of the city? The upper rooms are quietest; the no-smoking floor is so popular that you need to book at least 2–3 weeks in advance. The airport bus terminal is part of the complex; the U3 and U4 subway lines, trains, and buses stop at the terminal across the street; yet you're within an easy walk of the city center. ⊠ *Am Stadtpark, A–1030, ☎ 01/717–00–0, ℻ 01/713–0691. 600 rooms. 2 restaurants, bar, café, sauna, health club, parking. AE, DC, MC, V.*

$$$$ ⊞ Imperial. The hotel is as much a palace today as when it was completed in 1869. The emphasis is on old Vienna elegance and privacy;
★ heads of state stay here when they're in town. Service is deferential; the rooms have high ceilings and are furnished in classic antiques and Oriental carpets. The bath areas, in contrast, are modern and inviting; many are as large as guest rooms in lesser hotels. The staff will adjust the hardness (or softness) of the beds to your specific wants. Don't overlook the ornate reception rooms to the rear or the formal marble staircase to the right of the lobby area, newly restored to its original elegance. Rooms on the back overlooking the Musikverein are the quietest. ⊠ *Kärntner Ring 16, A–1010, ☎ 01/501–10–0, ℻ 01/501–10–410. 146 rooms. 2 restaurants, piano bar, no-smoking rooms. AE, DC, MC, V.*

$$$$ ⊞ InterContinental. This "first" among Vienna's modern hostelries (1964) has taken on the Viennese patina, and its public rooms, with glittering crystal and red carpets, suggest luxurious comfort. The guest rooms lean more toward the chain's norm, adequate though unexciting, but you will get either a view over the city park across the street (preferred) or over the city itself. The higher you go, the more dramatic the perspective. One of the hotel restaurants is the famed Vier Jahreszeiten. ⊠ *Johannesgasse 28, A–1030, ☎ 01/711–22–0, ℻ 01/713–4489. 492 rooms. 2 restaurants, bar, no-smoking rooms, sauna, exercise room, parking. AE, DC, MC, V.*

$$$$ ⊞ Palais Schwarzenberg. You will know from your first glimpse of
★ the elegant facade that this is no ordinary hotel. Set against a vast formal park, the palace, built in the early 1700s, seems like a country estate, and you can even jog in the garden. Your room will be furnished in genuine (but surprisingly comfortable) antiques, with some of the Schwarzenberg family's art on the walls. The baths are modern, although you might miss a shower curtain. Each room is individual; duplex suites 24 and 25 have upstairs bedrooms and views over the park; Room 26 has exquisite furniture, gorgeous draperies, and a winding stair leading up to the bedroom. If you have any reason to celebrate, do it here; this is the genuine old Vienna at its most elegant. ⊠ *Schwarzenbergpl. 9, A–1030, ☎ 01/798–4515–0, ℻ 01/798–4714. 38 rooms. Restaurant, bar, parking. AE, DC, MC, V.*

$$$$ ☷ **Sacher.** Few hotels in the world have been featured so often in films or in history; you'll sense the musty atmosphere of tradition when you arrive. This is the house where the legendary cigar-smoking Frau Sacher reigned; Emperor Francis Joseph was a regular patron. The Sacher dates from 1876; the patina remains (Room 329 exudes a sense of well-being) despite the elegant new baths installed in 1990. The corridors are a veritable art gallery, and the location directly behind the Opera House could hardly be more central. The staff is particularly accommodating; it has long been an open secret that the concierge at the Sacher can miraculously produce concert and opera tickets when all other possibilities are exhausted. The restaurant is disappointing and overpriced, more average than innovative say many critics, but the Tafelspitz remains legendary. The Café Sacher, of course, is legendary (☞ Exploring Vienna, *above*). ⊠ *Philharmonikerstr. 4, A–1010,* ☎ *01/514–56–0,* 𝔽𝔸𝕏 *01/514–57–810. 116 rooms, 112 with bath. Restaurant, 2 bars, café, no-smoking rooms. AE, DC, MC, V.*

$$$–$$$$ ☷ **Vienna Marriott.** The metal-and-glass exterior gives the impression of a giant greenhouse, borne out by the minijungle of trees and plants in the vast atrium lobby. Some guests object to the perpetual waterfall in the bar-café area, but for Vienna the effect is certainly original. Despite the size, a friendly atmosphere pervades. For a hotel built in 1984, the air-conditioned rooms and suites are unusually spacious and furnished with extra attention to detail; the corner suites (No. 24 on each floor) give a superb view out over the city park opposite. The upper rooms in back offer a panorama of the inner city; these and the rooms on the inner court are the quietest. You're an easy stroll from the city center. ⊠ *Parkring 12A, A–1010,* ☎ *01/515–18–0,* 𝔽𝔸𝕏 *01/515–18–6722. 310 rooms. 2 restaurants, 2 bars, café, no-smoking rooms, pool, sauna, exercise room, parking. AE, DC, MC, V.*

$$$ ☷ **Altstadt.** You're one streetcar stop or a short walk from the main
★ museums in this old-Vienna residential building. Each of the spacious rooms has individual decor focusing mainly on period furniture, with fine wood set against light and blue-gray walls. Upper rooms have views out over the city roofline. The management is particularly personable and helpful. ⊠ *Kirchengasse 41, A–1070,* ☎ *01/526–3399,* 𝔽𝔸𝕏 *01/523–4901. 25 rooms with bath or shower. Bar. AE, DC, MC, V.*

$$$ ☷ **Austria.** This older house, tucked away on a tiny cul-de-sac, offers
★ the ultimate in quiet and is only five minutes' walk from the heart of the city. The high-ceilinged rooms are pleasing in their combination of dark wood and lighter walls; the decor is mixed, with Oriental carpets on many floors. Rooms without full bath are in the $$ category. You'll feel at home here, and the staff will help you find your way around town or get opera or concert tickets. ⊠ *Wolfengasse 3 (Fleischmarkt), A–1010,* ☎ *01/515–23–0,* 𝔽𝔸𝕏 *01/515–23–505. 46 rooms, 42 with bath or shower. AE, DC, MC, V.*

$$$ ☷ **Biedermeier im Sünnhof.** This jewel of a hotel is tucked into a renovated 1820s house that even with all modern facilities still conveys a feeling of old Vienna. The rooms are compact but efficient, the public areas tastefully done in the Biedermeier style, and the service is friendly. The courtyard passageway around which the hotel is built has attracted a number of interesting boutiques and handicrafts shops, but at times there is an excess of coming and going as tour groups are accommodated. It's about a 20-minute walk or a six-minute subway ride to the center of the city. ⊠ *Landstrasser Hauptstr. 28, A–1030,* ☎ *01/716–71–0,* 𝔽𝔸𝕏 *01/716–71–503. 204 rooms. Restaurant, bar, parking. AE, DC, MC, V.*

$$$ ☷ **Europa.** The hotel cannot quite hide its 1957 vintage, and the garish blue-and-pink entry canopies don't help. But the rooms are comfortable without being luxurious, and the baths are modern. You couldn't find a more central location. Rooms on the Neuer Markt side are quieter than those on Kärntner Strasse. ⊠ *Neuer Markt 3/Kärntner Str. 18, A–1010,* ☎ *01/515–94–0,* 🖷 *01/513–8138. 102 rooms. Restaurant, bar, café. AE, DC, MC, V.*

$$$ 🏨 **Fürstenhof.** This turn-of-the-century building, directly across from the Westbahnhof, describes its large rooms as "old-fashioned comfortable," and you reach them via a marvelous hydraulic elevator. Furnishings are a mixed bag. The side rooms are quieter than those in front. Rooms without bath are in the $$ category. ⊠ *Neubaugürtel 4, A–1070,* ☎ *01/523–3267,* 🖷 *01/523–3267–26. 58 rooms, 39 with bath or shower. AE, DC, MC, V.*

$$$ 🏨 **König von Ungarn.** In a 16th-century house in the shadow of St. Stephen's Cathedral, this hotel began catering to court nobility in 1815. (Mozart lived in the house next door when he wrote *The Marriage of Figaro*). A superb redesign turned it into a modern hotel, and you could hardly hope for a happier result. The hotel radiates charm, from the greenery in the wood-paneled atrium lobby to the antiques of various periods and the pine country furnishings in the bedrooms. The rooms are not overly large, but each is individually and appealingly decorated. Those in back are somewhat quieter. Insist on written confirmation of bookings. ⊠ *Schulerstr. 10, A–1010,* ☎ *01/515–84–0,* 🖷 *01/515–84–8. 32 rooms. Restaurant, bar. DC, MC, V.*

$$$ 🏨 **Mailberger Hof.** This 14th-century house on a pedestrian street just
★ off the Kärntner Strasse was once a Baroque town palace. In 1976 it was turned into an intimate family-run hotel with great success and is a favorite of stars from the nearby State Opera House. The rooms are so attractively decorated it's hard to imagine you're in a hotel; colors and furniture have been coordinated without fussiness to create a setting you won't want to leave. You'll have to book about a month ahead to get a room. ⊠ *Annagasse 7, A–1010,* ☎ *01/512–0641,* 🖷 *01/512–0641–10. 40 rooms, 5 apartments with kitchenettes (available by month). Restaurant. AE, MC, V.*

$$$ 🏨 **Opernring.** This establishment's spacious, comfortable rooms, with
★ homelike furnishings and bright, attractive tiled baths, are only one reason guests come back. The unusually friendly, personal attention of the owner, Susie Riedl, makes you feel as though you're the only guest. The hotel has Best Western affiliation. The rooms on the inner courtyard are sunny and quieter but have a dreary outlook; disregard the traffic noise (there's no air-conditioning, so you may want the windows open) and enjoy the extraordinary view of the Opera House, diagonally across the Ring. ⊠ *Opernring 11, A–1010,* ☎ *01/587–5518,* 🖷 *01/587–5518–29. 35 rooms. AE, DC, MC, V.*

$$$ 🏨 **Wandl.** The restored facade identifies a 300-year-old house that has been in family hands as a hotel since 1854. You couldn't find a better location, tucked behind St. Peter's Church, just off the Graben. The hallways are punctuated by cheerful, bright openings along the glassed-in inner court. The rooms are modern, but some are a bit plain and charmless, despite parquet flooring and red accents. Ask for one of the rooms done in period furniture, with decorated ceilings and gilt mirrors; they're palatial, if slightly overdone. ⊠ *Peterspl. 9, A–1010,* ☎ *01/534–55–0,* 🖷 *01/534–55–77. 138 rooms. Bar. No credit cards.*

$$–$$$ 🏨 **Hotel-Pension Zipser.** This 1904 house, with an ornate facade and
★ gilt-trimmed coat of arms, is one of the city's better hotel values. It's in a fascinating district of small cafés, shops, jazz clubs, and excellent restaurants, yet within steps of the J streetcar line direct to the city center. The rooms are newly redone in browns and beiges, with modern furniture to match; the baths are elegant and well lit. The balconies of some of the back rooms overlook tree-filled neighborhood courtyards. The friendly staff will help get theater and concert tickets. Book ahead

a month or two to be sure of a room. ⊠ *Lange Gasse 49, A–1080,* ☎ *222/404–54–0,* 🕾 *01/408–5266–13. 47 rooms. Coffee shop, parking. AE, DC, MC, V.*

$$–$$$ 🏨 **Kärntnerhof.** Behind the "Schönbrunn yellow" facade of this ele-
★ gant 100-year-old house on a quiet cul-de-sac lies one of the friendliest small hotels in the center of the city. Don't let the dated and uninteresting lobby put you off; take the gorgeously restored Art Deco elevator to the rooms upstairs. They have been done over in either brown or white reproduction furniture, and the baths are modern. The staff is adept at getting theater and concert tickets for "sold out" performances and happily puts together special outing programs for guests. For a small fee, parking can be arranged in the abbey courtyard next door. ⊠ *Grashofgasse 4, A–1010,* ☎ *01/512–1923–0,* 🕾 *01/513–2228–33. 43 rooms. AE, DC, MC, V.*

$$–$$$ 🏨 **Pension Aclon.** On the upper floors of a gray but gracious older building just off the Graben (with the famous Café Hawelka downstairs), this family-run hostelry (complete with sheepdog) is attractively done up in old-Vienna style, with lots of plants, 19th-century furniture, dark woods, and elegant marble baths. Rooms on the inner court are quieter, though the street in front carries no through traffic. New rooms were added in 1996, the smaller ones in modern decor, the larger in period Biedermeier style. ⊠ *Dorotheergasse 6–8, A–1010,* ☎ *01/512–7940–0,* 🕾 *01/513–8751. 32 rooms, 21 with bath or shower. No credit cards.*

$$–$$$ 🏨 **Pension Nossek.** This family-run establishment on the upper floors of a 19th-century office and apartment building lies at the heart of the pedestrian and shopping area. The rooms have high ceilings and are eclectically but comfortably furnished; those on the front have a magnificent view of the Graben. Do as the many regular guests do and book early. ⊠ *Graben 17, A–1010,* ☎ *01/533–7041–0,* 🕾 *01/535–3646. 26 rooms, 22 with bath or shower. No credit cards.*

$$–$$$ 🏨 **Pension Pertschy.** Housed in a former town palace just off the Graben,
★ this pension is as central as you can get. A massive arched portal leads to a yellow courtyard, around which the house is built. Anybody who has stayed in Room 220 with its stylish old blue ceramic stove (just for show) would be happy again with nothing less. Most rooms are spacious with antique furniture of mixed periods, but even the small single rooms are charming. Baths are satisfactory. Use the elevator, but don't overlook the palatial grand staircase. ⊠ *Habsburgergasse 5, A-1010,* ☎ *01/534–49–0,* 🕾 *01/534–49–49. 43 rooms. DC, MC, V.*

$$ 🏨 **Ibis Wien.** About an eight-minute walk from the Westbahnhof and easily identifiable by its bronze metal exterior, the Ibis offers its standard chain accommodations in contemporary air-conditioned rooms that are compact, complete, and very good value. The blue and blue-gray accents are refreshing against the white room walls. The rooms on the shady Wallgasse side are more comfortable; those on the upper floors have a superb panoramic view. ⊠ *Mariahilfer Gürtel 22–24/Wallgasse 33, A–1060,* ☎ *01/599–98–0,* 🕾 *01/597–9090. 341 rooms. Restaurant, weinstube, parking. AE, DC, MC, V.*

$$ 🏨 **Pension Baroness.** One flight up, behind the drab facade of this turn-of-the-century apartment house, are comfortable rooms with contemporary furnishings, many quite spacious and many completely renovated in 1990. The front rooms are noisy, but the nearby streetcar stop is a convenience. ⊠ *Lange Gasse 61, A–1080,* ☎ *01/405–1061,* 🕾 *01/405–1061–61. 38 rooms. Bar. MC, V.*

$$ 🏨 **Pension Christina.** This quiet pension, just steps from Schwedenplatz and the Danube Canal, offers mainly smallish modern rooms, warmly decorated with attractive dark-wood furniture set off against beige walls.

⊠ *Hafnersteig 7, A–1010,* ☎ *01/533–2961–0,* ℻ *01/533–2961–11. 33 rooms. MC, V.*

$$ ⊞ **Pension City.** You'll be on historic ground here: In 1791 the play-
★ wright Franz Grillparzer was born in the house that then stood here; a
bust and plaques in the entryway commemorate him. On the second
floor of the present 100-year-old house, located about three minutes away
from St. Stephen's Cathedral, the rooms are newly outfitted in a suc-
cessful mix of modern and 19th-century antique furniture against white
walls. The baths are small but complete. ⊠ *Bauernmarkt 10, A–1010,*
☎ *01/533–9521,* ℻ *01/535–5216. 19 rooms. AE, DC, MC, V.*

$$ ⊞ **Pension Suzanne.** This 1950s building on a side street is just steps
★ away from the Opera House. The rooms are smallish but comfortably
furnished in 19th-century Viennese style; baths are modern, although
short on shelf space. Suzanne has regular guests who book months in
advance, so you'd be well advised to do the same. ⊠ *Walfischgasse 4,
A–1010,* ☎ *01/513–2507–0,* ℻ *01/513–2500. 19 rooms, 7 apartments with kitchenette. AE, DC, MC, V.*

$$ ⊞ **Rathaus.** This friendly hotel, under the same management as the
★ nearby Zipser, is in a 1908 building that has been attractively reno-
vated: The spacious rooms have contemporary furnishings. You'll be
within an easy walk of the main museums and close to public trans-
portation. ⊠ *Lange Gasse 13, A–1080,* ☎ *01/406–4302,* ℻ *01/408–
4272. 40 rooms. Garage. No credit cards.*

$$ ⊞ **Zur Wiener Staatsoper.** The hotel's florid facade, with oversize torsos supporting its upper bays, is pure 19th-century Ringstrasse style.
The rooms are less well defined in style, small yet comfortable. The
baths are adequate. And you'll find yourself within steps of the Opera
House and Kärntner Strasse. ⊠ *Krugerstr. 11, A–1010,* ☎ *01/513–
1274–0,* ℻ *01/513–1274–15. 22 rooms. AE, MC, V.*

$ ⊞ **Kugel.** This older but recently redecorated hotel halfway between
★ the Westbahnhof and the city center has rooms attractively furnished
in lighter woods and contrasting textiles. The newer baths are elegantly
tiled. Don't let the less appealing breakfast-TV room and reception areas
put you off; the rooms themselves are in invitingly pleasant contrast.
The staff is helpful and friendly. ⊠ *Siebensterngasse 43, A–1070,* ☎
01/523–3355, ℻ *01/523–1678. 38 rooms, 17 with bath or shower.
No credit cards.*

$ ⊞ **Pension Wild.** This friendly, family-run pension on several floors of
★ an older apartment house draws a liberal, relaxed, younger crowd to
one of the best values in town. Rooms are simple but modern, with
light-wood furniture and pine-paneled ceilings. Each wing has a kitchenette. The breakfast room/TV lounge is bright and attractive, and you're
close to the major museums. ⊠ *Lange Gasse 1, A–1080,* ☎ *01/406–
5174,* ℻ *01/402–2168. 14 rooms without bath. Sauna, exercise room.
AE, DC, MC, V.*

Seasonal Hotels

Student residences, which operate as hotels July–September, can provide excellent bargains in the inexpensive ($) category. They have sin-
gle or double rooms, all (unless noted) with bath or shower. You can
book by calling any of the Rosenhotels (☎ 01/911–4910, ℻ 01/910–
0269) or central booking for the student residence hotels of the Albertina group (☎ 01/521–7493, ℻ 01/521–1968). Unless otherwise
noted, credit cards are accepted.

⊞ **Academia.** Among this group, a fairly luxurious choice. ⊠ *Pfeilgasse 3a, A–1080,* ☎ *01/401–7655,* ℻ *01/401–7620. 368 rooms.
Restaurant, bar.*

⚐ **Accordia.** Belonging to the Albertina group, this is the newest of the seasonal hotels and is fairly close to the center. ⊠ *Grosse Schiffgasse 12, A-1020,* ☎ *01/212-1668. 95 rooms with shower.*

⚐ **Ambiente.** This accommodation is an Albertina member near the U.S. embassy, a quiet location. ⊠ *Boltzmanngasse 10, A-1090,* ☎ *01/310-3130-0. 50 rooms with shower.*

⚐ **Auge Gottes.** For bargain hunters, this choice is among the very cheapest. ⊠ *Nussdorfer Str. 75, A-1090,* ☎ *01/319-4488. 79 rooms without bath.*

⚐ **Avis.** This option even features its own restaurant and bar. ⊠ *Pfeilgasse 4, A-1080,* ☎ *01/408-3445,* FAX *01/405-6397. 72 rooms. Restaurant, bar. AE, MC, V.*

⚐ **Haus Technik.** An Albertina member, this place is fairly close to the center. ⊠ *Schäffergasse 2, A-1040,* ☎ *01/587-6560-0. 104 rooms with shower. Restaurant, parking.*

⚐ **Rosenhotel Burgenland 3.** For weary travelers, the restaurant is a boon, but tips the house into the $$ category. ⊠ *Bürgerspitalgasse 19, A-1060,* ☎ *01/597-9347,* FAX *01/597-9475-9. 140 rooms. Restaurant, bar, parking. AE, MC, V.*

⚐ **Studentenheim der Musikhochschule.** This choice offers the most central location of any of the seasonal hotels, in the heart of the city. ⊠ *Johannesgasse 8, A-1010,* ☎ *01/514-84-0,* FAX *01/514-84-49. 85 rooms, some with bath or shower.*

NIGHTLIFE AND THE ARTS

The Arts

Dance

Other than ballet companies in the opera and Volksoper, Vienna offers nothing in the way of dance. Under new directors, the ballet evenings that are on the opera house schedules (☎ 01/514-44-0) are now much improved, and finally up to international standards.

Film

Film has enjoyed a recent renaissance, with viewers seeking original rather than German-dubbed versions. Look for films in English at **Burgkino** (⊠ Opernring 19, ☎ 01/587-8406)—in summer, Carol Reed's classic *The Third Man* with Orson Welles is a regular feature; **de France** (⊠ Schottenring 5/Hessgasse 7, ☎ 01/317-5236); **English Cinema Haydn** (⊠ Mariahilfer Str. 57, ☎ 01/587-2262); **Top-Kino** (⊠ Rahlgasse 1, ☎ 01/587-5557); and **Votiv-Kino** (⊠ Währinger Str. 12, ☎ 01/317-3571). Art and experimental films are shown at the **Stadtkino** (⊠ Schwarzenbergpl. 8, ☎ 01/712-6276). The film schedule in the daily newspaper *Der Standard* lists foreign-language films (*Fremdsprachige Filme*) separately. In film listings, *OmU* means original language with German subtitles.

The **Filmmuseum** in the Albertina shows original-version classics like *Birth of a Nation, A Night at the Opera,* and *Harvey* and organizes retrospectives of the works of artists, directors, and producers. The monthly program is posted outside, and guest memberships (AS40 per day) are available. It is closed July, August, and September. ⊠ *Augustinerstr. 1,* ☎ *01/533-7054.* 🎟 *AS45.* 🕙 *Screenings Mon.–Sat. at 6 and 8.*

Galleries

A host of smaller galleries centers around the Singerstrasse and Grünangergasse, although there are many more scattered about the city.

Music

Vienna is one of the main music centers of the world. Contemporary music gets its hearing, but it's the hometown standards—the works of Beethoven, Brahms, Haydn, Mozart, and Schubert—that draw the Viennese public. A monthly program, put out by the city tourist board and available at any travel agency or hotel, gives a general overview of what's going on in opera, concerts, jazz, theater, and galleries, and similar information is posted on billboards and fat advertising columns around the city.

Vienna is home to four full symphony orchestras: the great Vienna Philharmonic, the outstanding Vienna Symphony, the broadcasting service's ORF Symphony Orchestra, and the Niederösterreichische Tonkünstler. There are also hundreds of smaller groups, from world-famous trios to chamber orchestras.

The most important concert halls are in the buildings of the Gesellschaft der Musikfreunde, called the **Musikverein** (⌷ Dumbastr. 3; ticket office at Karlspl. 6, ☏ 01/505–8190, ℻ 01/505–9409) and the **Konzerthaus** (⌷ Lothringerstr. 20, ☏ 01/712–1211, ℻ 01/712–2872). Both houses contain several halls; tickets bear their names: **Grosser Musikvereinssaal** or **Brahmssaal** in the Musikverein; **Grosser Konzerthaussaal, Mozartsaal,** or **Schubertsaal** in the Konzerthaus.

Concerts are also given in the small **Figarosaal** of Palais Palffy (⌷ Josefspl. 6, ☏ 01/512–5681–0), the concert studio of the broadcasting station (⌷ Argentinierstr. 30A, ☏ 01/501–01–8881), and the **Bösendorfersaal** (⌷ Graf Starhemberg-Gasse 14, ☏ 01/504–6651). Students of the music school regularly give class recitals in the school's concert halls during the academic year; look for announcements posted outside for dates and times (⌷ Seilerstätte 26 and Johannesgasse 8, ☏ 01/588–06–0).

Although the **Vienna Festival** (☏ 01/589–22–0), held early May to mid-June, wraps up the primary season, the summer musical scene is bright, with something scheduled every day. Outdoor symphony concerts are performed weekly in the vast arcaded courtyard of the Rathaus (entrance on Friedrich Schmidt-Pl.). You can catch musical events in the Volksgarten and in the St. Augustine, St. Michael's, Minorite, and University churches; at Schönbrunn Palace they're outside in the courtyard as well as part of an evening guided tour.

Mozart concerts are performed in 18th-century costume and powdered wigs in the large hall, or Mozartsaal, of the Konzerthaus (☞ *above*); operetta concerts are held in the Musikverein (☞ *above*), and the Hofburg and Palais Ferstel. There are no set dates, so inquire through hotels and travel and ticket agencies for availabilities. Note, however, that some of these concerts, including intermission lasting possibly an hour, are rather expensive affairs put on for tourists, and occasionally of disappointing quality.

Church music, the Mass sung in Latin, can be heard Sunday mornings during the main season at **St. Stephen's**; in the Franciscan church, **St. Michael's**; the **Universitätskirche**; and, above all, in the **Augustinerkirche.** The Friday and Saturday newspapers carry details. St. Stephen's also has organ concerts most Wednesday evenings from early May to late November.

The **Vienna Boys' Choir** (Wiener Sängerknaben) sing Mass at 9:15 AM in the **Hofburgkapelle** (⌷ Hofburg, Schweizer Hof, ☏ 01/533–9927) from mid-September to late June. Written requests for seats (standing room is free but limited) should be made at least eight weeks in advance to Hofmusikkapelle Hofburg, A–1010 Vienna. You will be sent a reservation card, which you exchange at the box office (in the Hofburg courtyard) for your tickets. Tickets are also sold at ticket agencies and at the box office every Friday at 5 PM, but you should be in line by 4:30. Each person is allowed a maximum of two tickets. If you've missed the Vienna Choirboys at the Sunday mass, you may be able to hear them in a more popular program in the Konzerthaus.

Most theaters now reserve tickets by telephone against a credit card; you pick up your ticket at the box office with no surcharge. The same applies to concert tickets. Ticket agencies charge a minimum 22% markup and generally deal in the more expensive seats. Expect to pay (or tip) a hotel porter or concierge at least as much as a ticket-agency markup for hard-to-get tickets. You might try **Vienna Ticket Service** (⊠ Postfach 160, A–1043, ☎ 01/587–9843–0, FAX 01/587–9844), **Carta Austria** (⊠ Goldschmiedgasse 10, ☎ 01/536–01), **American Express** (⊠ Kärntner Str. 21–23, A–1015, ☎ 01/515–40–0, FAX 01/515–40–70), **Kartenbüro Flamm** (⊠ Kärntner Ring 3, A–1010, ☎ 01/512–4225), or **Cosmos** (⊠ Kärntner Ring 15, A–1010, ☎ 01/515–33–0, FAX 01/513–4147). Tickets to musicals and some events including the Vienna Festival are available at the "Salettl" gazebo kiosk alongside the Opera House on the Kärntner Strasse. Tickets to that night's musicals are reduced by half after 2 PM (☎ 01/588–85).

Opera and Operetta

The **Staatsoper** (State Opera House, ⊠ Opernring 2, ☎ 01/51444–2656 or 01/514–44–0), one of the world's great opera houses, has been the scene of countless musical triumphs and a center of unending controversies over how it should be run and by whom. (When Lorin Maazel was unceremoniously dumped as head of the Opera not many years ago, he pointed out that the house had done the same thing to Gustav Mahler a few decades earlier.) A performance takes place virtually every night from September through June, drawing on the vast repertoire of the house, with emphasis on Mozart and Verdi. (Opera here is nearly always performed in the original language, even Russian.) Guided tours of the Opera House are held year-round. The opera in Vienna is a dressy event and even designer jeans are not socially acceptable. Evening dress and black tie, though not compulsory, are recommended for first-night performances and in the better seats.

Light opera and operetta are performed at the **Volksoper** (⊠ Währingerstr. 78, ☎ 01/51444–3318) outside the city center at Währingerstrasse and Währinger Gürtel (third stop on Streetcar 41, 42, or 43, from "downstairs" at Schottentor, U2, on the Ring). Prices here are significantly lower than in the main opera, and performances can be every bit as rewarding. Mozart is sung here, too, but in German, the language of the house.

You'll find musicals and operetta also at the **Theater an der Wien** (⊠ Linke Wienzeile 6, ☎ 01/588–30–0), the **Raimundtheater** (⊠ Wallgasse 18, ☎ 01/599–77–0), and **Ronacher** (⊠ Seilerstätte/Himmelpfortgasse, ☎ 01/514–02). Opera and operetta are performed on an irregular schedule at the **Kammeroper** (⊠ Fleischmarkt 24, ☎ 01/513–6702).

In summer, look for outdoor opera performances on the grounds of Schönbrunn Palace (☞ Exploring Vienna, *above*); Mozart's *Don Giovanni* here is a memorable experience. The 1996 *Magic Flute* is likely to be held over to 1997. Book early, since the Schönbrunn performances are regular sellouts. There's standing room available. Also in summer, light opera or operetta performances by the Kammeroper ensemble are given in the exquisite **Schlosstheater** at Schönbrunn. Ticket agencies will have details.

Tickets to the state theaters (**Opera, Volksoper, Burgtheater,** or **Akademietheater**) can be charged against your credit card. You can order them by phoning up to a month before the performance (☎ 01/513–1513) or buy them in person up to a month in advance at the *Theaterkassen,* the central box office. ⊠ *Theaterkassen, back of Opera, Hanuschgasse 3, in courtyard,* ☎ *01/514–44–2959 or 01/514–44–2960.* ⊙ *Weekdays 8–6, Sat. 9–2, Sun. and holidays 9–noon. Information and ticket office for Opera, Volksoper,* ⊠ *Kärntner Str. 40, Staatsoper arcade,),* ☎ *01/514–44–2958.* ⊙ *Weekdays 10–1 hr before performance, Sat. 10–noon.*

You can also write ahead for tickets. The nearest Austrian National Tourist Office can give you a schedule of performances and a ticket order form. Send the form (no payment is required) to the ticket office (⊠ Kartenvorverkauf Bundestheaterverband, Goethegasse 1, A–1010 Vienna), which will mail you a reservation card; when you get to Vienna, take the card to the main box office to pick up and pay for your tickets.

Theater

Vienna's **Burgtheater** (⊠ Dr. Karl Lueger-Ring 2, A–1010 Vienna; *see* state theaters, *above,* for ticket details) is one of the leading German-language theaters of the world. Its current director has replaced the German classics with more modern and controversial pieces. The Burg's smaller house, the **Akademietheater** (⊠ Lisztstr. 1), draws on much the same group of actors, for classical and modern plays. Both houses are closed during July and August.

The **Theater in der Josefstadt** (⊠ Josefstädterstr. 26, ☎ 01/402–5127, FAX 01/402–7631–60) stages classical and modern works year-round in the house once run by the great producer and teacher Max Reinhardt. The **Volkstheater** (⊠ Neustiftgasse 1, ☎ 01/523–3501–265) presents dramas, comedies, and folk plays. The **Kammerspiele** (⊠ Rotenturmstr. 20, ☎ 01/533–2833) does modern plays.

For **theater in English** (mainly standard plays), head for **Vienna's English Theater** (⊠ Josefsgasse 12, ☎ 01/402–1260). Another option is the equally good **International Theater** (⊠ Porzellangasse 8, ☎ 01/319–6272).

Nightlife

Balls

The gala Vienna evening you've always dreamed about can become a reality: among the many balls given during the Carnival season, several welcome the public—at a wide range of prices (at press time; subject to change). You can book tickets with a Eurocheck or through hotel concierges; there are also ticket agencies, including ATT (⊠ 6 Josefspl., A–1010, ☎ 0222/5124466, FAX 0222/5123355). Here is a run-down of some of the most popular Viennese balls. For a background on these festive events, *see* Stepping-Out in Three-Quarter Time *in* Pleasures and Pastimes, *above.*

Blumenball (⊠ Stadtgartenamt, 2B Am Heurmarkt, A–1030, ☎ 0222/71116, Extension 97247), or Florists Ball, January 12 at the Rathaus. Tickets are AS374. **Philharmonic Ball** (⊠ 12 Philharmoniker Bösendorferstr., A–1010, ☎ 0222/5056525), January 18 in the Goldmann Saal of the Vienna Musikverein; tickets are AS1305 (plus AS545 for a seat at a table). **Opera Ball** (⊠ 1 Opernballbüro Goethegasse, A–1010, ☎ 0222/51440), February 15 at the Opera House; tickets are AS2942 (plus AS2182 for a seat at a table, AS171 for standing room on stage, AS160 to AS749 for balcony seats). **Kaffeesiederball** (⌧ Club der Wiener Kaffeehausebesitzer Stubenring 8-10, A–1010, ☎ 0222/51450241), or Coffee Brewers' Ball, February 14 at the Hofburg Palace; tickets are AS706 (seats at tables from AS160). **Bonbon Ball** (⌧ Zentralverband der Schwarenhändler Österreichs Strasse, A–1020, ☎ 0222/3303121), February 16 at the Hofburg; tickets are AS492 (plus AS214 for a seat at a table).

Bars and Lounges

Vienna has blossomed in recent years with delightful and sophisticated bars. Head for the "Bermuda Triangle," an area in the First District roughly defined by Judengasse, Seitenstättengasse, Rabensteig, and Franz-Josefs-Kai. Here you will find dozens of bars, both intimate and large, like **Salzamt, Krah-Krah,** and **Ma Pitom.** Around Concordiaplatz and in Heinrichsgasse, **Puerto** and **Domicil** are highly popular. Back toward Stephansplatz, on Bäckerstrasse, check out **Weinorgel, Oswald & Kalb;** on Blutgasse, **Chamäleon;** on Singerstrasse, the **Galerie Bar. The American Bar** on Kärntner Durchgang has an original Adolf Loos turn-of-the-century interior.

Cabaret

Cabaret has a long tradition in Vienna. **Simpl** (⌧ Wollzeile 36, ☎ 01/512–4742) continues earning its reputation for barbed political wit but has had to give way to some newcomers at **K&K** (⌧ Linke Wienzeile 4, ☎ 01/587–2275) and **Kabarett Niedermair** (⌧ Lenaugasse 1A, ☎ 01/408–4492). To get much from any of these, you'll need good German with some Viennese vernacular as well plus knowledge of local affairs.

Casinos

Try your luck at the casino **Cercle Wien** (⌧ Kärntner Str. 41, ☎ 01/512–4836) in a former town palace redone in dark wood paneling and millions of twinkle lights. Games include roulette and blackjack. You'll need your passport for entry identification.

Discos

The disco scene is big in Vienna, and the crowd seems to follow the leader from one "in" spot to the next. A few continually draw full houses. Try **Atrium** (⌧ Schwarzenbergpl. 10, ☎ 01/505–3594); **Queen Anne,** still very much "in" (⌧ Johannesgasse 12, ☎ 01/512–0203); and **U–4,** popular with a mixed group, early thirties and younger (⌧ Schönbrunner Str. 222, ☎ 01/858–3185).

Jazz Clubs

Vienna is increasingly good for jazz, though places where it can be heard tend to come and go. Nothing gets going before 9 PM. Try **Jazzland** (⌧ Franz-Josefs-Kai 29, ☎ 01/533–2575); **Papa's Tapas** (⌧ Schwarzenbergpl. 10, ☎ 01/505–0311); and **Roter Engel** (⌧ Rabensteig 5, ☎ 01/535–4105), all of which offer live groups almost nightly. **Porgy & Bess** (⌧ Spiegelgasse 2, ☎ 01/512–8438–0) has gained a reputation for good jazz, although the future of the club is uncertain.

Nightclubs

Vienna has no real nightclub tradition, although there are a number of clubs in town. Most of the ones with floor shows are horribly expensive and not very good; some are outright tourist traps. The two where you run the least risk are **Casanova,** where singles can sit reasonably peacefully at the upstairs bar (⌧ Dorotheergasse 6, ☎ 01/512–9845), and upscale **Moulin Rouge** (⌧ Walfischgasse 11, ☎ 01/512–2130). The leading spots for dancing are the **Eden Bar,** which always has a live band and is for the well-heeled mature crowd (⌧ Liliengasse 2, ☎ 01/512–7450); **Chattanooga,** which often has a live band and draws a younger crowd (⌧ Graben 29, ☎ 01/533–5000); and **Volksgarten** (⌧ Volksgarten, Burgring 1, ☏ 01/533–0518–0), where a mixed younger set comes, particularly in summer for outdoor dancing.

OUTDOOR ACTIVITIES AND SPORTS

Participant Sports

Bicycling

Look for the special pathways either in red brick or marked with a stylized cyclist in yellow. Note and observe the special traffic signals at some intersections. You can take a bike on the subway (except during rush hours) for half fare, but only in cars with a blue shield on the door, and only on stairs or elevators with the "bike" shield, not the escalators. The city tourist office has a brochure in German with useful cycling maps, plus a leaflet "See Vienna by Bike" with tips in English. At most bookstores you can purchase a cycling map of Vienna put out by a local cycling organization known as ARGUS (⊠ Frankenberggasse 11, ☏ 01/505–8435). You can rent a bike starting at about AS40 per hour, leaving your passport or other identification as a deposit.

Rent a bike year-round at the Westbahnhof, Wien Nord (Praterstern), or Floridsdorf rail stations, or pick up a bike at **Radverleih Hochschaubahn,** mid-March through October (⊠ Prater amusement park, by Hochschaubahn, bear slightly right after you pass wheel, ☏ 12/729–5888); at **Radverleih Praterstern,** April–October (⊠ street level under Praterstern North rail station); or at **Hammermayer/Radsport Nussdorf** (⊠ Donaupromenade, next to Nussdorf DDSG dock, ☏ 01/374598). Other rental locations are available from tourist offices.

Boating

Both the **Alte Donau** (Old Danube), a series of lakes to the north of the main stream, and the **Neue Donau,** on the north side of the Donauinsel (the artificial island in the river), offer good waters for paddleboats, rowboats, kayaks, sailboats, and windsurfing. The Danube itself is somewhat fast-moving for anything but kayaks. Rent boats from **Auzinger Boote** (⊠ Laberlweg 22, ☏ 01/235788), **Karl Hofbauer** (⊠ Neue Donau at Reichsbrücke; ⊠ Obere Alte Donau 185, ☏ 01/204–3435–0), **Eppel** (⊠ Wagramer Str. 48, ☏ 01/235168), **Irzl** (⊠ Florian Berndl-Gasse 33 and 34, ☏ 01/203–6743), and **Newrkla** (⊠ Obere Alte Donau, ☏ 01/386105). For details about sailing and sailing events, check with **Haus des Sports** (⊠ Prinz-Eugen-Str. 12, ☏ 01/505–3742–0).

Golf

The top in-town golf course is at **Freudenau** in the Prater (☏ 01/728–9564–0, ℻ 01/728–5379). But this 18-hole par-70 course is so popular from April to November, even with the weekday AS800 fee, that you'll probably need to be invited or have an introduction from a member to play; on weekends, membership or an invitation is required. Alternatives are **Golfclub Am Wienerberg,** a 9-hole, par 35/70 course on the south side of Vienna, open March–Nov. (⊠ Gutheil Schoder-Gasse 9, ☏ 01/66123–0); **Brunn am Gebirge,** an 18-hole par-72 course about 10 kilometers (6 miles) to the southwest (⊠ Rennweg 50, ☏ 02236/33711, ℻ 02236/33863); **Ebreichsdorf,** 27 kilometers (17 miles) south of Vienna, an 18-hole par-72 course (⊠ Schlossallee 1, ☏ 02254/73888, ℻ 02254/73888–13); **Colony Club Gutenhof,** 10 kilometers (6 miles) to the southeast, with two courses of 18 holes, par 73 each, at Himberg (⊠ Gutenhof, ☏ 02235/87055–0, ℻ 02235/87055–14); or **Hainburg,** 50 kilometers (31 miles) east of Vienna, with 18 holes, par 72 (⊠ Auf der Heide, ☏ 02165/62628, ℻ 02165/65331); but these, too, are generally overbooked. Weekdays, of course, will be best for any of the courses, particularly those farther from Vienna.

Health and Fitness Clubs

Try **Fitness Center Stadtpark** (⊠ Kursalon, Johannesgasse 33, ☎ 01/714–7775), **Fitness Center Harris** (⊠ Niebelungengasse 7, ☎ 01/587–3710), or **Zimmermann Fitness** (⊠ Kaiserstr. 43, ☎ 01/526–2000; ⊠ Kreuzgasse 18, ☎ 01/406–4625). (The latter club is for women only.)

Ice Skating

The **Wiener Eislaufverein** (⊠ Lothringer Str. 22, behind InterContinental Hotel, ☎ 01/713–6353–0) has outdoor skating with skate rentals, October through March. Weekends are crowded. For indoor skating, check the **Wiener Stadthalle** (⊠ Vogelweidpl. 14, U6 to Urban Loritz-Pl., ☎ 01/981–00–0).

Jogging

Jogging paths run alongside the Danube Canal, and runners also frequent the Stadtpark and the tree-lined route along the Ring, particularly the Parkring stretch. Farther afield, in the Second District, the Prater Hauptallee, 4 kilometers (2½ miles) from Praterstern to the Lusthaus, is a favorite.

Riding

Splendid bridle paths crisscross the Prater park. To hire a mount, contact the **Reitclub Donauhof** (⊠ Hafenzufahrtstr. 63, ☎ 01/728–3646 or 01/728–9716), or **Reitclub Prater/Reitschule Sylvia Kühnert** (⊠ Dammhaufen 62, ☎ 01/728–1335).

Skiing

Nearby slopes such as **Hohe Wand** (Bus 49B from the Hütteldorf stop of the U4 subway), west of the city in the 14th District, offer limited skiing, with a ski lift and man-made snow when the heavens refuse, but serious Viennese skiers (that includes nearly everybody) will take a train or bus out to nearby Niederösterreich (Lower Austria), with the area around the **Semmering** (about an hour from the city) one of the favorite locations for a quick outing.

Swimming

Vienna has at least one pool for each of its 23 districts; most are indoor pools, but some locations have an outdoor pool as well. An indoor favorite is **Rogner's,** complete with water slide (⊠ Strohbachgasse 7–9, ☎ 01/587–0844–0). For a less formal environment, head for the swimming areas of the **Alte Donau** or the **Donauinsel.** The pools and the Alte Donau (paid admission) will be filled on hot summer weekends, so the Donauinsel can be a surer bet. Some beach areas are shallow and suitable for children, but the Donauinsel has no lifeguards, though there are rescue stations for emergencies. Changing areas are few, lockers nonexistent, so don't take valuables. And don't be tempted to jump into the Danube Canal; the water is definitely not for swimming, nor is the Danube itself, because of heavy undertows and a powerful current.

The city has information on all places to swim; contact City Hall (⊠ Rathaus, Friedrich Schmidt-Pl., ☎ 01/4000–5). Ask for directions to reach the following:

Donauinsel Nord. This huge free recreation area has a children's section and nude bathing. **Donauinsel Süd** is free and offers good swimming and boating and a nude bathing area. It's harder to get to and less crowded than other areas, and food facilities are limited. **Gänsehäufel.** This bathing island in the Alte Donau (☎ 01/235392) has paid admission, lockers, changing rooms, children's wading pools, topless and nude areas, and restaurants; on sunny weekends, it's likely to be full by 11 AM or earlier. **Krapfenwaldbad** is an outdoor park/pool tucked among the trees on the edge of the Vienna Woods (☎ 01/321501), full of Vienna's beautiful people and singles. Get there early on a sunny Sunday or you won't get in. **Stadionbad.** This huge sports complex is popular with the younger crowd; go early. There is no direct transportation; take the Bus 80B from U3/Schlachthausgasse to the Hauptallee stop, or, for the fun of it, ride the miniature railway (*Liliputbahn*) from behind the Ferris wheel in the Prater amusement park to the Stadion station and walk the rest of the way (✉ Prater, Marathonweg, ☎ 01/720–2102).

Tennis

Though Vienna has plenty of courts, they'll be booked solid. Try anyway; your hotel may have good connections. **Sportservice Wien-Sport** (✉ Bacherpl. 14, ☎ 01/545–1201–0) operates a central court-booking service (100 courts in summer, three halls in winter), and **Vereinigte Tennisanlagen** (✉ Prater Hauptallee, ☎ 01/728–1811) has courts in other locations as well. Or you can try **Tennisplätze Arsenal** (✉ Arsenalstr. 1, by Südbahnhof, ☎ 01/798–2132; ✉ Faradaygasse 4, ☎ 01/798–7265; ✉ Gudrunstr. 31, ☎ 01/602–1521), which has 57 sand courts; **Tennisplätze Stadionbad** (✉ Prater Hauptallee, ☎ 01/720–2070); or **Wiener Eislaufverein** (✉ Lothringer Str. 22, behind Inter-Continental Hotel, ☎ 01/713–6353–0).

Top businessmen and political leaders head to **Tennis Point Vienna** (✉ Nottendorfergasse/Baumgasse, ☎ 01/799–9997) for the 10 indoor courts, squash, sauna, and an outstanding fitness studio; there is a bar and an excellent and remarkably reasonable restaurant as well.

Spectator Sports

Football (Soccer)

Matches are played mainly in the **Ernst–Happel–Stadion** (stadium) in the Prater (✉ Meiereistr., ☎ 01/728–0854) and the **Hanappi Stadium** (✉ Keisslergasse 6, ☎ 01/914–3490–0). Indoor soccer takes place in the **Stadthalle** (✉ Vogelweidpl. 14, ☎ 01/981–00–01). Tickets can usually be bought at the gate, but the better seats are available through ticket agencies. At the **Vienna Ticket Service** (✉ Postfach 160, A–1060, ☎ 01/587–9843–0, 𝔽𝔸𝕏 01/587–9844), tickets must be ordered a month in advance. Otherwise try **American Express** (✉ Kärntner Str. 21–23, ☎ 01/515–40–0, 𝔽𝔸𝕏 01/515–40–70), **Cosmos** (✉ Kärntner Ring 15, A-1010, ☎ 01/515–33–0, 𝔽𝔸𝕏 01/513–4147), **Kartenbüro Flamm** (✉ Kärntner Ring 3, A-1010, ☎ 01/512–4225, 𝔽𝔸𝕏 01/513–9962), or **Österreichisches Verkehrsbüro** (✉ Friedrichstr. 7, ☎ 01/588–00–0, 𝔽𝔸𝕏 01/587–7142).

Horse Racing

The race track (flat and sulky racing) is in the Prater (Galopprennpl. Freudenau, ☎ 01/728–9535–0), and the season runs April–November. The highlight is the Derby, which takes place the third Sunday in June.

Tennis

Professional matches are played in the Prater or in the Stadthalle (☞ Football, *above*). Ticket agencies will have details.

SHOPPING

Shopping Districts

The **Kärntner Strasse, Graben,** and **Kohlmarkt** pedestrian areas claim to have the best shops in Vienna, and for some items, such as jewelry, some of the best anywhere, although you must expect high prices. The side streets within this area have developed their own character, with shops offering antiques, art, clocks, jewelry, and period furniture. **RingstrassenGalerie,** the new shopping plaza at Kärntner Ring 5-7, brings a number of shops together in a modern complex, although most of these stores have other, larger outlets elsewhere in the city. Outside the center, concentrations of stores are on **Mariahilfer Strasse** straddling the Sixth and Seventh districts; **Landstrasser Hauptstrasse** in the Third District; and, still farther out, **Favoritenstrasse** in the 10th District.

A collection of attractive small boutiques can be found in the **Palais Ferstel** passage at Freyung 2 in the First District. A modest group of smaller shops has sprung up in the **Sonnhof** passage between Landstrasser Hauptstrasse 28 and Ungargasse 13 in the Third District. The **Spittelberg** market, on the Spittelberggasse between Burggasse and Siebensterngasse in the Seventh District, has drawn small galleries and handicrafts shops and is particularly popular in the weeks before Christmas and Easter. Christmas is the time also for the tinselly **Christkindlmarkt** on Rathausplatz in front of city hall; in protest over its commercialization, smaller markets specializing in handicrafts have sprung up on such traditional spots as Am Hof and the Freyung (First District), also the venue for other seasonal markets.

Vienna's **Naschmarkt** (between Linke and Rechte Wienzeile, starting at Getreidemarkt) is one of Europe's great and most colorful food and produce markets. Stalls open at 5 or 6 AM, and the pace is lively until 1 or 2 PM. Saturday is the big day, when farmers come into the city to sell at the back end of the market. It's closed Sunday.

ANTIQUES

You will find the best antiques shops located in the First District, many clustered close to the Dorotheum auction house, in the **Dorotheergasse, Stallburggasse, Plankengasse,** and **Spiegelgasse.** You'll also find interesting shops in the **Josefstadt** (Eighth) district, with prices considerably lower than those in the center of town. Wander up Florianigasse and back down Josefstädter Strasse, being sure not to overlook the narrow side streets.

D&S (⊠ Dorotheergasse 12, ☎ 01/512–1011) specializes in old Viennese clocks. Look in at **Glasgalerie Kovacek** (⊠ Spiegelgasse 12, ☎ 01/512–9954) to see a remarkable collection of glass paperweights and other glass objects. You'll find paintings and furniture in many shops in this area, including **Kunst Salon Kovacek** (⊠ Stallburggasse 2, ☎ 01/512–8358). **Peter Feldbacher** (⊠ Annagasse 6, ☎ 01/512–2408) has items ranging from glass to ceramics to furniture. For Art Deco, look to **Galerie Metropol** (⊠ Dortheergasse 12, ☎ 01/513–2208). Another Art Deco option is **Galerie bei der Albertina** (⊠ Lobkowitzpl. 1, ☎ 01/513–1416).

Auctions

The **Dorotheum** (⊠ Dorotheergasse 17, ☎ 01/515–60–0) is a state institution dating to 1707, when Emperor Josef I determined that he didn't want his people being exploited by pawnbrokers. The place is intriguing, with goods ranging from furs to furniture auctioned almost daily. Information on how to bid is available in English. Some items are for immediate cash sale.

Flea Markets

Every Saturday (except holidays) rain or shine, from about 7:30 AM to 4 or 5, the **Flohmarkt** in back of the Naschmarkt, stretching along the Linke Wienzeile from the Kettenbrücken U4 subway station, offers a staggering collection of stuff ranging from serious antiques to plain junk. Haggle over prices.

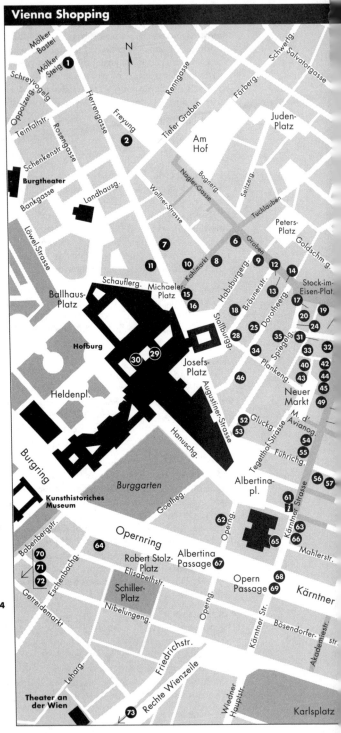

Vienna Shopping

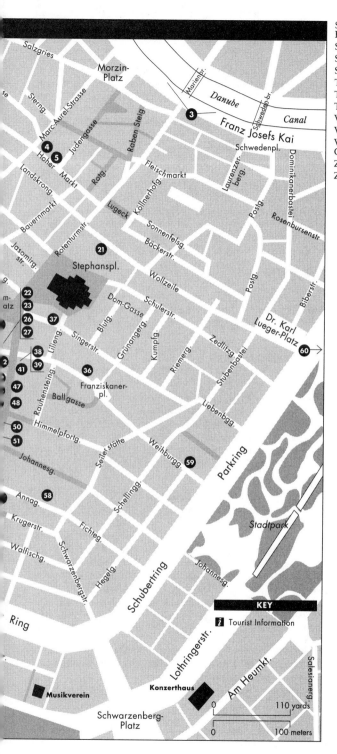

Salzgries

Morzin-
Platz

Marienbr.

Schwedenbr.

Danube

Canal

Franz Josefs Kai

Schwedenpl.

Sterng.

se

Marc-Aurel-Strasse

Judengasse

Raben Steig

Laurenzer-
berg.

Dominikanerbastei

Hoher

Markt

Rotg.

Fleischmarkt

Köllnerhofg.

Postg.

Rosenbursenstr

Landskrong.

Bauernmarkt

Rotenturmstr.

Lugeck

Sonnenfelsg.

Bäckerstr.

Jasomirg.

str.

Stephanspl.

Wollzeile

Postg.

Biberstr.

g.

m-

alz

Dom-Gasse

Schulerstr.

Blug.

Zedlitzg.

Dr. Karl
Lueger-Platz

Lilieng.

Singerstr.

Grünangerg.

Kumpfg.

Riemerg.

Stubenbastei

Rauhensteing.

Franziskaner-
pl.

Ball gasse

Liebenbgg.

Himmelpfortg.

Seilerstätte

Weihburgg.

Parkring

Johannesg.

Schellingg.

Stadtpark

Annag.

Krugerstr.

Fichteg.

Walfischg.

Schwarzenbergstr.

Hegelg.

Schubertring

Johannesg.

Ring

KEY

ℹ️ Tourist Information

Musikverein

Lothringerstr.

Am Heumkt.

Salesianerg

Konzerthaus

0   110 yards

0   100 meters

Schwarzenberg-
Platz

On Thursdays and Fridays from late spring to midfall, an outdoor combination arts-and-crafts, collectibles, and flea market takes place on Am Hof.

On Saturday and Sunday in summer from about 10 to 6 an outdoor **art and antiques market** springs up along the Danube Canal, stretching from the Schwedenbrücke to beyond the Salztorbrücke. Lots of books are sold, some in English, plus generally better goods and collectibles than at the Saturday flea market. Bargain over prices all the same.

Department Stores

The **Steffl** department store (✉ Kärntner Str. 19, ☎ 01/512–0685) is moderately upscale without being overly expensive. The larger department stores are concentrated in Mariahilfer Strasse. By far the best is **Herzmansky** (✉ Mariahilfer Str. 26–30, ☎ 01/521–58–0), definitely upscale; outstanding gourmet shops and restaurants are in the basement. Farther up the street you will find slightly cheaper goods at **Gerngross** (✉ Mariahilfer Str. and Kirchengasse, ☎ 01/521–80–0) and cheaper still at **Stafa** (✉ Mariahilfer Str. 120, ☎ 01/523–3483–0).

Specialty Stores

BOOKS

Several good stores whose stock includes books in English are on the Graben and Kärntner Strasse in the First District. For bookstores specializing in English-language books, *see* Contacts and Resources *in* Vienna A to Z, *below.*

CERAMICS AND PORCELAIN

Ceramics are anything but dull at **Berger** (✉ Weihburggasse 17, ☎ 01/512–1434). Gmunden primitive country ceramics are at **Pawlata** (✉ Kärntner Str. 14, ☎ 01/512–1764). More country ceramics can be found at **Plessgott** (✉ Kärntner Durchgang, ☎ 01/512–5824). Check out Viennese porcelain patterns at **Augarten** (✉ Graben/Stock-im-Eisen-Pl. 3, ☎ 01/512–1494) and **Albin Denk** (✉ Graben 13, ☎ 01/512–4439), **Rosenthal** (✉ Kärntner Str. 16, ☎ 01/512–3994), and **Wahliss** (✉ Kärntner Str. 17, ☎ 01/512–1729–0).

CRYSTAL AND GLASS

Select famous Vienna glassware at **Bakalowits** (✉ Spiegelgasse 3, ☎ 01/512–6351–0) and **Lobmeyr** (✉ Kärntner Str. 26, ☎ 01/512–0508–0), which also has a small museum of its creations upstairs; the firm supplied the crystal chandeliers for the Metropolitan Opera in New York City, a gift from Austria. **Berndorf** (✉ Wollzeile 12, ☎ 01/512–2944) and **Rasper & Söhne** (✉ Graben 15, ☎ 01/534–33–0) have the exquisite Riedl glass; so do **Albin Denk** (✉ Graben 13, ☎ 01/512–4439) and **Tabletop** (✉ Passage, Freyung 2, ☎ 01/535–4256; ✉ Weihburggasse/Hotel Marriott, ☎ 01/513–3895), though readers have reported that goods purchased here for shipment were never received.

GIFT ITEMS

Österreichische Werkstätten (✉ Kärntner Str. 6, ☎ 01/512–2418) offers outstanding and unusual handmade handicrafts, gifts, and quality souvenirs ranging from jewelry to textiles.

Souvenir in der Hofburg (✉ Hofburgpassage 1 and 7, ☎ 01/533–5053) is another source of more traditional gift items.

Niederösterreichisches Heimatwerk (☞ Women's Clothing, *below*) has handmade folk objects and textiles.

Wiener Geschenke (✉ Reitschulgasse 4/Michaelerpl., ☎ 01/533–7078; ✉ Lobkowitzpl. 1, ☎ 01/513–3773) has a nice selection of quality gift and traditional souvenir items and is open Sunday during part of the year.

JADE
Discover interesting pieces of Austrian jade at **Burgenland** (⊠ Opernpassage, ☎ 01/587–6266).

JEWELRY
Carius & Binder (⊠ Kärntner Str. 17, ☎ 01/512–6750) is good for watches.

Haban (⊠ Kärntner Str. 2, ☎ 01/512–6730–0; ⊠ Graben 12, ☎ 0222/ 512–1220) has a fine selection of watches and jewelry.

A. Heldwein (⊠ Graben 13, ☎ 01/512–5781) sells elegant jewelry, silverware, and watches.

A. E. Köchert (⊠ Neuer Markt 15, ☎ 01/512–5828–0) has outstanding original creations.

Eleonora Kunz (⊠ Neuer Markt 13, ☎ 01/512–7112) sells stunning modern pieces for men and women.

Schullin (⊠ Kohlmarkt 7, ☎ 01/533–9007–0) has some of the most original work found anywhere.

MEN'S CLOTHING
Clothing in Vienna is far from cheap but is of good quality. The best shops are in the First district: **Sir Anthony** (⊠ Kärntner Str. 21–23, ☎ 01/512–6835), **E. Braun** (⊠ Graben 8, ☎ 01/512–5505–0), **House of Gentlemen** (⊠ Kohlmarkt 12, ☎ 01/533–3258), **ITA** (⊠ Graben 18, ☎ 01/533–6004–0), **Malowan** (⊠ Opernring 23, ☎ 01/587–6296), **Silbernagel** (⊠ Kärntner Str. 15, ☎ 01/512–5312), **Teller** in the Third district (⊠ Landstrasser Hauptstr. 88–90, ☎ 01/712–6397) for particularly good value, **Venturini** (⊠ Spiegelgasse 9, ☎ 01/512–8845) for custom-made shirts.

For men's *Trachten,* or typical Austrian clothing, including lederhosen, try **Loden-Plankl** (⊠ Michaelerpl. 6, ☎ 01/533–8032), and go to **Collins Hüte** (⊠ Opernpassage, ☎ 01/587–1305) to get the appropriate hat.

NEEDLEWORK
For Vienna's famous petit point, head for **Petit Point Kovacec** (⊠ Kärntner Str. 16, ☎ 01/512–4886) or **Stransky** (⊠ Hofburgpassage 2, ☎ 01/533–6098).

RECORDS
Look for records and tapes at **Arcadia** (⊠ Kärntner Str. 40, Staatsoper arcade, ☎ 01/513–9568), which also features books and imaginative music-related souvenirs.

Carola is best for pop LPs and CDs (⊠ Albertinapassage by Opera House, ☎ 01/564114). **EMI** (⊠ Kärntner Str. 30, ☎ 01/512–3675) has a wide selection of pops plus classics upstairs.

Havlicek (⊠ Herrengasse 5, ☎ 01/533–1964) features classics and is particularly knowledgeable and helpful. **da Caruso** (⊠ Operngasse 4, ☎ 01/513–1326) specializes in classics, with an emphasis on opera.

SHOES AND LEATHER GOODS
Try **Humanic** (⊠ Kärntner Str. 51, ☎ 01/512–5892; ⊠ Singerstr. 2, ☎ 01/512–9101). For exclusive styles, go to **Zak** (⊠ Kärntner Str. 36, ☎ 01/512–7257), **Popp & Kretschmer** (⊠ Kärntner Str. 51, ☎ 01/512– 6421–0), and **Nigst** (⊠ Neuer Markt 4, ☎ 01/512–4303).

The couturier to Vienna is **Adlmüller** (⊠ Kärntner Str. 41, ☎ 01/512–6650–0). Check also **Flamm** (⊠ Neuer Markt 12, ☎ 01/512–2889), **E. Braun, ITA,** or **Malowan** (☞ Men's Clothing, *above*). You'll find modern young styling at **Maldone** (⊠ Kärntner Str. 4, ☎ 01/512–2761; ⊠ Kärntner Str. 12, ☎ 01/512–2234; ⊠ Graben 29, ☎ 01/533–6091; ⊠ Hoher Markt 8, ☎ 01/533–2555).

Check out the selection of dirndls and women's *Trachten,* the typical Austrian costume with white blouse, print skirt, and apron, at **Lanz** (⊠ Kärntner Str. 10, ☎ 01/512–2456), **Niederösterreichisches Heimatwerk** (⊠ Herrengasse 6–8, ☎ 01/533–3495), **Resi Hammerer** (⊠ Kärntner Str. 29–31, ☎ 01/512–6952), and **Tostmann** (⊠ Schottengasse 3a, ☎ 01/533–5331–0). (☞ Loden-Plankl *in* Men's Clothing, *above.*)

Weinhebers (wine dispensers with pear-shape glass containers) and other iron items can be found at **Franz Hamerle** (⊠ Annagasse 7, ☎ 01/512–4746) or **Zach** (⊠ Bräunerstr. 8, ☎ 01/533–9939).

VIENNA A TO Z

Arriving and Departing

By Boat

If you arrive in Vienna via the Danube, the DDSG/Blue Danube ship will leave you at **Praterlände** near Mexikoplatz (⊠ Handelskai 265, ☎ 01/727–50–0), although some upstream ships also make a stop at **Nussdorf** (⊠ Heiligenstädter Str. 180, ☎ 01/371257). The Praterlände stop is a two–block taxi ride or hike to or from the Vorgartenstrasse U1/subway station, or you can take a taxi directly into town.

By Bus

International long-distance bus service (Bratislava, Brno) and most postal and railroad buses arrive at the **Wien Mitte** central bus station (⊠ Landstrasser Hauptstr. 1b, ☎ 01/711–07–3850 or 01/711–01), across from the Hilton Hotel.

By Car

Vienna is 300 kilometers (187 miles) east of Salzburg, 200 kilometers (125 miles) north of Graz. Main routes leading into the city are the A1 Westautobahn from Germany, Salzburg and Linz, and the A2 Südautobahn from Graz and points south.

On highways from points south or west or from the airport, **Zentrum** signs clearly mark the route to the center of Vienna. From there, however, finding your way to your hotel can be no mean trick, for traffic planners have installed a devious scheme prohibiting through traffic in the city core (the First District) and scooting cars out again via a network of exasperating one-way streets. In the city itself a car is a burden, though very useful for trips outside town.

By Plane

Vienna's airport is at Schwechat, about 19 kilometers (12 miles) southeast of the city. For flight information, call 01/7007–2233. **Austrian Airlines** (☎ 01/717–99–0), **Air Canada** (☎ 01/515–55–31), **Delta** (☎ 01/512–6646–0), and **Lauda Air** (☎ 01/0660–6655) fly into Schwechat from North America. The North American services of Austrian, Delta, and Swissair are shared under joint flight numbers and may be flown in and out of Vienna by any of the three lines.

A **bus** leaves the airport every half hour from 5 AM to 6:30 AM, then every 20 minutes from 6:50 AM to 11:30 PM (the last bus is at midnight; after that, buses depart every hour to 5 AM), for the city air terminal (☎ 01/5800–35404 or 01/5800–33369) beside the Hilton Hotel. The trip takes about 25 minutes and costs AS70; you buy your ticket on the bus, so be sure to have Austrian money handy. A bus also runs every hour (every half-hour on weekends and holidays April–September) to the Westbahnhof (West Station) via the Südbahnhof (South Station); this bus might land you closer to your hotel, and taxis are available at the station. The introduction of improved rail service between the airport and the Wien-Mitte/Landstrasse rail station (opposite the Hilton) may bring changes to bus schedules this year.

Taxis will take about 30 minutes to most downtown locations, longer when traffic is heavy (weekdays 7–8:30 AM and 4:30–6:30 PM). Taxis from Vienna are not allowed to pick up passengers at the airport unless they've been ordered; only those from Lower Austria (where the airport is located, beyond the city limits) can take passengers into town. This means that taxis travel one way empty, so the meter fare is doubled; you'll end up with a bill of about AS350. You can cut the charge to about AS250 by phoning one of the Vienna cab companies from the airport (☎ 01/313–00, 01/601–60–0, or 01/401–00) and asking for a taxi to take you into town. They'll give you the last couple of digits of the taxi license, and you wait until it arrives. Be sure to arrange where the taxi will meet you. The same scheme applies when you leave: Not all Vienna cabs have permits for airport service, so call in advance to get one that can take you out for about AS300–AS320. The cheapest cab service is C+K Airport Service (☎ 01/60808), charging about AS270–AS300.

Mazur limos provide door-to-door transportation that's cheaper than a taxi. Look for the Mazur stand at the airport, or call 01/7007–6422, 01/604–9191, or 01/604–2233.

Fast **trains** run from the airport to the Wien Mitte station across the street from the Hilton Hotel and to the Wien Nord station, Praterstern, with service at half-hour intervals. The fare is AS30, or a Vienna streetcar ticket plus AS15. Check schedules, as the service is being expanded and changes are likely.

By Train
Trains from Germany, Switzerland, and western Austria arrive at the **Westbahnhof** (West Station), on Europaplatz, where the Mariahilfer Strasse crosses the Gürtel. If you're coming from Italy or Hungary, you'll generally arrive at the **Südbahnhof** (⊠ South Station, Wiedner Gürtel 1). The current stations for trains to and from Prague and Warsaw are **Wien Nord** (⊠ North Station, Praterstern) and **Franz-Josef Bahnhof** (⊠ Julius-Tandler-Pl.). Central train information will have details (☎ 01/1717; taped schedule information (in German) for trains to/from west, ☎ 01/1552; for trains to/from south, 01/1553).

Getting Around

Vienna is divided into 23 numbered districts. Taxi drivers may need to know which district you seek, as well as the street address. The district number is coded into the postal code with the second and third digits; thus A–1010 (the "-01-") is the First District, A–1030 is the Third, A–1110 is the 11th, and so on. Some sources and maps still give the district numbers, either in Roman or Arabic numerals, as Vienna X or Vienna 10.

Vienna is a city to tackle on foot. With the exception of the Schönbrunn and Belvedere palaces and the Prater amusement park, most sights are concentrated in the center, the First District (A–1010), much of which is a pedestrian zone anyway.

By Bus and Streetcar

Vienna's public transportation system is fast, clean, safe, and easy to use. Get public transport maps at a tourist office or at the transport-information offices (*Wiener Verkehrsbetriebe*), underground at Karlsplatz, Stephansplatz, and Praterstern. You can transfer on the same ticket between subway, streetcar, bus, and long stretches of the fast suburban railway, *Schnellbahn (S-Bahn)*. Buy single tickets for AS20 from dispensers on the streetcar or bus; you'll need exact change. The ticket machines at subway stations (*VOR-Fahrkarten*) give change and dispense 24-hour, 72-hour, and eight-day tickets, as well as single tickets separately and in blocks of two and five. At *Tabak-Trafik* (cigarette shops/newsstands) or the underground *Wiener Verkehrsbetriebe* offices you can get a block of five tickets for AS85, each ticket good for one uninterrupted trip in more or less the same general direction with unlimited transfers. Or you can get a three-day ticket for AS130, good on all lines for 72 hours from the time you validate the ticket; there's also a 24-hour ticket for AS50. If you're staying longer, get an eight-day ticket (AS265), which can be used on eight separate days or by any number of persons (up to eight) at any one time. These rates were valid at press time, but could be higher in 1997. A useful address is Tabak-Trafik Almassy (⊠ Stephanspl. 4, to the right behind cathedral, ☎ 01/512–5909); it is open every day from 8 AM to 7 PM and has tickets as well as film and other items. Ask at tourist offices or your hotel about a *Vienna-Card*; the card costing AS180 combines 72 hours' use of public transportation and discounts at certain museums and shops.

The first streetcars run about 5:15 AM, for those Viennese who start work at 8. From then on, service (barring gridlock on the streets) is regular and reliable, and most lines operate until about midnight. Where streetcars don't run, buses do; route maps and schedules are posted at each bus or subway stop.

Should you miss the last streetcar or bus, special night buses with an N designation operate at half-hour intervals over several key routes; the starting (and transfer) points are the Opera House and Schwedenplatz. The night-owl buses take a special fare of AS25, tickets available on the bus; normal tickets, your 72-hour or Vienna Card are not valid.

Within the heart of the city, bus lines 1A, 2A, and 3A are useful crosstown routes. These carry a reduced fare of AS8.50 per trip if you have bought the *Kurzstrecke* ticket (AS34), good for four trips or up to four people on one trip (with no transfer). The *Kurzstrecke* tickets are also valid for two stops on the subway or shorter distances on the streetcar lines.

By Car

Traffic congestion within Vienna has gotten out of hand and driving to in-town destinations generally takes longer than public transportation. City planners' solutions have been to make driving as difficult as possible, with one-way streets and other tricks, and a car in town is far more of a burden than a pleasure. Drivers not familiar with the city literally need a navigator. The entire First and Sixth through Ninth districts are limited parking zones and require that a "Parkschein," a paid-parking chit available at most newsstands and tobacconists, be displayed on the dash during the day. Overnight street parking in the First and Sixth through Ninth Districts is restricted to residents with special permits; all other cars are subject to expensive ticketing or even towing, so in these districts be sure you have off-street garage parking.

By Horse Cab

A *Fiaker,* or horse cab, will trot you around to whatever destination you specify, but this is an expensive way to see the city. A short tour of the inner city takes about 20 minutes and costs AS500; a longer one including the Ringstrasse takes about 40 minutes and costs AS800, for the whole Fiaker. The carriages accommodate four (five if someone sits next to the coachman). Starting points are Heldenplatz in front of the Hofburg, Stephansplatz beside the cathedral, and across from the Albertina, all in the First District. For longer trips, or any variation of the regular route, agree on the price first.

By Subway

Five subway lines (*U-bahn*), whose stations are prominently marked with blue *U* signs, crisscross the city. Karlsplatz and Stephansplatz are the main transfer points between lines. The last subway (U4) runs at about 12:30 AM.

By Taxi

Taxis in Vienna are relatively inexpensive. The initial charge is AS26 for as many as four people daytime, AS27 nighttime, weekends, and holidays. AS16 is added for radio cabs ordered by phone and for each piece of luggage that must go into the trunk, and a charge is added for waiting beyond a reasonable limit. It's customary to round up the fare to cover the tip. Taxis can be flagged on the street (when the roof light is on), taken from regular stands, or ordered by phone. To get a radio cab, call 01/313–00, 01/401–00, or 01/601–60–0. Service is usually prompt, but at rush hour, when weather is bad, or if you need to keep to an exact schedule, call ahead and order a taxi for a specific time. If your destination is the airport, ask for a reduced-rate taxi. For the cheapest taxi to the airport, *see* Between the Airport and City Center, *above.*

For a chauffeured limousine call **Tibor Adler** (☎ 01/216–0990), **Göth** (☎ 01/713–7196), **Mazur** (☎ 01/604–2233), or **Peter Urban** (☎ 01/713–5255 or 713–3781).

Contacts and Resources

Car Rentals

Rental cars can be arranged at the airport or in town. Major firms include **Avis** (✉ Airport, ☎ 01/7007–2700; ✉ Opernring 3–5, ☎ 01/587–6241), **Budget** (✉ Airport, ☎ 01/7007–2711; ✉ Hilton Hotel, Am Stadtpark, ☎ 01/714–6565–0), **EuroDollar** (✉ Airport, ☎ 01/7007–2699; ✉ Schubertring 9, ☎ 01/714–6717), **Hertz** (✉ Airport, ☎ 01/7007–2661; ✉ Kärntner Ring 17, ☎ 01/512–8677; international reservations, ☎ 01/713–1596), **National** (✉ Europcar/interRent at airport, ☎ 01/7007–3316; ✉ Denzel Autovermietung, Kärntner Ring 14, ☎ 01/505–4200; international reservations, 01/505–4166). **Buchbinder** (✉ Schlachthausgasse 38, ☎ 01/717–50–0) is a local firm with particularly favorable rates and clean cars.

Doctors and Dentists

If you need a doctor and speak no German, ask your hotel, or in an emergency, phone your consulate.

Embassies

U.S. embassy (✉ Boltzmanngasse 16). **U.S. consulate** (✉ Gartenbaupromenade, Parkring 12A, Marriott building). The telephone number for both is 01/313–39. **Canadian embassy** (✉ Fleischmarkt

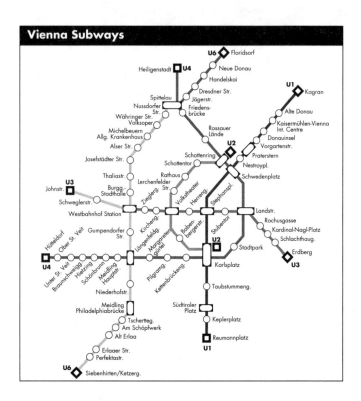

Vienna Subways

19/Laurenzerberg 2, ☎ 01/531–38–0). **U.K. embassy and consulate** (✉ Jauresgasse 12; embassy, ☎ 01/713–1575; consulate, ☎ 01/714–6117).

Emergencies

The emergency numbers are 133 for the **police,** 144 for an **ambulance,** 122 for the **fire department.**

English-Language Bookstores

The leading sources of books in English are **Big Ben Bookstore** (✉ Servitengasse 4a, ☎ 01/319–6412–0), **British Bookstore** (✉ Weihburggasse 24–26, ☎ 01/512–1945–0), and **Shakespeare & Co.** (✉ Sterngasse 2, ☎ 01/535–5053–0). **Pickwick's** (✉ Marc-Aurel-Str. 10–12, ☎ 01/533–0182) mainly rents videotapes.

English-Language Radio

"Blue Danube Radio" on FM at 103.8 and 91.0 MHz carries news, music, and information in English (and some in French) throughout the day and early evening, with major newscasts at 12 noon and 6 PM.

Guided Tours

BOAT TOURS

The **DDSG/Blue Danube Steamship Line** (☎ 01/727–50–0) runs a three-hour boat tour up the Danube Canal and down the Danube, from Schwedenbrücke, by Schwedenplatz, May through September, daily at 10:30 AM, 1, 2:30, and 4:30 PM. From early to late April and late September to the end of October, tours run daily at 1 PM. Check schedules and special cruise offerings, as the line has been under new management since last year, and trips as well as schedules are subject to change.

EXCURSIONS

All three bus tour operators (☞ Orientation Tours, *below*) offer short trips outside of the city. Check their offerings and compare packages and prices to be sure you get what you want. Your hotel will have brochures.

ORIENTATION TOURS

When you're pressed for time, a good way to see the highlights of Vienna is via a sightseeing-bus tour, which gives you a once-over-lightly of the heart of the city and allows a closer look at Schönbrunn and Belvedere palaces. **Vienna Sightseeing Tours** (⊠ Stelzhammergasse 4/11, ☎ 01/712–4683–0, FAX 01/712–4683–77) runs a 1¼-hour "get acquainted" tour daily, leaving from in front of the Opera House at 10:30 and 11:45 AM and 3 PM (AS220). **CityTouring Vienna** (⊠ Penzingerstr. 46, ☎ 01/894–1417–0, FAX 01/894–3239) runs a similar tour at 9:30 AM (AS180), leaving from the City Air Terminal by the Hilton Hotel, across from the Wien Mitte/Landstrasse U3/U4 subway station. You can cover almost the same territory on your own by taking either Streetcar 1 or 2 around the Ring, and then walking through the heart of the city (☞ Self-Guided Tours, *below*).

Vienna Sightseeing, CityTouring Vienna, and **Cityrama/Gray Line** (⊠ Börsegasse 1, ☎ 01/534–13–12, FAX 01/534–13–22) all have tours of about three hours (AS320), including brief visits to Schönbrunn and Belvedere palace grounds. If you want to see the Schönbrunn interior, you'll have to pay a separate entrance fee, with some operators offering a 30-minute or one-hour stop, or in some cases leaving you to find your way back to the center of town yourself. The CityTouring Vienna trip breaks the day into two halves, with the afternoon taking in the edge of the Vienna Woods via Grinzing and heading along the Danube past the UN-Center, the Prater amusement park, and the Hundertwasser House. Cityrama and Vienna Sightseeing tours start daily at 9:30 and 10:30 AM, and 2:30 PM; the CityTouring Vienna tours are at 11, 3:15, and 4. All three firms offer a number of other tours as well (your hotel will have detailed programs), and provide hotel pickup for most tours. For other than the "get acquainted" tours, the Vienna Sightseeing buses leave the central loading point in front of the Opera House 10 minutes before scheduled tour departures to make the hotel pickups. Cityrama tours start from Johannesgasse at the Stadtpark station on the U4 subway line, diagonally across from the InterContinental hotel. CityTouring Vienna tours originate at the City Air Terminal by the Hilton Hotel, opposite the Wien Mitte/Landstrasse station on the U4 and U3 subway lines.

STREETCAR TOURS

From early May through September, a 1929 vintage streetcar leaves each Saturday at 11:30 AM and 1:30 PM and Sunday, Monday, and holidays at 9:30 and 11:30 AM and 1:30 PM from the Otto Wagner Pavilion at Karlsplatz for a guided tour. For AS200 (AS180 if you have the *Vienna-Card*), you'll go around the Ring, out past the big Ferris wheel in the Prater and past Schönbrunn and Belvedere palaces in the course of the two-hour trip. The oldtimer trips are popular, so get tickets in advance at the transport-information office underground at Karlsplatz, weekdays 7 AM–6 PM, weekends and holidays 8:30–4 (☎ 01/7909–44026).

PERSONAL GUIDES

Guided walking tours (in English) are a great way to see the city highlights. Tour topics range from "Unknown Underground Vienna" to "1,000 Years of Jewish Tradition" and "Vienna Around Sigmund Freud." Tours take about 1½ hours, are held in any weather provided at least three people turn up, and cost AS108 plus any entry fees. No reservations are needed. Get a list of the guided-tour possibilities at the city information office at Kärntner Strasse 38 (☎ 01/513–8892). Ask for the monthly brochure "Walks in Vienna," which details the tours, days, times, and starting points. You can also arrange to have your own privately guided tour for AS1,116 for a half day.

SELF-GUIDED

Get a copy of "Vienna Downtown Walking Tours" by Henriette Mandl from any bookshop. The six tours take you through the highlights of central Vienna with excellent commentary and some entertaining anec-dotes, which most of your Viennese acquaintances won't know. The booklet "Vienna from A–Z" (in English, AS70; available at bookshops and city information offices) explains the numbered plaques attached to all major buildings.

Late-Night Pharmacies

In each area of the city one pharmacy stays open 24 hours; if a phar-macy is closed, a sign on the door will tell you the address of the near-est one that is open. Call 01/1550 for names and addresses (in German) of the pharmacies open that night.

Lost and Found

If you've lost something valuable, check with the police at the **Fundamt** (⊠ Wasagasse 22, ☎ 01/313–44–0 or 01/313–44–9211). If your loss occurred on a train, check the **Bundesbahn Fundamt** (⊠ railway lost property office, ☎ 01/5800). If you were coming in from Salzburg, call the office at the **Westbahnhof** (☎ 01/5800–32996) 8–noon; from Villach or the south, call the **Südbahnhof** (☎ 01/5800–35656). Losses on the subway system or streetcars can be checked by calling the **Zen-trale Fundstelle** (☎ 01/7909–43500).

Travel Agencies

The leading agencies are **American Express** (⊠ Kärntner Str. 21–23, ☎ 01/515–40–0, FAX 01/515–40–70), **Carlson/Wagon-Lits** (⊠ Kärnt-ner Ring 2, ☎ 01/501–60–0, FAX 01/501–60–65), **Cosmos** (⊠ Kärnt-ner Ring 15, ☎ 01/515–33–0, FAX 01/513–4147), **Ruefa Reisen** (⊠ Fleischmarkt 1, ☎ 01/534–04–0, FAX 01/534–04–394), and **Öster-reichisches Verkehrsbüro** (⊠ Friedrichstr. 7, opposite Sezession, ☎ 01/588–00–0, FAX 01/986–8533).

Visitor Information

The main point for information is the **Vienna City Tourist Office** (⊠ Fremdenverkehrsstelle der Stadt Wien), in back of the Opera House and around the corner from the Hotel Sacher, at Kärntner Strasse 38 (☎ 01/513–8892–0), open daily from 9 to 7.

If you need a room, go to **Information-Zimmernachweis** operated by the Verkehrsbüro in the Westbahnhof (☎ 01/892–3392) and in the Südbahnhof (☎ 01/505–3132). At the airport, the information and room-reservation office in the arrivals hall (☎ 01/7007–2828) is open daily 8:30 AM–9 PM. The information office at the DDSG dock on the Danube (☎ 01/727–50–0 or 01/218–0114) is open when ships are docking and embarking. None of these offices can arrange room book-ings by telephone; you must deal in person.

If you're driving into Vienna, get information or book rooms at **In-formation-Zimmernachweis** at the end of the Westautobahn at Wien-talstr./Auhof (☎ 01/979–1271) or at the end of the Südautobahn at Triesterstrasse 149 (☎ 01/616–0071 or 01/616–0070).

3 Side Trips from Vienna

From the Vienna Woods to the Weinviertel

Is it the sun or the soil? The dreamy castle-capped peaks? Whatever the reason, the idyllic regions outside Vienna have always offered perfectly pastoral escapes for Viennese. Rich in scenic splendor, this countryside is also saturated with musical history. Here, Beethoven was inspired to write his Pastoral Symphony, *Johann Strauss set the Vienna Woods to music, and a glass of intoxicating* Retzer Wein *urged Richard Strauss to compose the* Rosenkavalier Waltz. *From the elegant spa of Baden to mysterious Mayerling, this region is a day-tripper's delight.*

THE VIENNESE ARE UNDENIABLY LUCKY. Few populaces enjoy such glorious—and easily accessible—options for day-tripping. City residents in the droves tie their bicycles to the roof racks of their Mercedes on Saturdays and Sundays; Vacationers to Vienna can share in the natives' obvious pleasure in the city's environs any day of the week. For many the first destination is, of course, the Wienerwald, the fabled Vienna Woods. This is not a natural park or forest, as you would think from listening to Strauss or the tourist blurbs. The Wienerwald is a large range of rolling, densely wooded hills, extending from Vienna's doorstep to the outposts of the Alps in the south. This region is crisscrossed by country roads and hiking paths, dotted with forest lodges and inns, and solidifies every now and then into quaint little villages and market towns. In addition to such natural pleasures, the regions outside of Vienna offer something for everyone. Turning south to Mayerling leads you to the site where the successor to the Austrian throne presumably took his own life after shooting his secret love—a mystery still unresolved. You can opt to head northeast, into wonderfully encompassing woods and gently rolling hills sprinkled with elegant summer palaces, and, to the north, to take one long liquid adventure by exploring the Weinstrasse (Wine Road), along which vast expanses of vineyard produce excellent, mainly white, wines. Another choice is to follow the trail of the defensive castles that protected the land from invaders from the north, or you can even trace the early days of Masonry in Austria—both Haydn and Mozart were members of what was then a secret and forbidden brotherhood.

Updated by
Willibald
Picard

These subregions of Lower Austria are simple, mainly agricultural, country areas. People live close to the earth, and on any sunny weekend from March through October, you'll find whole families out working the fields. This isn't to suggest that fun is forgotten; just as often, you'll stumble across a dressy parade with the local brass band done up in *Lederhosen* and feathered hats. Sundays here are still generally days of rest, although this generally means that on Sunday morning, wives and daughters go to mass while husbands and older sons retire to discuss weather and politics at the local *Gasthaus,* the families to be reunited after services over a simple but filling meal. Whichever destination you choose, however, the lakes are waiting, the biking paths are open, and the lovely countryside cafés beckon.

Pleasures and Pastimes

Bicycling
The Carnuntum region and the southeast corner of the Weinviertel, a region known as the Marchfeld, offer outstanding cycling, with a number of marked routes. Cycle paths follow the southern bank of the Danube past Carnuntum (Petronell) through Bad Deutsch–Altenburg to Hainburg, and other parts of the region are flat enough to offer fine cycling without exertion. In the Marchfeld, another marked route close to the March river includes the Baroque castles at Marchegg, Schlosshof, and Niederweiden.

Castles
To take advantage of the fact that the Danube forms a natural line of defense, barons and baliffs decided centuries ago to fortify bluffs along the river. Castles were the best answer and a wonderful string of these more or less follows the course of the Thaya river, starting in Weitra and Heidenreichstein close to the Czech border, then eastward to Raabs, Riegersburg and Hardegg. The 17th- and 18th-century structures vary from turreted hilltop fortresses to more elegant moated bas-

tions, but all were part of a chain against invaders. Several are basically intact, the others restored, and all are impressive relics well worth visiting. Castle concerts have become popular during summer months, when the buildings are open for tours as well.

Dining

With very few exceptions, food in this region, while influenced by Vienna cuisine, is simple. The basics are available in abundance: roast meats, customary schnitzel variations, game in season, fresh vegetables, and standard desserts such as *Palatschinken,* crepes filled with jam or with nuts topped with chocolate sauce. Imaginative cooking is rare; this is not tourist country, and the local population demands little beyond reasonable quality and quantity.

Wines are equally taken for granted, although four of the areas included here are designated as separate wine regions—the Weinviertel, or wine quarter to the north of Vienna; the Kamptal, which divides the Weinviertel from the Waldviertel to the west; the Carnuntum–Petronell region just below the Danube to the southeast of Vienna, and the Thermen region south and southwest of the capital. The specialties are mainly white wines, with the standard types, Grüner Veltliner and Rieslings and increasingly Weissburgunder, predominating. Reds are coming more into favor, with lighter reds such as Zweigelt and even rosés to be found in the northern areas, the heavier reds such as Blaufränkisch and St. Laurent and the spicier Gewürztraminer and Müller–Thurgau whites in the south. Most of the vintners work small holdings, so output is limited. The wine market in Poysdorf, center of Austria's largest wine region, offers an opportunity to sample a wide choice of area wares.

Restaurant prices include taxes and a service charge, but it is customary to give the waiter an additional tip of 5%–7%, usually rounding up the bill to the nearest AS5 or 10.

CATEGORY	COST*
$$$$	over AS350
$$$	AS200–AS350
$$	AS100–AS200
$	under AS100

per person for a typical two-course meal, including a small glass of wine or beer but excluding an additional tip

Hiking and Walking

The celebrated Vienna Woods to the west and southwest of Vienna are crisscrossed by hundreds of easy hiking paths, numbered, color-coded, and marked for destinations. Excellent hiking maps available from most bookstores will give ideas and routes. Paths will take you through woods, past meadows and vineyards, alongside streams and rivers, with occasional *Waldschenke* hidden away deep in the woods where you can stop for refreshment or a cold snack. Deer, wild boar and a host of small animals inhabit these preserves. The area is protected, and development is highly restricted, making it ideal for pleasurable hiking.

Lodging

Accommodations in the countryside around Vienna are pretty basic. This is underdeveloped tourist territory, prime turf for the more adventuresome, with rooms frequently to be found as an adjunct to the local *Gasthaus*. Nearly all are family-run; the younger members will speak at least some school English. You'll probably have to carry your own bags, and elevators to upper floors are scarce. Booking ahead is a good idea, as most places have relatively few rooms, particularly rooms with full bath. Window screens are almost unknown in Austria as bugs are few, but in farming areas, both flies and occasionally mosquitoes can be a nuisance in the warmer seasons. Since you'll want windows open at night, take along a can of bug spray and you'll sleep more peacefully. The standard country bed covering is a down-filled feather bed, so if you're allergic to feathers or want more warmth, ask for blankets. Even the simpler hotels will be spotless, and almost without exception, you'll be offered a tasty breakfast which can range from fresh rolls with cold cuts and cheese and tea or coffee, to an ample buffet spread with cereals and fruit as well, included in the room price.

Hotel room rates include taxes and service, and usually breakfast—although check to be sure.

CATEGORY	COST*
$$$$	over AS1,000
$$$	AS800–AS1,000
$$	AS500–AS800
$	under AS500

All prices are for a standard double room for two, including taxes and service charge.

Exploring Vienna's Environs

The region surrounding Vienna divides itself logically into four areas. The Vienna Woods, that huge unspoiled belt of forest green stretching westward south of the Danube, was celebrated by composers Beethoven, Schubert, and Strauss, and remains a favorite of the Viennese today. The towns to the south, Mödling, Baden, and Bad Vöslau mark the east end of the rolling, wooded hills. There the fertile Vienna Basin begins, sweeping east to the low, wooded Leitha Mountains that shelter the Putzta Plain extending on into Hungary. The northern part of the basin widens into the Danube Valley, forming the Carnuntum agricultural and wine region, with Slovakia to the east.

North of the Danube, two great regions are divided by the Kamp River, with the wooded Waldviertel, or forest district, to the northwest adjoining the Czech Republic, and the rolling hills of the agricultural Weinviertel, or wine district, to the northeast, bordering in the north on the Czech Republic and in the east, where the March River flows into the Danube, on Slovakia.

Great Itineraries

The four districts surrounding Vienna are compact and each can be explored in a day or two. To pursue the lives of the famous composers Schubert and Beethoven, take the route to the south, to Mödling and Baden; for Haydn's birthplace, to the east to Rohrau, then possibly on to Eisenstadt (☞ Chapter 4). To tour a chain of defensive castles, head for the forested *Waldviertel*. For rolling hills, vast expanses of vineyards and to sample their output, seek out the *Weinviertel* to the north.

Baden and Environs

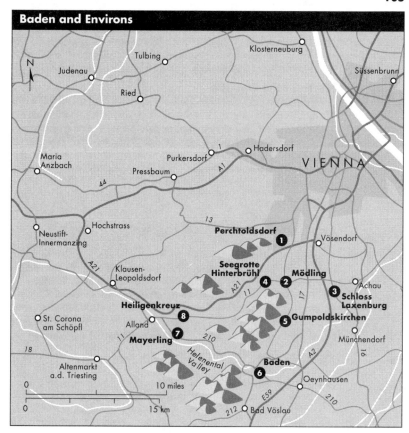

Numbers in the text correspond to numbers in the margin and on the Baden and Environs and the Waldviertel and the Weinviertel maps.

South of the Danube

IF YOU HAVE 1 DAY

To get a taste of the fringes of the Vienna Woods to the capital's south and west, head for **Mödling** ② and **Baden** ⑥. Both are smaller communities with unspoiled 17th-century town centers on a scale easy to assimilate. The route to Baden runs through the band of rolling wooded hills that mark the eastern edge of the Vienna Woods. The hills are skirted by vineyards forming a "wine belt," which also follows the valleys south of Vienna.

IF YOU HAVE 3 DAYS

With more time, you might spend two days in the Vienna Woods area, starting off with two particularly picturesque towns, **Perchtoldsdorf** ① and **Mödling** ②—with perhaps a look at the grand castle garden of **Laxenburg** ③—then following the scenic *Weinstrasse* ("wine road") through the lush vineyard country to the noted wine-producing village of

Gumpoldskirchen ⑤. Overnight in ⚏ **Baden** ⑥, then spend your second day taking in the sights of the fashionable spa town, including its grand Kurpark and Casino. Set out in the afternoon for mysterious ⚏ **Mayerling** ⑦. After an evocative dawn and morning here, set out for the great abbey at **Heiligenkreuz** ⑧, then head back to Vienna.

North of the Danube

IF YOU HAVE 1 DAY

The decision will have to be woods or wine, if you're tight on time. If woods, then head for **Waidhofen an der Thaya** ⑲, returning via picturesque **Raabs an der Thaya** ⑳ and **Geras** ㉓ and **Horn** ⑩. If wine, start at the bustling shipbuilding city of Korneuburg, then northward to the border town **Laa an der Thaya** ㉗, and return via **Poysdorf** ㉘, famous as a wine center.

IF YOU HAVE 3 DAYS

Spend a leisurely two days tracking the castles of the Waldviertel, starting at **Ottenstein** ⑫, moving on to **Zwettl** ⑬, with its magnificent abbey, overnighting at the noted castle-hotel/Masonic museum in ⚏ **Rosenau** ⑭, and on to **Weitra** ⑮, with its painted facades, for the start of the defensive castles route. The next mighty castle is at **Heidenreichstein** ⑱; follow the castle route with an overnight in ⚏ **Raabs an der Thaya** ⑳ and onward to **Riegersburg** ㉑ and **Hardegg** ㉒, overlooking the river forming the border with the Czech Republic. A stop in the ancient city of **Retz** ㉖ will give you a taste of the wine country; to end your excursion, head on to **Laa an der Thaya** ㉗ and **Poysdorf** ㉘.

When to Tour Vienna's Environs

Most of the regions around Vienna are best seen in the temperate seasons between mid-March and mid-November. The Waldviertel, however, with its vast stands of great forest offers picturebook scenery throughout the year. The combination of oaks and evergreens offers a color spectrum ranging from intense early spring green, through the deep green of summer into traces of autumn foliage, particularly in the Kamp River valley; in winter, occasional spectacular displays of hoar frost and snowswept vistas turn the region into a glittering three-dimensional Christmas card.

ON THE ROAD TO BADEN AND MAYERLING

This short, though history-rich, tour takes you to Baden through the legendary band of rolling wooded hills of the Vienna Woods (Wienerwald) that border Vienna on the west. The hills are skirted by vineyards forming a "wine belt," which also follows the valleys south of Vienna. You can visit this area easily in a day's outing, either by car or by public transportation, or you can spend the night in Baden, Mödling, or Alland for a more leisurely tour, visiting Mayerling, Heiligenkreuz, and a few other sights in the area.

By car from Vienna, head for Liesing (23rd District), then take Wiener Strasse to Perchtoldsdorf; from there, follow the signs south to Mödling and Baden. From Baden, take Route 210 (marked HELENENTAL) to Mayerling and on to Alland; return to Vienna via Route 11, stopping in Heiligenkreuz en route.

Perchtoldsdorf

❶ *12 km (7½ mi) southwest of Vienna center.*

Just over the Vienna city line to the southwest lies Perchtoldsdorf, a charmingly picturesque market town with many wine taverns, a 13th-century Gothic parish church, and the symbol of the town—an imposing stone tower completed in 1511, once forming a piece of the town's defense wall. Familiarly known as Pedersdorf, the town is a favorite excursion spot for the Viennese, who come mainly for the good local wines. Wander around the compact town square to admire the Renaissance houses, some with arcaded courtyards. The "Pestsäule" (Plague Column) in the center of the square, which gives thanks for rescue from the dread 16th century plague, was created by the famous Baroque architect Fischer von Erlach, and is similar to the Plague Column that adorns the Graben in Vienna. Without a car, you can reach Perchtoldsdorf from Vienna by taking the S-Bahn, or train, from the Westbahnbof, to Liesing, and then a short cab ride to the town.

Dining

$$$$ ✕ **Jahreszeiten.** This elegant, formal yet relaxed restaurant is in the capable hands of Günter Winter, whose reputation as a top chef continues to grow. The menu reflects international cuisine with an Austrian flair. You might be offered game and spring lamb in season, or try any of the fish offerings, perhaps sweet-sour shrimp on saffron rice. Finish with *Topfensouffle*, a delicately light cheesecake concoction. Beyond the kitchen, the atmosphere, like the tables, is set to perfection, and the menu is supplemented by wines from an outstanding cellar, international as well as local. ✉ *Hochstr. 17,* ☎ *0222/865–3129. Reservations essential. AE, DC, MC, V. Closed Mon., Easter week, and late July–early Aug. No lunch Sat. or dinner Sun.*

Mödling

❷ *20 km (12½ mi) southwest of Vienna.*

Founded in the 10th century, Mödling has a delightful town center, now a pedestrian zone. Here you can admire centuries-old buildings, most one- or two-story, which give the town an intimate feeling. Composers Beethoven and Schubert appreciated this in the early 1800s; Mödling was one of Beethoven's favored residences outside of Vienna. Note the domineering **St. Othmar Gothic parish church** on a hill overlooking the town proper, a Romanesque 12th-century charnel house (where the bones of the dead were kept), and the town hall, which has a Renaissance loggia. Later eras added Art Nouveau, which mixes happily with the several 16th- and 17th-century buildings.

❸ A few kilometers east of Mödling is **Schloss Laxenburg,** a complex consisting of a large Baroque Neues Schloss (New Castle), a small 14th-century Altes Schloss (Old Castle), and an early 19th-century neo-Gothic castle set into the sizable lake. The large park is full of birds and small game, such as roe deer and hare, and is decorated with statues, cascades, imitation temples, and other follies. The park and grounds are a favorite with the Viennese for Sunday outings. The Altes Schloss was built in 1381 by Duke Albrecht III as his summer residence, and several Habsburg emperors spent summers in the Neues Schloss, which now houses the International Institute of Applied Systems Analysis. Opposite is the large Baroque Convent of the Charitable Sisters. The castle is currently occupied by a research institute and is generally not open to the public, but the gardens are open daily. ⊠ *Schlosspl. 1,* ☎ *02236/ 712–26–0.*

❹ West of Mödling on Route 11 is the **Seegrotte Hinterbrühl,** a fascinating but now somewhat commercialized underground sea, created years ago when a mine filled up with water. You can take a 45-minute motorboat trip and look at the reflections through the arched caverns of the mine. ⊠ *Grutschgasse 2,* ☎ *02236/26364.* ⊠ *AS50.* ☉ *Apr.–Oct. daily 9–12, 1–5; Nov.–Mar. daily 9–12, 1–3.*

NEED A
BREAK? **Höldrichsmühle,** where a mill has turned since the 12th century, is now the spot for a famed 200-year-old country inn (⊠ Gaadner Str. 34, ☎ 02236/26274–0). Legend holds that the linden tree and the well found here inspired composer Franz Schubert to one of his better-known songs. Stop at this traditional restaurant for fish, game or various Champignon dishes in season.

Dining and Lodging

$$$$ ✕ ▥ **Babenbergerhof.** Rooms in this renovated, older hotel are comfortably up-to-date. You're in the quiet pedestrian zone (parking available), and upper rooms on the street side have views of the ancient parish church. The garden is particularly pleasant for summer dining; try the fried chicken or boiled beef. ⊠ *Babenbergergasse 6, A-2340,* ☎ *02236/22246,* FAX *02236/22246–6. 50 rooms. Restaurant, bar. AE, DC, MC, V.*

Gumpoldskirchen

From Mödling, follow the scenic "wine road" (an unnumbered road to the west of the rail line) through the lush vineyard country to the
❺ famous wine-producing village of **Gumpoldskirchen,** home of one of Europe's pleasantest white wines. This tiny village on the eastern slopes of the last Alpine rocks has lived for wine for two thousand years, and its white wines enjoy a fame that is widespread. At one stage, there was more Gumpoldskirchner on the world markets than the village could ever have produced—a situation reminiscent of the medieval glut of pieces of the True Cross. **Vintners' houses** line the main street, many of them with the typical large wooden gates that lead to the vine-covered courtyards where the Heuriger (wine of the latest vintage) is served by the owner and his family at simple wooden tables with benches. Gumpoldskirchen also has an arcaded Renaissance town hall, a market fountain made from a Roman sarcophagus, and the (private) castle of the Teutonic knights, whose descendants still own some of the best vineyard sites in the area.

Dining

$$ ✕ **Mautwirtshaus.** For a snack or a full meal, any of the various rooms in this country-style *Gasthaus* with its antique decor accents will be a good choice. Offerings range from lighter sausage and sauerkraut to the traditional roast pork or chicken, with surprise specialties when asparagus, game and geese are in season. Occasional Sunday jazz brunches add a contemporary note. ⊠ *Kaiserin-Elisabeth-Str. 22,* ☎ *02236/24481–0. DC, MC, V.*

Baden

❻ *32 km (20 mi) southwest of Vienna, 24 km (15 mi) north of Wiener Neustadt.*

The wine road brings you to the famous spa of Baden. Since antiquity, Baden's sulfuric thermal baths have attracted the ailing and the fashionable from all over the world. When the Romans came across the springs, they dubbed the town Aquae; the Babenbergs revived it in the 10th century, and when the Russian Czar Peter the Great visited in 1698, Baden's golden age began. Austrian Emperor Franz II spent 31 successive summers here: Every year for 12 years before his death in 1835, the royal entourage moved from Vienna for the season. Later in the century, Emperor Franz Josef II was a regular visitor, becoming the inspiration for much of the regal trappings the city still sports. In Baden, Mozart composed his "Ave Verum"; Beethoven spent 15 summers here and wrote large sections of his Ninth Symphony and *Missa Solemnis* when he lived at Frauengasse 10; here Franz Grillparzer wrote his historical dramas; and Josef Lanner, both Johann Strausses (father and son), Carl Michael Ziehrer, and Karl Millöcker composed and directed many of their waltzes, marches, and operettas.

The loveliest spot in Baden, and for many the main reason for a visit, is the huge and beautiful **Kurpark,** where occasional outdoor public concerts still take place. Operetta is performed under the skies in the Summer Arena (the roof closes if it rains); in winter, it is performed in the Stadttheater. People sit quietly under the old trees or walk through the upper sections of the Kurpark for a view of the town from above. The old Kurhaus, now enlarged and renovated, incorporates a convention hall. The ornate **Casino**—with a bar, restaurant, and gambling rooms— still includes traces of its original 19th-century decor, but has been enlarged and overlaid with glitz that rivals Las Vegas. ⊠ *Kurpark,* ☎ *02252/44496–0.* ☉ *Daily from 1 PM, gambling daily from 3 PM.*

Music lovers will want to visit the **Beethoven House** (⊠ Rathausgasse 10, ☎ 02252/86800–310). Admission is AS20, and hours are Tuesday–Friday 4–6, weekends and holidays 9–11 and 4–6. Children of all ages will enjoy the enchanting **Doll and Toy Museum** (⊠ Erzherzog Rainer-Ring 23, ☎ 02252/41020). Admission is AS20, and the museum is open Tuesday–Friday 4–6, weekends and holidays 9–11 and 4–6.

One of the pleasures associated with Baden is getting there. You can reach the city directly from Vienna by bus or, far more fun, interurban streetcar, in about 50 minutes—the bus departs from the Ring directly opposite the Opera House; the streetcar departs from the Ring across from the Bristol Hotel. Both drop you in the center of Baden. By car from Vienna, travel south on Route A2, turning west at the junction of Route 305. It is possible, with advance planning, to go on to Mayerling and Heiligenstadt on post office buses (☎ 0222/711–01).

Dining and Lodging

$$$$ ✕🏨 **Grand Hotel Sauerhof.** "Schönbrunn yellow" marks this appealing country house that's been elegantly renovated, with rooms in old-Vienna style. The hotel caters heavily to seminars and group activities, but individual guests are not ignored, and accommodations are comfortable and modern. The hotel's Rauhenstein restaurant is excellent (try the beef fillet with mushrooms, or for dessert, the famous house crepes) if occasionally inconsistent. ⊠ *Weilburgstr. 11–13, A-2500,* ☎ *02252/41251–0,* 🅵🅰🆇 *02252/48047. 88 rooms. Restaurant, bar, indoor pool, sauna, tennis court, exercise room. AE, DC, MC, V.*

$$$$ ✕🏨 **Schloss Weikersdorf.** You're in a restored renaissance castle, but just minutes away from the center of Baden. The setting on the edge of a vast public park offers bonuses of a rose garden and boating on the lake. Rooms and baths are luxuriously outfitted. ⊠ *Schlossgasse 9–1, A-2500,* ☎ *02252/48301,* 🅵🅰🆇 *02252/48301–150. 78 rooms, plus 26 rooms in the annex. Restaurant, bar, indoor pool, sauna, tennis courts, bowling. AE, DC, MC, V.*

$$$–$$$$ ✕⌂ **Krainerhütte.** This friendly house, in typical Alpine style, with balconies and lots of natural wood, has been family-run since 1876. The location on the outskirts of town is ideal for relaxing or exploring the surrounding woods. Facilities are up-to-date, and the restaurant offers a choice of cozy rooms or an outdoor terrace along with international and Austrian cuisine, with fish and game from the hotel's own reserves. ⊠ *Helenental, A–2500,* ☎ *02252/44511–0,* FAX *02252/44514. 60 rooms. Restaurant, indoor pool, sauna, tennis court. AE, MC, V. Closed mid-Jan.–early Feb.*

Mayerling

❼ *29 km (18 mi) west of Vienna, 11 km (7 mi) northwest of Baden.*

Scenic route 210 takes you through the quiet Helenental valley west of Baden to Mayerling, scene of a tragedy that is still impetuously discussed and disputed by the Austrian public, press, and historians at the slightest provocation as well as providing a torrid subject for movie-makers and novelists in many other parts of the world. On the snowy evening of January 28, 1889, the 30-year-old Habsburg heir, Crown Prince Rudolf, Emperor Franz Josef's only son, and his 17-year-old mistress, Baroness Marie Vetsera met a violent and untimely end at the emperor's hunting lodge at Mayerling. Most historians believe it was a suicide pact between two desperate lovers (the Pope had refused an annulment to Rudolf's own unhappy marriage). There are those, however, who feel Rudolf's pro-Hungarian political leanings might be a key to the tragedy. In an attempt to suppress the scandal—the full details are not known to this day—the baroness's body, propped up between two uncles, was smuggled back into the city by carriage (she was buried hastily in nearby Heiligenkreuz). The bereaved emperor had the hunting lodge where the suicide took place torn down and replaced with a rather nondescript Carmelite convent. Mayerling remains beautiful, haunted—and remote: the village is infrequently signposted.

Dining and Lodging

$$$$ ✕⌂ **Kronprinz Mayerling.** Close to both Mayerling and Heiligenkreuz, this stylish building set in a beautiful park has immaculate rooms, each with a whirlpool bath and balcony. The Kronprinz restaurant serves outstanding, adventuresome fare; each course is a concept unto itself, with inspiration coming from French and Chinese cuisine. Fish is particularly well handled, but you might find veal or lamb specialties offered. The associated Landgasthof Marienhof restaurant is simpler, cheaper, and generally far more crowded. ⊠ *Mayerling 1, A–2534 Alland,* ☎ *02258/2378,* FAX *02258/2379–41. 28 rooms. Restaurant, sauna, tennis court, exercise room. AE.*

Heiligenkreuz

❽ *14 km (8¾ mi) northwest of Baden, 14 km (8¾ mi) west of Mödling.*

Slightly northeast of Mayerling, in the heart of the southern section of the Vienna Woods, is Heiligenkreuz, a magnificent Cistercian abbey with a famous Romanesque and Gothic church, founded in 1135 by Leopold III. The church itself is lofty and serene, with beautifully carved choir stalls (the Cistercians are a singing order) surmounted by busts of Cistercian saints. The great treasure here is the relic of the Cross which Leopold V is said to have brought back from his crusade in 1188. The cloisters are interesting for the Chapel of the Dead, where the brothers lie in state guarded by four gesticulating skeletons holding a candelabra. The chapter house contains the tombs of Babenberg rulers. ⊠ *Heiligenkreuz 1,* ☎ *02258/2282.* ⊡ *AS35 (tours only).* ⊙ *Tours*

Mon.–Sat. 10, 11, 2, 3, 4 (summer only); Sun., hols., 11, 2, 3, 4 (summer only).

On a corner of the abbey grounds, follow the Baroque Stations of the Cross along chestnut and linden tree-lined paths. From Vienna, reach Heiligenkreuz by taking Route A21 southwest or via bus from Südtirolerplatz.

Dining and Lodging

$$$ ✕⊞ **Landgasthof Zur Linde.** In the heart of the Wienerwald, some 24 kilometers (15 miles) northwest of Mayerling, lies the small town of Laaben—equally distant (about 14 miles northwest of Mayerling) from Mayerling and Heiligenkreuz, in the shadow of the 2,900-foot Schöpfl Mountain. This charming, family-run country inn offers an excellent base from which to explore the countryside. Rooms are modest but complete and comfortable, with rustic decor. The popular restaurant, with its several wood-beamed rooms, sets the right atmosphere for international and regional cuisine, with seasonal specialties such as lamb, asparagus, and game featured. You might find roast pork marinated in apple cider or fresh local trout. ✉ *Hauptpl. 28, A-3053 Laaben,* ☎ *02774/8378–0,* ☏ *02774/8378–20. 10 rooms. Restaurant. No credit cards. Closed Tues., Wed., mid-Feb.–Mar., and 2 wks in Nov.*

THE WALDVIERTEL

The "Forest District" north of the Danube and to the northwest of Vienna was long dormant, out of the mainstream and cut off from neighboring Czechoslovakia by a sealed border until 1990. Today, with the reopening of many crossing points, the Waldviertel has reawakened. Here, gentle hills bearing stands of tall pine and oak are interspersed with small farms and friendly country villages. The region can be seen in a couple of days, longer when you pause to explore the museums, castles, and other attractions. Zwettl and Raabs an der Thaya, where facilities are more modest and much less expensive than those of the major tourism routes, make good bases for discovering this area.

The main rail line from Vienna to Prague passes through the Waldviertel, making the region accessible by train. In addition, post office buses cover the area fairly well and with reasonable frequency. Bus hubs are Horn, Waidhofen, and Zwettl. An express bus service runs between Vienna and Heidenreichstein via Waidhofen an der Thaya.

If you're traveling by car, signs for Prague will head you in the right direction out of Vienna. At Stockerau take Route 4 to Horn, Route 38 west to Zwettl, an unnumbered road to Weitra, Route 41 to Gmünd and Schrems, Route 30 north to Heidenreichstein, Route 5 to Waidhofen an der Thaya, an unnumbered road via Gross Siegharts to Raabs an der Thaya, Route 30 to Riegersburg, and an unnumbered road to Hardegg. Return on Route 30 to Geras, Route 4 to Horn, Route 34 down the Kamp Valley past Langenlois, and Route 3 back to Vienna.

Kleinwetzdorf/Heldenberg

❾ *52 km (32½ mi) northwest of Vienna, 32 km (20 mi) southeast of Horn.*

The celebrated Austrian field marshal Joseph Wenzel Graf von Radetsky (1766–1858) is buried at Heldenberg near the tiny village of Kleinwetzdorf, in elegant but lugubrious surroundings. The great field marshal was instrumental in defeating Napoléon in 1814, thus saving the Habsburg crown for the young Francis Joseph II. His tomb, arranged for by a wealthy uniform supplier, is marked by an obelisk set in a park studded with dozens of larger-than-life busts of Austrian roy-

The Waldviertel and the Weinviertel

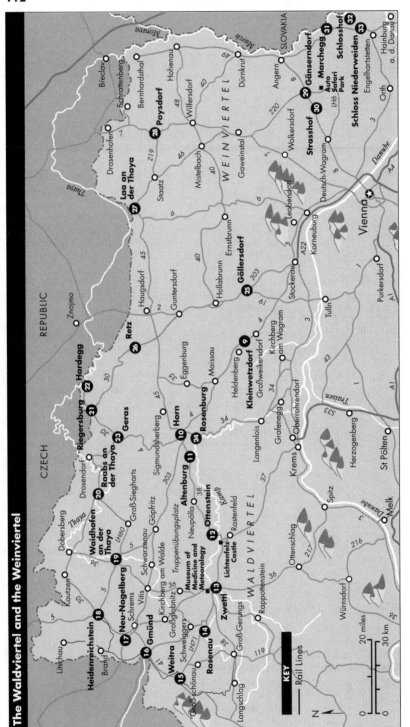

CZECH REPUBLIC

SLOVAKIA

WEINVIERTEL

WALDVIERTEL

KEY
Rail Lines

Lihtschau
Brand
Kautzen
Dobersberg
Drosendorf
Znojmo
Schrattenberg
Breclav
Bernhardsthal
Hohenau
Hohenau
Dürnkrut
Angern
SLOVAKIA
Hainburg a. d. Danau
Orth
Engelhartstetten
Deutsch-Wagram
Korneuburg
Stockerau
Tulln
Purkersdorf
St Pölten
Herzogenberg
Spitz
Melk
Würnsdorf
Langschlag
Groß-schönau
Groß-Gerungs
Roppoltstein
Ottenschlag
Rastenfeld
Neupölla
Langenlois
Krems
Grafenegg
Oberrohrendorf
Kirchberg am Wagram
Großweikersdorf
Heldenberg
Maissau
Eggenburg
Sigmundsherberg
Groß-Siegharts
Göpfritz
Schwarzenau
Kirchberg am Walde
Schweiggers
Großglobnitz
Vitis
Schrems
Gmünd
Weitra
Rosenau
Zwettl
Lichtenfels Castle
Museum of Medicine and Meteorology
Truppenübungsplatz
Altenburg
Raabs an der Thaya
Waidhofen an der Thaya
Geras
Riegersburg
Hardegg
Retz
Haugsdorf
Guntersdorf
Hollabrunn
Ernstbrunn
Mistelbach
Staatz
Laa an der Thaya
Wilfersdorf
Poysdorf
Drasenhofen
Gaweinstal
Wolkersdorf
Strasshof
Leobendorf
Vienna
Auto Safari Park
Marchegg
Gänserndorf
Schloss Niederweiden
Schlosshof
Göllersdorf
Rosenburg
Horn
Kleinwetzdorf

Thaya
Morava
March
Danube
Traisen
Kamp
Danube

9 Kleinwetzdorf
10 Horn
11 Altenburg
12 Ottenstein
13 Lichtenfels
14 Rosenau
15 Weitra
16 Gmünd
17 Neu-Nagelberg
18 Heidenreichstein
19 Waidhofen an der Thaya
20 Raabs an der Thaya
21 Riegersburg
22 Hardegg
23 Geras
24 Rosenburg
25 Göllersdorf
26 Retz
27 Laa an der Thaya
28 Poysdorf
29 Gänserndorf
30 Strasshof
31 Marchegg
32 Schlosshof
33 Schloss Niederweiden

0   20 miles
0   30 km

N

alty and nobility. Follow the marked path to the west back of the park past the memorial to young emperor Franz Josef II to reach the lion-guarded memorial to Radetzky's military campaigns in Italy and Hungary. The whole complex is a slighly eerie phantasmagoria—but historically fascinating. ⊠ *Heldenberg 46,* ☎ *02956/2372.* 🎟 *Free.* ☉ *Daily dawn–dusk.*

The small 17th-century Schloss Wetzdorf has a **Radetzky museum,** although of all the memorials to the field marshal, probably Johann Strauss father's "Radetzky March" is the best known. Half-hidden to the south of the castle is a free-standing arched gate surmounted with wonderful reclining lions. ⊠ *Kleinwetzdorf 1,* ☎ *02956/2751.* 🎟 *Tour AS30, parking free.* ☉ *Tour May–Oct., weekends and holidays at 2, 3, and 4.*

NEED A BREAK?

The **Schlosstaverne** in the Schloss Wetzdorf (☞ *above*) offers light snacks and basics such as Wiener schnitzel, coffee or a cooling drink (only open on weekends and holidays). The courtyard makes a delightful setting in good weather.

Dining and Lodging

$$–$$$ ✕🏨 **Restaurant Naderer.** A fine "food with a view" spot, the Naderer is located at the top of the hill above Maissau, 14 kilometers (9 miles) northwest of Kleinwetzdorf on Route 4. The cuisine is of a standard that draws guests from as far away as Vienna. You can expect the standards such as roast pork or chicken, but you'll also find excellent goose, duck, lamb and game in season. The cakes from the house kitchens are particularly good. Most of the excellent wines come from the surrounding vineyards. In summer, lunching on the terrace overlooking the valley can be a particularly pleasurable experience. Twelve hotel rooms are available for overnights. ⊠ *Am Berg 44, A-3712 Maissau,* ☎ *02958/82334. 12 rooms with bath. AE, DC, MC, V.*

Horn

⑩ *81 km (50½ mi) northwest of Vienna.*

Horn lies at the eastern edge of the Waldviertel. Remnants of the impressive fortification walls with its watchtowers built in 1532 to defend against invading Turks are still obvious. Wander through the core of the old city, which dates from the 15th century. Note the painted Renaissance façade on the house (1583) at Kirchenplatz 3. The **St. Stephen's parish church** on the edge of the cemetery out of the center boasts a Gothic choir and late Gothic stone chancel. The Baroque **Piaristen church,** built in 1660, features a 1777 altar painting by the renowned regional artist Kremser Schmidt. The castle, started in the 1500s and completely rebuilt in the 18th century, sits at the edge of the large, attractive Schlosspark. Horn is host to an international chamber music festival in summer.

⑪ About 5 kilometers (3 miles) west of Horn, at **Altenburg** on Route 38, **Altenburg abbey** was built in 1144 and rebuilt in 1645–1740 after its destruction by the Swedes. The library and the frescoed translucent ceilings by the master artist Paul Troger are glorious. ⊠ *Altenburg 1,* ☎ *02982/3451.* 🎟 *AS50 (tours only).* ☉ *Daily; tours Easter–Nov. 1, daily at 10, 11, and 4, and Nov. 2–Easter by appointment.*

⑫ Almost 35 kilometers (21 miles) west of Altenburg on Route 38, the castle at **Ottenstein,** now a hotel-restaurant, has a number of impressive reception rooms and parts dating to 1178. Ottenstein defied the invading Swedes in 1645 only to be devastated by the Russians in 1945. Sports enthusiasts will find boating and swimming in the reservoir-lake and golf at Niedergrünbach. The ruined Lichtenfels castle nearby can be explored. ☒ *Ottenstein 1,* ☎ *02826/254.*

Zwettl

⑬ *125 km (78 mi) northwest of Vienna, 52 km (32½ mi) northwest of Krems, 49 km (30¼ mi) west of Horn.*

Zwettl lies in the heartland of the forest district. The town center, squeezed between a river bend, is attractive for its gabled houses and colorful pastel façades. The city wall, dating from the Middle Ages, still includes eight defensive towers. But Zwettl is best known for the vast **Cistercian abbey,** dating from 1138, about 2¼ kilometers (1½ miles) west of the town. The Zwettl abbey, perched above the Kamp River, was established as an outpost of the abbey at Heiligenkreuz in the Wienerwald (☞ Heiligenkreuz, *above*). The imposing south gate in the cloisters remains from the original edifice; the church with its massive Gothic choir was completed in 1348. Later renovations added the glorious Baroque touches, with the west wall crowned by a 292-foot tower. An international organ festival is held here annually from the end of June to the end of July. ☎ *02822/550–17.* ✉ *AS50.* ☉ *Tour May and June, Mon.–Sat. at 10, 11, 2, and 3, and Sun. at 11, 2, and 3; July–Sept. additional tour daily at 4.*

About 2 kilometers (1 mile) north of Zwettl on Route 36, at Dürnhof, a fascinating **Museum of Medicine and Meteorology** is housed in a cloister chapel built in 1294. Exhibits follow the development of medicine from earliest times to the present, and the courtyard garden of medicinal herbs adds another dimension to the history. ☎ *02822/53180.* ✉ *AS40.* ☉ *May–Oct., Tues.–Sun. 10–6.*

Dining and Lodging

$$ ✕ **Stiftsrestaurant.** Set within the Zwettl abbey, this spacious tavern complex serves good Austrian country fare such as grilled chicken and roast pork with bread dumplings and occasional regional specialties such as Waldviertel potato dumplings. The outstanding beer, fresh from the nearby brewery, alone is alone worth a stop, as are the wines, which come from the abbey's own cellars. ☒ *Stift Zwettl,* ☎ *02822/550–36. No credit cards. Closed Tues. and Nov.–Easter.*

$$ ⊞ **Gasthof "Dichter Hamerling."** The cream-colored plain façade gives way to a relatively simple but modernized family-run hotel set somewhat to the east of the town center. Rooms are comfortable enough, and the buffet breakfast is ample. ☒ *Galgenbergstr. 3, A–3910,* ☎ *02822/54328,* ℻ *02822/52344–85. 24 rooms with bath. Parking. No credit cards.*

Rosenau

⑭ *8 km (5 mi) west of Zwettl.*

Schloss Rosenau, with its prominent central tower, is an impressive Renaissance structure built in 1590 with later Baroque additions. The castle was ravaged by the Soviets in 1945, then rebuilt as a hotel and museum complex housing the unique **Freemasonry Museum** (Freimaurer-Museum). A secret room once used for lodge ceremonies was discovered during the renovations and is now part of the museum. Displays show the ties of Haydn and Mozart to freemasonry, and many exhibits are in English, reflecting the origins of the brotherhood. ☎ *02822/58221.* ✉ *AS45.* ☉ *Mid-Apr.–Oct., daily 9–5.*

Dining and Lodging

$$$–$$$$ ✕⊡ **Schloss Rosenau.** Set in an elegant castle, this small hotel offers
★ country quiet and modern rooms furnished in period style. The wood-
paneled restaurant is one of the best in the area, featuring garlic soup,
bread soup, and lamb or game in season. In summer, food seems to
taste even better on the sunny outdoor terrace, which overlooks great
expanses of grain fields set about a jewel of a tiny castle. ⊠ *A–3924,*
☎ *02822/58221,* ⅎ⅍ *02822/58222–8. 18 rooms. Restaurant, indoor
pool, sauna, fishing. AE, DC, MC, V. Closed mid-Jan.–Feb.*

Weitra

⑮ *24 km (15 mi) northwest of Zwettl, 16 km (10 mi) southwest of
Gmünd.*

The small town of Weitra, set along the main road of LH71, is renowned
for its stunning ornate painted house façades (sgraffiti) dating from the
17th and 18th centuries. A charming small brewery has been in busi-
ness here since 1321! And the tradition is well founded: In 1645, 33
Weitra citizens held the right to operate a brewery. At the local Brauho-
tel, you can even take a course in brewing. The domineering 15th-cen-
tury defense **castle** with its Renaissance features is privately owned, but
following extensive renovations in 1993 parts are now open to the pub-
lic; the Rococo theater, ceremonial hall, the tower, and the extensive
Schlosskeller with an exhibition on beer brewing are particularly
worthwhile. This is the most westerly of the line of castles built to de-
fend against possible invaders from the north. ☎ *02865/3311 or
02856/2998.* ⊡ *AS60.* ⊙ *Mid-May–late Oct., Wed.–Sun. 10–5.*

Dining and Lodging

$$$ ✕⊡ **Brauhotel Weitra.** Riding on the town's tradition for beer brew-
ing, this new hotel is tucked behind an ancient façade, blending well
with the other buildings in the center. Rooms are comfortable and modern. The restaurant offers Austrian and regional standards plus some
surprises, often based on the use of beer in cooking. The house mini-
brewery keeps glasses filled, but wines are good, too. ⊠ *Rathauspl. 6,
A-3970,* ☎ *02856/2936–0,* ⅎ⅍ *02856/2936–222. 35 rooms. Restaurant, bar, sauna. No credit cards. Closed late Jan.–early Feb.*

Gmünd

⑯ *16 km (10 mi) north of Weitra, 55 km (34½ mi) northwest of Horn.*

The town of Gmünd was curiously divided in 1918 when the border
with Czechoslovakia was established. The actual line passes through
a few houses and backyards, but with the barbed-wire defenses removed,
the border is now a harmless affair. The core of the old town remains
in Austria, and is worth viewing for the painted façades (sgraffiti) around
the main square. Adjacent to the square is the once-moated (private)
castle which dates from the 16th century.

Railroad fans have a field day in Gmünd; the Czechs still use some steam
locomotives for switching, and on the Austrian side Gmünd is one of
↻ the main points on the delightful narrow-gauge **Waldviertler Bahn** (☎
02852/52588–365, 02852/51541, or 02812/228), which runs occasional steam excursions plus some regular services. The excursion runs
generally include a club car with refreshments.

↻ The **Naturpark Blockheide Gmünd-Eibenstein** nature park to the northeast of the town center, open free to the public all year, includes a ge-
ological open-air museum and a stone marking the 15th meridian east

of Greenwich. No one knows the source of the huge granite boulders that adorn the park. ✉ *Grillensteiner Str.,* ☎ *02852/54964.*

Northwest of Schrems, a detour west from Route 30, on Route 303, **⑰** leads to **Neu–Nagelberg,** pressed against the Czech border and a center of glass making since 1740. Among the operating glassworks you can visit to see how glass is made and blown is Glasstudio Zalto (✉ Neu–Nagelberg 58, ☎ 02859/7237–0). Another, Stölzle Kristall (✉ Hauptstr. 45, Alt–Nagelberg, ☎ 02859/7531–0), has a showroom and factory outlet.

Heidenreichstein

★ ☙ **⑱** *13 km (8¼ mi) north of Schrems, 51 ki (32 mi) northwest of Horn, 14 ki (9 mi) northwest of Waidhofen an der Thaya.*

The scenic route north from Schrems parallels the narrow-gauge railway to Heidenreichstein, noted for the massive moated **castle** with its corner towers, which has never been captured by enemy forces since it was built in the 15th century; some of the walls, 10 feet thick, went up in the 13th century. This is one of the most remarkable "water" castles in Austria. "Water"—or moated—castle were surrounded by a body of water (natural or artificial) for defense purposes whereas the "hill" castles used steep, often rocky and inaccessible, slopes for protection. The building is in remarkable condition, the best-preserved of all moated castles in Austria, and some of the rooms are furnished with pieces dating from the 15th and 16th centuries. ☎ *02862/52268.* ✉ *AS60 (tours only).* ☺ *Mid-Apr.–mid-Oct., Tues.–Sun. at 9, 10, 11, 2, 3, and 4.*

Waidhofen an der Thaya

⑲ *14 km (8¼ mi east of Heidenreichstein, 32 km (20 mi) north of Zwettl, 37 km (23¼ mi) northwest of Horn.*

Route 5 between Heidenreichstein and Waidhofen an der Thaya is particularly scenic. Waidhofen itself is a three-sided walled defense city typical of those of the 13th century. Fires destroyed much of the early character of the town, but the town square, rebuilt at the end of the 19th century, has a pleasing unity. The town is dominated by its Baroque parish church locally known as the "cathedral of the Thaya valley"; the Rococo chapel to Mary includes a Madonna of 1440 and distinguished portraits marking the Stations of the Cross. Outside the city walls, the **Bürgerspitalkapelle** has a side altar with a Gothic carved-wood relief of Madonna and child and 13 assistants, dating from about 1500.

Raabs an der Thaya

★ **⑳** *21 km (13 mi) northeast of Waidhofen an der Thaya, 42 km (26¼ mi) northwest of Horn.*

The Thaya River wanders leisurely thorough Raabs an der Thaya, an unusually attractive village watched over by an 11th-century castle perched dramatically on a rock outcropping and reflected in the river below. This was one of the chain of defensive castles through the Waldviertel region. The river is popular for fishing and swimming. ☎ *02846/365.* ✉ *AS50.* ☺ *June–Sept., weekends 10–5; call to confirm.*

The intriguing ruins of the Kollmitz castle to the southeast of Raabs can be explored, and a bit farther along are the ruins of Eibenstein castle, another link in the 16th- and 17th-century defense chain along the border with Bohemia.

Northeast of Raabs along Route 30 is the border town of Drosendorf, with a castle built in 1100 and an historic center typical of a small walled community. The encircling wall is virtually intact and complete with watchtowers.

Dining and Lodging

$$ ✕⛺ **Hotel Thaya.** A friendly, family-run hotel directly on the river, the
★ Thaya offers comfortable, modern if slightly spartan rooms in the new annex. Rooms directly overlooking the river are the favorites. The restaurant prepares such solid local specialties as roast pork and veal. ✉ *Hauptstr. 14, A–3820,* ☎ *02846/202–0,* 🖷 *02846/202–20. 25 rooms. Restaurant, bar, beer garden, sauna, exercise room, dance club, parking. No credit cards.*

$$ ⛺ **Pension Schlossblick.** This small modern pension has a homey atmosphere in its spacious lounge and cheery breakfast room. The rooms on the town side looking through the trees to the castle are the nicest. ✉ *Eduard Braith-Str. 7, A–3820,* ☎ *02846/437. 13 rooms. Restaurant, parking. No credit cards.*

Riegersburg

㉑ *28 km (17½ mi) east of Raabs, 33 km (20½ mi) north of Horn, 18½ km (11½ mi) northwest of Retz.*

The impressive **Schloss Riegersburg** was originally moated before the substantial edifice was given a Baroque makeover in 1731 and again virtually rebuilt after the Russians inflicted heavy damage in 1945. Note the window variations and the classic figures that ornament the roofline. The whole castle was renovated in 1992–93, highlighting the elegance of the public rooms and its period furnishings, now back in place. ☎ *02916/332.* 🎫 *Tour AS85, combination ticket with Hardegg AS130.* ⊘ *Apr.–June and Sept.–mid–Nov., daily 9–5; July and Aug., daily 9–7.*

☾ ㉒ **Hardegg,** about 6 kilometers (4 miles) east of Riegersburg on an unnumbered road, features a wonderfully eclectic **castle** that stands mightily on a rock promontory high above the Thaya River, watching over the Czech Republic. (The river midstream marks the boundary; as recently as 1990, the pedestrian bridge was unpassable, the border sealed, and Czech border defenses were concealed in the woods opposite.) The earliest parts of the castle date from 1140. The armory and armament collection, chapel, and the museum's exhibits on the emperor Maximilian in Mexico alone are worth a visit. In addition, the kitchen and other working rooms of the castle give a real feeling of the daily life of an earlier era. An English-speaking guide is available for small-group tours. ☎ *02949/8225.* 🎫 *AS65, tour AS25.* ⊘ *Apr.–June and Sept.–mid-Nov., daily 9–5; July and Aug., daily 9–6.*

Geras

㉓ *22 km (13¾ mi) north of Horn, 23 km (14½ mi) southeast of Raabs an der Thaya, 20 km (12½ mi) southwest of Hardegg.*

Another of the Waldviertel's great abbeys, the **Stift Geras,** is situated at Geras. Established in 1120, the impressive complex has had from its beginnings close ties to its agricultural surroundings. The abbey was given a glorious full-blown Baroque treatment in the course of rebuilding following a fire in 1730, including a translucent fresco by the noted Paul Troger in the 18th century Marble Hall, now often used for concerts. While the abbey still functions as a religious center, the complex is now also a noted school for arts and crafts. ✉ *Hauptstr. 1,* ☎

02912/345–289. ☐ AS50. ☉ Tour May–Oct., Tues.–Sat. at 10, 11, 2, 3, and 4; Sun. at 11, 2, 3, and 4.

Dining and Lodging

$$$ ✕🏨 **Stiftsrestaurant und Hotel "Alter Schüttkasten."** A former granary outbuilding of the abbey has been turned into a modern hotel with all the amenities. Rooms are comfortable; those on the front look out over the fields toward the abbey. The restaurant offers seasonal specialties such as fish and game in addition to pork, beef and other regional standards. ⊠ *Vorstadt 11, A–2093,* ☎ *02912/332,* 𝖥𝖠𝖷 *02912/332-33. 26 rooms. Restaurant, bar, sauna, parking. DC.*

Kamptal

The gloriously scenic Kamp River valley (Kamptal), running from Rosenburg in the north some 30 kilometers (19 miles) south roughly to Hadersdorf am Kamp, technically belongs to the Waldviertel, though for the amount of wine produced here, it might as well be a part of the Weinviertel, the wine district to the east. The river, road, and railroad share the frequently narrow and twisting route which meanders some 25 kilometers (15½ miles) through the valley from Rosenburg south to Langenlois. The villages along the route—Gars am Kamp, Schönberg am Kamp, Zöbing, Strass, and Langenlois—are all known for excellent wines, mainly varietal whites. Strass in particular has become an active center of viticulture, and many vintners offer wine tastings. Castle ruins dot the hilltops above the woods and vineyards; the area has been populated since well before 900 BC. Scattered through the valley are some noted eateries and hotels; the best are reviewed below, listed under their particular village.

Ⓒ ㉔ The massive defense castle at **Rosenburg** dates from 1200 and dominates the north entrance to the Kamptal Valley. Its features include the original jousting field as a forecourt and impressive reception rooms inside, where armor and other relics of the period are on display. Curious Renaissance balconies and small courtyards are incorporated into the design, although the variety in the 13 towers added in the 15th century is the touch that immediately catches the eye. ☎ *02982/2911.* ☐ *AS65, including tour; falconry demonstration AS65; combination ticket for tour and demonstration AS100. ☉ Apr.–mid-Nov., daily 9– 5; falconry demonstration Apr.–Nov., daily at 11 and 3; tour begins 1 hr before demonstration.*

Dining and Lodging

GARS AM KAMP

$$–$$$ ✕ **Pfiffig.** The ruins of the ancient castle above Gars am Kamp provide the dramatic setting for this excellent family-run restaurant serving regional specialties and other choices such as *Tafelspitz* (delicate boiled beef). The rooms are elegant and offer a showcase for local artists. The excellent wines understandably come from the neighborhood. ⊠ *A–3571 Gars am Kamp,* ☎ *02985/30500. No credit cards. Closed Mon., Tues., and Jan.*

GRAFENEGG

$$–$$$ ✕🏨 **Schlosstaverne Mörwald.** Beyond the golden facade of this elegant tavern across from Schloss Grafenegg you'll find a friendly and ★ welcoming atmosphere. Rooms are comfortably furnished in beiges and reds. The restaurant offers game in season and local cuisine with international touches. The strawberries in early summer taste even better outdoors on the sunny dining terrace. ⊠ *A–3485 Haitzendorf,* ☎ *02735/2616,* 𝖥𝖠𝖷 *02735/2298–6. 6 rooms. Restaurant. MC, V. Closed Jan. and Feb.*

$$$$ ✕ **Gut Oberstockstall.** A former cloister in Oberstockstall, just north
★ of Kirchberg am Wagram, houses this country inn where the rustic setting indoors is charming and the courtyard garden idyllic in summer.
Nearly all ingredients come from the farm itself, guaranteeing top
freshness; preparation is individual and imaginative. The specialties of
the house include beef, lamb, duck, game in season, and delicious
desserts—all to the accompaniment of the house's own outstanding
wines. ✉ *A–3740 Kirchberg am Wagram,* ☎ *02279/2335. No credit
cards. Closed Sun.–Tues.; mid-Dec.–Feb.; and last 2 wks of Aug.*

$–$$ ✕ **Brundlmayer.** This country Heuriger in the center of Langenlois of-
fers outstanding wines from one of Austria's top vintners, as well as a
tasty hot-and-cold buffet, all in an indoor rustic setting, or outdoors
in the Renaissance courtyard. The simple but delicious fare might include variations on Schinkenfleckerl, the popular dish of baked ham
and noodles, goat cheese, or dried, lightly-smoked ham. ✉ *Walterstr.
14, A–3550 Langenlois,* ☎ *02734/2883. No credit cards. Closed
Mon.–Wed. and mid-Dec.–early Mar.*

Route 34 takes you through more vineyards to Kollersdorf, where Route
3 east will return you to Vienna.

THE WEINVIERTEL

Vines have a tendency to thrive in beautiful surroundings and, as attractive buildings and towns often develop close to vineyards, a journey through any wine region can be an alluring prospect. Luckily, Austria
has been largely neglected by the "experts," and its deliciously fresh
wines form an ideal treasure trove to reward those who enjoy drinking wine and dislike the all-too-frequent nonsense that goes with it.
That's especially the case with the rustic and delightful "Wine District,"
the rolling countryside north of Vienna, which earns its name from the
terrain and climate of the region, ideal for the cultivation of wine.

The Weinviertel is bounded by the Danube on the south, the Thaya
River and the reopened Czech border on the north, the March River
and Slovakia to the east. No well-defined line separates the Weinviertel from the Waldviertel to the west; the Kamp River valley, officially
part of the Waldviertel, is an important wine region. Whether wine,
crops, or dairying, this is farming country, its broad expanses of vineyards and farmlands broken by patches of forest and neat villages. A
tour by car, just for the scenery, can be made in a day; you may want
two or three days to savor the region and its wines—these are generally on the medium-dry side. Don't expect to find here the elegant facilities found elsewhere in Austria; prices are low by any standard, and
village restaurants and accommodations are mainly *Gasthäuser* that
meet local needs. This means that you'll rub shoulders over a glass of
wine or a beer with country folk.

Göllersdorf

㉕ *10 km (6¼ miles) north of Stockerau West interchange on Rte. 303/E59.*

The rolling hills and agricultural lands of the southwest Weinviertel
around Hollabrunn offer little excitement other than panoramas and
scenic pleasures, but one exception is the **Schloss Schönborn** about 2
kilometers (1¼ mile:south of Göllersdorf. The castle was laid out in
1712 by that master of Baroque architecture, Johann Lukas von Hildebrandt. Today the castle is in private hands, but the harmony of de-

sign can be appreciated from the outside. The parish church in Göllers-dorf is also a Baroque Hildebrandt design of 1740 overlaid on a Gothic structure dating to the mid-1400s.

Retz

★ ㉖   *70 km (43¾ mi) north of Vienna, 29 km (18¼ mi) northeast of Horn, 13 km (8¼ mi) southeast of Hardegg.*

Retz, at the northwest corner of the Weinviertel, is a charming town with an impressive rectangular central square formed by buildings mainly dating to the 15th century. Retz is best known for its red wines. Here you can tour **Austria's largest wine cellar**, tunneled 65 feet under the town, and at the same time taste wines of the area. Some of the tunnels go back to the 13th century, and at the end of the 15th century each citizen was permitted to deal in wines and was entitled to storage space in the town cellars. Efforts to use the cellars for armaments production during World War II failed because of the 88% humidity. The temperature remains constant at 8°C–10°C (47°F–50°F). Entrance to the cellars is at the Rathauskeller. ☏ *02942/2700.* ✉ *Tour AS70.* ✉ *Tour Mon.–Sat. at 10:30 and 2, Sun. at 10:30, 2, and 4; call to confirm tour times.*

Take time to explore Retz's tiny streets leading from the town square; the oldest buildings and the wall and gate tower defenses survived destruction by the Swedish armies in 1645 during the Thirty Years' War. The Dominican church (1295) at the southwest corner of the square survived, and it is interesting for its long, narrow design. The pastel Biedermeier façades along with the sgraffiti add appeal to the square, which is further marked by the impressive city hall with its massive Gothic tower in the center.

Dining and Lodging

$$$$ ✕🏠 **Althof Retz/Hotel Burghof.** A new hotel has been tucked into an ancient estate building just off the town square. Take your choice of the upscale Hotel Burghof or the slightly less expensive Althof, which also serves as a training hotel. Both are done in whites and light wood. Rooms are modern, comfortable and with all facilities. The restaurant has been less successful, but the standards and regional specialties are fine. The excellent wines naturally come mainly from the area. ✉ *Althofgasse 14, A–2070,* ☏ *02942/3711–0,* 🆕 *02942/3711–55. 65 rooms. Restaurant, parking. No credit cards.*

Laa an der Thaya

㉗   *65 km (40¼ mi) north of Vienna, 39 km (24¼ mi) east of Retz, 26 km (16¼ mi) northwest of Mistelbach.*

From 1948 until about 1990, Laa an der Thaya, was a town isolated by the Cold War, directly bordering then–Czechoslovakia. Laa is considerably livelier now that the border is open. (As long as you have your passport with you, you can cross into the Czech Republic and return without complication.) The town's huge central square is adorned with a massive neo-Gothic city hall, in stark contrast to the low, colorful buildings that form the square. If you're traveling from Retz to Laa an der Thaya, retrace your way south on Route 30 to Route 45.

Laa boasts a **Beer Museum,** located in the town fortress, that traces the history of beer (the nearby Hubertus brewery has been in business since 1454) and maintains an imposing collection of beer bottles. ☏ *02522/2501–29.* ✉ *AS20.* ☉ *May–Sept., weekends and holidays 2–4.*

Dining

$$ ✕ **Restaurant Weiler.** Light woods and country accessories set the tone
★ in this family-run restaurant, and in summer dinner is served in the out-
door garden. Try the delicate cream of garlic soup or the house specialty,
game in season. For dessert, the delicious cakes of the house are tempt-
ingly displayed in a showcase. ⊠ *Staatsbahnstr. 60,* ☎ *02522/379–2379.*
No credit cards. Closed Mon., 2 wks in Feb., and July. No dinner Sun.

Poysdorf

㉘ *61 km (38¼ mi) north of Vienna, 22 km (13¼ mi) southeast of Laa an*
der Thaya.

Poysdorf is considered by many the capital of the Weinviertel. Wine-
making here goes back to the 14th century. Poysdorf vintages, mainly
whites, rank with the best Austria has to offer. Narrow paths known
as *"Kellergassen"* ("cellar streets") on the northern outskirts are lined
with wine cellars set into and under the hills. A festival in early Septem-
ber marks the annual harvest. At the wine market in the center of town,
you can taste as well as buy (⊠ Singerstr. 2); the market is open Mon-
day–Thursday 8–5, Friday 8–6, and weekends and holidays 10–noon
and 2–6. The town museum includes a section on viticulture and
wine-making. ⊠ *Brunner Str. 9,* ☎ *02552/2200–17.* 🎟 *AS40.* ⊙
Easter–Oct., Mon.–Wed. 9–noon and 1–5; call to confirm.

Dining

MISTELBACH

$$–$$$ ✕ **Zur Linde.** This friendly family-run restaurant with rustic decor 16
★ kilometers (10 miles) south of Poysdorf is setting higher standards for
such traditional fare as roast pork, stuffed breast of veal, flank steak,
and fresh game in season. Desserts are excellent; try the extraordinary
Apfelstrudel. A major attraction here is the remarkable range of wines
from the neighborhood at altogether reasonable prices. ⊠ *Bahnhof-*
str. 49, A–2130 Mistelbach, ☎ *02572/2409. AE, DC, MC, V. Closed*
Mon.; late Jan.–mid-Feb., and late July–mid-Aug. No dinner Sun.

POYSDORF

$$ ✕ **Gasthaus Schreiber.** Choose the shaded garden under huge trees or
the country rustic decor indoors. The typical Austrian fare—roast
pork, stuffed breast of veal, boiled beef, filet steak with garlic—is
commendable, as is the house-made ice cream. The wine card lists more
than 60 area labels. ⊠ *Bahnstr. 2, A–2170,* ☎ *02552/2348. No credit*
cards. Closed Tues. and late Jan.–mid-Feb. No dinner Mon.

Gänserndorf

☾ **㉙** *30 km (18¾ mi) northeast of Vienna.*

Three kilometers (2 miles) south of Gänserndorf, the **Safari-Park und**
Abenteuerpark (Safari Park and Adventure Park) allows visitors to drive
through re-created natural habitats of live wild animals, many of which
(lions and tigers) are hardly indigenous to Austria. The adventure
takes five to six hours, allowing time for the petting zoo and the extra
animal shows, which start every half hour. For those without a car, a
safari bus leaves for the circuit every hour. ⊠ *Siebenbrunner Str.,* ☎
02282/70261–0, 🗷 *02282/70261–27.* 🎟 *AS162.* ⊙ *Palm Sun.–Oct.,*
weekdays 9:30–4, weekends and holidays 9–4:30.

Strasshof

㉚ *3 km (2 mi) southwest of Gänserndorf.*

Ⓒ The **Heizhaus** north of Strasshof is a fascinating private collection of dozens of steam locomotives and railroad cars stored in a vast engine house. Enthusiasts have painstakingly rebuilt and restored many of the engines; steam locomotives are up and running on the first Sunday of each month. The complex includes transfer table, water towers, and coaling station, and visitors can climb around among many of the locomotives awaiting restoration. The collection includes—at least for the time being—many of the operative locomotives from the Technical Museum in Vienna, now closed for extensive renovations. ⊠ *Siller-str. 123,* ☎ *02287/3027.* ⌑ *AS60, steam days AS70, including parking and tour.* ⊙ *Mid-Apr.–Oct., Sun. and holidays 10–4.*

The area to the north of Gänserndorf includes one of Austria's few gas and oil fields, where operating pumps patiently pull up crude to be piped to the refinery about 20 kilometers (12½ miles) south. Underground, exhausted gas wells serve as natural storage tanks for gas coming to Western Europe from Russia.

Dining

$$$$ ✕ **Marchfelderhof.** Located in nearby Deutsch Wagram, this sprawling complex, with its eclectic series of rooms bountiously decorated with everything from antiques to hunting trophies, has a reputation for excess in the food department as well. The menu's standards—Wiener schnitzel, roast pork, lamb—are more successful than the more expensive efforts at innovation. Deutsch Wagram is 12 kilometers (7 miles) southwest of Gänserndorf on Route 8, 17 kilometers (11 miles) northeast of Vienna on Route 8. ⊠ *Bockfliesser Str. 31, A–2232 Deutsch Wagram,* ☎ *02247/2243–0. AE, DC, MC, V. Closed Mon. and late Dec.–early Feb.*

Marchegg

㉛ *11 ki (7 mi) southeast of Gänserndorf.*

The tiny corner of the lower Weinviertel to the southeast of Gänserndorf is known as the Marchfeld, for the fields stretching east to the March River, forming the border with Slovakia. In this region—known as the granary of Austria—three elegant Baroque castles in the area are worth a visit; all have been totally renovated in recent years and given over to changing annual exhibits, concerts, and other public activities. These country estates have lost none of their gracious charm over the centuries. The northernmost of the group is the **castle** at Marchegg, the oldest parts dating to 1268. What you see today is the Baroque overlay added in 1733 to the basic building of the middle ages. The castle now houses a hunting museum. To reach Marchegg from Gänserndorf, take Route 8a 6 kilometers (4 miles) east to Route 49, then Route 49 10 kilometers (6 miles) south. ☎ *02285/224.* ⌑ *AS30.* ⊙ *Mid-Mar.–Nov., Tues.–Sun. 9–noon and 1–5.*

㉜ The castle at **Schlosshof** is a true Baroque gem, a product of that master designer and architect Johann Lukas von Hildebrandt, who in 1732 reconstructed the four-sided castle into an elegant U-shaped building, opening up the eastern side to a marvelous Baroque formal garden that gives way toward the river. The famed Italian painter Canaletto captured the view before the reconstruction. The castle—once owned by Empress Maria Theresa—is now used for changing annual exhibits, but you can walk the grounds without paying admission. The castle is about 8 kilometers (5 miles) south of Marchegg. ☎ *02285/6580.* ⌑ *AS50, tour AS20, combination ticket with Schloss Niederweiden AS80.* ⊙ *Apr.–Oct., daily 10–5.*

㉝ **Schloss Niederweiden,** about 4 kilometers (2½ miles) southwest of Schlosshof and north of Engelhartstetten, was designed as a hunting lodge and built in 1694 by that other master of the Baroque, Fischer von Erlach. This jewel was subsequently owned by Prince Eugene and Empress Maria Theresa, who added a second floor and the mansard roofs. Annual exhibits now take place here in summer, and in a vinothek you can sample the wines of the surrounding area. ☎ 02214/2803. ✉ *AS50, tour AS20, combination ticket with Schlosshof AS80.* ☉ *Apr.–Oct., daily 10–5; Vinotek weekends and holidays 10–6.*

SIDE TRIPS FROM VIENNA A TO Z

Arriving and Departing

By Car

The autobahn A1 traverses the Wienerwald in the west; the A2 autobahn runs through the edge of the Wienerwald to the south. The A4 autobahn is a quick way to reach the Carnuntum region. The Waldviertel and Weinviertel are accessed by major highways but not autobahns.

By Plane

Vienna's Schwechat airport serves the surrounding region as well.

By Train

The main east–west train line cuts through the Wienerwald; the main north–south line out of Vienna traverses the eastern edge of the Wienerwald. The main line to Prague and onward runs through the Waldviertel. Train service in the Weinviertel is regular to Mistelbach, irregular after that. The rail line east out of Vienna to the border town Wolfstal cuts through the Carnuntum region. The line to the north of the Danube to Bratislava runs through the middle of the Marchfeld.

Getting Around

By Bus

Buses are a good possibility for getting around, although if you're not driving, a combination of bus and train is probably a better answer in many cases. Frequent scheduled bus service runs between Vienna and Baden, departing from across from the Opera House in Vienna to the center of Baden. Connections are available to other towns in the area. Bus service runs between Vienna and Carnuntum–Petronell, and on to Hainburg. Service to the Waldviertel is less frequent, but is available between Vienna and Horn, Zwettl, Waidhofen, and Raabs an der Thaya. From these points, you can get buses to other parts of the Waldviertel. An express bus service runs between Vienna and Heidenreichstein via Waidhofen an der Thaya. In the Weinviertel, bus service is fairly good between Vienna and Mistelbach, Laa an der Thaya, and Poysdorf.

By Car

Driving through these regions is by far the best way to see them, since you can wander the byways and stop whenever and wherever you like. Roads are good and generally well marked. To explore the Vienna Woods, from Vienna head for Liesing (23rd District), then take Wiener Strasse to Perchtoldsdorf; from there, follow the signs south to Mödling and Baden. From Baden, take Route 210 (marked HELENENTAL) to Mayerling and on to Alland; return to Vienna via Route 11, stopping in Heiligenkreuz en route.

Carnuntum–Petronell is easy to reach: from Vienna, simply follow signs to AIRPORT/BRATISLAVA (A4). Leave the divided highway for the more scenic

Route 9, which will be marked to Hainburg. At Petronell, you will have to take a sharp left off the bypass road, but signs are clear for the Roman ruins (Carnuntum), as they are for the other destinations in the region.

For the Waldviertel, signs for Prague will head you in the right direction out of Vienna. At Stockerau take Route 4 to Horn, Route 38 west to Zwettl, an unnumbered road to Weitra, Route 41 to Gmünd and Schrems, Route 30 north to Heidenreichstein, Route 5 to Waidhofen an der Thaya, an unnumbered road via Gross Siegharts to Raabs an der Thaya, Route 30 to Riegersburg, and an unnumbered road to Hardegg. Return on Route 30 to Geras, Route 4 to Horn, Route 34 down the Kamp valley past Langenlois, and Route 3 back to Vienna. If you're headed out of Vienna toward Langenlois and the lower Kamp Valley, follow signs to Krems; the turnoff onto Route 3 at Stockerau West is a bit tricky.

You've a choice of routes when heading out to the Weinviertel. One is to head out of Vienna to Stockerau on Route 3 or the autobahn A22/E49/E59, following the signs to Prague. After Stockerau, turn north on Route 303 to beyond Hollabrunn, then Routes 2 and 30 to Retz. From Retz, backtrack on Route 30 to Route 45 and head east to Laa an der Thaya. Then follow Route 46 to Staatz, Route 219 to Poysdorf, Route 7/E461 south beyond Gaweinstal, Route 220 to Gänserndorf, and Route 8 back to Vienna. The alternative is to take Route 7/E461 from Vienna/Floridsdorf north via Wolkersdorf; beyond Gaweinstal there's a choice of routes that will bring you to Mistelbach and on to Laa an der Thaya, or to Poysdorf.

By Train
Take the interurban train between Vienna and Baden for a delightful variation on the car or bus routine. Local trains on the Westbahn (main east–west line) will drop you off at stations in the Wienerwald, but connections can be tricky unless you plan on an "out-and-back" excursion.

The suburban trains (*Schnellbahn*) running from Wien-Mitte (Landstrasser Hauptstrasse) stop at Petronell, with service about once an hour. Carnuntum is about a 10-minute walk from the Petronell station. Trains go on to Hainburg, stopping at Bad Deutsch-Altenburg.

The main rail line from Vienna to Prague passes through the Waldviertel, making the region accessible by train, but you'll need a bus connection to reach the smaller towns.

Train service into the Weinviertel is fairly good but selective in the destinations you can reach on a direct trip. The suburban express line (*Schnellbahn*) runs between Vienna and Mistelbach, and to Gänserndorf and beyond to Bernhardsthal on the Czech border.

Contacts and Resources
Bicycle Rentals
The best bicycling territories in the regions surrounding Vienna are the Weinviertel, the Carnuntum–Petronell area and the Marchfeld. Larger towns have shops that rent bicycles, as do the key rail stations, but demand is great, so reserve in advance. The Lower Austrian information office (⌧ Heidenschuss 2, A-1010 Vienna, ☎ 01/533–3114–0) can assist.

Car Rentals
Cars can be rented from all leading companies at the Vienna airport (☞ Vienna A to Z *in* Chapter 2) or in Baden, from Autoverleih Buchbinder (☎ 02252/48693) or Autoverleih Schmidt (☎ 02252/47047).

Emergencies

Police, ☎ 133, **fire,** ☎ 122. For **ambulance** or medical emergency, ☎ 144.

Guided Tours

The Wienerwald is one of the standard routes offered by the sightseeing-bus tour operators in Vienna, and it usually includes a boat ride through the "underground sea" grotto near Mödling. For details, check with your hotel or with **Cityrama** (☎ 01/534–13–12), **Vienna Sightseeing Tours** (☎ 01/712–4683–0), or **CityTouring Vienna** (☎ 01/894–1417–0). These short tours give only a quick taste of the region; if you have more time, you'll want to investigate further.

With the opening of the Czech and Slovak republics, more tours may be offered to the Waldviertel and Weinviertel regions of Lower Austria, but for now this is one area you'll probably have to explore on your own.

Visitor Information

Get information in Vienna before you start out, at the tourist office of Lower Austria (✉ Heidenschuss 2, ☎ 01/533–3114–0, ℻ 01/535–0319). There are several helpful regional tourist offices. **Wienerwald** (✉ Hauptpl. 11, A-3002 Purkersdorf, ☎ 02231/2176, ℻ 02231/5510). **March–Donauland** (✉ Hauptpl. 4, A-2405 Bad Deutsch–Altenburg, ☎ 02165/64820, ℻ 02165/65322). **Waldviertel** (✉ Gartenstr. 32, A-3910 Zwettl, ☎ 02822/54109, ℻ 02822/54144). **Weinviertel** (✉ Liechtensteinstr. 1, A-2170 Poysdorf, ☎ 02552/3515, ℻ 02552/3715).

Local tourist offices are generally open weekdays. Here are the offices for the Wienerwald region. **Perchtoldsdorf** (☎ 01/869–7634–34). **Mödling** (✉ Elisabethstr. 2, ☎ 02236/26727, ℻ 02236/41632). **Gumpoldskirchen** (✉ Schrannenpl. 1, ☎ 02252/62101–0). **Baden** (✉ Hauptpl. 2, ☎ 02252/44531–57, ℻ 02252/80733).

The Waldviertel district has numerous tourist offices. **Gars am Kamp** (✉ Hauptpl. 82, ☎ 02985/2680). **Horn** (✉ Wiener Str. 4, ☎ 02982/2372). **Zwettl** (✉ Dreifaltigkeitspl. 1, ☎ 02822/52233). **Gmünd** (✉ Stadtpl. 19, ☎ 02852/53212, ℻ 02852/54713). **Waidhofen an der Thaya** (✉ Hauptpl. 1, ☎ 02842/503–17). **Raabs an der Thaya** (✉ Hauptstr. 25, ☎ 02846/365–0, ℻ 02846/365–21).

The Weinviertel region has several tourist centers. **Retz** (✉ Hauptpl. 30, ☎ 02942/2700). **Laa an der Thaya** (✉ Rathaus, ☎ 02522/2501–0). **Mistelbach** (✉ Hauptpl. 6, ☎ 02572/2515–248). **Poysdorf** (✉ Singergasse 2, ☎ 02552/2200–17). **Gänserndorf** (✉ Rathauspl. 1, ☎ 02282/2651–0).

4 The Danube Valley

A tonic in any season, a trip up the Austrian Danube unveils a parade of storybook-worthy sights: fairytale castles-in-air, medieval villages, and Baroque abbeys crowned with "candle-snuffer" cupolas. The Danube itself is a marvel—on a summer day it even takes on the proper shade of Johann Strauss blue. Along its banks, you'll discover the beautiful Wachau Valley, and cheery Linz, whose pastry shops produce the best Linzertortes around.

By George
Hamilton

Updated by
Willibald
Picard

TO THE SIGHTSEER, a trip along the Austrian Danube unfolds rather like a treasured picture book of history. Roman ruins (some built by Emperor Claudius), remains of medieval castles-in-air, and Baroque monasteries crowned with "candle-snuffer" cupolas perch precariously above the river, compelling the imagination with their legends and myths. This is where Isa—cousin of the Lorelei—lured sailors to the shoals, where Richard the Lion-Hearted was locked in a dungeon for years, and where the Nibelungs—immortalized by Wagner—caroused operatically in battlemented forts. Once, Roman sailors used to throw coins into the perilous whirlpools around Grein to placate Danubius, the river's tutelary god. Today, thanks to the technology of modern dams, travelers have the luxury of seeing this part of Austria from the tame deck of a comfortable river steamer. In clement weather, the nine-hour trip upriver to Linz is highly rewarding. If you have more time to spare, the voyage onward to Passau may be less dramatic but gives more time to take in the picturesque vineyards and the castles perched like so many eagles' aeries on crags above bends in the river.

Even more of the region's attractions can be discovered traveling by car or bus. You can explore plunging Gothic streets, climb Romanesque towers, and linger over a glass at vaulted Weinkellers. River and countryside form an inspired unity here, with fortress-topped outcroppings giving way to broad pastures that swoop down to the very river banks. Many visitors classify this tour as one of Europe's great trips: here you feel you can almost reach out and touch the riverside towns and soak up the intimacy unique to this stretch of the valley. In this chapter, we follow the course of the Danube upstream from Vienna as it winds through Lower Austria (Niederösterreich) and a bit of Upper Austria (Oberösterreich) to Linz, past monasteries and industrial towns, the riverside vineyards of the lower Weinviertel, and the fragrant expanses of apricot and apple orchards.

Linz, Austria's third largest city (and its most underrated), is a key industrial center. It's also a fine town for shopping; the stores are numerous and carry quality merchandise, often at more reasonable prices than in Vienna or the larger resorts. Concerts and operas performed at Linz's modern *Brucknerhaus* make every bit as good listening as those in Vienna or Salzburg.

It is, however, the Danube, originating in Germany's Black Forest and emptying into the Black Sea, that is our focal point: The route that brought the Romans to the area and contributed to its development remains one of Europe's important waterways, with four national capitals on its banks—Vienna, Bratislava, Budapest, and Belgrade. It was not only the Romans who posited "Whoever controls the Danube, controls all Europe." The "Kuenringer"—the robber knights who built many of the hilltop castles—thrived by sacking the baggage caravans of the early Crusaders; later, castles were financed through slightly more legitimate means—Frederick Barbarossa, leading his army downstream, had to pay a crossing toll at Mauthausen. Subsequently, cities sprang up to serve as ports for the salt, wood, ores, and other cargo transported on the river. Today, modern railroads and highways parallel most of the Blue Danube's course.

This is a wonderful trip to take in early spring or in the fall after the grape harvest, when the vineyards turn reddish blue and a bracing chill settles over the Danube; the Empress Maria Theresa would arrive in Linz in May, just as the fruit trees were about to bloom. No matter when you come, be sure to try some of those fruits in a *Linzertorte*—a filling of brandy-flavored apricots, raspberries or plums under a latticed pastry crust—a treat as satisfyingly rich and copious as the Danube Valley itself.

Pleasures and Pastimes

Abbeys

While castles galore dot the area—ranging from crumbling mountaintop ruins to wonderfully restored edifices replete with gargoyles—the real gems in these environs are the abbeys, majestic relics of an era when bishops were as influential as kings. The greatest are Melk, Klosterneuburg, Kremsmünster, St. Florian and Göttweig, all of which have breathlessly imposing scope and elegance.

Bicycling

The trail along the Danube must be one of the great bicycle routes of the world. For much of the way (the exception being the Korneuburg–Krems stretch) you can bike on either side of the river. Some small hotels will even arrange to pick up you and your bike from the cycle path. You'll find bicycle rentals at most riverside towns and at rail stations. The terrain around Linz is relatively level, and within the city there are 89 kilometers (55 miles) of marked cycle routes. In the areas of Eferding, St. Florian, through the Enns River valley, and around Steyr, the territory is generally good for cycling, with gentle hills and special routes.

Dining

Wherever possible, restaurants capitalize on the river view, and alfresco dining overlooking the Danube is one of the region's unsurpassed delights. Simple *Gasthäuser* are everywhere, but better dining is more often found in the country inns. The cuisine is basically Austrian, although desserts are often brilliant local inventions, including the celebrated Linzertorte, basically a jam tart—almost a pie—topped with a lattice crust, and Linzer Augen, jam-filled cookies with three "eyes" in the top cookie.

Wine is very much the thing in the lower part of the Weinviertel, particularly in the Wachau region on the north bank of the Danube. Here you'll find many of Austria's best white wines, slightly dry and with a touch of fruity taste. In some of the smaller villages, you can sample the vintner's successes directly in his cellars. Restaurants, from sophisticated and stylish to plain and homey, are often rated by their wine offerings as much as by their chef's creations.

CATEGORY	COST*
$$$$	over AS500
$$$	AS300–AS500
$$	AS200–AS300
$	under AS200

per person for a typical three-course meal with a glass of house wine

Hiking

You could hardly ask for better hiking country: From the level ground of the Danube Valley, hills rise on both sides, giving great views when you reach the upper levels. There are *Wanderwege* (marked hiking paths) virtually everywhere; local tourist offices have maps and route details. Around Linz you might retrace the route of the Linz–Budweis horse-drawn tramway, Continental Europe's first railway, or trek from one castle to another. You can hike in the Mühlviertel from Freistadt to Grein and even get your pack transferred from hotel to hotel.

Lodging

Accommodation options range from castle hotels where you'll be treated like a king, to quieter but elegant, usually family-run country inns, to standard city hotels, in Linz. The region is compact, so you can easily stay in one place and drive to a nearby locale to try a different restaurant. Rates understandably reflect the quality of service and amenities and usually include breakfast, which may range from a fast to a feast.

CATEGORY	COST*
$$$$	over AS1,500
$$$	AS1,000–AS1,500
$$	AS700–AS1,000
$	under AS700

All prices are for a standard double room, including tax and service.

Exploring the Danube Valley

Although much of the river is tightly wedged between steep hills rising from a narrow valley, the north and south banks of the Danube present differing vistas. The hills to the north are terraced so that the vineyards can catch the sun; the orchards, occasional meadows, and shadowed hills on the south are as visually appealing if less dramatic. Upstream from the Wachau region the valley broadens, giving way to farmlands and the industrial city of Linz straddling the river.

Great Itineraries

The Wachau section of the Danube valley is a favorite outing for Viennese seeking a pleasant Sunday drive and a glass or two of good wine, but for foreign visitors to treat the region this casually would cause them to miss some of Austria's greatest treasures. Once there, castles and abbeys beckon, picturesque villages beg to be explored, and the vine-covered wine gardens prove nearly irresistible.

Numbers in the text correspond to numbers in the margin and on the Lower Danube Valley, Upper Danube Valley, and Linz maps.

IF YOU HAVE 3 DAYS

Start out early from Vienna, planning for a stop to explore the medieval center of **Krems** ③. The Vinotek Und's eponymous Kloster will give you a good idea of the regions's best wines. From Krems, you can scoot across the river to visit **Stift Göttweig** ㊹ or you can leave it until the return trip. Spend a night in a former cloister, now an elegant hotel, in ☒ **Dürnstein** ⑤ in the shadow of the ruined castle where Richard the Lion-Hearted was imprisoned. An early-morning climb up to the ruin, or a jog along the Danube shoreline will reward you with great views. Take time to explore the town before heading along the Danube, crossing to ☒ **Melk** ㊸, rated one of the greatest abbeys in Europe. This is high baroque at its most glorious. Follow the river road on to ☒ **Stift Göttweig** ㊹ and have lunch on the terrace. The Stift's Baroque chapel is breathtaking. Continuing eastward, follow the river as closely as possible (signs indicate Zwentendorf and Tulln) to **Klosterneuburg** ㊼, an imposing abbey once seat of the powerful Babenburger kings, and onward to Vienna.

IF YOU HAVE 5 DAYS

A more leisurely schedule would follow the same basic route but permit a visit at either **Burg Kreuzenstein** or **Schloss Grafenegg** before stopping in **Krems** ③ and Und, and an overnight in ☒ **Dürnstein** ⑤. Spend the morning exploring the town, including the colorfully restored baroque Stiftskirche. In the afternoon, discover the wine villages of **Weis-**

Lower Danube Valley

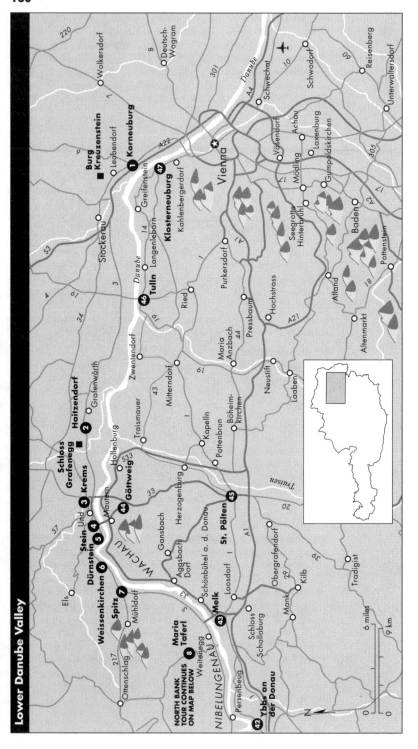

Wolkersdorf
Deutsch-Wagram
Korneuburg
Burg Kreuzenstein
Leobendorf
Greifenstein
Klosterneuburg
Kahlenbergerdorf
Vienna
Schwechat
Vösendorf
Achau
Mödling
Loxenburg
Gumpoldskirchen
Schwadorf
Unterwaltersdorf
Reisenberg
Baden
Pottenstein
Seegrotte Hinterbrühl
Stockerau
Tulln
Purkersdorf
Ried
Hochstrass
Pressbaum
Atland
Allenmarkt
Zwentendorf
Maria Anzbach
Neustift
Laaben
Haitzendorf
Grafenwörth
Mitterndorf
Böheim-kirchen
Traismauer
Kapelln
Potenbrun
Schloss Grafenegg
Hollenburg
Krems
Göttweig
Herzogenburg
St. Pölten
Mautern
Stein Und
Dürnstein
Gansbach
Aggsbach Dorf
Schönbühel a. d. Donau
Obergrafendorf
Tradigist
Els
Weissenkirchen
Spitz
Mühldorf
Loosdorf
Mank
Kilb
Maria Taferl
Weitenegg
Melk
Schloss Schallaburg
Ottenschlag
NIBELUNGENGAU
Persenbeug
Ybbs an der Donau

NORTH BANK TOUR CONTINUES ON MAP BELOW

WACHAU

Danube

Traisen

6 miles

9 km

N

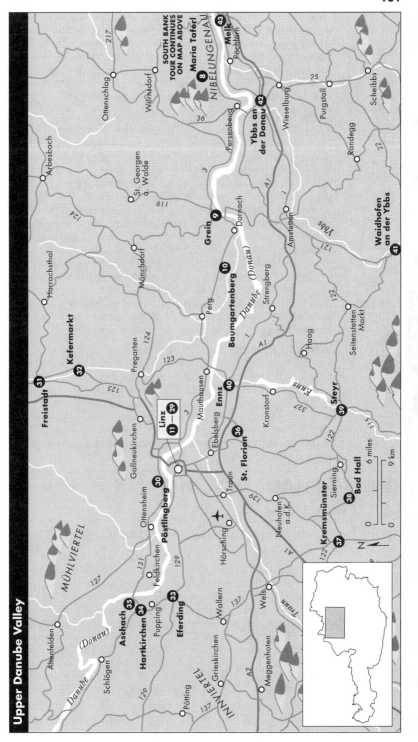

Upper Danube Valley

217

Ottenschlag

Wörnsdorf

SOUTH BANK
TOUR CONTINUES
ON MAP ABOVE

Maria Taferl

Melk 43

8

NIBELUNGENAU

Pöchlarn

36

Persenbeug

25

Wieselburg

Purgstall

Scheibbs

**Ybbs an
der Donau** 42

Randegg

22

Arbesbach

St. Georgen
a. Walde

3

A1

Amstetten

1

121

Ybbs

**Waidhofen
an der Ybbs** 41

119

Grein 9

Dornach

Harrachsthal

Mönchdorf

124

Danube (Donau)

Strengberg

122

Haag

10

Baumgartenberg

Perg

Seitenstetten
Markt

Kefermarkt 32

Pregarten

124

123

1

A1

Steyr

Enns

31

Freistadt

125

Mauthausen

Enns

40

Kronstorf

337

39

115

Gallneukirchen

Linz

11 — 29

3

Ebelsberg

36

St. Florian

Kremsmünster

122

Bad Hall

Sierning

38

Ottensheim

30

Pöstlingberg

Traun

139

Neuhofen
a.d.K.

A1

122

37

N

Feldkirchen

129

Hörsching

Wallern

137

Wels

Trun

6 miles

9 km

MÜHLVIERTEL

Altenfelden

127

131

Pupping

Aschach

Harkirchen 34

35

Eferding 33

Grieskirchen

Meggenhofen

A2

Schlögen

(Donau)

Danube

129

Pöting

137

INNVIERTEL

senkirchen ⑥ and **Spitz** ⑦. Plan on two overnights in ⊡ **Linz** ⑪, to discover the city itself and to fit in a side trip across the river north to the
walled city of **Freistadt** ㉛ and then on to **Kefermarkt** ㉜, to view the
42-foot high intricately carved wood winged altar dating to 1497. On
day four, take in **Kremsmünster** ㊲ and **St. Florian** ㊱, then proceed to
⊡ **Melk** ㊸. The fifth day will be full, but start with the Melk abbey,
then **Stift Göttweig** ㊹, and onward to **Klosterneuburg** ㊼.

IF YOU HAVE 7 DAYS

Additional time would allow far better acquaintance with this region.
Located to the northwest of the Wachau, the Mühlviertel—the mill region north of Linz—turned out thousands of yards of linen from flax
grown in the neighboring fields in the last century. You might follow
the "textile trail," which takes you to museums tracing this bit of history. On your way along the northern Danube bank, visit the fascinating theater in **Grein** ⑨ and view the curious chancel in the church
at **Baumgartenberg** ⑩. From ⊡ **Linz** ⑪, take trips upriver to **Eferding** ㉝,
Hartkirchen ㉞, and **Aschach** ㉟, and south to **Steyr** ㊴; you might also
consider an overnight in this charming medieval city with its vast center square framed in pastel facades. From Steyr, attractive back roads
will bring you to the walled town of **Waidhofen an der Ybbs** ㊶, parts
of which date to the Turkish invasion of the 1600s. Rather than try to
pack three abbeys into one day, spread out the pleasures, dining in
Mautern and overnighting in ⊡ **Tulln** ㊻ before heading on to
Klosterneuburg ㊼ and, finally, returning to Vienna.

When to Tour the Danube Valley

The Wachau—both north and south Danube banks—are packed wall-
to-wall with visitors in late-April–early May, but of course there's a
reason: the apricot and apple trees are in glorious blossom. Others prefer the chilly early to mid-autumn days, when a blue haze cradles the
vineyards. Throughout the region, winter is drab. Seasons hardly with-
standing, crowds jam the abbey at Melk; you're best off going first thing
in the morning, before the tour buses arrive, or at midday when the
throngs have receded.

THE WACHAU, NORTH BANK
OF THE DANUBE

Storybook Castles and Wagnerian Legends

Unquestionably the most lovely stretches of the Danube's Austrian course
run from the outskirts of Vienna, through the narrow defiles of the
Wachau to the Nibelungengau—the region where the mystical race of
dwarfs, the Nibelungs, are supposed to have settled, at least for a
while. If you're taking the tour by train, take Streetcar D to Vienna's
Franz Josefs Bahnhof, where you'll depart. If you're driving, the trick-
iest part may be getting out of Vienna. Follow signs to Prague to get
across the Danube. Once across, avoid the right-hand exit marked
Prague, which leads to the autobahn, and continue ahead, following
signs for Prager Strasse and turning left at the traffic light. Prager
Strasse (Route 3) heads you toward Langenzersdorf and Korneuburg.

Korneuburg

❶ *18 km (11¼ mi) northwest of Vienna.*

Until recently, Korneuburg was the center of Austrian shipbuilding, where
river passenger ships, barges, and transfer cranes were built for Russia, among other customers. Stop for a look at the imposing neo-

Gothic city hall (1864), which dominates the central square and towers over the town.

★ Atop a hillside 3 kilometers (2 miles) beyond Korneuburg along Route 3 sits **Burg Kreuzenstein,** a castle with fairy-tale turrets and towers. Using old elements and Gothic and Romanesque bits and pieces brought to this site of a previously destroyed castle, Count Wilczek built Kreuzenstein from 1879 to 1908, to house his late-Gothic collection of art objects. You would never suspect the building wasn't absolutely authentic if the tour guides weren't so forthcoming. You'll see rooms full of armaments, the festival and banquet halls, library, chapel, even the kitchens. You can also reach Kreuzenstein via the suburban train (*S-Bahn*) to Leobendorf and a ¾-hour hike up to the castle. ⊠ *Leobendorf bei Korneuburg,* ☎ 02262/66102. ⬚ *AS80.* ⊘ *Tour mid-Mar.–mid-Nov., Tues.–Sun. 9–5; last tour at 4.*

Haitzendorf

❷ *51 km (38½ mi) west of Korneuburg, 12 km (7½ mi) east of Krems.*

The tiny farming community of Haitzendorf—To reach it from Korneuburg, take Route 3, 33 kilometers (21 miles) past Stockerau, then turn right at Graftenwörth—features a church dating to the 14th century, but it best known for turreted Schloss Grafenegg nearby. In early summer, the vast strawberry fields surrounding the town yield a delicious harvest which you can pick yourself. A lush meadow and woodland area also surrounds **Schloss Grafenegg.** The moated Renaissance castle dating to 1533 was stormed by the Swedes in 1645 and rebuilt from 1840 to 1873 in the English Gothic Revival style. Greatly damaged during the 1945–1955 occupation, it was extensively restored in the 1980s. Look for such fascinating details as the gargoyle waterspouts, and don't miss the chapel. ☎ 02735/2205–14. ⬚ *AS60.* ⊘ *Mid-Apr.–Oct., Tues.–Sun. daily 10–5.*

NEED A BREAK?	The **Schlosstaverne Mörwald** (☎ 02735/2616–0) offers excellent food in a delightful setting, either in the Biedermeier-style dining room or under an umbrella in the garden.

Krems

★ ❸ *80 km (50 mi) northwest of Vienna, 26 km (16¼ mi) north of St. Pölten.*

Krems marks the beginning (when traveling upstream) of the Wachau section of the Danube. This delightful old town along Route 3 celebrated its 1000th birthday in 1995 and is closely tied to Austrian history; here the ruling Babenbergs set up a dukedom in 1120, and the earliest Austrian coin was struck in 1130. In the Middle Ages, Krems looked after the iron trade, while neighboring Stein traded in salt and wine, and over the years Krems became a center of culture and art. Today the area is the heart of a thriving wine production, and narrow streets, a Renaissance Rathaus, a parish church that is one of the oldest in Lower Austria, and a pedestrian zone make Krems an attractive city to wander through. Among the sights of Krems is the **Steiner Tor,** the massive square gate once set into the wall of the moated city, flanked by two stubby round towers and capped by candle-snuffer roofs. The oldest part of town is to the east. Along the **Obere and Untere Landstrasse,** you'll spot dozens of eye-catching buildings in styles ranging from Gothic to Baroque. It's easy to pick out the heavy Gothic **Piaristenkirche,** begun in 1470, with its distinctive square tower, central peak, and minitowers at each corner. The main altar and most of the side altars incorporate paintings by the local artist Martin Johann Schmidt (1718–1801), popularly known as Kremser Schmidt, whose translucent works you will repeatedly come across in the course of this trip. Close by is the parish church of **St. Veit,** completed in 1630. The interior is surprisingly spacious; Schmidt did the ceiling frescoes. On the entry portal of the **Bürgerspitalkirche** at Obere Landstrasse 15, you'll spot Friedrick III's legend *A.E.I.O.U.*, reputedly standing for *Austria Erit In Orbe Ultima,* Latin for "Austria will reach to the ends of the earth."

A 14th-century former Dominican cloister, farther along the street, now serves as the **Historisches Museum der Stadt Krems** (city historical museum), with a wine museum that holds occasional tastings. ⊠ *Körnermarkt 13,* ☎ *02732/801–338.* ☑ *AS30.* ⊙ *Easter–late Oct., Tues.–Sat. 9–noon and 2–5; Sun. and holidays 9–noon.*

Dining and Lodging

$$$ ╳ **Zum Kaiser von Österreich.** At this landmark located in the Old City district, you'll find excellent regional cuisine along with an outstanding wine selection (some of these vintages come—literally—from the backyard). The inside rooms are bright and pleasant but the outside tables in summer are even more inviting. Owner-chef Haidinger learned his skills at Bacher, across the Danube in Mautern, so look for fish dishes along with specialties such as potato soup and roast shoulder of lamb with scalloped potatoes. ⊠ *Körnermarkt 9, A-3500,* ☎ *02732/86001. DC, MC, V. Closed Mon.*

$$$ ╳▥ **Am Förthof.** An inn has existed on the riverside site of this mod-
★   ern hotel for hundreds of years. The rooms are comfortable and balconied; those in front have a view of the Danube and Göttweig abbey across the river—and the sounds of the traffic. The dining room and in summer the inviting courtyard garden offer good regional cuisine; the chef's ambitions occasionally surpass his achievements, but the sumptuous breakfasts are an assured culinary experience. ⊠ *Förthofer Donaulände 8, A-3500,* ☎ *02732/83345 or 02732/81348,* ℻ *02732/83345–40. 20 rooms. Restaurant, pool, sauna. DC, MC, V.*

$–$$ ╳▥ **Alte Post.** You're allowed to drive into the pedestrian zone to this romantic house in the heart of the old town, next to the Steinener Tor (Stone Gate). The rooms are in comfortable country style (full baths are scarce), but the real feature here is dining on regional specialties or sipping a glass of the local wine in the arcaded Renaissance courtyard. The staff is particularly friendly, and cyclists are welcome. ⊠ *Obere Landstr. 32, A-3500,* ☎ *02732/82276–0,* ℻ *02732/84396. 26 rooms, 7 with bath. Restaurant, bicycles. No credit cards. Closed Jan.–mid-Mar.*

En Route   Between Krems and Stein, in a beautifully restored Capuchin cloister
★   in the tiny town of Und, is the **Weinkolleg Kloster Und.** The building also houses the tourist office and a small wine museum, where you can taste (and buy) more than 100 Austrian wines. ⊠ *Undstr. 6, Krems–Stein,* ☎ *02732/73073,* ℻ *02732/73074–85.* ☑ *AS130, including tasting.* ⊙ *mid-Jan.–Dec. 24, daily 11–7.*

Stein

❹   *5 km (2 mi) east of Krems.*

A frozen-in-time hamlet that has become over time virtually a suburb of the adjacent city of Krems, Stein is dotted with lovely 16th-century houses, many on the hamlet's main street, Steinlanderstrasse. The former 14th-century **Minoritenkirche,** just off the main street in the pedestrian zone, now serves as a museum with changing exhibits. A few steps beyond the Minoritenkirche, an imposing square Gothic tower identifies the 15th-century **St. Nicholas parish church,** whose altar painting and ceiling frescoes were done by Kremser Schmidt. The upper part of the Gothic charnel house (1462), squeezed between the church and the hillside, has been converted to housing. Notice, too, the many architecturally interesting houses, among them the former tollhouse, with rich Renaissance frescoes. Stein was the birthplace of Ludwig Köchel, the cataloger of Mozart's works, which are referred to by their Köchel numbers.

Dürnstein

❺ *90 km (56 mi) northwest of Vienna, 9 km (5½ mi) west of Krems, 34 km (21¼ mi) northeast of Melk.*

If a beauty contest was held among the towns along the Wachau Danube, chances are Dürnstein would be the winner, hands down—as you'll see when you arrive along with droves of tourists. Set among terraced vineyards, the town is landmarked by its gloriously Baroque **Stiftskirche,** dating from the early 1700s, which sits on a cliff overlooking the river—this cloister church's combination of luminous blue facade and stylish Baroque tower is considered the most beautiful of its kind in Austria. More than 100 tiny angels decorate the heavens of its ceiling, and couples come from near and far to be married in the romantic setting. After taking in the Stiftskirche, most visitors head up the hill, climbing 500 feet over the town, to the famous **Richard the Lion-Hearted Castle** where Leopold V held Richard the Lion-Hearted of England, caught on his way back home from the Crusades. In the tower of this castle, Richard was imprisoned (1192–93) until he was rescued by Blondel, the faithful minnesinger. It's said that Blondel was able to locate his imprisoned king when he heard his master's voice completing the verse of a song he was singing. The rather steep 30-minute climb to the ruins will earn you a breathtaking view up and down the Danube Valley and over the hills to the south. The town is small; leave the car at one end and walk the narrow streets.

Dining and Lodging

$$$ ✕ **Loibnerhof.** Here, in an idyllic setting on the banks of the Danube, you'll dine on inventive variations on regional themes: Wachauer fish soup, crispy roast duck, and various grilled fish or lamb specialties. The house is famous for its *Butterschnitzel,* an exquisite variation on the theme of ground meat (this one's pan-fried veal with a touch of pork). The garden is enchanting in summer, but on weekends it's packed, and service tends to suffer. ✉ *Unterloiben 7,* ☎ *02732/82890–0,* ℻ *02732/82890–3. No credit cards. Closed Mon., Tues., and mid-Jan.–mid-Feb.*

$$ ✕ **Zum Goldenen Strauss.** This onetime post station, long a simple *Gasthaus,* has ambitions to be something more. You'll be offered substantial portions of very good Austrian fare, prepared with a flair that helps compensate for the occasionally slow service. Try the garlic soup followed by *Tafelspitz,* tasty boiled beef. The dining rooms inside are cozy, the terrace a delight. ✉ *A–3601,* ☎ *02711/267. No credit cards. Closed Tues. and mid-Jan.–early Mar.*

$$$$ 🏨 **Richard Löwenherz.** The impressive vaulted reception and dining rooms
★ of this former convent are beautifully furnished with antiques, reflecting the personal warmth and care of the family management. The inviting open fire, stone floors, and friendly touches make this one of the most romantic of the Romantik Hotels group. Though all rooms are spacious and comfortable, the balconied guest rooms in the newer part

of the house are more modern in decor and furnishings. Wander through the grounds and gardens, admiring the crumbling ruined walls from earlier centuries. A terrace overlooking the Danube offers stunning views. The outstanding restaurant is known for its regional specialties and local wines. ⊠ *A–3601,* ☎ *02711/222,* 𝔽𝔸𝕏 *02711/222–18. 40 rooms. Restaurant, bar, pool. AE, DC, MC, V. Closed Nov.–mid-Mar.*

$$$$ 🏨 **Schlosshotel Dürnstein.** This 17th-century early Baroque castle, on a rocky terrace with exquisite views over the Danube, offers genuine elegance and comfort. The best rooms look onto the river, but all are unusually bright and attractive; of moderate size, they have comfortable seating and country antiques throughout. Half board is standard. The kitchen is not up to the quality of the excellent wines from the area, but the setting makes terrace dining a memorable experience. ⊠ *A–3601,* ☎ *02711/212,* 𝔽𝔸𝕏 *02711/351. 37 rooms. Restaurant, bar, indoor and outdoor pools, sauna, exercise room. AE, DC, MC, V. Closed Nov.–Mar.*

$$$ 🏨 **Sänger Blondel.** Behind the yellow facade is a very friendly, traditional family hotel with elegant country rooms of medium size that have attractive paneling and antique decorations. The staff is particularly helpful and can suggest excursions in the area. The hotel is known for its restaurant, which features local specialties and a wide range of salads and lighter dishes. ⊠ *A–3601,* ☎ *02711/253–0,* 𝔽𝔸𝕏 *02711/253–7. 16 rooms. Restaurant. No credit cards. Closed mid-Nov.–mid-Mar. and 1 wk in early July.*

Weissenkirchen

❻ *14 km (8¾ mi) southwest of Krems, 22 km (13¾ mi) northeast of Melk.*

Tucked among vineyards, just around a bend in the Danube, is Weissenkirchen, a picturesque town that was fortified against the Turks in 1531. A fire in 1793 laid waste to much of the town, but the 15th-century parish church of **Maria Himmelfahrt,** built on earlier foundations, largely survived. The south nave dates to 1300, the middle nave to 1439, the chapel to 1460. The madonna on the triumphal arch goes back to the Danube school of about 1520; the Baroque touches date to 1736; and to complete the picture, the Rococo organ was installed in 1777. On the Marktplatz, check out the 15th-century **Teisenhoferhof,** which has a charming Renaissance arcaded courtyard. The building now houses the Wachau museum and contains many paintings by Kremser Schmidt. ☎ *02715/2268.* 🎫 *AS20.* ☉ *Apr.–Oct., Tues.–Sun. 10–5.*

Dining and Lodging

$$$ ✕ **Jamek.** Josef Jamek is known for his outstanding wines; his wife, ★ Edeltraud, for what she and her chefs turn out in the kitchen of this fine restaurant, which is also their home. You dine in one of several rooms tastefully decorated with 18th-century touches. Creative variations on typical Austrian specialties are emphasized; lamb and game in season are highlights. Wines are from the nearby family vineyards. ⊠ *Joching 45,* ☎ *02715/2235,* 𝔽𝔸𝕏 *02715/2483. Reservations essential. No credit cards. Closed Sun., Mon., mid-Dec.–mid-Feb., and 1st 2 wks of July; but call, as closing times may vary. No dinner Thurs.*

$$$ ✕ **Prandtauerhof.** The Baroque facade is the work of Jakob Prandtauer, ★ the architect responsible for many of the greatest buildings in the area. Ornate details are carried over into the cozy guest rooms and the inner court; a sense of history pervades the house. The kitchen delivers excellent traditional cuisine such as stuffed breast of veal, and there's a separate fish menu. You'll also find game in season, tempting desserts such as rhubarb strudel, and wines from the house vineyards. ⊠

Joching 36, ☎ *02715/2310,* FAX *02715/2310–9. Reservations essential. No credit cards. Closed Tues.; Sun. and holiday evenings; and mid-Nov.–early Mar.*

$$ ✕ **Heinzle.** The tree-shaded terrace overlooking the Danube is idyllic but the main dining room—with red tile floor and dark wood ceiling—is no less pleasant. This is a favorite on weekends and holidays, so come during the week or book ahead. The excellent fresh fish would be the logical (but not only) choice; start with a cream soup of smoked fish, and plan on one of the rich desserts. ✉ *Donaulände 280,* ☎ *02715/2231. Reservations essential. No credit cards. Closed Jan.; Mon. in summer; and Mon. and Tues. in winter.*

$$$ 🏨 **Raffelsbergerhof.** This stunning Renaissance building (1574), once
★ a shipmaster's house, has been tastefully converted into a hotel with every comfort. The rooms are attractively decorated without being overdone. The family management is particularly friendly, and there's a quiet garden to complement the gemütlich public lounge. ✉ *A-3610,* ☎ *02715/2201,* FAX *02715/2201–27. 12 rooms. MC. Closed Nov.–Apr.*

Spitz

➐ *17 km (10½ mi) southwest of Krems, 17 km (10½ mi) northeast of Melk.*

Picturesque Spitz is set off the main road and back from the Danube, sitting like a jewel in the surrounding vineyards and hills. One vineyard, the "thousand bucket" hill, is said to produce that much wine in a good year. A number of interesting houses in Spitz go back to the 16th and 17th centuries. The late-Gothic 15th-century parish church contains Kremser Schmidt's altar painting of the martyrdom of St. Mauritius. Note the carved wood statues of Christ and the 12 apostles, dating to 1380, on the organ loft. Just beyond Spitz and above the road is the ruin of the castle Hinterhaus, to which you can climb. A side road here marked to Ottenschlag (Route 217) leads up the hill, and about 7 kilometers (4½ miles) beyond Mühldorf, to **Burg Oberranna,** a well-preserved castle surrounded by a double wall and dry moat. The original structure dates to 1114–1125, the St. George chapel possibly even earlier. Part of the castle has been renovated into a hotel (☞ *below*). ✉ *Ober-Ranna 1, Mühldorf,* ☎ *02713/8221.* 🎫 *AS20.* 🕐 *May–Oct., Sat. 3–5, Sun. and holidays 2–6.*

Lodging

$$$ 🏨 **Burg Oberranna.** This 12th-century castle—a noted historic sight in itself (☞ *above*)—has been successfully turned into a charming and comfortable hotel, great as a base for hiking and also perfect for those who just want to get away. Rooms include a kitchenette. ✉ *Ober-Ranna 1, A-3622,* ☎ *02713/8221,* FAX *02713/8366. 11 rooms with bath or shower and 4 apartments. Restaurant. AE, V. Closed Nov.–Apr.*

$$ 🏨 **Wachauer Hof.** This appealing traditional house, set near the vineyards, has been under family management for generations. You can enjoy the wines in the *Gaststube,* the shaded garden, or the restaurant, which offers basic Austrian fare. The medium-size rooms have comfortable chairs, ample pillows, and rustic decor. ✉ *Hauptstr. 15, A-3620,* ☎ *02713/2303–0,* FAX *02713/2403. 30 rooms with bath or shower. Restaurant. MC. Closed mid-Dec.–mid-Feb.*

En Route The vistas are mainly of the other side of the Danube, looking across at Schönbühel and Melk, as you follow a back road via Jauerling and Maria Laach to Route 3 at Aggsbach. Shortly after Weitenegg the Wachau ends, and you come into the part of the Danube Valley known as the Nibelungenau, where the Nibelungs—who inspired the great saga, the *Nibelungenlied,* source of Wagner's Ring—are supposed to have settled for a spell. If you have always thought of the Nibelungs as a mythical race of dwarfs known only to old German legends and Wagner, dismiss that idea here. The Nibelungs existed, though not as Wagner describes them, and this area was one of their stamping grounds.

Maria Taferl

❽ *13 km (8¼ mi) west of Melk, 7½ km (4½ mi) northeast of Persenbeug/Ybbs an der Donau.*

Crowning a hill on the north bank is the two-towered **Maria Taferl,** a pilgrimage church with a spectacular outlook. It's a bit touristy, but the church and the view are worth the side trip. About 5 kilometers (3 miles) up a back road is **Schloss Artstetten,** a massive square castle with four round defense towers at its corners. This is the burial place of Archduke Franz Ferdinand and his wife, Sophie, whose double assassination in 1914 in Sarajevo was one of the triggers that set off World War I. ☎ 07413/8302. ◻ *AS58; combination ticket available with Melk abbey and Schloss Schallaburg* (☞ *below*). ⊙ *Apr.–Oct., daily 9–5:30.*

Lodging

$$$ ◻ **Krone–Kaiserhof.** Two hotels under the same family management share each other's luxurious facilities. The Krone looks out over the Danube Valley, while the Kaiserhof has views of the nearby Baroque pilgrimage church. Both have rooms done a bit slickly in country style, and the restaurants are popular. An associated guest house ($) is less elegant but also shares facilities. Cyclists staying overnight will be picked up free at Marbach or Klein Pöchlarn landing stations on the Danube. ◻ *A-3672,* ☎ *07413/6355–0 or 07413/6358,* ◻ *07413/6355–83. 72 rooms. 2 restaurants, bar, café, indoor and outdoor pools, sauna, miniature golf, exercise room. V. Closed Jan. and Feb.*

Grein

❾ *34 km (21¼ mi) east of Mauthausen, 20 km (12½ mi) west of Persenbeug/Ybbs an der Donau.*

Set above the Danube, Grein is a picture-book town complete with castle. The river bend below, known for years as "the place where death resides," was one of the most hazardous stretches of river until the reefs were blasted away in the late 1700s. Take time to see the intimate Rococo **Stadttheater** in the town hall, built in 1790 by the populace and still occasionally used for concerts or plays. ◻ *Rathaus,* ☎ *07268/6680.* ◻ *AS25.* ⊙ *Tour Apr.–late Oct., daily at 9, 10:30, and 2:30.*

NEED A   **Kaffeesiederei Blumensträussl** (◻ Stadtpl. 6) is a lovely spot for coffee
BREAK?   and cake, amid the Viennese Biedermeier decor in winter or outdoors in
             the café garden in summer. The *Mozarttorte* is renowned.

Baumgartenberg

❿ *11 km (6¼ mi) west of Grein, 17½ km (11 mi) east of Mauthausen.*

The small village of Baumgartenberg is worth a visit for its ornate Baroque parish church—note the lavish stucco-work and exquisitely carved 17th-century pews—and the unusual chancel supported by a tree trunk. The church is the only reminder of a once-famed Cistercian abbey, founded in 1141 by Otto von Machland, that used to thrive here. Outside the town is the picturesque castle of Klam, which used to belong to playwright August Strindberg; it now contains a small museum.

LINZ

The Rich Town of the River Markets

🕚 *130 km (81¼ mi) east of Salzburg, 185 km (115½ mi) west of Vienna.*

The capital of Upper Austria, set where the Traun River flows into the Danube, Linz has a fascinating old city core and an active cultural life. In 1832 it had a horse-drawn train to Czechoslovakia that was the first rail line on the Continent. Once known as "The Rich Town of the River Markets" because of its importance as a medieval trading post, it is today the center of Austrian steel and chemical production, both started by the Germans in 1938. A city of contrasts, Linz has Austria's largest medieval square and is home to one of the country's most modern multipurpose halls, the Brucknerhaus, which is used for concerts and conventions.

With the city's modern economic success, Linz's attractions for tourists have been generally overlooked. Nevertheless, Linz boasts beautiful old houses on the Hauptplatz, a Baroque cathedral with twin towers and a fine organ over which composer Anton Bruckner once presided, and its "city mountain," the Pöstlingberg, with a unique railway line to the top. Extensive redevelopment, restoration, and the creation of traffic-free zones continue to transform Linz. The heart of the city—the Altstadt (Old City)—has been turned into a pedestrian zone; either leave the car at your hotel or use the huge new parking garage under the main square in the center of town. Distances are not great, and you can take in the highlights in the course of a two-hour walking tour.

⓬ The lower end of the main square is marked by the **Altes Rathaus,** the old city hall. Although the original 1513 building was mainly destroyed by fire and replaced in 1658–59, its octagonal corner turret and lunar clock, as well as some vaulted rooms, remain, and you can detect traces of the original Renaissance structure on the Rathausgasse facade. The present exterior dates from 1824. The approach from Rathausgasse 5, opposite the Keplerhaus, leads through a fine arcaded courtyard. On the facade here you'll spot portraits of Emperor Friedrich III, the mayors Hoffmandl and Prunner, the astronomer Johannes Kepler, and the composer Anton Bruckner. ⊠ *Hauptpl.*

⓭ One of the symbols of Linz is the 65-foot Baroque **Pillar to the Holy Trinity** in the center of the Hauptplatz square. Completed in 1723 of white Salzburg marble, the column offers thanks by an earthly trinity—the provincial estates, city council, and local citizenry—for deliverance from the threats of war (1704), fire (1712), and plague (1713). From March through October, there's a flea market here each Saturday (except holidays), from 7 AM to 2 PM.

⓮ The **Minorite Church,** once part of a monastery, sits at the end of the Klosterstrasse. The present building dates from 1752–1758 and has a delightful Rococo interior with side altar paintings by Kremser Schmidt and the main altar by Bartolomeo Altomonte. The church is open October–June, Monday–Saturday 7:30–11 AM and Sunday 7:30–noon, and July–Sept., daily 7:30–4. The early-Renaissance monastery
⓯ adjoining the Minorite Church is now the **Landhaus,** with its distinctive tower, seat of the provincial government. Look inside to see the arcaded courtyard with the 1852 Planet Fountain and the Hall of Stone on the first floor, above the barrel-vaulted hall on the ground floor; for a more extensive look at the interior, inquire at the local tourist office for their scheduled guided tours. The beautiful Renaissance doorway (1570) is of red marble. ⊠ *Klosterstr. 7.*

Linz

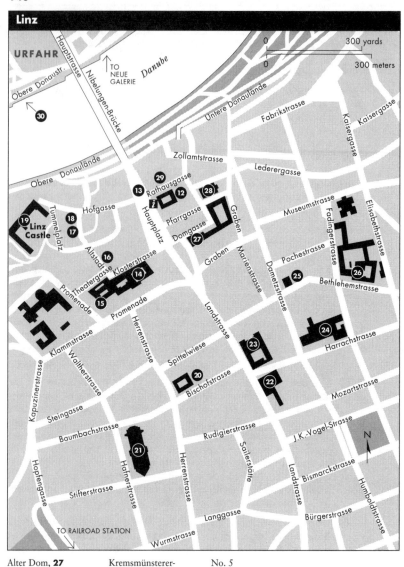

URFAHR

TO NEUE GALERIE

Danube

Alter Dom, **27**
Altes Rathaus, **12**
Bischofshof, **20**
Carmelite Church, **22**
Deutschordens-kirche, **24**
Elisabethinen-kirche, **26**

Kremsmünsterer-haus, **18**
Landhaus, **15**
Linz Castle, **19**
Minorite Church, **14**
Mozart Haus, **16**
Neuer Dom, **21**
Nordico (City Museum), **25**

No. 5 Rathausgasse, **29**
Pillar to the Holy Trinity, **13**
Pöstlingberg, **30**
Stadtpfarrkirche, **28**
Ursuline Church, **23**
Waaghaus, **17**

16 The three-story Renaissance **Mozart Haus** has a later Baroque facade and portal. Actually the Thun Palace, Mozart arrived here in 1783 with his wife to meet an especially impatient patron (Mozart was late by 14 days). As the composer forgot to bring any symphonies along with him, he set about writing one in the space of four days. The result: the sublime *Linz* symphony in 1783. The palace now houses the local tourist office and private apartments, but the courtyard can be viewed. ⊠ *Altstadt 17.*

17 The **Waaghaus,** bought by the city in 1524, is in the heart of the Altstadt on the tiny street of the same name. Once the public weighing office, it's now an indoor market. Emperor Friedrich III is said to have

18 died in the **Kremsmünstererhaus** (⊠ Altstadt 10) in 1493. The building was done over in Renaissance style in 1578–1580, and a story was added in 1616, with two turrets and onion domes. There's a memorial room to the emperor here; his heart is entombed in the Linz parish church, but the rest of him is in St. Stephen's cathedral in Vienna. The traditional rooms are now home to one of Linz' best restaurants, the Kremsmünsterer Stuben (☞ Dining and Lodging, *below*).

19 The massive four-story building in Tummelplatz is the **Linz Castle,** rebuilt by Friedrich III about 1477, literally on top of a castle that dated from 799. Note the **Friedrichstor,** the Friedrich gate, with the same *A.E.I.O.U.* monogram also found in Krems, and the two interior courtyards. The castle houses the Upper Austrian provincial museum—weapons, musical instruments, nativity scenes, Upper Austrian art, and prehistoric and Roman relics. ⊠ *Tummelpl. 10,* ☎ *0732/774419.* ⊞ *AS40.* ⊙ *Tues.–Fri. 9–5, weekends and holidays 10–4.*

20 At the intersection of Herrenstrasse and Bischofstrasse is the **Bischofshof** (Bishop's Residence), which dates from 1721. Graced by a fine wrought-iron gateway, this remains the city's most important Baroque profane building. The design is by Jakob Prandtauer, the architectural genius responsible for the glorious Melk and St. Florian abbeys. In 1862 the bishop of Linz engaged one of the architects of the Cologne cathedral to develop a design for a cathedral in neo-Gothic French-cathedral style and modestly ordered that its tower not be higher than that

21 of St. Stephen's in Vienna. The result was the massive **Neuer Dom** (new cathedral), its 400-foot tower shorter than St. Stephen's by a scant 6½ feet. ⊠ *Baumbachstr..* ⊙ *Daily 7:30–7.*

22 The **Carmelite Church,** on Landstrassem, was modeled on St. Joseph's in Prague and is a magnificent Baroque church (open daily 7–11:30 and 3–6). Across the street from the Carmelite Church is another

23 Baroque wonder, the **Ursuline Church** (open daily 1–6). Its double-figured towers are one of the identifying symbols of Linz (open daily 8–6). Inside is a blaze of gold and crystal ornament. Note the Madonna figure wearing a hooded Carmelite cloak with huge pockets used to

24 collect alms for the poor. The former **Deutschordenskirche** (seminary church, 1723) is a beautiful yellow-and-white Baroque treasure with an elliptical dome, designed by Johann Lukas von Hildebrandt, who also designed its high altar. ⊠ *Harrachstr..* ⊙ *Daily 8–6.*

At the corner of Dametzstrasse and Bethlehemstrasse, you'll find the
25 **Nordico** (city museum, 1610). Its collection follows local history from pre-Roman times to the mid-1880s. ⊠ *Bethlehemstr. 7,* ☎ *0732/2393–1912.* ⊞ *Free, except for special exhibits.* ⊙ *Weekdays 9–6, weekends 2–5.*

26 The **Elisabethinenkirche** (⊠ Bethlehemstr.) dates to the mid-18th century. Note the unusually dynamic colors in the dome fresco by Altomonte. Hidden away off the Graben, a narrow side street off of the Taubenmarkt above the Hauptplatz, sits the Baroque **Alter Dom** (old cathedral, 1669–78), whose striking feature is the single nave together with the side altars. Anton Bruckner was organist here from 1856 to 1868. ⊙ *Daily 7–noon and 3–7.*

28 The **Stadtpfarrkirche** (city parish church) dates to 1286 and was rebuilt in Baroque style in 1648. The tomb in the right wall of the chancel contains Friedrich III's heart. The ceiling frescoes are by Altomonte, and the figure of Johann Nepomuk (a local saint) in the chancel is by Georg Raphael Donner, in a setting by Hildebrandt. ⊠ *Domgasse.* ⊙ *Mon.–Sat. 8–7, Sun. 9–7.*

29 At **No. 5 Rathausgasse,** the astronomer Johannes Kepler lived from 1622 to 1626; Linz's first printing shop was established in this house in 1745.

★ **30** For a splendid view over Linz and the Danube, ride up the **Pöstling-berg** on the electric **Pöstlingbergbahn.** To reach the base station for the railway, take Streetcar 3 across the river to Urfahr, Linz's left bank. Note the railway's unusual switches, necessary because the car wheel flanges ride the outside of the rails rather than the (usual) inside. When the line was built in 1898, it boasted the steepest incline of any noncog railway in Europe. In summer, the old open-bench cars are used. On a clear day the view at the top takes in a good deal of Upper Austria south of the Danube, with a long chain of the Austrian Alps on the horizon. At the Pöstlinberg summit is the **Church of Sieben Schmerzen Mariens,** an immense and splendidly opulent twin-towered Baroque pilgrimage church (1748), visible for leagues as a landmark of Linz. With a chilled glass of white wine, drink in the grand vista at one of the flower-hung restaurants located near the church. ☎ *0732/2801–7002.* ⊠ *Round-trip AS35, combined ticket with streetcar Line 3 AS48.* ⊙ *Daily every 20 min 5:30 AM–8:20 PM.*

☾ A kid's treat at the top of the Pöstlinberg (that's entertaining for the rest of the family) is the **fairytale-grotto railroad,** which runs through a colorful imaginary world. ⊠ *AS40.* ⊙ *Sat. before Palm Sunday–Apr. and Oct., daily 9–4:45; May–Sept., daily 9–5:45.*

The exceptional **Neue Galerie,** across the river in the Urfahr district, is one of Austria's best modern art museums. The fine collection is well balanced, featuring mainly contemporary international and Austrian artists. ⊠ *Blütenstr. 15, Urfahr,* ☎ *0732/2393–3600.* ⊠ *AS40.* ⊙ *May–Oct., Mon.–Wed. and Fri. 10–6, Thurs. 10–10, Sat. 10–1; Nov.–Apr., Fri.–Wed. 10–6, Thurs. 10–10.*

Dining and Lodging

$$$$ ✕ **Der neue Vogelkäfig.** In 1992 Georg Essig moved his restaurant, exotic bird cages and all, from an idyllic suburban location into this small house in an unfashionable part of town; the main trace of country remaining is the lovely garden under chestnut trees. But the interior setting, with its pastel colors, is both intimate and friendly. The kitchen is imaginative and up to Linz's highest standard, featuring such dishes as a selection of delicate fish filets or fillet of beef rolled with herbs. ⊠ *Holzstr. 8,* ☎ *0732/770193. AE, DC, MC, V. Closed weekends and 3 wks weeks in Aug.*

$$$$ ✕ **Kremsmünsterer Stuben.** In a beautifully restored historic house in
★ the heart of the Old City you'll find an attractive wood-paneled restaurant offering everything from regional specialties to a six-course dinner. You might choose from saddle of hare or fillet of venison as a main course as you relax in the comfortable, traditional ambience of the city's best restaurant. ⊠ *Altstadt 10,* ☎ *0732/782111,* FAX *0732/784130. Reservations essential. Jacket and tie. AE, DC, MC, V. Closed Sun., Mon., 2 wks in Jan., and 2 wks in Aug.*

$$$$ ╳ **Verdi.** Linz's favored dinner restaurant is in Lichtenberg, about 3 kilometers (2 miles) north of the center, off Leonfelder Strasse. The cuisine is regional Austrian, with Italian and French overtones; the name refers to the opulent green-hued decor. Some complain of overemphasis on presentation, but this hardly deters the many regulars. Choose game in season or tender lamb. ⊠ *Pachmayrstr. 137,* ☎ *0732/733005. No credit cards. Closed Sun., Mon., and 3 wks in Jan.*

$$ ╳ **Stadtwirt.** First-class regional food is served along with colorful, genuinely local atmosphere (since 1622) unspoiled by frills, and at remarkably reasonable prices. If you long for a proper veal schnitzel, try it here—although the house specialty is variations on Tafelspitz. The strudels are outstanding, the service by the inexperienced staff less so. ⊠ *Landstr./Bismarckstr. 1,* ☎ *0732/785122–0,* ⅢX *0732/785122–75. No credit cards. Closed Sun.*

$$ ╳ **Traxlmayr.** Proud with the patina of age, this is one of Austria's great
★ old-tradition coffeehouses. You can linger all day over one cup of coffee, reading the papers (*Herald Tribune* included) in their bentwood holders, and then have a light meal. All Linz gathers on the terrace in summer. Ask for the specialty, *Linzer Torte*, with your coffee. ⊠ *Promenade 16,* ☎ *0732/773353. No credit cards. Closed Sun.*

$$ ╳ **Zum Klosterhof.** This complex in the former Kremsmünster abbey gives you a choice of upstairs and downstairs rooms that range from fairly formal to rustic-country to completely informal. The fare is traditional Austrian, and the beverage of choice is Salzburger Stiegl beer. ⊠ *Landstr. 30,* ☎ *0732/773373–0,* ⅢX *0732/773373–21. AE, DC, MC, V.*

$$$$ ⊞ **Schillerpark.** You're close to the south end of the pedestrian zone but still reasonably near the center and the sights in this very modern complex (glass outside, marble and air-conditioned inside). The rooms have clean lines, with contemporary furnishings. The casino is in the same building. ⊠ *Rainerstr. 2–4,* ☎ *0732/6950–0,* ⅢX *0732/6950– 9. 111 rooms. 2 restaurants, 2 bars, café, sauna. AE, DC, MC, V.*

$$$ ⊞ **Trend.** In this multistory modern hotel, you'll be directly on the Danube, next to the Brucknerhaus concert hall, and within reasonable walking distance of the center. The rooms are compact, modern, and attractively decorated; ask for an upper room on the river side for the superb views. ⊠ *Untere Donaulände 9,* ☎ *0732/7626–0,* ⅢX *0732/ 7626–2. 176 rooms. Restaurant, bar, café, indoor pool, sauna, exercise room, nightclub. AE, DC, MC, V.*

$$–$$$ ⊞ **Wolfinger.** This charming, traditional hotel in an old building is a
★ favorite of regular guests, in part because of the friendly staff, and its location couldn't be more central. The medium-size rooms have been recently modernized, with comfortable new furniture and bright fabrics. Those in the front are less quiet but give a view of city activities. ⊠ *Hauptpl. 19,* ☎ *0732/773291–0,* ⅢX *0732/773291–55. 45 rooms. AE, DC, MC, V.*

$$ ⊞ **Zum Schwarzen Bären.** The "Black Bear" is a fine, traditional house near the center of the Old City, a block from the pedestrian zone, and incidentally was the birthplace of the renowned tenor Richard Tauber (1891–1948). The rooms are smallish and well worn, but the baths (most with shower) are modern, if compact. ⊠ *Herrenstr. 9–11,* ☎ *0732/772477–0,* ⅢX *0732/772477–47. 35 rooms, 29 with bath. Restaurant, bar, weinstube. AE, DC, MC, V.*

Nightlife and the Arts

Linz is far livelier than even most Austrians realize. The local population is friendlier than that in either Vienna or Salzburg, and much less cliquish than in those top resort towns. Nor has Linz lagged behind other Austrian cities in developing its own hot section, known as the "Bermuda Triangle." Around the narrow streets of the Old City (Klosterstrasse, Altstadt, Hofgasse) are dozens of fascinating small bars and lounges, and as you explore, you'll probably meet some Linzers who can direct you to the current "in" location. A good starting point, where both the young and the older will feel comfortable, is **S'Linzerl** (⊠ Hofberg 5), which is open Monday–Saturday 9 PM–3 AM.

The Linz casino, with roulette, blackjack, poker, and slot machines, is in the **Hotel Schillerpark;** the casino complex includes a bar and the Rouge et Noir restaurant. A passport is required for admission. ⊠ *Rainerstr. 2–4,* ☎ *0732/654487–0,* FAX *0732/654487–24.* ☉ *Dec. 25–Oct. and Nov. 2–Dec. 23, daily 3 PM–3 AM.* ▱ *AS210, including 5 AS50 tokens.*

The tourist office's monthly booklet "Was ist los in Linz und Oberösterreich" ("What's on in Linz and Upper Austria") will give you details of theater and concerts. Two **ticket agencies** are Linzer Kartenbüro (⊠ Herrenstr. 4, ☎ 0732/778800) and Ruefa (⊠ Landstr. 67, ☎ 0732/662681–0, FAX 0732/662681–33).

The Linz **opera** company is talented and often willing to mount venturesome works and productions. Most performances are in the Landestheater, some in the Brucknerhaus. Concerts and recitals are held in the **Brucknerhaus,** the modern hall on the banks of the Danube. From mid-September to early October, it's the center of the International Bruckner Festival. In mid-June, the hall hosts the biggest multimedia event in the area, the Ars Electronica, a musical and laser-show spectacle ⊠ *Untere Donaulände 7,* ☎ *0732/775230,* FAX *0732/783745.* ☉ *Box office weekdays 10–6.*

Don't overlook the casual **wine gardens** set under huge trees on the north bank of the Danube (Urfahr district), west of the new city hall. This is anything but tourist territory, and you'll toast the friendly Linzers with mugs of wine on pleasant summer afternoons and evenings.

Shopping

Linz is a good place to shop; prices are generally lower than those in resorts and the larger cities, and selections are varied. The major shops are found in the main square and the adjoining side streets, in the old quarter to the west of the main square, in the pedestrian zone of the Landstrasse and its side streets, and in the Hauptstrasse of Urfahr, over the Nibelungen Bridge across the Danube. For local handmade items and good-quality souvenirs, try **O.Ö. Heimatwerk** (⊠ Landstr. 31, Linz, ☎ 0732/773376–0), where you'll find silver, pewter, ceramics, fabrics, and some clothing. Items from clothing to china are sold at the **Flea Market** (open March–mid-November, Saturday 7–2) on the Hauptplatz (main square). From mid-November through February the market moves across the river next to the new city hall and runs from 8–2, also on Saturdays. The state-run **Dorotheum auction house** is at Fabrikstrasse 26 (☎ 0732/773132–0). Auctions take place every Wednesday at 1:30.

For **antiques** head for the old city, on the side streets around the main square. Try **Otto Buchinger** (⊠ Bethlehemstr. 5, ☎ 0732/770117), **Richard Kirchmayr** (⊠ Bischofstr. 3a, ☎ 0732/797711), **Kunsthandlung Kirchmayr** (⊠ Herrenstr. 23, ☎ 0732/774667), and **Ute Pastl** (⊠ Wischerstr. 26, Urfahr, ☎ 0732/737306). For **jewelry,** try **Pfaffenberger** (⊠ Landstr. 42, ☎ 0732/772495) or **Wild** (⊠ Landstr. 49, ☎ 0732/774105–0).

Sports and Outdoor Activities

Buy tickets for sports events at **Kartenbüro Ruefa** (✉ Landstr. 67, ☎ 0732/662681–0, ℻ 0732/662681–33). The office is open weekdays 8:30–noon and 2–6 and Saturday 8:30–noon.

BICYCLING

Cyclists appreciate the relatively level terrain around Linz, and within the city there are 89 kilometers (55 miles) of marked cycle routes. Get the brochure *Cycling in Linz* from the tourist office. You can **rent a bike** through **Fahrradzentrum B7** (✉ Oberfelderstr. 12, ☎ 0732/330550); **LILO Bahnhof** (✉ Coulinstr. 30, ☎ 0732/600703); or at the **Hauptbahnhof** (✉ main rail station, Bahnhofstr. 3, ☎ 0732/6909–385).

GOLF

Fairly close to Linz is the 9-hole, par-72 **Golfclub St. Oswald-Freistadt** (✉ St. Oswald bei Freistadt, ☎ 07945/7938). The 18-hole, par-72 **Böhmerwald Golfpark** is near Linz (Ulrichsberg, ☎ 07288/8200). East of Linz is the relatively new 18-hole, par-71 **Linzer Golf Club Mühlviertel,** playable mid-March to November (✉ Luftenberg a.d. Donau, ☎ 07237/3893).

ICE SKATING

Linz is an ice-skating city; from late October to late February, there's outdoor skating at the **city rink** (daily 2–5 and Friday–Wednesday 6–9, weekends and holidays also 9–noon) and indoors at the adjoining indoor sports complex, the **Eishalle,** from late September to April, Wednesday 9–noon, Saturday 2–5, and Sunday 10–noon, 2–5, and 6–9. Hockey and skating competitions are also held in the Eishalle. ✉ *Untere Donaulände 11,* ☎ *0732/778513.*

SOCCER

Soccer matches are played in Linz in the **Stadion** (✉ Roseggerstr. 41, ☎ 0732/660670 or 0732/601115).

TENNIS

Tennis matches and other sports events are held at the **Stadthalle** (☎ 0732/657311–0).

WATER SPORTS

The Danube is not suitable for swimming, but alternatives exist. The closest swimming is at **Pleschinger Lake**; to get there, take Tram 1 to Urfahr/Reindlstrasse and Bus 32 to the lake. This is a pleasant spot for family swimming, although it tends to be crowded on sunny, warm weekends. The **Kral Waterskiing School** (✉ Talgasse 14, ☎ 0732/731494) offers waterskiing and other water sports.

EXCURSIONS FROM LINZ

Into the Hinterland

Many travelers find Linz the most practical point of departure for visits to the Mühlviertel and the Gothic and Baroque sights found in the towns of St. Florian, Kremsmünster, and Steyr, although Steyr certainly merits an overnight itself. The **Mühlviertel** (mill district now in the agricultural, not industrial, sense) north of Linz toward the Czech border is made up of meadows and gentle wooded hills interspersed with towns whose appearance has changed little since the Middle Ages. To the west of Linz, south of the Danube, lies the **Innviertel,** named for the Inn River (which forms the border with Germany before it joins the Danube), a region of broad fields and meadows, and enormous woodland tracts, ideal for cycling, hiking, and riding. To the south, the hilly landscape introduces the foothills of the Austrian Alps.

Freistadt

★ ㉛ *41 km (25¼ mi) northeast of Linz.*

To get to Freistadt, a preserved walled city in the eastern part of the Mühviertel, cross the Danube to Linz-Urfahr and turn right onto Freistädter Strasse (Route 125/E55). Freistadt developed as a border defense city on the salt route into Bohemia (now the Czech Republic), which accounts for the wall, towers, and gates, still wonderfully preserved today. Look at the late-Gothic **Linzertor,** the Linz Gate, with its steep wedge-shaped roof, and the **Böhmertor,** on the opposite side, leading to Bohemia. A walk around the wall gives an impression of how a city in the Middle Ages was conceived and defended; it takes about a half hour. The city's central square, aglow with pastel facades, is virtually the same as it was 400 years ago; only the parked cars intrude into the picture of antiquity. Pause for a local beer; the town's first brewery dated to 1573. While wandering through the alleys behind the **central square,** note the wealth of architectural details; plus, many of the arcades contain interesting small shops. The 15th-century parish **church of St. Catherine**'s was redone in Baroque style in the 17th century but retains its slender tower, whose unusual balconies have railings on all four sides. The late-Gothic castle to the northeast of the square now houses the **Mühlviertel Heimathaus** (district museum); the display of painted glass in the chapel and the hand tools in the 163-foot tower are especially interesting. ☎ 07942/2274. 🖃 AS10. ☉ *Tour May–Oct., Tues.–Sat. at 10 and 2, Sun. and holidays at 10; Nov.–Apr., Tues.–Fri. at 10, Tues. and Thurs. also at 2.*

Dining and Lodging

$$ ✕🏨 **Deim/Zum Goldenen Hirschen.** This romantic and atmospheric 600-year-old house full fits perfectly into the Old City. The rooms are up-to-date and attractive. The stone-arched ceiling adds to the elegance of the dining room, where you'll find international and local specialties and game in season. ⊠ *Böhmergasse 8, A–4240,* ☎ *07942/2258–0, 07942/2111,* 🖷 *07942/2258–40. 32 rooms. Restaurant. DC. Closed 1st 2 wks of Jan.*

$$ ✕🏨 **Zum Goldenen Adler.** Here you'll be in another 600-year-old
★ house; it has been run by the same family since 1807, so tradition runs strong. The medium-size rooms are modern yet full of country charm; hotel service is exceptionally accommodating. The newly renovated garden, with a piece of the old city wall as background, is a delightful oasis. The restaurant can be variable but is known for regional specialties such as *Böhmisches Bierfleisch,* a cut of beef cooked in beer. The desserts are outstanding. ⊠ *Salzgasse 1, A–4240,* ☎ *07942/2112–0,* 🖷 *07942/2112–44. 30 rooms. Restaurant, pool, sauna, exercise room. AE, DC, MC, V.*

Kefermarkt

㉜ *9 km (5¼ mi) south of Freistadt, either via marked back roads or by turning east off of Rte. 125/E14.*

The late-Gothic **church of St. Wolfgang** boasts one of Austria's great art treasures, a 42-foot-high winged altar intricately carved from linden wood, commissioned by Christoph von Zelking, and completed in 1497. So masterly is the carving that it has been ascribed to famous 15th-century sculptors Veit Stoss and Michael Pacher, but most historians now attribute it to Jürg Huber and Martin Kriechbaum. Some figures, such as the St. Christopher, are true masterpieces of Northern Renaissance sculpture. The church also has some impressive 16th-century frescoes.

Eferding

③③ *25 km (15¼ mi) west of Linz, 22 km (13¾ mi) north of Wels.*

Eferding, a centuries-old community with an attractive town square, lies west of Linz. You can easily drive the 25 kilometers (16 miles) on Route 129, but the more adventurous route is via the *LILO* (Linzer Lokalbahn) interurban railway from Coulinstrasse 30 (☎ 0732/654376), near the main rail station. In the town itself, the double door in the south wall of the 15th-century **church of St. Hippolyte** is a gem of late-Gothic stonecutting, with the Madonna and Child above flanked by Saints Hippolyte and Agyd. Inside, note the Gothic altar with its five reliefs and the statues of Saints Wolfgang and Martin. Visit the **Spitalskirche** (built in 1325) and note the Gothic frescoes in the Magdalen chapel, which date to about 1430.

Dining and Lodging

$$$$ ✕ **Dannerbauer.** Two kilometers (1½ miles) north of Eferding, on the
★ road to Aschach and directly on the Danube, is one of the area's best restaurants. It serves many species of fish—some you probably never heard of—to your taste: poached, grilled, broiled, or fried. Many of the fish come from the river; some are raised in the house ponds, to ensure freshness. There are meat dishes, too, and game in season, and the soups (try the nettle soup) are excellent. The place has a pleasant outlook with lots of windows. ⊠ *Brandstatt bei Eferding,* ☎ *07272/2471. AE, DC. Closed Mon., Tues., and mid-Jan.–mid-Feb.*

$ ⊞ **Zum Goldenen Kreuz.** The golden facade indicates a typical country-style hotel, simple and with the appealing charm of a family-run establishment. You'll sleep under fluffy feather-bed coverlets. The restaurant is known for its good regional cuisine, and there are occasional specialty weeks. ⊠ *Schmiedstr. 29, A–4070,* ☎ *07272/4247–0,* ℻ *07272/4249. 21 rooms. Restaurant. AE, DC, MC. Closed Christmas wk.*

Hartkirchen

③④ *12 km (7½ mi) north of Eferding, 26 km (16¼ mi) northwest of Linz.*

The **parish church** at Hartkirchen is worth a visit to see fine Baroque wall and ceiling frescoes, dated 1750, that create the illusion of space and depth. To reach Hartkirchen, take Rte. 130 north from Eferding to Pupping and continue 3 km (2 mi).

Aschach

③⑤ *9 km (5½ mi) north of Eferding, 21 km (13¼ mi) northwest of Linz.*

Two kilometers (1 mile) farther (Route 131) along the Danube from Hartkirchen is Aschach, a small village that was once a river toll station and long famed as the birthplace of Leonard Paminger, one of the most noted 16th-century Austrian composers. It features several gabled-roof burghers' houses, a castle, and a late-Gothic church that are all well preserved. Less intact is the castle, now semi-ruined, that once belonged to the regal Counts of Harrach, located near the town.

Lodging

$$ ⊞ **Faust Schlössl.** Once a toll-collection station belonging to the
★ Schaunberg family (ruins of the family castle are nearby), this castle is on the river directly across from Aschach. Rumor has it that the place is haunted by the Devil, who is said to have built it in a single night for Dr. Faustus. Ignore the tale and enjoy simple but modern comfort in the towers and turrets of the converted castle. ⊠ *Oberlandshaag 2,*

A–4082 Feldkirchen, ☎ *07233/7402–0,* FAX *07233/7402–40. 25 rooms. Restaurant, pool, fishing, bicycles. AE, MC, V.*

$$ 🏨 **Zur Sonne.** The welcome of the bright yellow facade carries over to the comfortable traditional decor inside. You're right on the Danube here, and the best rooms have a river view. This popular restaurant offers regional specialties and, of course, fish, including fresh trout. ✉ *Kurzwernhartpl. 5, A–4082 Aschach/Donau,* ☎ *07273/6308. 12 rooms with bath or shower. Restaurant. No credit cards.*

St. Florian

★ ❸❻ *13 km (8¼ mi) southeast of Linz.*

St. Florian is best known for the great Augustinian abbey, considered among the finest Baroque buildings in Austria. Composer Anton Bruckner (1824–96) was organist for 10 years and is buried in the abbey. Take the road south to Kleinmünchen and Ebelsberg, or for a more romantic approach, try the **Florianer Bahn,** a resurrected electric interurban tram line, which runs museum streetcars on Sundays and holidays from May through the end of September, 6 kilometers (nearly 4 miles) from Pichling to St. Florian (☎ 07224/4333); streetcars depart at 10:40, 2:10, and 3:40.

Guided tours of the **Abbey of St. Florian** include a magnificent figural gate encompassing all three stories, a large and elegant staircase leading to the upper floors, the imperial suite, and one of the great masterworks of the Austrian Baroque, Jakob Prandtauer's **Eagle Fountain courtyard,** with its richly sculpted figures. In the splendid **abbey church,** where the ornate decor is somewhat in contrast to Bruckner's music, the Krismann organ (1770–74) is one of the largest and best of its period. Another highlight is the **Altdorfer Gallery,** which contains several masterworks by Albrecht Altdorfer, the leading master of the 16th-century Danube School and ranked with Durer and Grunewald as one of the greatest Northern painters. ✉ *Stiftstr. 1,* ☎ *07224/8902–10.* 🎟 *AS58.* ☉ *1½-hr tour Apr.–Oct., daily at 10, 11, 2, 3, and 4.*

Nightlife and the Arts

Summer concerts are held in June and July at the Kremsmünster (☞ *below*) and St. Florian abbeys; for tickets, contact Oberösterreichische Stiftskonzerte (✉ Domgasse 12, ☎ 0732/776127). A chamber music festival takes place at Schloss Tillysburg in July (☎ 0732/775230). In July and August, a series of concerts on the Bruckner organ is given on Sunday afternoons at 4 in the church (☎ 07224/8903).

Kremsmünster

❸❼ *36 km (22½ mi) south of Linz, 9 km (5½ mi) northwest of Bad Hall, 18 km (11¼ mi) southeast of Wels.*

The vast Benedictine **abbey** at Kremsmünster was established in 777 and remains one of the most important cloisters in Austria. Most travelers arrive there by taking Route 139 (or the train) heading southwest from Linz. Inside the church is the Gothic memorial tomb of Gunther, killed by a wild boar, whose father, Tassilo, duke of Bavaria (and nemesis of Charlemagne) vowed to build the abbey on the site. Centuries later, a Baroque extravaganza replaced the initial structures. There are magnificent rooms: the **Kaisersaal** and the frescoed library with more than 100,000 volumes, many of them manuscripts. On one side of the **Prälatenhof** courtyard are Jakob Prandtauer's elegant fish basins, complete with sculpted saints, holding squirming denizens of the deep, and opposite is the **Abteitrakt,** whose art collection includes the Tassilo Chalice, from about 765. The eight-story observatory houses an early museum of science. ☎ 07583/275–216. 🖾 *Rooms and art gallery AS45, observatory and tour AS50. ☉ Rooms and art gallery tour (minimum 5 people) Easter–Oct., daily at 10, 11, 2, 3, and 4; Nov.–Easter at 11 and 2. Observatory tour (minimum 5 people) May, June, Sept., and Oct., daily at 10 and 2; July and Aug., daily at 10, 2, and 4).*

🕘 The castle at **Kremsegg,** on Route 139 near Kremsmünster, has a collection of old-fashioned cars and motorcycles. ☎ *07583/247–14.* 🖾 *AS70. ☉ Sat. 1–5; Sun., holidays, and July–Aug., 10–noon, 1–5.*

Bad Hall

㊳ *36 km (22½ mi) south of Linz, 18 km (11¼ mi) west of Steyr.*

Bad Hall is a curious relic from earlier days when "taking the cure" was in vogue in Europe. It's still a spa and its saline-iodine waters are prescribed for internal and external application, but you can enjoy the town for its turn-of-the-century setting. Since those on the cure need amusement between treatments, the town lays on numerous sports offerings—during warm weather, there are especially excellent opportunities for golf and tennis—and an operetta festival in summer.

Lodging

$$$$ 🏨 **Schlosshotel Feyregg.** You'll be in an exclusive setting in this Baroque ★ castle just outside town, once the elegant summer residence of an abbot. The comfortable, spacious guest rooms on the ground floor are furnished in period style. The golf course is within an easy stroll. ⊠ *A–4540 Bad Hall/Feyregg-Pfarrkirchen,* ☎ *07258/2591. 11 rooms. Bar. No credit cards.*

$$$–$$$$ 🏨 **Herzog Tassilo Kurhotel.** The yellow exterior of this turn-of-the-century villa reflects the sunny attitude within. Rooms are comfortable if not luxurious, but the main attractions are the vast park in which the hotel is set and the opportunity to "take the cure" under medical supervision for eye, heart, or circulation complaints. Minimum half board is required. ⊠ *Parkstr. 4, A–4540 Bad Hall,* ☎ *07258/2611– 0,* 🖷 *07258/2611–5. 85 rooms. Restaurant, bar, café, indoor pool, sauna, exercise room. AE, DC, MC, V.*

Steyr

★ **㊴** *40 km (25 mi) south of Linz, 20 km (13½ mi) south of Enns.*

Steyr, a stunning Gothic market town, watches over the confluence of the Steyr and Enns rivers. If you travel from Kremsmünster, follow Route 139 until it joins Route 122 and take the road another 17 kilometers (10½ miles). Today the **main square** is lined with pastel facades, many with Baroque and Rococo trim, all complemented by the castle that sits above. The Bummerlhaus at No. 32, in its present form dating to 1497, has a late-Gothic three-story effect. On the Enns side, steps and narrow passageways lead down to the river. In Steyr you are close to the heart of Bruckner country. He composed his *Sixth Symphony* in the Parish House here, and there is a Bruckner room in the **Meserhaus** where he composed his "sonorous music to confound celestial spheres." So many of the houses are worthy of attention that you will need to take your time and explore. Given the quaintness of the town center, you'd hardly guess that Steyr in 1894 had Europe's first electric street lighting. The **Steyrertalbahn,** a narrow-gauge vintage railroad, wanders 17 kilometers (10½ miles) from Steyr through the countryside on weekends June–September (☎ 07252/46569 or 0732/250345). The **industrial museum** set in former riverside factories is a reminder of the era when Steyr was a major center of ironmaking and armaments pro-

duction; hunting arms are still produced here, but the major output is
powerful motors for BMW cars, including those assembled in the
United States. ⌧ *Wehrgrabengasse 7,* ☎ *07252/77351–0.* ⌧ *AS55.*
𝕆 *Tues.–Sun. 10–5.*

Dining and Lodging

$$$ ✕ **Rahofer.** You'll have to search out this intimate restaurant, which
is hidden away in one of the passageways off the main square down
toward the river. The choice is limited but the Italian specialties are
usually excellent; try the saltimbocca or lamb fillet broiled au gratin
with herbs and olive oil. Soups and desserts are praiseworthy. ⌧
Stadtpl. 9, ☎ *07252/54606. AE, DC, V. Closed Sun. and Mon.*

$$$ ✕🏨 **Minichmayr.** From this traditional hotel the view alone—out over
the confluence of the Enns and Steyr rivers, up and across to Schloss
Lamberg—will make your stay memorable. Ask for a room on the river
side, but check before you register, since tradition has unfortunately,
in some cases, become an excuse for shabbiness. No caveats apply to
the excellent restaurant's creative, light cuisine and regional specialties. The hotel is one of the Romantik Hotel group. ⌧ *Haratzmüller-
str. 1–3, A–4400,* ☎ *07252/53410–0,* 🗚 *07252/48202–55. 51 rooms.
Restaurant, bar, weinstube, sauna, exercise room, bicycles. AE, DC,
MC, V.*

$$ 🏨 **Mader/Zu den Drei Rosen.** In this very old family-run hotel with
★ small but pleasant modern rooms, you're right on the attractive town
square. The restaurant offers solid local and traditional fare, with out-
door dining in a delightful garden area within the ancient courtyard.
⌧ *Stadtpl. 36, A–4400,* ☎ *07252/53358–0,* 🗚 *07252/53358–6. 53
rooms. Restaurant, weinstube. AE, DC, MC, V.*

THE WACHAU ALONG THE SOUTH BANK OF THE DANUBE

South of the Danube and east of Linz, the gentle countryside is crossed
by rivers that rise in the Alps and eventually feed the Danube. Little
evidence remains today, in this prosperous country of small-industry
and agriculture, that the area was heavily fought over in the final days
of World War II. From 1945 to 1995, the river Enns marked the bor-
der between the western (U.S., British, and French) and the eastern (Rus-
sian) occupying zones.

Enns

40 *20 km (12½ mi) southeast of Linz.*

A settlement has continuously existed at Enns since at least AD 50; the
Romans set up a major encampment shortly after that date. Contem-
porary Enns is dominated by the 184-foot square city tower (1565–
68) that stands in the town square. A number of Gothic buildings in
the center have Renaissance or Baroque facades. Guided tours of the
town's highlights, starting at the tower, are available for a minimum
of three persons daily at 9:15 and 10:30, May–mid-September (☎
07223/3261). Visit the **St. Laurence basilica,** built on the foundations
of a far earlier church, west of the town center, to view the glass-en-
cased archaeological discoveries from earlier civilizations. And outside,
look for the Baroque carved-wood Pontius Pilate disguised as a Turk,
alongside a bound Christ, on the balcony of the old sanctuary.

Lodging

$$$ ⊞ **Lauriacum.** You might overlook this plain contemporary building, set as it is among Baroque gems in the center of town, but it's the best place to stay. The bright rooms offer modern comfort, and the quiet garden is a welcoming spot. ⊠ *Wiener Str. 5–7, A–4470,* ☎ *07223/2315,* FAX *07223/2332–29. 30 rooms. Restaurant, bar, café, sauna. MC, V.*

Waidhofen an der Ybbs

④ *30 km (18¾ mi) east of Steyr, 25 km (15¾ mi) south of Amstetten.*

Waidhofen an der Ybbs is well worth a slight detour from the more traveled routes. This picturesque river town developed early as an industrial center, turning Styrian iron ore into swords, knives, sickles, and scythes. These weapons proved successful in the defense against the invading Turks in 1532; marking the decisive moment of victory, the hands on the north side of the town tower clock remain at 12:45. In 1871, Baron Rothschild bought the collapsing castle and assigned Friedrich Schmidt, architect of the Vienna city hall, to rebuild it in neo-Gothic style. Stroll around the two squares in the Altstadt to see the Gothic and Baroque houses, and to the Graben on the edge of the old city for the delightful Biedermeier houses and the churches and chapels. From Enns, take the A1 autobahn or Route 1 east from Enns to just before Amstetten, where Route 121 cuts south paralleling the Ybbs River and the branch rail line for about 25 kilometers (16 miles).

Dining

$$$ ✕ **Türkenpfeiferl.** A relaxed atmosphere marks this restaurant. Set in a handsomely restored town house within the heart of the Old Town, it serves excellent regional standards. Try the breast of chicken, grilled trout with garlic butter, or lamb with creamed celery sauce. The wine cellar includes far more than is on the list, so ask for advice. The garden is particularly pleasant for summer dining, and children are welcome. ⊠ *Hoher Markt 23,* ☎ *07442/53507. DC, MC. Closed Mon., Tues., and 1st wk of July.*

Ybbs an der Donau

④ *25 km (15¾ mi) northeast of Amstetten, 13 km (8¼ mi) west of Melk.*

Floods and fires have left their mark on Ybbs an der Donau, but many 16th-century houses remain, their courtyards vine-covered and shaded. The parish church of St. Laurence has interesting old tombstones, a gorgeous gilded organ, and a Mount of Olives scene with clay figures dating to 1450. To get to Ybbs an der Donau from Waidhofen an der Ybbs, make your way back to the Danube via Routes 31 and 22 east, then Route 25 north thorugh the beer-brewing town of Wieselburg.

Melk

★ **④** *22 km (13¾ mi) east of Ybbs an der Donau, 18 km (11¼ mi) west of St. Pölten, 33 km (20¾ mi) southwest of Krems.*

The ideal time to approach the magnificent abbey of Melk is mid- to late afternoon, when the sun sets the abbey's ornate Baroque yellow facade aglow. As one heads eastward paralleling the Danube, the classic view of the abbey, shining on its promontory above the river, comes into view—unquestionably one of the most impressive sights in all Austria. The glories of the abbey tend to overshadow the town—located along Route 1—but the riverside village of Melk itself is worth exploring. A self-guided tour (in English, from the tourist office) will head you toward the highlights and the best spots from which to photograph the abbey.

The **Abbey of Melk** by any standard is a Baroque masterpiece. Here the story of Umberto Eco's historical novel and film *The Name of the Rose* took place, and in fact, as in fiction, the monastery did burn in 1297, in 1683, and again in 1735. The Benedictine abbey was established in 1089; the building you see today dates to architect Jakob Prandtauer's reconstruction, completed in 1736, in which some earlier elements are incorporated. Part palace, part monastery, part opera set, Melk is a classic vision thanks greatly to the upward-reaching twin towers, capped with Baroque helmets and cradling a 208-foot-high dome, and a roof bristling with Baroque statuary. Symmetry here beyond the towers and dome would be misplaced, and much of the abbey's charm is due to the way the early architects were forced to fit the building to the rocky outcrop which forms its base. A tour of the building includes the main public rooms: a magnificent library, with more than 70,000 books, 2,000 manuscripts, and a superb ceiling fresco by the master Paul Troger; the marble hall, whose windows on three sides enhance the ceiling frescoes; the glorious spiral staircase; and the church of Saints Peter and Paul, an exquisite example of the Baroque style. ⊠ *Abt Berthold Dietmayr-Str. 1, ☏ 02752/2312. ☐ AS50; with tour AS65; combination ticket available with Schloss Artstetten (☞ Maria Taferl, above) and Schloss Schallaburg (☞ below). ⊙ Apr.–Sept., daily 9–5 (50-min tour hourly; last tour 1 hr before closing); Apr.–Oct., daily 9–5; tour Nov.–Mar., daily at 11 and 2.*

NEED A BREAK?   The **Stiftsrestaurant** at the abbey of Melk (☞ *above*) offers standard fare, but the abbey's excellent wines elevate a simple meal to a lofty experience—particularly on a sunny day on the terrace. Closed November–April.

Dining and Lodging

$$–$$$ ✕🏨 **Stadt Melk.** This traditional hotel in the heart of town offers plain but adequate accommodations in smallish rooms (look before you register), but the main feature here is the excellent and attractive restaurant. The cuisine ranges from regional traditional to creative light; try one of the cream soups, stuffed chicken breast, or rack of lamb in an olive crust to enjoy the contrasts; dishes here are individually prepared. ⊠ *Hauptpl. 1, A–3390, ☏ 02752/2475, FAX 02752/2475–19. 16 rooms. Restaurant. AE, DC, MC, V. Closed mid-Nov.–mid-Dec.*

$$ 🏨 **Goldener Ochs.** Here in the center of town you're in a typical village *Gasthof* with the traditional friendliness of family management. The rather small rooms were renovated in 1990, and the restaurant offers solid, standard fare. ⊠ *Linzer Str. 18, A–3390, ☏ 02752/2367–0, FAX 02752/2367–6. 35 rooms, 25 with bath. Restaurant, sauna, exercise room, bicycles. AE, DC, MC, V.*

Schallaburg

6 km (3¾ mi) south of Melk.

From Melk, take a road south marked to Mank to arrive at the restored Protestant castle of **Schloss Schallaburg** (dating from 1573), which features an imposing two-story arcaded courtyard that is held to be the area's finest example of Renaissance architecture. Its ornate, warm brown terra-cotta decoration is unusual. The yard once served as a jousting court. Many centuries have left their mark on the castle: inside, the Romanesque living quarters give way to an ornate Gothic chapel. The castle now houses changing special exhibits. ☎ 02754/6317. 🖃 AS60; *tour AS20 per person extra; combined ticket with Melk abbey AS75, with Schloss Artstetten AS95.* ☾ *May–Oct., weekdays 9–5, weekends and holidays 9–6; last admission 1 hr before closing.*

En Route   To return to the Wachau from Schallaburg, head back toward Melk and take Route 33 along the south bank. This route, attractive any time of the year, is spectacular (and thus heavily traveled) in early spring, when apricot and apple trees burst into glorious blossom. Among the palette of photogenic pleasures is **Schönbühel an der Donau,** whose unbelievably picturesque castle, perched on a cliff overlooking the Danube, is unfortunately not open to visitors. Past the village of Aggsbach Dorf you'll spot, on a hill to your right, the romantic ruin of 13th-century Aggstein castle, reportedly the lair of pirates who preyed on river traffic.

Mautern

1 km (½ mi) south of Stein.

Mautern, opposite Krems, was a Roman encampment mentioned in the tales of the Nibelungs. The old houses and the castle are attractive, but contemporary Mautern is known for one of Austria's top restaurants (☞ Dining and Lodging, *below*), in an inn run by Lisl Bacher; in nearby Klein-Wien there's another culinary landmark—also excellent—run by her sister (☞ Göttweig, *below*).

Dining and Lodging

$$$$ ✕🏠 **Landhaus Bacher.** Lisl Bacher's creative, light cuisine has elevated
★   this attractive restaurant to one of the top half-dozen in the country. Quality is consistently outstanding and the setting is delightful. The light-flooded rooms are elegant but not pretentious, and there's an attractive garden for al fresco dining. Offerings change regularly, reflecting the season and Bacher's remarkable inventiveness—simply perfection in the combination of ingredients and courses. Among main dishes, you might find local lamb with olives and artichoke hearts or guinea-fowl with truffles. Ask for advice on wines; the choice is wide. There are a few small and cozy rooms in an adjoining guest house. ⊠ *Südtirolerpl. 208,* ☎ *02732/82937–0 or 02732/85429,* **FAX** *02732/74337. Reservations essential. DC, V. Closed Mon. and Tues. Nov.–Apr., and mid-Jan.–mid-Feb. No lunch Mon. and Tues. May–Oct.*

Göttweig

★ ④   *7 km (4½ mi) south of Krems, 18 km (11¼ mi) north of St. Pölten.*

You're certain to spot **Stift Göttweig** as you come along the riverside road: The vast Benedictine abbey high above the Danube Valley watches over the gateway to the Wachau. To reach it, go along Route 33, turn right into the highway south (marked to Stift Göttweig and St. Pölten), and turn right again (marked to Stift Göttweig) at the crest of the hill. Göttweig's exterior was redone in the mid-1700s in the classical style, which you'll note from the columns, balcony, and relatively plain side towers. Inside, it is a monument to Baroque art, with marvelous ornate decoration against the gold, brown, and blue. The stained-glass windows behind the high altar date to the mid-1400s. The church is open independent of guided tours. The public rooms of the abbey are splendid, particularly the Kaiserzimmer (emperor's rooms), in which Napoléon stayed in 1809, reached via the elegant emperor's staircase. ⊠ *Furth bei Göttweig,* ☎ *02732/85581–0.* 🖃 *AS40.* ☾ *Tour (minimum 8 people) Easter–Oct., daily at 10, 11, 2, 3, and 4.*

Dining

$$$ ✕ **Schickh.** This restaurant, tucked away among lovely old trees below
★ the north side of the Göttweig abbey, is worth looking for. Creative
ideas out of the kitchen transform seasonal and regional specialties.
You might be offered asparagus wrapped in smoked lamb or tender
roast baby lamb. In summer you'll dine in the garden, probably rub-
bing elbows with the knowledgeable Viennese elite. There's a handful
of guest rooms available for overnights. ⊠ *Avastr. 2, A–3511 Klein-
Wien/Furth bei Göttweig,* ☎ *02736/218–0,* ℻ *02736/218–7. Reser-
vations essential. No credit cards. Closed Wed., Thurs., and Mar.*

$–$$ ✕ **Stiftsrestaurant.** The terrace restaurant on the abbey grounds offers
not only good standard Austrian cuisine but, on a fine day, a spectac-
ular view. It's a great spot for lunch, coffee, or a drink. The grilled chicken
can be recommended without reservation. You might try—and buy by
the bottle—the excellent wines produced by the abbey. ⊠ *Stift Göttweig, A–3511 Furth bei Göttweig,* ☎ *02732/84663. AE, DC, MC, V.
Closed Nov.–Mar.*

St. Pölten

45 *65 km (40¾ mi:west of Vienna, 26 km (16¼ mi) south of Krems.*

St. Pölten, Lower Austria's capital to the south of the Danube, is a city
of comfortable contrasts and, for some, will be worth a detour 20 kilometers (12½ miles) to the south of the main stretch of the Wachau. The
old municipal center, now mainly a pedestrian zone, shows a distinctly
Baroque face. The originally **Romanesque cathedral** on Domplatz has a
rich Baroque interior; the Rococo **Franciscan church** at the north end of
the Rathausplatz has four altar paintings by Kremser Schmidt. The Institute of English Maidens (a former convent, completed in 1769) on nearby
Linzer Strasse is one of the finest Baroque buildings in the city. The east
side of the river is abuzz with new glass and steel construction associated with the regional capital, which is moving here after centuries in
Vienna. The capital is moving because of a political decision—supported
by a one-sided referendum back in the mid-1980s—at enormous expense
and rather against the current will of most Lower Austrian residents, who
prefer the central convenience of Vienna. When completed in 1998, the
St. Pölten government district will be a memorial to one of Lower Austria's powerful conservative politicians who initiated the project.

In a moated castle north of Pottenbrunn, 6½ kilometers (4 miles) east
of St. Pölten, there's a fascinating museum, the ***Zinnfigurenmuseum***
devoted to authentically detailed tin soldiers. Imagine a bird's-eye view
of entire armies in battle formation; you'll see thousands of soldiers at
their posts in the battles of Leipzig (1813), Berg Isel (Innsbruck, 1809),
Vienna (1683), and World War I. ⊠ *Pottenbrunner Hauptstr. 77,* ☎
02785/2337. ▣ *AS50.* ⊙ *Apr.–Oct., Tues.–Sun. 9–5.*

Dining and Lodging

$$$ ✕ **Galerie.** Mellow furnishings from long-gone dining rooms and ho-
tels lend atmosphere to this stylish restaurant. In contrast to the an-
tiques, the kitchen strives to do new things—generally successfully—with
Austrian standards like pork fillet or turkey breast. ⊠ *Fuhrmanngasse
1,* ☎ *02742/351305. AE, DC, MC, V. Closed Sun., Mon., and 2 wks
around Easter.*

$$$ ▥ **Metropol.** Slick modern styling marks this new hotel on the edge of
the pedestrian zone at the heart of the Old City. Rooms are comfort-
able, if lacking a broken-in quality. ⊠ *Schillerpl. 1, A–3100,* ☎
02742/70700–0, ℻ *02742/70700–133. 100 rooms. Restaurant, bar,
sauna, parking. AE, DC, MC, V.*

OFF THE
BEATEN PATH

HERZOGENBURG – The great Augustinian cloister of Herzogenburg is 11 kilometers (6¾ miles) north of St. Pölten (take Wiener Strasse/Route 1 out of St. Pölten heading east for 12 kilometers, or 8 miles, to Kapelln, then turn left to Herzogenburg). The present buildings date mainly to the mid-1700s. Fischer von Erlach was among the architects who designed the abbey. The church, dedicated to Saints George and Stephen, is wonderfully Baroque, with exquisitely decorated ceilings. ☎ 02782/3112-0. ✉ AS40. ☉ 1-hr tour Apr.–Oct., daily 9–11 and 2–5 on the hr.

En Route Small rural villages abound on the south bank plain, some quaint, some typical. Head north on Route S33 or the parallel road, marked to Traismauer, and pick up Route 43 east. If you're ready for back roads (too well marked for you to get lost), cut off to the left to Oberbierbaum (Upper Beer Tree!) and then on to Zwentendorf (there's a fascinating black madonna in the side chapel of the parish church here). If you follow Route 43, it will land you on Route 1 at Mitterndorf; drive east and after 4 kilometers (2½ miles), turn left off Route 1 onto Route 19, marked for Tulln.

Tulln

❹❻ *41 km (25¾ mi) northeast of St. Pölten, 42 km (26¼ mi) west of Vienna.*

At Tulln, you'll spot a number of charming Baroque touches in the attractive main square. There's a new **Egon Schiele Museum** to honor the great modern artist, who was born here (1890–1918); the museum showing a selection of his works is in the one-time district prison, with a reconstruction of the cell in which Schiele—accused of producing "pornography"—was locked up in 1912. ✉ *Donaulände 28,* ☎ *02272/ 4570.* ✉ *AS30.* ☉ *Tues.–Sun. 9–noon and 2–6.*

A former **Minorite cloister** now houses a collection of museums. Among the more interesting are the **Limesmuseum,** which recalls the early Roman settlements in the area, and the **Landesfeuerwehrmuseum,** documenting rural firefighting. Also look inside the well-preserved, late-Baroque (1750) Minorite church next door. ✉ *Minoritenpl. 1,* ☎ *02272/61915.* ✉ *AS30.* ☉ *Weekdays 3–6, Sat. 2–6, Sun. 10–6.*

The Romanesque **St. Stephan Stadtpfarrkirche** (parish church) on Wiener Strasse is noteworthy for its west door and the six figures carved in relief circles on each side (presumably the 12 apostles). Alongside the church, the unusual combined chapel (upstairs) and charnel house (below) is in a structure that successfully combines late-Romanesque and early Gothic.

Dining and Lodging

$$$$
★
✗ **Zum Roten Wolf.** In an unpretentious but attractive rustic restaurant (one of Austria's top 20) in Langelebarn, 4 kilometers (2½ miles) east of Tulln, the stylishly elegant table settings complement the consistently outstanding food. Neither preparation nor presentation leaves anything to be desired. Try any of the lamb variations or the breast of duck. The service is especially friendly; ask for advice on the wines. You can get here by local train from Vienna; the station is virtually at the door. ✉ *Bahnstr. 58,* ☎ *02272/2567. Reservations essential. AE, DC, MC, V. Closed Mon. and Tues.*

$$
🏠 **Zur Rossmühle.** From the abundant greenery of the reception area to the table settings in the dining room, you'll find pleasing little touches in this attractively renovated hotel on the town square. The rooms are done in grand-old yet brand-new Baroque. Take lunch in

the courtyard garden; here, as in the more formal dining room, you'll be offered Austrian standards. ⊠ *Hauptpl. 12–13, A-3430,* ☎ *02272/2411,* ℻ *02272/2411–33. 55 rooms. Restaurant, bar, sauna, horseback riding. AE, DC, V.*

Greifenstein

East of Tulln on Route 14; turn left at St. Andrä-Wördern and stay on the Danube shoreline.

Atop the hill at Greifenstein, yet another **castle** with spectacular views looks up the Danube and across to Stockerau. Its earliest parts date to 1135, but most of it stems from a thorough but romantic renovation in 1818. The view is worth the climb, even when the castle and inexpensive restaurant are closed. ⊠ *Kostersitzgasse 5,* ☎ *02242/32353 or 02243/88105.* ⊙ *Mar.–Dec., Wed.–Sun.*

Klosterneuburg

47 *13 km (8¼ mi) northwest of Vienna.*

The great Augustinian **abbey** dominates the scene at Klosterneuburg. The structure has changed many times since the abbey was established in 1114, most recently in 1892, when Friedrich Schmidt, architect of Vienna's city hall, added neo-Gothic features to its two identifying towers. Klosterneuburg was unusual in that until 1568 it housed both men's and women's religious orders. In the abbey church, look for the carved wood choir loft and oratory and the large 17th-century organ. Among Klosterneuburg's treasures are the beautifully enameled 1181 Verdun Altar in the Leopold Chapel, stained-glass windows from the 14th and 15th centuries, Romanesque candelabra from the 12th century, and gorgeous ceiling frescoes in the great marble hall. In an adjacent outbuilding there's a huge wine cask over which people slide. The exercise, called *Fasslrutsch'n,* is indulged in during the *Leopoldiweinkost,* the wine-tasting around St. Leopold's day, November 15. ⊠ *Stiftspl. 1,* ☎ *02243/36210–212.* ⊠ *AS50.* ⊙ *1-hr tour Mon.–Sat. hourly 9–11 and 1:30–4:30, Sun. and holidays at 11 and hourly 1:30–4:30.*

Dining

$$ ✕ **Stiftskeller.** The main dining rooms are on the ground floor, but instead seek out the atmospheric underground rooms in a historic part of the abbey. This is an authentic cellar in every sense of the word, with some of the fine wines even carrying the Klosterneuburg label. You can sample them along with standard Austrian fare, from Wiener schnitzel to rump steak with onions. ⊠ *Albrechtsbergergasse 1,* ☎ *02243/32070. No credit cards.*

OFF THE BEATEN PATH
KAHLENBERGERDORF – Near Klosterneuburg and just off the road tucked under the Leopoldsberg promontory, is the charming small vintners' village of Kahlenbergerdorf, an excellent spot to stop and sample the local wines. You're just outside the Vienna city limits here, which accounts for the crowds on weekends.

DANUBE VALLEY A TO Z

Arriving and Departing

By Boat

Large riverboats with sleeping accommodations ply the route between Vienna and Linz and between Passau on the German border and Linz, from late spring to early fall. Smaller day boats go between Vienna and the Wachau valley, and there you can change to local boats that criss-cross the river between the colorful towns. For information on boat schedules, contact **DDSG/Blue Danube Schiffahrt** (✉ Handelskai 265, A–1020 Vienna, ☎ 0222/727–50–440, ℻ 0222/218–9238; ✉ Untere Donaulände 10, A–4010 Linz, ☎ 0732/783607, ℻ 0732/783607–9); for Linz–Passau service, **Wurm & Köck** (✉ Höllgasse 26, D–94032 Passau, ☎ 0049851/929292, ℻ 0049851/35518); for Linz–Ottensheim and excursions, **Fitzcaraldo Donauschiffahrt** (✉ Ottensheimer Str. 37, A–4010 Linz, ☎ 0732/710008, ℻ 0732/710009). Danube boat services from Melk to Krems with stops between within the Wachau region are operated by **Brandner Schiffahrt** (✉ Ufer 50, A–3313 Wallsee, ☎ 07433/2590–0, ℻ 07433/2590–25.

By Car

A car is certainly the most comfortable way to see this region, as it conveniently enables you to pursue the byways. The main route along the north bank is Route 3; along the south bank, there's a choice of autobahn Route A1 or a collection of lesser but good roads.

By Plane

Linz is served mainly by **Austrian Airlines, Lufthansa, Swissair,** and **Tyrolean.** Regular flights connect with Vienna, Amsterdam, Berlin, Düsseldorf, Frankfurt, Paris, Stuttgart, and Zürich. The Linz airport (☎ 07221/72700–0) is in Hörsching, about 12 kilometers (7½ miles) southwest of the city. Buses run between the airport and the main railroad station according to flight schedules.

By Train

Rail lines parallel the north and south banks of the Danube. Fast services from Vienna run as far as Stockerau; beyond that, service is less frequent. The main east–west line from Vienna to Linz closely follows the south bank for much of its route. Fast trains connect German cities via Passau with Linz.

Getting Around

By Bicycle

A bicycle trail parallels the Danube for its entire length in Austria, in most stretches on both north and south banks. Tourist offices (☞ Visitor Information, *below*) have information, maps, and recommendations for sightseeing and overnight and mealtime stops.

By Boat

Bridges across the river are few along this stretch, so boats provide essential transportation; service is frequent enough that you can cross the river, visit a town, catch a bus or the next boat to the next town, and cross the river farther up- or downstream. You can take a day trip from Vienna and explore one of the stops, such as Krems, Dürnstein, or Melk. Boats run from May to late September.

By Bus

If you link them together, bus routes will get you to the main points in this region and even to the hilltop castles and monasteries, assuming you have the time. If you coordinate your schedule to arrive at a point by train or boat, you can usually make reasonable bus connections to outlying destinations. In Vienna you can book bus tours (☞ Guided Tours, *below*); in Linz, ask at the municipal bus station (✉ Bahnhofpl. 12, ☎ 0732/1671).

By Car

A car is certainly the most hassle-free way to get around. Roads are good and well marked, and you can switch over to the A1 autobahn, which parallels the general east–west course of the route (☞ Driving *in* the Gold Guide).

By Train

Every larger town and city in the region can be reached by train, but the train misses the Wachau Valley along the Danube's south bank. The rail line on the north side of the river literally clings to the bank in places, but service is infrequent. You can combine rail and boat transportation along this route, taking the train upstream and crisscrossing your way back on the river. From Linz, the delightful LILO interurban line (☎ 0732/654376) makes the run up to Eferding. A charming narrow-gauge line meanders south to Waidhofen an der Ybbs.

Contacts and Resources

Bicycle Rentals

For details on the scenic Danube river route, ask for the folder "Danube Cycle Track" (in English, from Niederösterreich-Information, ⊠ Heidenschuss 2, A–1010 Vienna, ☎ 0222/533–3114–0 or 0222/53110–6200, ℻ 0222/535–0319) for hints on what to see and where you'll find "cyclist-friendly" accommodations, repairs, and other services. You'll find bicycle rentals at Aggsbach–Markt, Dürnstein, Grein, Krems, Mautern, Melk, Persenbeug–Gottsdorf, Pöchlarn, Schönbühel/Aggsbach Dorf, Spitz, Weissenkirchen, and Ybbs. The terrain around Linz is relatively level, and within the city there are 89 kilometers (55 miles) of marked cycle routes. Ask for the brochure "Cycling in Linz" from the tourist office. You can rent a bike through **Fahrradzentrum B7** (⊠ Oberfelderstr. 12, ☎ 0732/330550); **LILO Bahnhof** (⊠ Coulinstr. 30, ☎ 0732/600703); or at the **Hauptbahnhof** (⊠ main rail station, Bahnhofstr. 3, ☎ 0732/6909–385). Bicycles can be rented at the railroad stations in Freistadt (☎ 07942/2319) and Steyr (☎ 07252/595–385), or privately in Kremsmünster at **Tenniscenter Stadlhuber** (☎ 07583/7498–0). The brochure "Radfahren" is in German but lists contact numbers for cycle rentals throughout Upper Austria.

Canoeing

The Danube is fast and tricky, so you're best off sticking to the calmer waters back of the power dams (at Pöchlarn, above Melk, and near Grein). You can rent a canoe at Pöchlarn. You can also canoe on an arm of the Danube near Ottensheim, about 8 kilometers (5 miles) west of Linz. For information call Ruderverein Donau (☎ 0732/236250) or Ruderverein Ister-Sparkasse (☎ 0732/774888).

Car Rentals

Cars can be rented at the airports in Vienna or Linz. Linz contacts: **Avis** (⊠ Schillerstr 1, ☎ 0732/662881); **Buchbinder** (⊠ Untere Donaulände 15, ☎ 0732/773051); **EuroDollar** (⊠ Coulinstr. 13, ☎ 0732/658360); **Hertz** (⊠ Bürgerstr. 19, ☎ 0732/784841–0).

Emergencies

Police, ☎ 133. **Fire,** ☎ 122. **Ambulance,** ☎ 144. If you need a doctor and speak no German, ask your hotel how best to obtain assistance.

Fishing

This is splendid fishing country. Check with the town tourist offices about licenses and fishing rights for river trolling and fly-casting in Aggsbach-Markt, Dürnstein, Emmersdorf, Grein, Kleinpöchlarn, Krems, Mautern, Mauthausen, Persenbeug–Gottsdorf, Pöchlarn, Schönbühel/Aggsbach Dorf, Spitz, Waidhofen/Ybbs, and Ybbs. In Linz, check **Fischereiverband** (⊠ Kärntnerstr. 12, ☎ 0732/650507), **Fischerhof AMBO** (⊠ Landwiedstr. 69, ☎ 0732/670257), or **Weitgasser** (⊠ Figulystr. 5, ☎ 0732/656566). In the streams and lakes of the area around Linz, you can fly-cast for rainbow and brook trout and troll for pike and carp. For details, contact the tourist offices or the numbers listed below: In Attersee, **Esso Station Nussdorf** (☎ 07666/80634); Bad Hall, **Gasthof Schröck "Hofwirt"** (hotel guests only, ☎ 07258/2274); Freistadt, **Sportgeschäft Gutenbrunner** (☎ 07942/2720) and **Sportgeschäft Juch** (☎ 07942/2532); Grein, **Die Erste Sparkasse Mauthausen** (☎ 07268/203); Kremsmünster, **Gerhard Fleck** (☎ 07583/6103); Steyr, **Angelsportverein Steyr** (☎ 07252/615443).

Golf
In addition to courses listed with towns, there are greens in Bad Ischl, Mondsee, and Wels.

Guided Tours
Tours out of Vienna take you to Melk and back by bus and boat in eight hours, with a stop at Dürnstein. Bus tours operate year-round except as noted, but the boat runs only April–October. Operators include: **Cityrama/Gray Line** (⊠ Börsegasse 1, ☎ 0222/534–13–0, ℻ 0222/534–13–22), for AS760; **Vienna Sightseeing Tours** (⊠ Stelzhammergasse 4/11, ☎ 0222/712–4683–0, ℻ 0222/712–4683–77), for AS890; and **Citytouring Vienna** (⊠ Penzinger Str. 46, ☎ 0222/894–1417–0, ℻ 0222/894–3239), for AS950, including a light snack.

Day boat trips with loudspeaker announcements in English run daily to and through the Wachau from Vienna from May through September. Contact the **DDSG/Blue Danube schiffahrt** (⊠ Handelskai 265, ☎ 0222/727–50–440, ℻ 0222/218–9238). The cruise trips leave from Schwedenbrücke, by Schwedenplatz, in Vienna, daily at 10:30, 1, 2:30, and 4:30. For information on daytime and evening excursions out of Linz, check with the tourist office or Fitzcaraldo Donauschiffahrt (☞ Getting Around by Boat, *above*).

Hiking
Local tourist offices have maps and route details of the fabulous trails in the area, and in Linz you can get the booklet "Urban Hiking Paths in Linz." For information on the Mühlviertel from Freistadt to Grein, call ☎ 0732/735020.

Tennis
You'll find tennis courts—indoors and out—in nearly every town. Ask at the tourist offices in Aggsbach–Markt, Dürnstein, Grein, Krems, Maria Taferl, Mautern, Persenbeug–Gottsdorf, Pöchlarn, Spitz, Waidhofen/Ybbs, and Weissenkirchen. In Linz, ask the tourist office about possible available courts.

Travel Agencies
In Linz, leading travel agencies include **American Express** (⊠ Bürgerstr. 14, ☎ 0732/669013, ℻ 0732/655334); **Carlson Wagonlit Travel** (⊠ Bismarckstr. 8, ☎ 0732/771492–0, ℻ 0732/771492–9); **Kuoni** (⊠ Hauptpl. 14, ☎ 0732/771301, ℻ 0732/775338); and **Oberösterreichisches Landesreisebüro** (⊠ Hauptpl. 9, ☎ 0732/771061–0, ℻ 0732/771061–49).

Visitor Information
For general information on the area, check with the following district tourist offices. **Lower Austria** (⊠ Heidenschuss 2, A–1010 Vienna, ☎ 0222/533–3114–0, ℻ 0222/535–0319). **Upper Austria** (⊠ Schillerstr. 50, A–4010 Linz, ☎ 0732/771264, ℻ 0732/600220). **Linz** (⊠ Hauptpl. 5, ☎ 0732/7070–1777, ℻ 0732/772873), where you can pick up the latest *Linz City News* in English as well as German.

Most towns have local *Fremdenverkehrsamt* (tourist offices). **Bad Hall** (⊠ Kurhaus, A–4540, ☎ 07258/2031–0, ℻ 07258/2031–25). **Dürn-**

stein (✉ Parkpl. Ost, A–3601, ☎ 02711/200, 02711/219, ℻ 02711/422). **Eferding** (✉ Stadtpl. 1, A–4070, ☎ 07272/5555–20, ℻ 07272/5555–33). **Freistadt** (✉ Hauptpl. 12, A–4240, ☎ 07942/2974, ℻ 07942/3207). **Grein** (✉ Hauptstr. 3, A–4360, ☎ 07268/6680 or 07268/7290, ℻ 07268/7290). **Klosterneuburg** (✉ Niedermarkt 4, A–3400, ☎ 02243/32038, ℻ 02243/86773). **Krems/Stein** (✉ Undstr. 6, A–3500, ☎ 02732/82676, ℻ 02732/70011). **Melk** (✉ Babenbergerstr. 1, A–3390, ☎ 02752/2307–32, ℻ 02752/2307–37). **Pöchlarn** (✉ Regensburger Str. 11, A–3380, ☎ 02757/2310–30, ℻ 02757/2310–66). **St. Pölten** (✉ Rathauspl. 1, A–3100, ☎ 02742/353354, ℻ 02742/333–2819). **Steyr** (✉ Stadtpl. 27, A–4400, ☎ 07252/53229 or 48154, ℻ 07252/48154–15). **Tulln** (✉ Albrechtsgasse 32, A–3430, ☎ 02272/5836, ℻ 02272/5838). **Wachau** (✉ Undstr. 6, A–3500 Krems, ☎ 02732/85620, ℻ 02732/87471). **Waidhofen an der Ybbs** (✉ Obere Stadtpl. 28, A–3340, ☎ 07442/511–165, ℻ 07442/511–77). **Weissenkirchen** (✉ Gemeinde Weissenkirchen, A–3610, ☎ 02715/2232–11 or 02715/2600, ℻ 02715/2232–22).

5 Portraits of Austria

The Land of the Waltz

The Law of the Heuriger

Books and Videos

THE LAND OF THE WALTZ

THE VIENNESE traditionally live in two countries. One is on the map. The other is the imaginary region where wine flows, love triumphs, and everything is silk-lined. This is the land of the waltz.

A century ago, during the sunset years of Austria's 1,000-year-old empire, there was no clear demarcation between the real world and that mythical land of the waltz. The two realms merged along the hazy boundary that never quite separates fact from fancy in Vienna.

This region of the Viennese mind is not just a shallow, sybaritic fantasy. Like Viennese music itself, it embodies a substantial premise. If melody could be translated, a Viennese waltz would add up to 100 ways of saying that, all considered, and with due allowance for everything, simply being alive is a cause for celebration.

At its surprising best—in such creations as "The Blue Danube," the "Emperor Waltz," or "Tales from the Vienna Woods"—the waltz is perhaps the closest description of happiness ever attained in any art.

Paradoxically, the music is not merry. A haze of wistfulness lies over the sunniest tunes, and their sweetness sometimes touches on melancholy. Though the dance is a swirling embrace, the music countermands sensual abandonment. It insists on grace; it remains pensive in the midst of pleasure. And in this blending of the sensual with the reflective, the Viennese waltz expresses and creates a condition of durable bliss—a measured joy.

For almost 100 years, while the last Habsburg emperors ruled the real Austria, the land of the waltz had its own dynasty— the Waltz Kings. Both were named Johann Strauss.

Johann Strauss I ruled over this mythical realm of music during the first part of the 19th century. A generation later, his son, Johann Strauss II, extended the scope of the waltz to symphonic proportions, writing dance music in the form of orchestral tone poems that transformed the ballroom into a concert stage.

These two men welded their city and their music into a single identity, making Vienna and the waltz almost a single thought. Viennese historians are fond of florid metaphors suggesting that Johann Strauss— father and son—did not so much compose their waltzes as ineffably transmute their city into music. Such notions seem altogether plausible to the romantic Viennese, including the younger Strauss himself. "If it is true that I have talent," he wrote during the latter part of his life, "I owe it, above everything else, to my beloved city of Vienna . . . in whose soil is rooted my whole strength, in whose air float the melodies which my ear has caught, my heart has drunk in, and my hand has written down."

Sentimental, yes. Unrealistic, no. Strauss's own assessment of his creative act is probably accurate. *Zeitgeist* and *genius loci*— the spirits of time and place—have always whispered to the creative imagination, and Strauss, being a musician, surely had a fine ear for such promptings.

It is impossible to weigh such ephemeral influences, but one can hardly dispute the perceptive comment made by Marcel Brion on Vienna's matchless array of musicians: "They would not have been what they were, what they had to be, if chance had forced them to live anywhere but in Vienna."

Music, like wine, takes its flavor from the soil and the season in which it grows, and the roots of the waltz were nourished by a moment of history in which an aging civilization had reached the peak of mellowness. No other city has ever been so suffused by an art as Vienna was by music. Painting, perhaps, was of similarly intense concern to the Florentines of the Renaissance. But this enthusiasm was confined to a relatively small circle of aristocratic sponsors centering around the Medicis, and it seems unlikely that painting played a major part in the life of the ordinary Florentine.

By contrast, Vienna's involvement with music was shared by its shopkeepers and janitors. The barriers between serious and popular music had not yet become impassable. There was no "music business" in the modern sense, for commercial pressures had not yet debased and polarized public taste. In the crowds who thronged to hear performances of Beethoven symphonies, Haydn oratorios, or Mozart operas, burghers and artisans easily joined princes of the realm. Conversely, in the little rustic inns tucked among the hillsides of the Vienna Woods, members of the nobility mixed quite casually with lesser folk to dance to the sweet and giddy folk tunes of the region. Here lay the tree-shaded courtyards of the *Heurigen,* the vintners' houses where the Viennese sampled the new wine. And if the white wines that grow along the Danube lack the finesse of more famous vintages from the Rhine or the Moselle, they have a tart freshness and a light headiness that make them all the more inviting for casual tippling.

During the long spring and fall seasons, and during the mild summers, these spacious gardens and courtyards were filled daily from about four in the afternoon until the early hours, and their mood of easy conviviality shaped the pattern of Viennese leisure. Drunkenness was not tolerated; the typical Viennese was a thoughtful drinker who made a glass last a long time by puffing, between sips, on a pencil-thin, foot-long cigar that he smoked through a straw. Groups of strolling musicians would pass from one to another of these inns, entertaining the patrons with tunes of the Austrian countryside—the lilting *Ländler,* which was the rural precursor of the not yet invented waltz, and the *Schnadahüpfl,* a jaunty country hop. Here, too, the sound of music created an instant democracy of manners, and class barriers melted in the balmy atmosphere of relaxed hedonism.

This aspect of Vienna's life invariably amazed foreign visitors, particularly those from France, where such casual friendliness between people of widely different social standing was unthinkable either before or after the revolution. "Ancestors and rank seem to be forgotten," reports one traveler, "and aristocratic pride laid aside. Here we see artisans, artists, merchants, councillors, barons, counts and excellencies dancing together with waitresses, women of the middle class, and ladies."

At private concerts, too, there was congenial mingling of persons from different social strata. Tradespeople with sincere musical interests often found access to the musical soirées which were the chief entertainment in the Baroque town houses of the high bourgeoisie.

In an ancient monarchy whose minutely graded class structure might otherwise have calcified into social arthritis, music thus served a vital limbering function. In an order where stratus—being mostly fixed by birth—could rarely be achieved, music provided the safety valve that kept the pressure of social unrest from building up and enabled absolutism to maintain its sway over Austria long after the American and French revolutions had shaken other thrones.

FOR CENTURIES, the Habsburg rulers maintained a tradition of fostering the arts. The theater, as long as it confined itself to entertainment and did not become a platform for ideas, received royal encouragement, as did the pictorial arts; sculpture; and, above all, music, architecture, and landscaping.

The implicit tenet was that beauty begets pleasure, and pleasure begets contentment. The great cities of imperial Austria—Vienna, Prague, Salzburg, and Budapest—owe their splendor to the endearing assumption that civic beauty is the key to civic tranquillity.

To accuse the Habsburgs of prostituting art for political aims would be unjust. Its furtherance was no cynically contrived policy. In fact, it was no policy at all, never having been consciously formulated. The state of the arts in Austria sprang quite naturally from a naïvely mystic faith—not uncommon in Catholic countries—that aesthetic grace was akin to divine grace and that to invest a country with outward beauty would somehow bestow civic virtues that would hold it together inwardly. This sort of intuition is legitimate to statecraft. What, after all, is a nation but an agreement on style and a cohesive sharing of myths?

Under these conditions, the whole country seemed pervaded by a certain musicality—an innate, casual feeling for form and harmony. It was evident in the visual charm of the Austrian Baroque that left its mark not alone on the great cities but also on many of the smaller towns and villages.

A feeling for the Baroque and its later, lighter variants, with their graceful, almost melodic lines, was by no means confined to the leading architects employed in the design of palaces and manors. It filtered down to the humblest mason molding garlanded cherubs above the gate of an ordinary house. It shaped the vision of the local builder who quite matter-of-factly bestowed an exquisite harmony of proportions. It guided the hand of the cabinetmaker who filled the house with the playful curves of Rococo and Biedermeier furniture. It influenced the gardener and blacksmith alike, one arranging flowerbeds like calligraphy, the other echoing the scrolls in wrought iron. The tailor and the pastry cook shared a concern for graceful shape, and even the gestures of ordinary citizens reflected a certain elegance as they went about their business.

Industrial manufacture had not yet cast its equalizing pall on the design of objects that fill the household and pass through hands in daily use. Far longer than the more industrialized countries to the west, Austria retained the practice and attitudes of individual craftsmanship. The decorative merit of a product ranked at least as high as its utility. Beauty had market value, and the combination of commercial worth and aesthetic joy bestowed on tradesmen and their customers alike a measure of dignity and satisfaction.

In such an ambience, the ear, too, became attuned to the refinements and delights of form. Music derived from the surroundings. It was inescapable. It lay before the eyes.

Vienna, and much of Austria, thus became a natural breeding ground for musicians. A contemporary chronicler, Eduard Bauernfeld, observes that "every hole is full of musicians who play for the people. Nobody wants to eat his *Bratl* at the inn if he can't have table music to go with it." No feast or celebration was complete without a special overture composed for the occasion. Virtually every bourgeois family could muster a passable string quartet among its members, creating a constant demand for new scores. More than 60 piano

factories flourished in the city, which numbered a mere 250,000 inhabitants, and next to good looks and a dowry, musical talent was considered a girl's chief asset.

EVERY SUNDAY, the churches resounded with musical settings of the Mass—"operas for the angels," as Mozart called them. Performed by choirs and orchestras of remarkable proficiency, these compositions by Mozart, Haydn, and Schubert were splendidly melodic, and the occasion, despite its ecclesiastical setting, was often more of a public concert than a divine service. The clergy never objected to mixing devotion and enjoyment. In fact, the monasteries owned some of the best vineyards and maintained some of the coziest inns to dispense their wine. Austrian Catholicism had been spared the more Puritan notions of sin that had shaped the restrictive attitudes of northern Europe. It had also escaped much of the cruel virulence of the Counter Reformation. Austria's faith, touchingly expressed in countless sculptures of smiling, childlike Madonnas, never really clashed against that other trinity in Vienna's heaven—wine, women, and song.

Perhaps the most significant aspect of Vienna's musical life was the attitude of the typical listener. In Paris or London, for example, music was regarded as an entertainment. Not so in Vienna. Here it was a personal necessity, an indispensable part of everyday life. In its lighter forms, music was a needed refreshment; in its more demanding forms, an exercise of the spirit in search of illumination.

It is hardly surprising that such a society left considerable room for individuality. The forces of regimentation and efficiency were traditionally resisted, thus preparing the ground for Vienna's famed *Gemütlichkeit*, the characteristic attitude of unhurried bonhomie.

No doubt the most benign economic influence on the social climate was the virtual absence of extreme poverty. To be sure, Vienna had its share of improvidents and people suffering ill fortune. But the causes of their plight were personal rather than built into an exploitative system. Hence their number was small and they did not constitute an embittered group endangering the balance of the community.

Where in Paris a Jacobin majority marshaled the envy and fear of the deprived into an orgy of class hatred, the Viennese joined all classes in self-indulgent epicureanism.

Even lowly citizens ate well in Vienna. A surviving restaurant menu lists a complete meal for 13 *Kreuzer*—the equivalent of about 25¢. For this modest sum one could regale oneself on soup, smothered liver, roast beef, vegetables, bread, and a quarter-liter of wine. A remarkable document survives in the City Archives showing that during one typical year (1786) some 200,000 Viennese managed to do away with 42,197 oxen, 1,511 cows, 66,353 calves, 43,925 sheep, 164,700 lambs, 96,949 pigs, 12,967 suckling pigs, 454,063 buckets of local wine, 19,276 buckets of Hungarian and Tirolean wine, and 382,478 buckets of beer. No one seems to have made per-capita comparisons, but this document is generally taken as historic proof of an ample appetite.

Such statistics are not irrelevant to music, for they bespeak a love of life and a general greediness for good things, be they products of art or of the kitchen.

WITH COMFORTS of mind and body abundant and readily available, economic incentive never was honed to an irritant edge. Material possessions alone could not change one's social standing in a fixed-status society, and since the public environment was generally delightful, there was less need for private luxury. Consequently, acquisitive drive, the dominant motivating force in open and industrial societies, rarely inspired the Viennese. Their motivation was not so much material success but satisfaction with the task at hand, or, quite often, simply the leisurely enjoyment of the day. To the Viennese, this was the utmost practicality and realism.

As long as external conditions supported this mode of existence, remarkably little cruelty or vulgarity crept to the surface of Austrian life. The feral substrate at the bottom of any society remained nicely covered. And those who, by dark intuition, knew it was there said nothing of it.

Of course, not even an unfailing surfeit of music and Wiener schnitzel could remove all challenges from life, but in an age of indulgent epicureanism, these challenges could usually be surmounted by not trying too hard. That, too, lies in the music. The cardinal rule for playing a waltz is the same as for mastering other phases of life in Vienna: Don't push it—and keep the tempo loose.

Its cushioned resilience made Vienna relatively crisis-proof—at least until the final, cataclysmic collapse of the empire. Nonchalant self-irony lent Vienna, and all Austria, the buoyancy to clear minor hurdles. For example, during a government scandal involving payoffs at the ministerial level, the noted Viennese journalist Karl Kraus soothed tempers by explaining that the accused civil servant "took such small bribes as to border on incorruptibility."

Scanning 1,000 years of Austrian history, John Gunther observed that the country "in its own inimitable, slippery way wriggled out of any difficulty. Something of the very softness of the Austrian character had been a factor of strength, because the horns of a crisis were apt to disappear through absorption—the crisis lost its point, melted in the prevailing solvent of easygoing compromise."

This is hardly a country to be admired by moralists. Philosophers may not find it much to their liking, either. But poets and musicians have always felt at home there, for the land pulses with the heartbeat of humanity.

Johann Strauss felt that pulse and shaped it into a special music that lifted Vienna from its moorings on the map, wafting the city across that misty line between reality and dream into the land of the waltz.

—Hans Fantel

A native of Austria and longtime resident of the United States, Hans Fantel is currently a syndicated columnist for the *New York Times*.

THE LAW OF THE HEURIGER

MARIA THERESA'S SON, Emperor Joseph II (1741–90), who wanders in and out of the play and movie *Amadeus* muttering, "Well, there you are," uttered far more enduring words on August 17, 1784, when he proclaimed to the Austrian people that "we give every man the freedom to sell or dispense—year-round, in any form, at any time, and at whatever price he wants—food, wine, or fruit juice that he has produced himself."

Handed this entrepreneurial key by royalty, the farmers of the Vienna Woods unlatched the *Heuriger:* a unique wine tavern that proliferates in the capital and eastern Austria. *Heuriger* is a noun derived from an adjective meaning "this year's," which applies not only to young wines, but also to such crops as cabbage and potatoes. To the thirsty, however, the only real Heuriger is the farmhouse facade adorned by a sprig of pine, a branch of fir, or a wreath of holly and a plaque on the door signifying that the new wine is in and has been pressed on the premises. Open that door in summer and you'll feast your eyes upon an inviting courtyard lined with picnic tables and crowded with Austrians making merry (which, often as not, means intense intellectual conversations about trivia), frequently hoisting glasses for toasting or refilling, and occasionally lifting voices, too, in song.

Inside the house you'll usually find a buffet from which you can buy hot or cold food and, in those that stay open year-round, a cozy hearth around which you can also eat, drink, and revel. In the larger heurige (plural) or posher ones that cater to tourists and businesspeople, you'll find live music— usually *Schrammelmusik,* named after a 19th-century family who composed, played, sang, and ordained the wistful sound of music still heard in the heuriger.

Rendered by violins, guitar, and clarinet or accordion and sung in an impenetrable Austrian dialect, the songs counterpoint the conversation by treating such earthy themes as a lover's lane in the Vienna Woods that's too small for one person but big enough for two, or lamenting that "the old cog-wheel railway is scrap iron now," or wrestling with the dilemma of a would-be lover who's making headway but watching the clock in the knowledge that the last streetcar leaves soon and he doesn't have money for the taxi ride that would clinch his case. This song is called "The Little Blue Light," and, while the last No. 38 streetcar from the wine suburb of Grinzing no longer wears a blue lamp on its tail, its illuminated destination signs bear equally ominous blue squares of cardboard.

In Grinzing, in particular, one must be wary of places where the Vienna-by-night tour buses draw up every half hour and the *schrammel* musicians drop everything to play "Deep in the Heart of Texas" or "If I Were a Rich Man." Stick around there and you won't be rich for long. Far better to follow a Viennese drinking song with lyrics that list virtually every wine village within easy reach, starting with "a little Grinzing, a little Sievering, a little Neuwaldegg, Nussdorf, Ottakring and Petersdorf." Or play it safe at the elegantly rustic Grinzinger Hauermandl, where the music, chicken, and wine are consistently first-rate.

Today, within the city limits of Vienna, there are some 800 families growing wine on more than 1,800 acres to produce about 12 million quarter-liter glasses of wine per year. Heuriger wine is mostly white: clear, sparkling, dry, and, thanks to its high acidity, possessed of a fresh bite that can bite back the morning after. It is wise to switch, after a couple of glasses, from new wine to old (*alt*). The price may be a dime more tonight, but tomorrow's pain will be less.

The Vienna Tourist Board once published a brochure, "Heurige in Wien," listing 150 of them by neighborhood. There are at least five times that many, and one of the charms of a summer night is to discover your own. Even the farsighted Joseph II, "the People's Emperor" who encouraged Mozart and tried to democratize the Habsburg monarchy, might be astonished at how the cottage industry he envisioned has

166   Portraits of Austria

become a backbone of both Austrian tourism and Viennese life.

"During the warm season, from May to September, people go early, around six o'-clock in the evening," says Traudl Lessing, a Viennese chronicler and connoisseur of Heuriger living. "They take their children and dogs along, as both provide excellent starting points for conversation and friendly relations. As soon as the benches around the rough wooden tables have filled, people sit down with strangers and begin to confide in each other. They tell their unknown friends about the wife's illness, the cranky boss, and how they avoid the burdens of taxation."

FRAU LESSING and her husband, Erich, gave their daughter Hannah's wedding party indoors recently at the spacious and lively Heuriger Schübel-Auer in the Heiligenstadt neighborhood. Beethoven once lived in this district and cursed the church bells he could see tolling but not hear. In fact, just around the corner, a 17th-century house where the peripatetic composer resided for part of 1817 is now one of Vienna's most famous heurige: Mayer am Pfarrplatz.

After Joseph II's 1784 proclamation, known in Vienna as "the law of the heuriger," farmers started selling pork, poultry, and sometimes beef from their own livestock in the front rooms where their customers used to sample their wines. Farmers' daughters found work at home as cooks and waitresses instead of migrating to the city or marrying for survival. Soon, whole families were making cheese and peddling their produce to a market that came to them.

Early in the 20th century, this laissez-faire law of the heuriger was modified for the only time in its 207-year history. Its provisions had spawned too many child alcoholics and adult workaholics—the former souring on not-always-unfermented grape juice; the latter missing church—so certain soft drinks were sanctioned (usually Almdudler Limonade, which tastes like ginger ale), and farmers were forbidden to sell their wines on more than 300 days a year. The amendment also permitted ham and cheese and fowl to be sold by wine farmers who didn't have their own pigs and cows and

chickens. Even today, though, a wine tavern peddling beer, coffee, or Coca-Cola isn't an authentic heuriger and shouldn't be displaying the symbolic green bush outside.

During and after two devastating world wars, the heuriger assumed a new social role in Viennese lives. Rather than entertain in cramped, shabby, or bomb-damaged quarters, hosts invited their guests to meet them at "our Heuriger," where they would buy drinks and sometimes dinner—though it is still good form in many heurige to bring your own picnic and buy just wine. If the coffeehouse, a tradition a century older than the Heuriger, remains the living room of the Viennese—"neither at home nor in the fresh air," they like to say—the Heuriger is their summer garden and year-round retreat.

How the heuriger has kept pace with modern times, trends, and thinking can be experienced most happily on a visit to Gumpoldskirchen, a wine village some seven miles outside the city. On the dividing line between the slopes of the *Wienerwald* (Vienna Woods, the northeastern foothills of the Alps) and the *puszta* (the flat Hungarian plain that begins in Austria), Gumpoldskirchen is a more early-to-sing, early-to-bed place than Grinzing—and the prices are better. If you arrive around 3 or 4 PM, there is ample light to explore some of the 100 charming courtyards behind welcoming green laurels and tarry perhaps in the Renaissance sobriety of the Benedictine monks' Heuriger or the cozy nook carved out of a wine barrel in Schabl's Pressehaus (both on the main street) before bearing left at the onion-domed church around which the town was built several centuries ago.

This will put you on a *Weinwanderweg* through the vineyards: a 30-to 45-minute circle walk designed and decorated in 1975 by the vintners of Gumpoldskirchen. An ancient wine press looms up on a hillside like a gallows. A modern metal sculpture of an insect magnifies and gentrifies the *Reblaus* (phylloxera), a plant pest that came over from California in the 1870s and destroyed most of Europe's wines; the vines were restored only when reblaus-resistant strains were also imported from California.

Along its way, the Weinwanderweg relates the history of Austrian wines from the third century, when the Roman Emperor Probus first allowed grapes to be grown outside Italy, up through Joseph II to the present day, when Gumpoldskirchen leads all of Austria in the production of Zierfandler, another white wine deceptively called Rotgipfler, and Blauer Portugieser, which is red and Austrian.

Somehow, one develops a thirst along the Weinwanderweg, and in gathering darkness, dozens of pine bushes of Gumpoldskirchen are already illuminated and beckoning below. Safely down, you should head for one of the twin Heurige of the Bruckberger family at Wienerstrasse 1 and Kirchenplatz 1, where the music has already started and the partying has been going on for hours.

The Bruckbergers have been in the wine business for more than three centuries. They slaughter their homefed livestock once a week. Apple-cheeked young Hans Bruckberger presides over the noisy, happy, 800-seat heuriger that bears the family name on the main street. A couple of blocks away, right where the Weinwanderweg begins and ends, his sister Elisabeth runs a more intimate cellar heuriger for romantic dining by candlelight and softer music. The wine, music, and strudel in both places are just right—and so are the duck at Elisabeth's and the crisp bread and spicy Liptauer cheese, roast chicken, and steamy pigs' knuckles at Hans's.

Hans's and Elisabeth's sister, Hansi, runs a *Heuriger-proviant*, a food-supply store adjacent to the larger Heuriger. Here you can buy cold cuts and bread for snacking along the Weinwanderweg or on a Wienerwald hike or if you just don't feel like hacking the buffet in the Heuriger. At the end of an evening, when a Bruckberger patron expresses the need for a cup of coffee before heading back to the real world, particularly by car, the dirndled wine waitress will respond demurely with: "That would be against the law of the Heuriger. But we can send out. Give me the money and I'll go next door and buy you one."

Taking your schillings and accepting a small tip, she strides through Hans's kitchen into Hansi's store. As a shopkeeper, Hansi is allowed to brew and sell coffee. The law of the Heuriger has been circumvented, but if it helps a drinker to arrive home safely, well, as Joseph II might say, there you are.

— Alan Levy

BOOKS AND VIDEOS

Many readers find *A Nervous Splendor,* Frederic Morton's profile of late 19th-century Vienna (Little, Brown/Penguin, 1979) one of the most impressive takes on the Austrian gestalt. For a comprehensive overview, check out Richard Rickett's *A Brief Survey of Austrian History* (Heinemann, 1983) and Edward Crankshaw's *The Habsburgs* (Weidenfeld & Nicolson, 1972), a good and brief history of the royal house that ruled Austria from 1278 to 1918.

Joseph Wechsberg's beautifully written book on the Strauss musical dynasty, *The Waltz Emperors* (Viking, 1969) contains some of this author's most inspired passages on Viennese style. There are libraries filled with books on the many musical geniuses who lived in Vienna; for a compact guide to those musicians who helped make Vienna the musical capital of the world, see *Music and Musicians in Vienna* (Heinemann, 1973), also by Richard Rickett. Of the many tomes devoted to Wolfgang Amadeus Mozart, *In Mozart's Footsteps: A Travel Guide for Music Lovers,* by Harrison James Wignall (Paragon, 1991) is a particularly helpful and delightful guide for the tourist. For more in-depth coverage, read Wolfgang Hildeschimer's *Mozart* (Farrar, Strauss, 1982)

and the many volumes of H.C. Robbins Landon, including his *1791: Mozart's Last Year* (Schirmer, 1988). More personal takes on "Wolfi"" can be found in Peter Schaffer's play, *Amadeus* (the Academy Award–winning film of 1984, unfortunately, was filmed in Prague) and in Anthony Burgess's *On Mozart* (Ticknor & Fields, 1992).

For Vienna coverage, see Henriette Mandl, *In Search of Vienna: Walking Tours of the City* (Brandstätter, 1995) and Christian Nebehay, *Vienna 1900* (Brandstätter, 1984), a set of profusely illustrated guides to architecture, painting, music, and literature in turn-of-the-century Vienna. Carl E. Schorske's landmark *Fin-de-Siècle Vienna: Politics and Culture* (Vintage/Random House, 1981) helps unravel today's Vienna and Austria. The 20th-century artistic efflorescences of Vienna, the Jugendstil and the Wiener Werkstatte are covered in Kirk Varnedoe's Vienna 1900: Art, Architecture, and Design (Museum of Modern Art, 1986) and in J. Schwieger's *Wiener Werkstatte* (Abbeville, 1984). Sarah Gainham's *Night Falls on the City* (Collins, 1967) remains an extraordinary novel about the struggle of an actress to hide her Jewish husband from the Nazis in wartime Vienna.

GERMAN VOCABULARY

To people who have studied only Romance languages in school, the very sight of written German is terrifying—particularly when it's printed in that Gothic script that resembles old English lettering. Take heart, you are not alone. Mark Twain once wrote a funny piece called "The Horrible German Language," expounding on the German habit of tacking pieces of words together until the result fills an entire line. But never mind—you won't be required to speak it, and the section below will help.

Remember that the Austrians sometimes have just as much trouble speaking (and writing) English as you do with German. Witness the sign in a ski-resort hotel:

Not to perambulate the corridors
in the hours of repose
in the boots of ascension

An asterisk (*) denotes common usage in Austria.

English	German	Pronunciation

Basics

English	German	Pronunciation
Yes/no	Ja/nein	yah/nine
Please	Bitte	**bit**-uh
May I?	Darf ich?	darf isch?
Thank you (very much)	Danke (vielen Dank)	**dahn**-kuh (**fee**-len dahnk)
You're welcome	Bitte, gern geschehen	**bit**-uh, gairn ge**shay**-un
Excuse me	Entschuldigen Sie	ent-**shool**-di-gen zee
What? (What did you say?)	Wie, bitte?	vee, **bit**-uh?
Can you tell me?	Können Sie mir sagen?	kunnen zee meer **sah**-gen?
Do you know . . . ?	Wissen Sie . . . ?	**viss**-en zee
I'm sorry	Es tut mir leid.	es toot meer lite
Good day	Guten Tag	**goo**-ten tahk
Goodbye	Auf Wiedersehen	owf **vee**-der-zane
Good morning	Guten Morgen	**goo**-ten **mor**-gen
Good evening	Guten Abend	**goo**-ten **ah**-bend
Good night	Gute Nacht	**goo**-tuh nahkt
Mr./Mrs.	Herr/Frau	hair/frow
Miss	Fräulein	**froy**-line
Pleased to meet you	Sehr erfreut.	zair air-**froyt**
How are you?	Wie geht es Ihnen?	vee **gate** es **ee**-nen?
Very well, thanks.	Sehr gut, danke.	sair goot, **dahn**-kuh
And you?	Und Ihnen?	oont **ee**-nen?
Hi!	*Servus!	**sair**-voos
Hello! (on the telephone)	Hallo!	**hah**-lo

Numbers

1 eins	eints			6 sechs	zex		
2 zwei	tsvy			7 sieben	**zee**-ben		
3 drei	dry			8 acht	ahkt		
4 vier	fear			9 neun	noyn		
5 fünf	foonf			10 zehn	tsane		
11 elf	elf			16 sechszehn	**zex**-tsane		
12 zwölf	tsvoolf			17 siebzehn	**zeeb**-tsane		
13 dreizehn	**dry**-tsane			18 achtzehn	**ahkt**-tsane		
14 vierzehn	**fear**-tsane			19 neunzehn	**noyn**-tsane		
15 fünfzehn	**foonf**-sane			20 zwanzig	**tsvahn**-tsig		
30 dreissig	**dry**-tsig			80 achtzig	**ahkt**-sig		
40 vierzig	**fear**-tsig			90 neunzig	**noyn**-tsig		
50 fünfzig	**foonf**-zig			100 hundert	**hoon**-dairt		
60 sechszig	**zex**-sig			500 fünfhun-	**foonf**-		
70 siebzig	**zeeb**-sig			dert	hoon-dairt		

Colors

black	schwarz	schvarts	pink	rosa	**row**-sa
blue	blau	blauw	purple	violett	vee-o-**let**
brown	braun	brown	red	rot	wrote
green	grün	groohn	white	weiss	vice
orange	orange	o-**rahnj**	yellow	gelb	gelb

Days of the Week

Sunday	Sonntag	**zohn**-tahk
Monday	Montag	**moan**-tahk
Tuesday	Dienstag	**deens**-tahk
Wednesday	Mittwoch	**mitt**-voak
Thursday	Donnerstag	**doe**-ners-tahk
Friday	Freitag	**fry**-tahk
Saturday	Samstag	**zahm**-stahk

Months

January	Januar	**yahn**-yu-ar
	*Jänner	**ye**-ner
February	Februar	**feb**-ru-ar
	*Feber	**fe**-ber
March	März	mayrts
April	April	ah-**pril**
May	Mai	my
June	Juni	**yoo**-nee
July	Juli	**yoo**-lee
August	August	ow-**goost**
September	September	sep-**tehm**-ber
October	Oktober	oc-**toe**-ber
November	November	no-**vehm**-ber
December	Dezember	day-**tsem**-ber

Useful Phrases

Do you speak English?	Sprechen Sie Englisch?	**shprek**-hun zee **eng**-glisch?
I don't speak German.	Ich spreche kein Deutsch.	isch **shprek**-uh kine doych

Please speak slowly.	Bitte sprechen Sie langsam.	**bit**-uh **shprek**-en zee **lahng**-zahm
I don't understand	Ich verstehe nicht	isch fair-**shtay**-uh nicht
I understand	Ich verstehe	isch fair-**shtay**-uh
I don't know	Ich weiss nicht	isch vice nicht
Excuse me/sorry	Entschuldigen Sie	ent-**shool**-di-gen zee
I am American/ British	Ich bin Amerikaner(in)/Engländer(in)	isch bin a-mer-i-**kahn**-er(in)/**eng**-len-der(in)
What is your name?	Wie heissen Sie?	vee **high**-sen zee
My name is . . .	ich heiße . . .	isch **high**-suh
What time is it?	Wieviel Uhr ist es? *Wie spät ist es?	**vee**-feel oor ist es **vee** shpate ist es
It is one, two, three . . . o'clock.	Es ist ein, zwei, drei . . . Uhr.	es ist ine, tsvy, dry . . . oor
Yes, please/ No, thank you	Ja, bitte/ Nein, danke	yah **bi**-tuh/ **nine** dahng-kuh
How?	Wie?	vee
When?	Wann? (as conjunction, als)	vahn (ahls)
This/next week	Diese/nächste Woche	**dee**-zuh/**nehks**-tuh **vo**-kuh
This/next year	Dieses/nächstes Jahr	**dee**-zuz/ **nehks**-tuhs yahr
Yesterday/today/ tomorrow	Gestern/heute/ morgen	**geh**-stern/ **hoy**-tuh/**mor**-gen
This morning/ afternoon	Heute morgen/ nachmittag	**hoy**-tuh **mor**-gen/ **nahk**-mit-tahk
Tonight	Heute Nacht	**hoy**-tuh nahkt
What?	Was?	vahss
What is it?	Was ist es?	**vahss** ist es
Why?	Warum?	vah-**rum**
Who/whom?	Wer/wen?	vair/vehn
Who is it?	Wer ist da?	vair ist dah
I'd like to have . . .	Ich hätte gerne . . .	isch **het**-uh gairn
a room	ein Zimmer	ine **tsim**-er
the key	den Schlüssel	den **shluh**-sul
a newspaper	eine Zeitung	i-nuh **tsy**-toong
a stamp	eine Briefmarke	i-nuh **breef**-mark-uh
a map	eine Karte	i-nuh **cart**-uh
a city map	ein Stadtplan	ine **staad**-plahn
I'd like to buy . . .	ich möchte . . . kaufen	isch **merhk**-tuh **cow**-fen
cigarettes	Zigaretten	tzig-ah-**ret**-ten
matches	Streichholzer *Zünder	**shtrike**-hult-suh **zoon**-der

a dictionary	ein Wörterbuch	ine **vert**-tair-book
soap	Seife	**sigh**-fuh
a toothbrush	eine Zahnbürste	i-nuh **tsahn**-burst-tuh
toothpaste	Zahnpaste	**tsahn**-pasta
a magazine	eine Zeitschrift	i-nuh **tsite**-shrift
a newspaper	eine Zeitung	i-nuh **tsi**-tung
paper	Pepier	pa-**peer**
an envelope	ein Briefumschlag	ine **breef**-um-schlag
	*ein Kuvert	ine **koo**-vair
a postcard	eine Postkarte	i-nuh **post**-car-tuh
I'd like to exchange . . .	Ich möchte . . . wechseln	isch **merhk**-tuh . . . **vex**-eln/
dollars to schillings	Dollars in Schillinge	dohl-lars in **shil**-ling-uh
pounds to schillings	Pfunde in Schillinge	pfoonde in **shil**-ling-uh
How much is it?	Wieviel kostet das?	**vee**-feel **cost**-et dahss?
It's expensive/ cheap	Es ist teuer/billig	es ist **toy**-uh/**bill**-ig
A little/a lot	ein wenig/sehr	ine **vay**-nig/zair
More/less	mehr/weniger	mair/**vay**-nig-er
Enough/too much/ too little	genug/zuviel/ zu wenig	geh-**noog**/tsoo-**feel**/ tsoo **vay**-nig
Telegram	Telegramm	tel-eh-**gram**
I am ill/sick	Ich bin krank	isch bin krahnk
I need . . .	Ich brauche . . .	isch **brow**-khuh
a doctor	einen Arzt	I-nen artst
the police	die Polizei	dee po-lee-**tsai**
help	Hilfe	**hilf**-uh
Stop!	Halt!	hahlt
Fire!	Feuer!	**foy**-er
Caution/Look out!	Achtung!/Vorsicht!	**ahk**-tung/**for**-zicht
Is this bus/train/ subway going to . . . ?	Fährt dieser Bus/ dieser Zug/ diese U-Bahn nach . . . ?	fayrt **deez**er buhs/ **deez**-er tsook/ **deez**-uh oo-bahn nahk . . .

Getting Around

Where is . . .	Wo ist . . .	**vo** ist
the train station?	der Bahnhof?	dare **bahn**-hof
the subway station?	die U-Bahn- Station?	dee **oo**-bahn- **staht**-sion
the bus stop?	die Bushaltestelle?	dee **booss**-hahlt-uh-**shtel**-uh
the airport?	der Flugplatz? *der Flughafen?	dare **floog**-plats dare **floog**-hafen

the post office?	die Post?	dee **post**
the bank?	die Bank?	dee **banhk**
the American/ British/Canadian consulate?	das Amerikanische/ Britische/ Kanadische Konsulat?	dahs a-mare-i-**kahn**-ish-uh/**brit**-ish-uh/ kah-**nah**-dish-eh cone-soo-**laht**
the police station?	die Polizeistation?	dee po-lee-**tsai**-staht-**sion**
the . . . hotel?	das . . . Hotel?	dahs . . . ho-**tel**
the store?	das Geschäft?	dahs geh-**sheft**
the cashier?	die Kasse?	dee **kah**-suh
the . . . museum?	das . . . Museum	dahs moo-**zay**-um
the hospital?	das Krankenhaus?	dahs **krahnk**-en-house
the elevator?	der Aufzug?	dare **owf**-tsoog
the telephone?	das Telefon?	dahs te-le-**fone**
the rest room?	die Toilette?	dee twah-**let**-uh
a hairdresser/ barber?	ein Friseur?	ine frih-**zerh**
a supermarket? (self-service)	ein Supermarkt? SB-Geschäft?	ine zoo-per-**mahrkt/** es-bay geh-**sheft**
here/there	hier/da	here/dah
open/closed	offen/geschlossen	**off**-en/ge-**schloss**-en
left/right	links/rechts	links/**recktz**
straight ahead	geradeaus	geh-**rah**-day-owws
is it near/far?	ist es in der Nähe/ist es weit?	ist es in dare **nay**-uh? ist es vyte?
highway	Autobahn	**ow**-two-bahn
road	Landstrasse	**land**-strah-suh
paved highway	asphaltierte Strasse	asfal-**teer**-tuh **strah**-suh
route	Strecke, Route	**strek**-keh, **roo**-tuh
road	Strasse	**strah**-suh
street	Strasse, Gasse	**strah**-suh, **gah**-suh
tree-lined boulevard	Allee	ahl-**lay**
square	Platz	plats
main square	Hauptplatz	**howpt**-plats
the zoo	der Tiergarten	dare **teer**-gahr-ten
church	die Kirche	dee **keerkh**-uh
cathedral	der Dom	dare dome
neighborhood	der Gegend, die Umgebung	dare **geh**-gend, dee oom-**geh**-boong
foreign exchange	Geldwechsel	**geld**-vek-sel
department store	ein Kaufhaus	ine **kowf**-house

city hall	das Rathaus	dahs **raht**-house
marketplace	der Markt, Marktplatz	dare markt, **markt**-plats
taxi	Taxi	**tahk**-see

Dining Out

A bottle of . . .	eine Flasche . . .	I-nuh **flash**-uh
A cup of . . .	eine Tasse . . .	I-nuh **tahs**-uh
A glass of . . .	ein Glas . . .	ein glahss
Appetizers	Vorspeisen	**for**-shpys-en
Ashtray	der Aschenbecher	dare **ahsh**-en-bekh-er
Bill/check	die Rechnung	dee **rekh**-nung
Breakfast	Frühstück	**fruh**-stuck
Cheers!	Prost! (for wine, zum Wohl!)	prost (tsoom **vole**)
Cocktail	Cocktail	**cock**-tail
Coffee shop	Kaffeehaus	kah-**fay**-house
Cold	kalt	kahlt
Depending on the season	je nach Saison	yay nahk say-**zone**
Desserts	Nachspeisen	**nakh**-shpy-zen
Dinner	Abendessen	**ah**-bund-**es**-en
Dish	Speise	**shpy**-zeh
Dish of the day	Tagesmenü	**tah**-guhs-meh-**nyuh**
Do you have . . . ?	Haben Sie . . . ?	**hah**-ben zee
Drink included	Getränke inbegriffen	geh-**trehn**-kuh in-beh-grif-en
Enjoy	Geniessen Sie	geh-**nee**-sen zee
Entrées	Hauptspeisen	**howpt**-shpy-zen
Extra charge	*Zuschlag	**zoo**-shlag
Fixed-price menu	Menü	meh-**nyuh**
Food	Essen	**es**-en
A fork	eine Gabel	i-nuh **gah**-bul
Homemade	Hausgemacht	**house**-geh-mahkt
Hot	heiß	hice
I am a diabetic.	Ich bin Diabetiker.	isch bin dee-ah-**bet**-ik-er
I am on a diet.	Ich halte Diät.	isch **hahl**-tuh dee-**ate**

MENU GUIDE

English	German

Breakfast

Toast	Toast
Bread	Brot
Roll(s)	Brötchen
Sweet rolls or bread	Plundergebäck
White bread	Weißbrot
Whole-wheat bread	Vollweizenbrot
Butter	Butter
Jam, marmalade	*Marmelade, Konfitüre
Honey/syrup	Honig/Sirup
Eggs	Eier
Boiled egg	Gekochtes Ei
Scrambled eggs	*Eierspeise, Rühreier
Bacon	Speck
Bacon and eggs	Ei mit Speck
Ham and eggs	*Schinkeneierspeise
Fried eggs	Spiegelei
Orange juice	Orangensaft
Lemon	Zitrone
Sugar	Zucker

Soups

Stew	Eintopf
Semolina dumpling soup	Grießnockerlsuppe
Goulash soup	Gulaschsuppe
Chicken soup	Hühnersuppe
Potato soup	Kartoffelsuppe
Garlic soup	Knoblauchsuppe
Liver dumpling soup	Leberknödelsuppe
Oxtail soup	Ochsenschwanzsuppe
Tomato soup	Tomatensuppe
Onion soup	Zwiebelsuppe

Methods of Preparation

Bleu (boiled in salt and vinegar)	Blau
Baked, roasted	Gebraten
Fried, deep-fried	Gebacken
Steamed	Gedämpft
Grilled (broiled)	Gegrillt
Boiled	Gekocht
Sautéed	In Butter geschwenkt
Breaded	Paniert
Raw	Roh

When ordering steak, the English words "rare, medium, (well) done" are used and understood in German. The German equivalents in Austria are: sehr Englisch (very rare), Englisch (rare), etwas durch (medium), durch (done), sehr durch (well done). When you want a steak rare or medium rare, you'll have to insist on it; the usual preparation is done to well done.

Vegetables

Eggplant	*Melanzani, Aubergine
Cauliflower	*Karfiol, Blumenkohl
Beans	Bohnen
green	*Fisolen, *grüne* Bohnen
white	*weiße*
Button mushrooms	Champignons
Peas	Erbsen
Cucumber	Gurke
Cabbage	*Kraut, Kohl, Weisskohl
Lettuce	*Salat, Kopfsalat
Leek	*Poree, Lauch
Peas and carrots	*Englisches Gemüse
Corn	Mais
Corn on the cob	*Kukuruz, Maiskolben
Carrots	*Karotten
Peppers	Paprika
Chanterelle mushrooms	Pfifferlinge
Mushrooms	Champignons
Brussels sprouts	*Kohlsprossen
Red beets	*Rote Ruben
Red cabbage	Rotkohl(kraut)
Celery	Sellerie
Asparagus (tips)	Spargel(spitzen)
Tomatoes	*Paradiser, Tomaten
Onions	Zwiebeln
Garlic	Knoblauch
Potatoes	*Erdäpfel, Kartoffel
salad, oil and vinegar	Kartoffelsalat
salad, mayonnaise	Mayonnaisesalat
fried with onion	Röstkartoffeln

Fish and Seafood

Eel	Aal
Oysters	Austern
Trout	Forelle
Flounder	Scholle, Flunder
Prawns	Garnelen
Halibut	Heilbutt
Lobster	Hummer
Scallops	Jakobsmuscheln
Cod	Kabeljau
Crawfish	Krebs
Salmon	Lachs
Spiny lobster	Languste
Mackerel	Makerele
Herring	Matjes, Heringe
Mussels	Muscheln
Red sea bass	Rotbarsch
Sole	Seezunge
Squid	Tintenfisch
Tuna	Thunfisch

Catfish	Wels
Carp	Karpfen

Meat

Mutton	Hammel
Veal	Kalb(s)
Lamb	Lamm
Beef	Rind(er)
filet	*Lungenbraten
roast beef	*Beiried
rump steak	*Röstbraten
ground beef	*Faschiertes, Hackfleisch
Pork	Schwein(e)
Ham	Schinken
Goat	Kitz

Game and Poultry

Duck	Ente
Pheasant	Fasan
Goose	Gans
Chicken	*Hendl, Huhn
Hare	Hase
Deer	Hirsch
Rabbit	Kaninchen
Capon	Kapaun
Venison	Reh
Pigeon	Taube
Turkey	*Pute, Truthahn, Indianer
Quail	Wachtel

Fruits

Apple	Apfel
Orange	*Orange(n)
Apricot	*Marillen, Aprikose
Blueberry	*Heidelbeere
Blackberry	Brombeere
Strawberry	Erdbeere, *Ananas
Raspberry	Himbeere
Cherry	Kirsche
Grapefruit	*Grapefruit, Pampelmuse
Cranberry	Preiselbeere, Moosbeere
Raisin	Rosine
Grape	Trauben, Weintraube
Pineapple	(Hawaii-) Ananas

Beverages

coffee	Kaffee
with milk, cream	braun
black	Schwarz
decaffeinated	koffeinfrei
water, tap water	Wasser, Leitungswasser
mineral water	Mineralwasser
soft drink	*Limonade, Soda
fruit juice	Fruchtsaft

milk	Milch
tea	Tee
beer	Bier
draft beer	Bier vom Fass
a dark beer	Ein Dunkles
chilled	eiskalt
with/without ice	mit/ohne Eis
with/without water	mit/ohne Wasser
straight	pur
room temperature	Zimmertemperatur
. . . brandy	. . . geist
whiskey	Whisky (Scotch, Bourbon)
. . . liqueur	. . . likör
. . . schnapps	. . . schnapps
Scotch	Scotch
Egg liquor	Eierlikör
Mulled claret	Glühwein
Caraway flavored liquor	Kümmel
Fruit brandy	Obstler
Vermouth	Wermut
1/8 liter (usually wine)	Achterl
1/4 liter (usually wine)	Viertel
1/3 liter beer	*Seidl
1/2 liter beer	*Krügerl

When ordering a martini, you have to specify "gin (vodka) and vermouth"; otherwise you will be given a vermouth (Martini & Rossi).

INDEX

X = restaurant, 🏨 = hotel

NOTES

Fodor's Travel Publications

Available at bookstores everywhere, or call 1–800–533–6478, 24 hours a day.

Gold Guides

U.S.

Alaska

Arizona

Boston

California

Cape Cod, Martha's Vineyard, Nantucket

The Carolinas & the Georgia Coast

Chicago

Colorado

Florida

Hawai'i

Las Vegas, Reno, Tahoe

Los Angeles

Maine, Vermont, New Hampshire

Maui & Lāna'i

Miami & the Keys

New England

New Orleans

New York City

Pacific North Coast

Philadelphia & the Pennsylvania Dutch Country

The Rockies

San Diego

San Francisco

Santa Fe, Taos, Albuquerque

Seattle & Vancouver

The South

U.S. & British Virgin Islands

USA

Virginia & Maryland

Washington, D.C.

Foreign

Australia

Austria

The Bahamas

Belize & Guatemala

Bermuda

Canada

Cancún, Cozumel, Yucatán Peninsula

Caribbean

China

Costa Rica

Cuba

The Czech Republic & Slovakia

Eastern & Central Europe

Europe

Florence, Tuscany & Umbria

France

Germany

Great Britain

Greece

Hong Kong

India

Ireland

Israel

Italy

Japan

London

Madrid & Barcelona

Mexico

Montréal & Québec City

Moscow, St. Petersburg, Kiev

The Netherlands, Belgium & Luxembourg

New Zealand

Norway

Nova Scotia, New Brunswick, Prince Edward Island

Paris

Portugal

Provence & the Riviera

Scandinavia

Scotland

Singapore

South Africa

South America

Southeast Asia

Spain

Sweden

Switzerland

Thailand

Tokyo

Toronto

Turkey

Vienna & the Danube

Fodor's Special-Interest Guides

Alaska Ports of Call

Caribbean Ports of Call

The Complete Guide to America's National Parks

Family Adventures

Fodor's Gay Guide to the USA

Halliday's New England Food Explorer

Halliday's New Orleans Food Explorer

Healthy Escapes

Ballpark Vacations

Kodak Guide to Shooting Great Travel Pictures

Nights to Imagine

Rock & Roll Traveler USA

Sunday in New York

Sunday in San Francisco

Walt Disney World, Universal Studios and Orlando

Walt Disney World for Adults

Wendy Perrin's Secrets Every Smart Traveler Should Know

Where Should We Take the Kids? California

Where Should We Take the Kids? Northeast

Worldwide Cruises and Ports of Call

Affordables
Caribbean
Europe
Florida
France
Germany
Great Britain
Italy
London
Paris

Bed & Breakfasts and Country Inns
America
California
The Mid-Atlantic
New England
The Pacific Northwest
The South
The Southwest
The Upper Great Lakes

The Berkeley Guides
California
Central America
Eastern Europe
Europe
France
Germany & Austria
Great Britain & Ireland
Italy
London
Mexico
New York City
Pacific Northwest & Alaska
Paris
San Francisco

Compass American Guides
Alaska
Arizona
Boston
Canada
Chicago
Colorado
Hawaii
Idaho
Hollywood
Las Vegas
Maine
Manhattan
Minnesota
Montana
New Mexico
New Orleans
Oregon
Pacific Northwest
San Francisco
Santa Fe
South Carolina
South Dakota
Southwest
Texas
Utah
Virginia
Washington
Wine Country
Wisconsin
Wyoming

Citypacks
Atlanta
Berlin
Chicago
Hong Kong
London
Los Angeles
Montréal
New York City
Paris
Prague
Rome
San Francisco
Tokyo
Washington, D.C.

Fodor's Español
Caribe Occidental
Caribe Oriental
Gran Bretaña
Londres
Paris

Exploring Guides
Australia
Boston & New England
Britain
California
Canada
Caribbean
China
Costa Rica
Egypt
Florence & Tuscany
Florida
France
Germany
Greek Islands
Hawai'i
Ireland
Israel
Italy
Japan
London
Mexico
Moscow & St. Petersburg
New York City
Paris
Prague
Provence
Rome
San Francisco
Scotland
Singapore & Malaysia
South Africa
Spain
Thailand
Turkey
Venice

Fodor's Flashmaps
Boston
New York
San Francisco
Washington, D.C.

Fodor's Gay Guides
Los Angeles & Southern California
Pacific Northwest
San Francisco and the Bay Area
USA

Fodor's Pocket Guides
Acapulco
Atlanta
Barbados
Budapest
Jamaica
London
New York City
Paris
Prague
Puerto Rico
Rome
San Francisco
Washington, D.C.

Mobil Travel Guides
America's Best Hotels & Restaurants
California & the West
Frequent Traveler's Guide to Major Cities
Great Lakes
Mid-Atlantic
Northeast
Northwest & Great Plains
Southeast
Southwest & South Central

Rivages Guides
Bed and Breakfasts of Character and Charm in France
Hotels and Country Inns of Character and Charm in France
Hotels and Country Inns of Character and Charm in Italy
Hotels and Country Inns of Character and Charm in Paris
Hotels and Country Inns of Character and Charm in Portugal
Hotels and Country Inns of Character and Charm in Spain

Short Escapes
Britain
France
New England
Near New York City

Fodor's Sports
Golf Digest's Places to Play
Skiing USA
USA Today The Complete Four Sport Stadium Guide

Fodor's Vacation Planners
Great American Learning Vacations
Great American Sports & Adventure Vacations
Great American Vacations
Great American Vacations for Travelers with Disabilities
National Parks and Seashores of the East
National Parks of the West